International Conflict and National Public Policy Issues

**Applied
Social Psychology
Annual
Volume 6**

Publication of the APPLIED SOCIAL PSYCHOLOGY ANNUALS is sponsored by the
SOCIETY FOR THE PSYCHOLOGICAL STUDY OF SOCIAL ISSUES (SPSSI),
Division 9 of the American Psychological Association. Founded in 1936, SPSSI
established as its goal the application of behavioral science research to major social
problems of the time. Drawing upon the intellectual traditions of Kurt Lewin, his
colleagues, and his successors, SPSSI has consistently sought to promote research that
is socially useful *and* theoretically meaningful. Following these aims, SPSSI has
undertaken the editorial responsibility for this annual series—focusing on the broad area
where social psychological research interfaces with social issues and problems.

International Conflict and National Public Policy Issues

Applied Social Psychology Annual 6

STUART OSKAMP, EDITOR
Claremont Graduate School

Sponsored by the Society for the
Psychological Study of Social Issues (SPSSI)

SAGE PUBLICATIONS
Beverly Hills   London   New Delhi

For information address:

SAGE Publications, Inc.
275 South Beverly Drive
Beverly Hills, California 90212

SAGE Publications India Pvt. Ltd.
M-32 Market
Greater Kailash I
New Delhi 110 048 India

SAGE Publications Ltd
28 Banner Street
London EC1Y 8QE
England

Printed in the United States of America

International Standard Book Number 0-8039-2474-7
International Standard Book Number 0-8039-2475-5 (pbk.)
International Standard Series Number 0196-4151

FIRST PRINTING

CONTENTS

STUART OSKAMP

1

INTRODUCTION:
Social Psychology, International
Affairs, and Public Policy

The topic of peace versus war has had a major resurgence in the attention of social scientists since the beginning of the 1980s. Though peace has always been an important concern of social psychologists, it received most research attention in the years following World War II and then again during the Vietnam War (McGrath, 1980a). Perhaps the recently renewed interest was due to the approach of Orwell's prophetic year of 1984, or perhaps to the strain and stridency of recent superpower relations. In any case, the last few years have seen a surprising surge in the number of social psychologists studying and writing about international conflict, peace, and war.

This volume is both a result of that increased interest and an intended stimulus to further attention to these topics. In this introductory chapter I will briefly sketch the kinds of research that have been done in this area and indicate how the contents of this volume fit into this picture. The authors represented here are all authorities in the areas that they are describing and, in addition, they have been encouraged to write in an informal, easily readable style, so that the volume will be interesting to and usable by undergraduate students and professional psychologists alike. This *Annual* series is sponsored by the Society for the Psychological Study of Social Issues (SPSSI), an organization that, since its founding in 1936, has pioneered in encouraging behavioral science research on the major social problems of the time. Assuredly, the maintenance of peace and avoidance of a nuclear holocaust must qualify as *the* preeminent social issue of the present day.

EARLY PEACE-WAR RESEARCH

Among the psychologists most concerned with issues of international conflict were the founders of SPSSI. Some of them were refugees from Nazi persecution in Europe, and all of them were appalled at the atrocities perpetrated there, as well as at the wastefulness of war as a way of settling national disputes. Thus peace became one of the enduring themes of social issues research, as shown over four decades in the pages of the *Journal of Social Issues,* the SPSSI journal (McGrath, 1980a). Within a few years after World War II, the journal published issues on "Citizen Participation in World Affairs" and "Social Science and the Atomic Crisis," and it followed them in the 1950s with discussions of "Psychological Impediments to Effective International Cooperation," "Research Approaches to the Study of War and Peace," and "The Role of the Psychologist in International Affairs." The 1960s began with the well-known contributions of Bronfenbrenner (1961) on the mirror image in United States-Soviet relations and of Osgood (1962) on his GRIT proposal for reducing international tensions. During this decade there were more editions of the *Journal of Social Issues* addressed to issues of nuclear policies and international conflict, and the Vietnam War stimulated several extended discussions of violence and war. However, since the end of that war, there has been a ten-year hiatus in which American social psychologists have largely ignored issues of international affairs, despite the prevalence of armed conflict in Lebanon, Iran, Afghanistan, and other nations of the Middle East, Northern Ireland, Central America, the Falkland Islands, Chad, and many other other troubled lands.

One reason that has been suggested for the drop-off in social psychological research on international affairs is a growing disillusionment among social scientists as to whether they had useful knowledge to offer to policymakers (McGrath, 1980b). In addition, there is considerable controversy about whether policymakers will listen, even to the best research evidence, and about how to make them more receptive to it (Oskamp, 1984). These issues are discussed afresh in the following chapter, by B. F. Skinner, and in the final two chapters of this volume.

RECENT CONCERN ABOUT NUCLEAR WAR

The recent return of psychologists to research on international conflict has been paralleled and supported by an upswelling of research and publication about these issues from other disciplines as well, as illustrated in the following examples. Physicians have called attention to the catastrophic public health problems that would follow even a single nuclear explosion, let alone a full-scale war (Chivian, Chivian, Lifton, & Mack, 1982). Physicians for Social Responsibility, begun by Dr. Helen Caldicott, has become a model for other professional groups who want to disseminate their particular insights about the folly of nuclear war (see Caldicott, 1980). Biological and physical scientists have pooled their knowledge of the effects of a major nuclear exchange and demonstrated the likelihood of a resulting "nuclear winter," in which huge stratospheric dust clouds would cause continuous subfreezing temperatures, resulting in the extermination of most human, animal, and plant life on the globe (Ehrlich, Sagan, Kennedy, & Roberts, 1985; Turco, Toon, Ackerman, Pollack, & Sagan, 1983). Animal researchers have made detailed comparisons of aggression in various animal species with warfare among humans (Cordes, 1984). From a religious perspective, Chernus (1982) has written about the mythologies behind national nuclear postures, and groups such as the U.S. Conference of Catholic Bishops (1983) have proposed policies to promote world peace.

Other advocacy groups have sprung up in many countries to try to influence national policies on nuclear warfare. In the United States the long-standing antinuclear organizations, such as SANE, the Union of Concerned Scientists, and the Council for a Livable World, have recently been joined by many others, such as Beyond War, Ground Zero, and Mobilization for Survival, to name but a few. In addition, individual psychologists like Paul Nelson, and people from many other disciplines have dedicated their lives full time to peace work (Nelson, 1984).

As a result of these efforts, many Americans have an increased awareness of the threat of nuclear war. A 1983 Harris poll found that 86 percent of U.S. adults are worried about the prospect of a future nuclear war, and 67 percent believe that there is a likelihood of a "third world war using nuclear weapons breaking out in the next twenty years" (Plous, 1984). Increasing numbers of Americans are learning that our Pershing II nuclear missiles now installed in Germany can reach the U.S.S.R. in six minutes, which is less time than it took our officials to discover that several nuclear alerts in 1979 and 1980 were false alarms caused by computer errors (Caldicott, 1980). If a full-scale nuclear war should occur, the estimated number of deaths in the United States within the first 30 days ranges from 75 million to 145 million (that is, from one-third to two-thirds of the population), even in the highly unlikely case of the population being sheltered as fully as possible. "However, deaths from burns, injuries, and radiation sickness can be expected to continue far beyond this particular [30-day] interval" (U.S. Congress, 1979, p. 97). In fact, even in the most limited nuclear war, in which "only one city is attacked, and the remaining resources of the nation are available to help, medical facilities would be inadequate to care for the injured" (U.S. Congress, 1979, p. 6). Even in such a limited attack, the entire amount of U.S. blood supplies for a year might be needed within the first 24 hours (Chivian et al., 1982). Such facts give ample cause for public alarm!

TYPES OF PSYCHOLOGICAL RESEARCH

Faced with such horrific eventualities, concerned psychologists have responded with several kinds of research efforts, which are briefly described below.

Public Opinion Studies

Perhaps the most widespread use of social science is in conducting public opinion polls, aimed at informing the populace or officials of people's attitudes, beliefs, fears, and desires. The results of opinion polls are also important factors in shaping public attitudes, and they often constitute an important input to government decisions.

In addition to the nationwide commercial polls like Gallup and Harris, which frequently publish data on people's war/peace-related attitudes, many more in-depth studies have focused specifically on attitudes about nuclear war. A complete issue of the *Journal of Social Issues* on "Images of Nuclear War" reported a variety of studies on people's beliefs, fears, expectations, and behavior concerning nuclear war (Fiske, Fischhoff, & Milburn, 1983). In the foreign policy journal *Foreign Affairs*, Yankelovich and Doble (1984) reported on the public mood regarding nuclear weapons. They found 89 percent of Americans believe "there can be no winner in an all-out nuclear war; both the United States and the Soviet Union would be completely destroyed" (p. 33-34); 83 percent agree that "we cannot be certain that life on earth will continue after a nuclear war" (p. 34); and 83 percent believe "there can be no such thing as a limited nuclear war; if either side were to use nuclear weapons, the conflict would inevitably escalate into all-out war" (p. 37). The authors concluded that the U.S. public has "an impatient awareness that the old responses are not good enough, and a sense of urgency about finding new responses" (p. 33). As policy implications, they stressed that most Americans now want negotiations, not confrontations, with the Soviet Union, that reconsideration of the United States' policy of reliance on nuclear weapons is badly needed; and that "Americans are prepared—somewhat nervously—to take certain risks for peace" (p. 45).

A more detailed study of public feelings about a nuclear freeze (Milburn, Watanabe, & Kramer, 1984) similarly concluded that support for a nuclear freeze was consistently high across varied political and social groups, despite presidential opposition to the freeze movement. Klineberg (1984) has summarized trends in public opinion about nuclear war, including the growth of organizational and legislative support for a change in U.S. nuclear weapons policies. Klineberg stressed the marked increase in public commentators' mentions of the psychological aspects of the problem, and he suggested over a dozen aspects of international affairs to which the work of psychologists is intrinsically relevant. Chapter 4 in this volume, by Ralph K. White, presents a similar sort of analysis of psychologists' possible contributions, and Chapter 8, by Seymour Feshbach and colleagues, provides an example of research on nuclear armaments attitudes.

Attitude Change Research

Attitude change research is a major field in which psychologists have relevant knowledge, and is one of the preeminent areas of social psychology. A host of experimental findings in this area are potentially relevant to changing nuclear attitudes just as much as any other kind of attitude (see Oskamp, 1977; Petty & Cacioppo, 1981). There have been some studies aimed specifically at trying to change attitudes toward nuclear war (e.g., Granberg & Faye, 1972a). However, it seems that there has been a good deal more research assessing and measuring nuclear attitudes than trying to change them. In this volume, Chapter 3 by John A. Nevin and Chapter 8 by Stuart Oskamp and colleagues adopt an attitude-change approach.

**Children's Fears
of the Nuclear Threat**

An attitude area that has received considerable specific attention is children's fears of nuclear war, recently reviewed by Duncan and Kraus (1984) and Yudkin (1984). One of the first researchers to investigate them, reporting data from 1961 through 1982, was Milton Schwebel (1982). He emphasized the prevalence of children's denial of the nuclear threat, but found that children who did think about the possibility of nuclear war typically felt helpless and powerless or resentful toward adults, who they felt had created the threat. In annual surveys from 1976 to 1982, Bachman (in press) has found a steady increase in the percentage of teenagers who worry about nuclear war. A nationwide poll of over 2000 high school students disclosed that 87 percent thought there would be a nuclear war in the next 20 years, and that 90 percent of those thought that if such a war occurred, the world would not survive (Goodman, Mack, Beardslee, & Snow, 1983).

An intriguing glimpse of some adolescents' fears regarding nuclear war is provided by results of a student referendum at Brown University, where 60 percent of the student voters called on the school administration to stockpile cyanide pills for use in the event of a nuclear war ("Campus Concern,"1984).

A unique comparison of Russian children's nuclear views with those of American children was presented in a study in which American researchers were able to interview and give questionnaires to over 300 Soviet children in summer youth camps (Chivian, Mack, & Waletzky, 1983). The authors found that, by age 8, Soviet children have learned quite a lot about nuclear weapons' effects in school, through the media, and in discussions at home. These children showed sharp contrasts with a comparable survey of U.S. children, as follows:

	Percentage of Soviet children	Percentage of U.S. children
Felt worried or very worried about nuclear war	99	58
Believed they and their parents could survive a nuclear war	3	17
Believed the U.S. and U.S.S.R. would not survive a nuclear war	79	38
Felt a nuclear war between the U.S. and U.S.S.R. could be prevented	93	65

Thus, the Soviet children were more worried and pessimistic about survival in a nuclear war, but more optimistic about preventing one.

Perceptions of International Situations

Another approach to research on international conflict is to emphasize the differing perceptions of various groups and nations. This was a major theme of Bronfenbrenner's (1961) exposition of the mirror image in United States-Soviet relations and of Osgood's (1962) GRIT proposal for reducing international tensions. The gap between perception and reality in international affairs is often emphasized by referring to *images* of other nations and peoples, as in Kelman's (1965) social psychological analysis of international behavior. Similarly, White (1966) has discussed international disagreements about the meaning of the terms "socialism" and "capitalism," and has presented a detailed analysis of misperception of the Vietnam War (White, 1970).

Current analyses of international relations that stress perceptual aspects include White's (1984) book *Fearful Warriors*, about United States-Soviet relations, and articles by Moyer (1985), Plous and Zimbardo (1984), and Stagner (1984). In this volume, Chapter 4 by Ralph K. White extends this theme. Perception of other groups or situations is also a key concept in Chapter 10 on terrorism by Ariel Merari and Nehemia Friedland, Chapter 11 on post-traumatic stress disorder by Laura M. Davidson and Andrew Baum, and Chapter 12 on resolving policy disputes by Kenneth R. Hammond and Janet Grassia.

Leaders' Personalities

Political scientists and historians, as well as psychologists, have often analyzed international events in terms of the personalities of the national leaders involved. One example is Tucker's (1973) study of Stalin's personality and actions as the leader of Russia, and Wrigley (1984) has combined personality characteristics and general principles of social behavior in discussing the actions of policymakers. In Chapter 9 of this volume, Lawrence S. Wrightsman adopts this type of approach in discussing the effectiveness of U.S. presidents, carefully maintaining a social-psychological level of analysis by stressing the crucial nature of the fit between a president's personality and the task situation that he faces.

Research on Group Processes

A major social-psychological emphasis over many decades has been the study of interaction processes in small groups and organizations. One psychologist who is famous for applying this approach to the study of international crisis situations is Janis (1982; Janis & Mann, 1977), as in his books analyzing group decision making and the ways in which it frequently deteriorates into the inferior process that he calls "groupthink." Another aspect of intergroup processes is negotiation and bargaining behavior, an area that has been well summarized by Pruitt (1981; Pruitt & Lewis, 1977). A third way of viewing group interaction patterns is in terms of the reward structures inherent in the situation. Among the pioneers of this approach were Deutsch's (1949) work on the nature of cooperative and competitive interaction, Hardin's (1968) influential article on the "tragedy of the commons," and Platt's (1973) discussion of "social traps," in which short-range rewards motivate people to act in opposition to their long-range interests. A worthy successor to those forerunners is Axelrod's (1984) book, *The Evolution of Cooperation*, which used a multiperson, mixed-motive (i.e., non-zero-sum) game situation to test hypotheses about how best to stimulate interpersonal cooperation. This research found that, in the long run, a simple tit-for-tat strategy of responding to one's co-participants is the best way to encourage them to cooperate.

In this volume, Chapter 5 by Irving L. Janis summarizes and extends his past analyses of problems of decision making in international crisis situations. The area of negotiation and bargaining is represented in Chapter 6 by Peter Carnevale, on the process of mediation as applied to international disputes. Other chapters that bear on group-process issues include Chapter 10 on terrorism, by Ariel Merari and Nehemia Friedland, and Chapter 12 on resolving policy disputes, by Kenneth R. Hammond and Janet Grassia.

International Workshops

A particularly intriguing way of trying to defuse international disputes through group-process methods is to get representatives (middle-level leaders and intellectuals) from two or more contending groups together in a several-day long, intensive workshop, where they discuss both the cognitive and emotional sides of the dispute as well as possible avenues for diminishing it. This approach has been used with promising results in the Greek-Turkish dispute on Cyprus, by Carl Rogers in the Northern Ireland Catholic-Protestant conflict ("Rogers," 1984), and in the Arab-Israeli conflict (Kelman, 1977; Kelty, 1984). Some of the basic principles of this approach were also invoked when President Carter brought President Anwar Sadat of Egypt and Prime Minister Menachem Begin of Israel together and hammered out the Camp David agreement.

Consequences of War and Conflict

One of the most studied consequences of war, stress, and conflict situations is the occurrence of post-traumatic stress disorder (PTSD), as it is now known—formerly called shell-shock, combat fatigue, and various other terms. Because of unique characteristics of the Vietnam War, PTSD seems to have been particularly frequent in that war, and most of the research on it has been done with Vietnam veterans (e.g., Figley, 1978). Relatively recent studies have measured PTSD symptoms in other groups, such as prison-camp survivors from World War II (Waid, 1984). Researchers have also found similar, though milder, physiological and psychological reactions after civilian crisis situations such as the nuclear accident at the Three Mile Island power plant (Davidson, Fleming, & Baum, 1984; Dohrenwend, Dohrenwend, Fabrikant, et al., 1979) and the toxic waste leakage at Love Canal in Niagara Falls, New York (Levin, 1982).

In this volume, Chapter 11 by Laura M. Davidson and Andrew Baum gives an up-to-date review of social psychological research on PTSD, stemming from both war and civilian crises. Some of the consequences of stress are also touched on in Chapter 10 on terrorism, by Ariel Merari and Nehemia Friedland.

Policy Implications and Advocacy

Probably the most important aspect of psychological research on war-peace issues is the implications it may have for public policy decisions. These implications have been discussed at length by many authors. To name only a few, White (1983, 1984) has described ways in which United States-Soviet relations could be improved by developing more empathy for the viewpoint of the other side. From his background of research on processes of cooperation versus competition, Deutsch (1983) has proposed rules to guide diplomatic and military actions of the superpowers. In preparation for a Carnegie Corporation conference on the prevention of nuclear war, Kahan and colleagues (1983) have suggested several areas of behavioral science research—in particular, negotiation, decision making, and interpersonal perception—which can have important implications for helping to avoid nuclear conflict.

All of the areas of research mentioned in the preceding pages have their own implications for public policy, and each of the following chapters discusses them in its own way. The question of whether social researchers should become involved in advocacy of particular policy actions is discussed by Seymour Feshbach and colleagues in Chapter 7, with the recommendation that we should do so when the data and the value issues involved are reasonably clear-cut. Two especially important issues are taken up in the last two chapters of the volume by Leonard Saxe and Denise Dougherty and by Paul R. Kimmel—namely, how is social science information used by policymakers, and how can its appropriate use be increased? If this volume can add even a small amount to the use of relevant research findings in policy decisions, it will have established its value as a contribution to policy science.

CONTENTS OF THIS VOLUME

This volume's variety of contributions to understanding and avoiding international conflict, and to related public policy issues, demonstrates emphatically the keen interest of many social psychologists in these difficult-to-study but crucially important issues of our time. The thirteen following chapters are divided into two groups. The first group deals directly with aspects of international conflict, war, and peace; and the second group considers related questions such as terrorism, presidential leadership, some of the results of war and other stressful situations, and the ways in which social science information can be used in resolving policy disputes and influencing public policy. Further information about the contents of each chapter is given in the introductions to Part I and Part II of the volume.

In brief, the theme of this whole volume is that psychologists have knowledge, skills, and values that can contribute appreciably to solving international conflict issues and to other important national public policy questions. What more important application of social science could there be?

REFERENCES

Axelrod, R. (1984). *The evolution of cooperation.* New York: Basic Books.

Bachman, J. (in press). American high school seniors view the military, 1976-1982. *Armed Forces and Society.*

Bronfenbrenner, U. (1961). The mirror image in Soviet-American relations: A social psychologist's report. *Journal of Social Issues, 17* (3), 45-56.

Caldicott, H. (1980). *Nuclear madness: What can you do?* New York: Bantam.

Campus concern: Who's afraid of the bomb? (1984, October 29). *Time,* p. 78.

Chernus, H. (1982). Mythologies of nuclear war. *The Journal of the American Academy of Religion, 50,* 255-273.

Chivian, E., Chivian, S., Lifton, R. J., & Mack, J. E. (Eds.). (1982). *Last aid: The medical dimensions of nuclear war.* San Francisco: Freeman.

Chivian, E., Mack, J., & Waletzky, J. (1983). *What Soviet children are saying about nuclear war.* Unpublished manuscript, International Physicians for the Prevention of Nuclear War and Harvard Medical School, Department of Psychiatry.

Cordes, C. (1984, November). Findings debunk aggression as evolutionary inheritance. *APA Monitor, 15* (11), 17.

Davidson, L. M., Fleming, I., & Baum, A. (1984, August). *Chronic stress and Three Mile Island: The role of toxic exposure and uncertainty.* Paper presented at American Psychological Association meeting, Toronto.

Deutsch, M. (1949). A theory of cooperation and competition. *Human Relations, 2,* 129-151.

Deutsch, M. (1983). The prevention of World War III: A psychological perspective. *Political Psychology, 4,* 3-31.

Dohrenwend, B. P., Dohrenwend, B. S., Fabrikant, J. I., et al. (1979). Report of the public health and safety task group on behavioral effects. In *Staff reports to the President's Commission on the*

Accident at Three Mile Island (pp. 257-308). Washington, DC: U.S. Nuclear Regulatory Commission.

Duncan, B. L., & Kraus, M. A. (1984, August). *Children, families, and nuclear proliferation: A systems perspective.* Paper presented at the American Psychological Association meeting, Toronto.

Ehrlich, P. R., Sagan, C., Kennedy, D., & Roberts, W. O. (1985). *The cold and the dark: The world after nuclear war.* New York: Norton.

Figley, C. R. (Ed.). (1978). *Stress disorders among Vietnam veterans: Theory, research and treatment.* New York: Brunner/Mazel.

Fiske, S. T., Fischhoff, B., & Milburn, M. A. (Eds.) (1983). Images of nuclear war. *Journal of Social Issues, 39* (1), 1-180.

Goodman, L. A., Mack, J. E., Beardslee, W. R., & Snow, R. M. (1983). The threat of nuclear war and the nuclear arms race: Adolescent experience and perceptions. *Political Psychology, 4,* 501-530.

Granberg, D., & Faye, N. (1972). Sensitizing people by making the abstract concrete: Study of the effect of "Hiroshima-Nagasaki." *American Journal of Orthopsychiatry, 42,* 811-815.

Hardin, G. (1968). The tragedy of the commons. *Science, 162,* 1243-1248.

Janis, I. L. (1982). *Victims of groupthink* (2nd ed.). Boston: Houghton Mifflin.

Janis, I. L., & Mann, L. (1977). *Decisionmaking.* New York: Free Press.

Kahan, J. P., Darilek, R. E., Graubard, M. H., Brown, N. C., Platt, A., & Williams, B. R. (1983, December). *Preventing nuclear conflict: What can the behavioral sciences contribute?* Unpublished manuscript, Santa Monica, CA: Rand Corporation.

Kelman, H. C. (Ed.). (1965). *International behavior: A social-psychological analysis.* New York: Holt, Rinehart & Winston.

Kelman, H. C. (1977). The problem-solving workshop in conflict reduction. In M. Berman & J. E. Johnson (Eds.), *Unofficial diplomats.* New York: Columbia University Press.

Kelty, E. J. (1984, January). *A psychological approach to the Arab-Israeli conflict.* Unpublished manuscript, Rockville, MD: National Institute of Mental Health.

Klineberg, O. (1984). Public opinion and nuclear war. *American Psychologist, 39,* 1245-1253.

Levine, A. G. (1982). *Love Canal: Science, politics, and people.* Lexington, MA: D. C. Heath.

McGrath, J. E. (1980a). What are the social issues? Timeliness and treatment of topics in the *Journal of Social Issues. Journal of Social Issues, 36* (4), 98-108.

McGrath, J. E. (1980b). Social science, social action, and the *Journal of Social Issues. Journal of Social Issues, 36* (4), 109-124.

Milburn, M. A., Watanabe, P. Y., & Kramer, B. M. (1984, August). *The nature of attitudes toward a nuclear freeze.* Paper presented at the American Psychological Association meeting, Toronto.

Moyer, R. S. (1985, January). The enemy within. *Psychology Today, 19* (1), 30-37.

Nelson, A. (1984). *Psychological equivalence: Awareness and response-ability in our nuclear age.* Unpublished manuscript, Santa Cruz, CA.

Osgood, C. E. (1962). *An alternative to war or surrender.* Urbana: University of Illinois Press.

Oskamp, S. (1977). *Attitudes and opinions.* Englewood Cliffs, NJ: Prentice-Hall.

Oskamp, S. (1984). *Applied social psychology.* Englewood Cliffs, NJ: Prentice-Hall.

Petty, R. E., & Cacioppo, J. T. (1981). *Attitudes and persuasion: Classic and contemporary approaches.* Dubuque, IA: Brown.

Platt, J. (1973). Social traps. *American Psychologist, 28,* 641-651.

Plous, S. (1984). *Psychological and strategic barriers in present attempts at nuclear disarmament: A new proposal.* Unpublished manuscript, Stanford University, Department of Psychology.

Plous, S., & Zimbardo, P. G. (1984, November). The looking glass war. *Psychology Today, 18* (11), 48-59.

Pruitt, D. G. (1981). *Negotiation behavior.* New York: Academic Press.

Pruitt, D. G., & Lewis, S. A. (1977). The psychology of integrative bargaining. In D. Druckman (Ed.), *Negotiations: Social-psychological perspectives.* Beverly Hills, CA: Sage.

Rogers calls peace results "surprising." (1984, November). *APA Monitor, 15* (11), p. 15.

Schwebel, M. (1982). Effects of the nuclear war threat on children and teenagers: Implications for professionals. *American Journal of Orthopsychiatry, 52,* 608-617.

Stagner, R. (1984, August). *Egocentrism, "doublethink," and political dispute settlement.* Paper presented at the American Psychological Association meeting, Toronto.

Tucker, R. C. (1973). *Stalin as revolutionary, 1879-1929: A study in history and personality.* New York: Norton.

Turco, R. P., Toon, O. B., Ackerman, T. P., Pollack, J. B., & Sagan, C. (1983). Nuclear winter: Global consequences of multiple nuclear explosions. *Science, 222,* 1283-1292.

U.S. Conference of Catholic Bishops. (1983). *The challenge of peace: God's promise and our response.* Boston: Daughters of St. Paul.

U. S. Congress, Office of Technology Assessment. (1979). *The effects of nuclear war.* Washington, DC: Author.

Waid, L. R. (1984, August). *Japanese prison camp survivors: Psychic scarring.* Paper presented at the American Psychological Association meeting, Toronto.

White, R. K. (1966). "Socialism" and "capitalism": An international misunderstanding. *Foreign Affairs, 44,* 216-228.

White, R. K. (1970). *Nobody wanted war: Misperception in Vietnam and other wars* (rev. ed.). Garden City, NY: Doubleday.

White, R. K. (1983). Empathizing with the rulers of the USSR. *Political Psychology, 4,* 121-137.

White, R. K. (1984). *Fearful warriors: A psychological profile of U.S.-Soviet relations.* New York: Free Press.

Wrigley, C. (1984, August). *Personality and social factors in the making of policy.* Paper presented at the American Psychological Association meeting, Toronto.

Yankelovich, D., & Doble, J. (1984). The public mood: Nuclear weapons and the U.S.S.R. *Foreign Affairs, 63,* 33-46.

Yudkin, M. (1984). When kids think the unthinkable. *Psychology Today, 18* (4), 18-25.

PART

I

War-Peace Issues

This group of chapters deals directly with aspects of international conflict, war, and peace. Though B. F. Skinner, the author of Chapter 2, is not a social psychologist, many of his empirical and theoretical contributions have very extensive social psychological implications. In this chapter he issues a challenge to social scientists who seek to advance the cause of peace. Skinner is pessimistic about whether psychology can noticeably influence the powerful institutions in our society: government, religion, and business. Yet he is optimistic that we have the knowledge to modify "human nature"—that is, the continuing behavior of millions of citizens.

Chapter 3, by John A. Nevin, responds to Skinner's challenge in the most direct way possible, for Nevin also writes from a behavioral perspective, and he shows how reinforcement principles can develop a class of operant behavior, which he terms "peace activism." Moreover, his own personal experience as a peace activist provides supportive observations for his perspective.

Chapter 4 broadens the preceding theoretical perspective by pointing out ten different psychological principles, all of them stemming from the research literature, which can be helpful in preventing future wars. Its author, Ralph K. White, is internationally known for his longtime focus on peace-war issues, and his balanced discussion in this chapter of the strengths and weaknesses of the doctrine of deterrence in international affairs is particularly important.

In Chapter 5, Irving L. Janis focuses specifically on governmental leader's decision-making in international crises, and he offers ten prescriptions for counteracting the widely prevalent tendency toward "groupthink" in such situations. His primary research method in this area is an intensive case study of past crises, such as the Cuban missile crisis or the abortive Iranian hostage rescue attempt.

In the next chapter, Peter J. Carnevale discusses how international disputes are mediated and what psychologists can contribute to knowledge in this area. He describes strategies, motivations, and tactics involved in international mediation, and he illustrates the psychological principles involved with real-world examples as well as with findings from laboratory studies.

Extending the research-oriented discussion of the previous chapters, Chapter 7, by Seymour Feshbach and colleagues, considers the role of psychologists in social advocacy on issues such as nuclear armament policies. The authors make the case that advocacy by individual psychologists and by psychological organizations should be considered an obligation when key social issues are consonant with the values held by psychologists and when our training and skills are relevant to the issues.

The final chapter in this section, by Stuart Oskamp and colleagues, investigates how the mass media can influence public attitudes on nuclear war issues. They studied the impact of a unique media event, the television film about nuclear war, *The Day After*. Because their findings indicate that the media can have important effects on public war-peace viewpoints, it seems desirable for psychologists to monitor these impacts just as carefully as they have studied the effects of media violence or pornography.

B. F. SKINNER

2

TOWARD THE CAUSE
OF PEACE:
What Can
Psychology Contribute?

Near the end of World War II, I received from SPSSI a letter telling me that "in the opinion of competent advisors, an enclosed statement, if signed by a large number of psychologists and released at the proper time, might have a considerable influence on public and even official opinion. At the very least, it would serve an educational purpose in leading people to think about the conditions essential for a sound peace." The statement began, "Humanity's demand for a lasting peace leads us as students of human nature to assert ten pertinent and basic principles which should be considered in planning the peace," and among the principles were these: War can be avoided. It is not born in men, it is built into them. Racial, national, and group hatreds can, to a considerable degree, be controlled. If properly administered, relief and rehabilitation can lead to self-reliance and cooperation; if improperly, to resentment and hatred. The trend of human relationships is toward ever-wider units of collective security (Human Nature and the Peace (1945).[1]

Well, that sounded a bit like Gordon Allport and Hadley Cantril, who had been my *betes noires* when I was at Harvard a few years before, and I wrote a rather nasty reply: "While I subscribe wholeheartedly to every one of your ten points as a citizen, I will not put my name to them as a psychologist. It is a plain question of intellectual honesty. I do not believe we have the slightest scientific evidence of the truth of at least nine of these propositions, and I do not propose to join in an effort to make the public believe we have."

I think I've grown more mellow in the forty years that have passed since then, but I find myself again taking a rather deviant line on a similar

AUTHOR'S NOTE: This chapter was delivered at an SPSSI-sponsored symposium with the same title, chaired by Jeffrey Z. Rubin, at the 1983 American Psychological Association convention. Symposium participants were asked to respond to a series of questions about the specific ways in which psychologists' knowledge and skills could contribute to a more peaceful world.

issue. I stated it last year at the American Psychological Association meeting in a paper called "Why We Are Not Acting To Save the World." The questions we are asked to answer in the symposium today bring to mind a famous passage in Shakespeare's *Henry IV, Part I:* Glendower has boasted "I can call spirits from the vasty deep," and Hotspur replies, "Why, so can I. And so can any man. But will they come when you do call to them?" I think we *can suggest* remedies for the problems in the world today, but can those who are in power actually put them into effect?

Peace is thought of these days as mainly a matter of nuclear weapons, and of course they are the greatest threat the human race has ever faced. But peace is also a matter of overpopulation, of the exhaustion of crucial resources, and of the pollution of the environment. All these things lead to war in one way or another, whether nuclear or conventional. And it is actually no problem at all to suggest solutions. For example, we can absolutely guarantee that there will never be a nuclear holocaust simply by destroying all nuclear weapons. We can stop the growth of the population and even go into a phase of zero or negative population growth simply by having fewer children. We can certainly cut back on the fantastic pace with which we are exhausting the fossil fuels laid down during hundreds of millions of years simply by designing a style of life that makes fewer demands. The same move will ease the problem of pollution.

These measures would solve our problems, but they must be carried out by the three great agencies that control almost all of what we do. We are to some extent still controlled by the natural environment but less and less so as the centuries pass. Beyond that, we are mainly living under contingencies of reinforcement arranged by governments, religions, and capital (if I may use "capital" without calling the spirit of Karl Marx from the vasty deep—I mean business and industry). These agencies have built the world we are in at this moment—they have brought you all here, they will send you all away at the end of the meeting to other spheres of action. But can they take any real action with respect to the more remote future we are considering here?

As a specialist in the experimental analysis of behavior, I believe that what we do is determined primarily by its consequences, and these three agencies are themselves controlled by consequences that are either indifferent to, or in conflict with, the desired consequences we are concerned with here. Governments can't really act effectively with respect to a remote future. No congressperson or senator could strongly back a measure that would *really* cut down our consumption of energy; he or she would be out of office at the next election. Governments as a whole are competing with other governments. There is no world government; competition is the thing and competition means current strength rather than eventual security.

Religions are in a curious position, at least those that talk about a future world. I have discussed this with colleagues at the Harvard Divinity School, and they agree that you shouldn't look to religion for much help. The notion of a second coming of Christ, which dominated the Middle Ages, implied that this world was expendable. It wouldn't be used after a while; there was no point in worrying about its future. And if you are concerned mainly with a future in heaven, you won't spend much time on the future here. The Pope—interested now in maximizing the number of souls in heaven—is encouraging people to breed children who will, quite predictably, die a painful death of starvation.

Capital is even more securely bound by the immediate future than government. It is said that Detroit looks five years ahead where Japan looks ten, but we're talking about the consumption of critical resources and pollution far beyond that. We can't ask Detroit to build a car that will *really* save energy. A company that did that would not be selling cars.

There is a fourth group, and it used to be called the Fourth Estate. It consists of scholars, scientists, teachers, and writers. To the extent that they are not controlled by governments, religions, or capital they are free to look ahead, and indeed they are the people who are looking ahead now. They include us. We are free to predict what is probably going to happen 10, 20, or 100 years from now and even to propose what should be done to make a viable future come to pass.

But what can we do? What steps can we take? By definition we are powerless; that's why we are a fourth estate. We have to turn to governments or religions or capital to get any kind of action. You may say that we can turn to the people and organize protests and marches, but please note that the marchers march to Washington; they go to government, but government can't move. The people can't go beyond those who have the power and control the variables.

The people, too, create obstacles to world peace. Probably we are all to some extent instinctively aggressive. Skillful aggressive maneuvers that hurt others should have had great survival value, even as recently as a few thousand generations ago, and I don't think that has all been wiped out by subsequent evolution. When my older granddaughter was nine months old, I was playing with her and she started to reach for something that I didn't want her to touch; it was dangerous. Instead of slapping her hand, I gently restrained her by drawing her hand back. I did it several times—whereupon she bit me. My wife was shocked. "She *bit* you!" she cried, as if our granddaughter was some kind of little monster. But was it not a perfectly natural thing for an active member of a species that has emerged triumphant by treating all other species in the world aggressively? (I hasten to say that our granddaughter is now a talented, peaceful, college freshman.) Unfortunately, reasons for aggression also develop during the lifetime of the individual. If you are strong enough, you will get what you want by taking it away from others, and usually with a bit of aggression.

In short, there are many reasons why we so often turn to punitive measures. We see them in every walk of life. As I have said many times, students study mainly to avoid the punitive consequences of not studying. Wages in industry are usually thought of as rewards, but that's true only for the schedules involved in piecework pay. A weekly wage is not a reward. The check on Friday afternoon does not reinforce working on Monday morning. You work on Monday morning because a supervisor will cut you off from that check on Friday if you don't. You are a wage slave—you work to avoid losing a standard of living. In daily life we turn almost immediately to criticism, ridicule. As parents we tend to spank our children. Walk through any supermarket and see how people treat their children when they are out in public. How they often treat them in private is finally coming to attention under the name of child abuse. Punishment is a way to get what we want; it is warlike, not peaceful.

Perhaps there is something that we as the Fourth Estate can do. I am not offering it as *the* answer to our problem today, but it is worth trying. We can build a better way of life apart from governments, religions, or capital by learning to treat each other well. There are alternatives to aggression and punishment, and as psychologists, we can find them. As teachers, as therapists, as designers of a culture we can show people how to control both the natural and the conditioned tendencies to punish. It will not be easy. Punishment works immediately, positive reinforcement takes a little time; hence it is hard to see the advantage in the latter. But we can promote peace in a very real way by designing cultural practices in which people are induced by positive reinforcement to produce the goods they need and to treat each other well.

You may say, "Oh, that's utopian, and you're talking about *Walden Two* again." But it is at least something that *can* be done. As psychologists we can design a way of life that is peaceful in its very nature. You may object that other countries won't follow suit and we'll be lost if we don't remain warlike, somehow or other. But that is to confess failure at the very start. If we can show that there is a way of life in which old aggressive tendencies—whether innate or learned—can be suppressed, it will be a much happier world, a more peaceful and productive world, and it will be emulated; it will be copied. I think it is worth a try.

I have given you my only personal answer to the questions about how psychologists can contribute to world peace. If there are other answers, I shall be as delighted as any of you to discover them.

NOTE

1. Human Nature and the Peace (1945) was a statement drafted by a SPSSI committee and circulated to members of the American Psychological Association for signatures. Over 2000 psychologists signed it, whereas 13 refused to do so. The wording of the ten principles (each of which was followed by a paragraph of elaboration) was as follows:

(1)   War can be avoided: War is not born in men; it is built into men.
(2)   In planning for permanent peace, the coming generation should be the primary focus of attention.
(3)   Racial, national, and group hatreds can, to a considerable degree, be controlled.
(4)   Condescension toward "inferior" groups destroys our chance for a lasting peace.
(5)   Liberated and enemy peoples must participate in planning their own destiny.
(6)   The confusion of defeated people will call for clarity and consistency in the application of rewards and punishments.
(7)   If properly administered, relief and rehabilitation can lead to self-reliance and cooperation; if improperly, to resentment and hatred.
(8)   The root-desires of the common people of all lands are the safest guide to framing a peace.
(9)   The trend of human relationships is toward ever wider units of collective security.
(10) Commitments now may prevent postwar apathy and reaction.

REFERENCE

Human nature and the peace: A statement by psychologists. (1954). *Newsletter of the Society for the Psychological Study of Social Issues, 2*(2), 4-6.

JOHN A. NEVIN

3

BEHAVIOR ANALYSIS, THE NUCLEAR ARMS RACE, AND THE PEACE MOVEMENT

Twenty years ago, the physicists Jerome B. Wiesner and Herbert F. York wrote: "Both sides of the (nuclear) arms race are . . . confronted by the dilemma of steadily increasing military power, and steadily decreasing national security" (1964, p. 35). I heard virtually identical language in the recent TV production *In Our Defense,* while I was transforming an APA talk into this chapter. Despairing, I asked myself: Has nothing changed, except the absolute levels of power and insecurity? Can the U.S. and the U.S.S.R. ever find a way out of this dilemma? The morning radio news did nothing to lift the dark mood as it announced yet another failure of half-hearted efforts toward arms control negotiations.

Wiesner and York (1964, p. 35) went on to say, "*It is our considered professional judgment that this dilemma has no technical solution*" (italics in original). Perhaps one of the reasons that the nuclear dilemma has eluded solution despite widespread concern is that many of those working for arms control and disarmament have approached the dilemma from the standpoint of the physical sciences, or from prescientific conceptions of human behavior. Perhaps if the young but rapidly growing science of behavior were to join in the search for solutions, the dilemma might be easier to resolve. As a behavior analyst, I am a professional optimist (at least after the effects of the morning news have dissipated). Behavior analysts have taught complex conceptual relations to pigeons, social interaction to withdrawn schizophrenics, and healthful ways of living to their clients and themselves. Why not peaceable behavior to humanity?

AUTHOR'S NOTE: This chapter is based on an invited address to the American Psychological Association, August 1984. It is dedicated to the many students and friends at the University of New Hampshire and the surrounding community who have contributed to the movement for disarmament and peace. Victor Benassi, Ken Fuld, Mandy Merrill, Christine Prunier, and Carole Renselaer were especially encouraging as I worked on the text, and Jan Robinson and Liz Cook were invaluable in the process of getting it ready for publication. B. F. Skinner provided the impetus for the analyses and activities described here with his early ideas about response classes (1938), and with a

THE BEHAVIORAL PERSPECTIVE

The science of behavior, as developed by B. F. Skinner and his followers, attempts to provide a scientific, deterministic account of behavior by reference to an individual's past history, current environment, and genetics—and nothing else. To change behavior, on this view, it suffices to alter those variables of which it is a function; no deep, inner, private processes need to be addressed. However, we do need to identify the controlling variables in order to proceed. For example, psychiatric patients often engage in disruptive behavior that prevents effective treatment. This behavior may or may not be related to whatever factors led to the patient's admission; it may, for example, be maintained inadvertently by attention from the nursing staff. One must determine whether this is true by withholding attention for some particular form of disruptive behavior and seeing if it decreases. If so, a controlling variable has been identified, and one can now go on to use staff attention systematically, withholding attention for any form of disruptive behavior, and giving lots of attention for positive activities such as self-care and social interaction on the ward.

Behavior analysis is highly pragmatic in application. Although its practices may be guided by laboratory-based principles (as in the attention example above), behavior analysis does not adhere rigidly to programs that *should* work, but casts about for programs that *do* work. Its goals are specific and concrete: Thus, a behavior therapist does not so much seek to help a client become "healthy and self-actualizing," as to eliminate, say, a problem with substance abuse and to teach techniques for working effectively alone or with others. Moreover, a problem like substance abuse is not seen as symptomatic of some deep-seated, underlying problem—the substance abuse *is* the problem. It may turn out that the substance-abuse problem cannot be alleviated without addressing some other, concurrent aspects of the client's life, but this is a matter for exploration and analysis in each individual case. The application of behavior analysis works very well in many areas of therapy and education, and its scope and effectiveness are steadily expanding (see, for example, Leitenberg, 1976; and recent issues of the *Journal of Applied Behavior Analysis*).

What does all this have to do with the nuclear arms race? Clearly, the arms race is the cumulative outcome of the actions (or even more, the

---

personal communication (1982) that concluded: "It is just possible that an experimental analysis of behavior has arrived on the scene in time. It offers, I think, the only possible means of solving our problems. What a magnificent contribution that would be."

failures to act) of individual human beings, lots of them, in government, industry, the military—and lots and lots of ordinary citizens. Thus, at its core it is a behavioral problem, despite the near-magical technology and countertechnology (and jargon) that it has spawned. It may be seen as arising from the modern system of national states, each striving to control access to resources; and maybe permanent nuclear disarmament cannot be achieved without radical alterations in this system. But from an immediate pragmatic standpoint, the arms race is the problem. It simply must be halted and reversed.

THE DANGERS OF THE NUCLEAR ARMS RACE

The original impetus for the arms race, of course, was deterrence: the notion that the United States could prevent war, that the Soviet Union would never dare to use nuclear weapons against us and could not even credibly threaten their use to blackmail us, if our nation was so powerfully armed that it could destroy the Soviet Union even after taking a first strike. To maintain a stable world situation in the absence of international authority, according to the logic of deterrence, the Soviet Union had to be in the same position. The Soviets, of course, agreed with this logic and responded in kind to each new development in the United States' inventory of weapons and delivery systems. As long as each side acts to match the other, on "worst case" assumptions because of incomplete information about the opponent's plans and potential, the arms race must go on—and on, and on—in the name of mutual deterrence.

But history is not kind to the notion of deterrence when each side strives to equal or exceed an opponent's military power. A study by Wallace (1979) identified 99 serious international disputes between 1816 and 1965, in which troops were moved to the borders, ports blockaded, ambassadors withdrawn, and the like. Wallace then determined which of these disputes had been preceded by arms races between the contending parties—presumably intended to *prevent* armed conflict—and which ones eventuated in wars. The results, shown in Table 3.1, demonstrate a strong association between arms races and wars. Observe especially that 96 percent of serious disputes were settled without armed conflict in the absence of prior arms races, whereas only 18 percent of roughly similar disputes were settled without recourse to war if the dispute had been preceded by an arms race. As conservative, scientific psychologists, we should not draw conclusions about causality here. Many other variables may be

TABLE 3.1

The Association Between Arms Races Preceding Serious Disputes Between Nations, and the Escalation of Those Disputes to Armed Conflict

		Arms Race Before Dispute	
		Yes	No
Dispute Escalates	Yes	23 (82%)	3 (4%)
to War	No	5 (18%)	68 (96%)
	Total	28 (100%)	71 (100%)

SOURCE: Adapted from Wallace (1979).

operating, and the problem by its nature precludes experimental analysis and systematic replication. Nevertheless, I conclude with Wallace that investment in arms by one or more powers to deter attacks by others not only fails to reduce the chances of war, but actually predisposes the contending parties to go to war when a serious dispute arises.

The source of this bias toward war is probably reciprocal fear of each other's growing military power. In the nuclear age, with weapons that can destroy cities within minutes, and especially with the development of first-strike weapons that threaten the opponent's weapons, this may translate into the so-called Schelling syndrome: "He, thinking I was about to kill him in self-defense, was about to kill me in self-defense, so I had to kill him in self-defense" (Schelling, 1960, p. 232). The war doesn't have to be about anything in this view; the current dispute merely provides an occasion for a war that is waiting to happen.

It is now obvious that a nuclear war, once started, would be so disastrous that these weapons can *never* be used rationally, over *any* conceivable issue. The physicists have warned us for years about the destructive power of these weapons and the dangers of ever more sophisticated and destabilizing delivery systems. More recently, the physicians have described the disastrous medical consequences of nuclear explosions over population centers. Most recently, the earth scientists and biologists have shown that a nuclear exchange could darken the face of the earth, and leave *everyone*—not just the people of the U.S. and U.S.S.R.—starving and freezing in the dark. I quote from Ehrlich and his many colleagues (1983, p. 1299): "In any large-scale exchange between the superpowers, global environmental changes sufficient to cause the extinction of a major fraction of the plant and animal species on the Earth are likely. In that event, the possibility of the extinction of *Homo sapiens* cannot be excluded."

The danger to our species is clear. To me and many others, it seems that the only way to avoid catastrophe is total nuclear disarmament, forever, by all the nations and political groups on this earth. Indeed, I will go further: As global resources come under increasingly heavy pressure, as inequitable distribution makes violent conflict ever more likely, and as even "conventional" weapons become more and more devastating, our species can no longer afford to engage in competitive military activity in any form. Readers may or may not agree with these views, but surely all will agree that the prevention of nuclear war deserves continuous high priority for humanity, because all other problems become irrelevant if a nuclear war occurs.

How can we, as psychologists, contribute to the prevention of nuclear war? What can we do to help resolve the Wiesner-York dilemma? Collectively, we are dedicated to research on the determinants of behavior in the laboratory and in natural and social settings, and to application of our methods and findings to real, pressing individual and social problems. We do not, as professionals, have the same sort of expertise on nuclear issues as physicists, medical doctors, earth scientists, or ecologists, but we are experts in individual human action. We can and must use that expertise, at the local and individual level, to confront the nuclear peril and prolong the life of our species.

THE ARMS RACE AND
THE TRAGEDY OF THE COMMONS

Let's start by trying to characterize the arms race at a global level in relation to a familiar behavioral paradigm. The paradigm I suggest is set forth in Garrett Hardin's well-known article, "The Tragedy of the Commons" (1968). Hardin begins his piece with the Wiesner-York quotation and then characterizes the population problem by analogy to the behavior of herdsmen sharing common pastureland. Although the argument is well known, it is worth recalling:

As a rational being, each herdsman seeks to maximize his gain. . . . The utility [of adding one more animal to his herd] has one positive and one negative component. . . . Since the herdsman receives all the proceeds from the sale of the additional animal, the positive utility is nearly + 1. . . . Since the effects of overgrazing are shared by all the herdsmen, the negative utility is only a fraction of –1. . . . [Thus] the only sensible course is to add another animal to his herd. And another, and another. . . . But this is the conclusion reached by each and every rational herdsman sharing a commons. Therein is the tragedy. Each man is locked into a system that compels him to increase his herd without limit—in a world that is limited. Ruin is the destination toward which all men rush, each pursuing his own best interest in a society that believes in the freedom of the commons. Freedom in a commons brings ruin to all. (Hardin, p. 1244)

In a language familiar to experimental and social psychologists, the tragedy of the commons can be restated as the problem of "self-control" or "implusiveness" versus "delay of gratification." Hardin's herdsman is faced with a choice: (1) Add a cow and gain relatively immediate reward, with deferred and distributed but ultimately disastrous costs, or (2) Refrain from adding a cow (and by implication, persuade his fellow herdsmen also to refrain), with immediate costs in the loss of potential income and the effort required to persuade neighbors to behave likewise, but with the long-term gain of maintaining the commons and establishing what would now be called a sustainable steady-state agriculture. It is important to understand that there is no advantage, either individual or social, in refraining from adding a cow unless all other herdsmen do likewise.

From a behavioral perspective, there seems to be no real choice: The probability of persuading others is too low, and the deferred advantages of refraining are too remote to control behavior. Thus, in order to survive, society is led to what Hardin calls mutual coercion, mutually agreed upon—in this case, social arrangements, laws, and enforcement mechanisms that define private property and protect the commons from destruction. Presumably, these arrangements, although unjust in some local settings, are maintained by the long-term preservation of resources on which our lives depend, where the rules and sanctions are essential to bridge the delay. In the self-control literature (e.g., Rachlin, 1974), the institution of private property or other forms of "mutual coercion, mutually agreed upon" would be construed as commitment responses at a societal level.

Let me draw out the parallel to the problem of the nuclear arms race with two quotations. First, from Jonathan Schell's statement of the choice in *The Fate of the Earth* (1982, p. 148): "One response is to decline to face the peril, and go on piling up the instruments of doom, year after year until, by accident or design, they go off. The other response is to recognize the peril, dismantle the weapons, and arrange the political affairs of the earth so that the weapons will not be built again." Second, from Freeman Dyson's *Weapons and Hope* (1984, p.

286): "The world seems now to be approaching a fork in the road, a fork with two ways out, marked by conspicuous signposts, one marked 'Ban the Bomb!,' the other marked 'Don't Rock the Boat!' . . . 'Ban the Bomb' says that our existing weapons and strategy are unacceptably dangerous. 'Don't Rock the Boat' says that it would be unacceptably dangerous to upset the political equilibrium which has grown up around our existing weapons and strategy."

Both authors agree that the nations of the world are offered a choice between continuing uninterrupted the present system of armed nation states—each striving for power in a world that provides immediate material advantage to the powerful—but with the eventual consequence of a nuclear holocaust and, perhaps, human extinction; or facing the immediate risks and disruptions of political and economic life that might follow from the abolition of nuclear weapons and warfare, with the long-term consequence of human survival in a more prosperous and peaceful world. As with the commons dilemma, choosing the latter does not solve the problem unless all nations are persuaded to go along; and again, the low probability of persuading all nations to join in nuclear disarmament, and the remoteness of the consequences, make the latter choice—survival and well-being—quite unlikely.

To illustrate the likely outcome of the conflict between immediate goods that entail long-term risks, and vice versa, consider the fate of the McCloy-Zorin Principles for Disarmament Negotiations, worked out in 1961 at the initiative of President Kennedy (see Price, 1983). The Principles called for eliminating all national military establishments (except internal police forces); giving the United Nations power to resolve disputes, with a peace force to back up its authority; and setting up an International Disarmament Organization with unrestricted rights of access for onsite inspection to ensure compliance with the agreements. An idealistic document, to be sure, but a hopeful one. In 1964, the Soviets accepted these principles, after much discussion over the onsite inspection provision, as the basis for further, more detailed negotiations; but at this point, according to Price (1983), the Pentagon began to object and the United States withdrew from negotiations, rationalizing its withdrawal with an analysis by Wolfers et al. (1966) of all the possible disadvantages that could arise from worst case situations in a disarmed world. Evidently, the immediate political risks and the economic costs to the military-industrial complex outweighed the remote and shining vision of peace and disarmament under international authority. We might paraphrase Hardin: "Each nation is locked into a system that compels it to increase its armaments without limit.

Armageddon is the destiny to which all nations rush, each seeking security and advantage in a limited world." Hardin's solution of "mutual coercion, mutually agreed upon," as it might be embodied in substantial disarmament agreements enforced by the United Nations, seems too unlikely to give us much hope. And so we sit as the audience in a theater, and wait for the great cathartic moment as the tragedy moves relentlessly toward its conclusion. But wait a minute—stop the show! We're not only the audience, but also the victims of this tragedy. This is no time for purely academic analysis of the remorseless workings of complex behavioral processes. We must act. (See Humphrey, 1983, for a powerful statement of this theme.)

ON POLITICAL ACTION

Although we can no more alter behavioral processes than we can repeal the law of gravity, we can alter the internal contingencies and consequences, the utilities if you prefer, on which those processes operate. Prompted by the danger of extinction, we can enter the political arena. Individually, or collectively as a professional association, we can attempt to influence our leaders through letters, petitions, deputations, and so forth; but we are likely to fail because we don't control the backup reinforcers—power and money. However, if we can alter the behavior of the great aggregate of the people, and if the behavior of leaders is a function of the behavior of citizens in sufficient numbers, then we can do some good.

Is the behavior of leaders in fact related to the behavior of citizens? Individually, case by case,the answer seems to many people to be no. How often, after all, are we reinforced for writing a thoughtful, well-argued recommendation to a Senator or Representative by seeing a change of his or her vote? We need to look at a more molar level. From the last five years' voting records for the House of Representatives, I extracted items dealing specifically with appropriations for nuclear weapons systems such as MX, B1, and Trident, and the nuclear freeze, and simply pooled all votes on these items as favorable or unfavorable to disarmament. Figure 3.1 shows that the ratio of favorable to unfavorable votes has shifted gradually and is now approaching the point at which favorable votes will be the majority. The May 31, 1984 vote blocking funds for the MX missile until April 1985 suggests that the line has been crossed, by 199 to 196. Is this shift the result of widespread citizen action? One cannot be sure, of course, but it is worth noting that the number of groups organized at the grass-roots level and lobbying

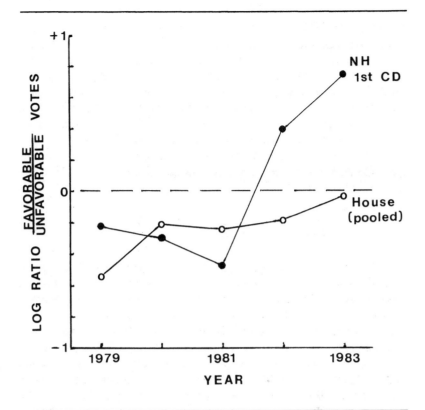

Figure 3.1   Pooled votes in the House of Representatives on funding for nuclear weapons systems or the nuclear freeze (categorized by SANE as favorable or unfavorable to nuclear arms control and disarmament, for the past five years). The y-axis represents the log ratio of favorable to unfavorable votes; zero represents exact equality. The voting record of a single representative from the author's home district is also shown.

actively against the military establishment has increased from about 10, five years ago, to over 20 at present.

Consistent with the tradition of studying the individual organism in the experimental analysis of behavior, I also present the voting behavior of one congressman—Norman D'Amours, from my home district in New Hampshire—in Figure 3.1. Note the clear shift in his votes between 1981 and 1982. This shift can be traced specifically to his appearances in several small towns in his district during the late fall and winter of 1981-1982. The Carroll County Freeze Group had organized to ensure that Freeze supporters would attend these meetings and speak out; and our congressman rather suddenly found himself confronted with people whose principal concern was not the security of their jobs or pensions, but the security of their world. In March 1982, a lot of New Hampshire towns discussed and adopted Freeze resolutions at their annual town meetings, and our congressman clearly got the message (as noted in a personal communication from A. Alpert, 1984). I conclude, not surprisingly, that the behavior of elected representatives is indeed a function of the behavior of citizens. Given enough sustained activity by the people at large, then, it may actually be possible to shift the immediate payoffs for the national leadership so as to make choices favoring the disarmament alternative more likely.

OBSTACLES TO ACTION

Now, we're down at the level of the individual citizen—the level where we, as professionals, may have something very important to contribute. The goal must be to establish and maintain an effective worldwide peace movement, a movement that embraces many diverse people and persists through shifts in national and global situations. Episodic events like the mass demonstration at the United Nations in 1982 or single-issue efforts like the Freeze movement won't suffice in the long run—and it is likely to be a very long run indeed, because the knowledge of how to make and deliver nuclear weapons will never go away. The movement must develop and sustain the power to make national leaders explore new ways to resolve their conflicts. But again, the commons problem arises. Faced with the overwhelming magnitude and complexity of the nuclear disarmament problem, any rational individual who contemplates devoting time and resources to its resolution is likely to refrain, for reasons similar to those driving Hardin's herdsman: The costs to one's individual career, personal life, and pocketbook are certain, substantial, and immediate, whereas the shared positive outcome of a disarmed world is improbable and remote. Moreover, the latter outcome will only be achieved if one persuades many, many others to join in.

Unfortunately, other factors operate to make persuasion ineffective. We've all heard repeated warnings of nuclear extinction from many eloquent and expert speakers and writers; but at the same time, our daily lives continue pretty much as usual. Because we have no experience of these warnings actually being followed by a single nuclear explosion—let alone a major exchange that would threaten our extinction—the warnings have little validity (in the technical sense of being highly correlated with the predicted consequences) and thus lose their potency. Moreover, the warnings themselves are highly aversive. It is, after all, profoundly disturbing to contemplate the utter devastation of the world we know, and the loss of all that we care for; so it is reinforcing to escape or avoid such discussions.

Finally, many people profess to be powerless in the face of threatened nuclear extinction. The arms race seems to be driven by remote, impersonal forces that are far beyond individual influence. Realistically, they say, what can one do? This sense of powerlessness may have its roots in their histories. For example, many people have been involved in various local or national causes in which their participation had little or no immediate effect, and so they dropped out. This sort of history of ineffective action makes efforts in related causes less likely—an outcome sometimes called "learned helplessness" (Seligman, 1975).

OVERCOMING THE OBSTACLES

All in all, the behavioral deck seems to be stacked against sustained involvement by any significant number of individuals; but in fact the peace movement is growing, here and abroad. It is instructive to consider how this may be.

I suggest that the peace movement is growing because it is based locally, focused on specific issues, highly diversified, and maintained by relatively minor successes. The fact that major cultural shifts can occur cumulatively, if perhaps haphazardly, through a series of small steps has some useful behavioral aspects, termed "the psychology of small wins" by Weick (1984, p. 43). I quote some characteristics of small wins from his article:

A small win is a concrete, complete, implemented outcome of moderate importance. By itself, one small win may seem unimportant. A series of wins at small but significant tasks, however, reveals a pattern that may attract allies, deter opponents, and lower resistance to subsequent proposals. . . . Small wins often originate as solutions that single out and define as problems those specific, limited conditions for which they can serve as the complete remedy. I emphasize the importance of limits for both the solution and the problem to distinguish the solutions of small wins from the larger, more open-ended solutions that define problems more diffusely (e.g., burn the system down).

The similarities of this viewpoint to behavior-analytic pragmatism are striking. Weick goes on to comment that "Small wins do not combine in a neat, linear, serial form, with each step being a demonstrable step closer to some predetermined goal . . . (but) cohere only in the sense that they move in the same general direction or all move away from some deplorable condition" (p. 43)—a perfect characterization of the peace movement. When compared with occasional big wins, Weick suggests that small wins are easier to comprehend and more pleasurable to experience. Perhaps these aspects of "small wins" can outweigh the processes that keep so many individuals from involvement in the peace movement.

PEACE ACTIVISM AS OPERANT BEHAVIOR

Let me now get concrete about individual human behavior, with reference to some representative instances in my recent experience. Time and again—for example, after the TV showing of *The Day After*— I have heard people say in effect, "Hey, I'm persuaded that a nuclear war would be horrible, and I'd love to end the arms race right now, but I can't, so please leave me alone while I get on with the business of my life"—a clear case of defining the problem at a global level, plus the operation of the tragedy of the commons. If, for such a person, the problem can be restated in small-wins fashion—not as ending the arms race, but as (for example) collecting six signatures on a Freeze petition this week, without implying that these signatures will end the arms race, or even that the entire Freeze movement will necessarily end the arms race—just go out and get six signatures—then a contribution to a cumulative, persistent movement can be established. If this person is placed where signatures are easy to get—say, a Jesse Jackson rally (my example comes from the fall of 1984)—success is virtually guaranteed. Coupled with the cheers of other participants in the petition campaign, and the obvious delight of the campaign coordinator as the signatures flow in, this success—and I really don't care how one thinks about the reinforcement process here—unquestionably makes more of the same activity likely. Indeed, one can easily establish "petition addicts" in this way. But that, of course, is not enough. Whether the petition campaign succeeds or fails, it will surely end, and then what?

To pursue this fictional but representative case, suppose this same person (who has a talent for neat hand-lettering) is asked to make up posters announcing an upcoming peace rally. And behold, after photocopying and posting them all over the community and campus, there is his or her work, drawing comments—more reinforcement, but of a different sort, and for a different particular response. Then, this person might be encouraged to take full responsibility for the publicity for the next rally—press releases, phone calls to reporters, making sure that others prepare and distribute the posters, the whole works—and if there is a large turnout, with good media coverage, another particular group of responses is reinforced in yet another way. Finally, try a political variation—say, encourage participation in a "bird-dogging" group that attends campaign appearances and asks critical questions about the candidate's views on nuclear-weapons issues. With a bit of luck (and some advice on sitting near the audience microphone), the person will manage to ask a question, the candidate will respond, and the candidate's response will be discussed later—and perhaps the so-called bird-dogging program itself will attract some attention. Again, various different reinforcers have been obtained more or less immediately for yet another kind of activity.

The outcome of all this, I suggest, is the establishment of an open-ended repertoire—a molar response class—that might be termed "peace activism." If a few members of the class are maintained by at least occasional reinforcers, then the entire class is maintained, and one may expect some novel variants to emerge. For example, I have known individuals who never before faced an audience to give powerful public statements on disarmament after just such a history as I've described; or even, in some cases, law-abiding citizens who have rarely so much as parked illegally to engage in systematic, sustained, and public civil disobedience such as war-tax resistance.

The notion of a molar response class may need some elaboration. Any action that is altered by its effect on the environment is really a class, not a single action. Successive instances always differ in detail, and reinforcement should properly be said to raise the probability, not of the particular response that produced the reinforcer, but of the class to which that instance belongs. The identification of a coherent response class is not always easy, but a number of different particular responses may be regarded as members of a class if reinforcement of a few instances leads to increases in other instances as well. For example, if a child receives reinforcers after mimicking a few specific adult activities, and as a result some new, not-yet reinforced instances of mimickry occur, one can speak of "imitating adults" as an open-ended, molar response class (see Baer & Sherman, 1964). There is not much research on this question, but it seems likely that wide variations in particular reinforced responses are necessary for the establishment of an open-ended class such as "peace activism."

For some people, "peace activism" may already be established as a response class, perhaps on the basis of exposure to others engaging in diverse activities that constitute a class because of common naming and common consequences. In that case, raising the probability of a single response, such as signature-gathering, should activate the entire class. I have seen that, too, in the sudden peace activism of individuals who seemed to have all the right background (a Quaker upbringing, for example) but who were inactive. From a practical standpoint, the sole difference between building a molar response class and tapping into a preexisting class is time and effort—it is simply faster and easier in the latter case.

Although I have not attempted anything even approximating systematic research along these lines, I believe that the rapid growth and high activity level of the University of New Hampshire Coalition for Disarmament and Peace—which involves about 100 students, faculty, staff, and community people as of October 1984, after starting at zero in November 1983—have resulted from the fact that it operates in exactly this way. Opportunities for action are described, instructions and models are provided, and a supportive group provides reinforcers for some relevant activity even if a project fails. Now, with a number of people deeply involved in frequent and varied educational projects and political activities; with social support from regular meetings, vigils, and group fasts; and with fairly regular notice in the area newspapers, the group is self-sustaining, building the appropriate repertoires for tapping into preexisting response classes as new people come along.

The techniques that produce this sort of activity are instruction, modeling, and shaping through differential reinforcement: standard operating procedures for behavior analysts. Of course these are exactly the same techniques used, on a common-sense basis, by many effective and durable organizations. The current growth of the peace movement probably depends on their use. A behavioral approach does not necessarily do anything radically different, but it can do more, better, and faster, by being specific in its goals and systematic in its methods.

At this point, an ethical and philosophical objection may arise (e.g., Vassaf, 1984). The systematic use of behavioral principles may seem to contravene the sense of autonomy and personal responsibility on which any movement for social liberation depends: It smacks of 1984-style Orwellian manipulation. How can a just and peaceful world be established and maintained by such manipulative means? I think the question can be answered by analogy to education. The elementary schools place children in environments designed to make it as easy as possible for them to learn to read. Reinforcers for the pupils derive from their new-found ability to enjoy stories in books, and the society at large profits from having a literate population. No one objects to a systematic reading program because there is no hidden agenda: The idea is simply to help people to read well. In like fashion, a systematic program can help people who are concerned about survival in the nuclear age to become active and effective in the peace movement. Their individual reinforcers include a new-found and decidedly positive sense of "empowerment," while society profits from having a vigorous peace movement. No ethical objection arises because the purpose is right up front: joyous participation in the unending struggle for survival and well-being.

THE RELEVANCE OF RESEARCH

Vigorous involvement in the peace movement by many hundreds of thousands of people is probably necessary for survival, but it is not sufficient. Which of the diverse activities of all these individuals and local groups in fact make a difference? Which of them are critical for maintaining a high level of peace-related action by individuals, for effectiveness in recruiting others, or for accomplishing stated goals such as changing congressional votes? No behavior analyst would ever pursue a therapeutic program without measuring changes in behavior during the course of treatment, and relating them to changes in the program. We need to do the same here, at a local level, in order to avoid wasting time and energy on ineffective action.

No matter how well we design programs to help those concerned about the arms race to become active and effective, there is a prerequisite: concern. One needs a reasonable understanding of the threat posed by nuclear weapons, and a healthy level of fear that they might be used. This is a task for education—to provide the requisite information without generating indifference or apathy. There is a lot of research in social psychology on how to maximize the effectiveness of persuasive messages about smoking and health, safe driving, and the like, much of it dealing with the characteristics of the messages and the context in which they are presented. I recently found one example (thanks to Victor Benassi and Vern Padgett) that seems especially appropriate here. Leventhal, Watts, and Pagano (1976) divided college student smokers into groups that saw a moderately arousing, mostly factual film about smoking and health, or that same film plus a graphic color film of the surgical removal of a blackened lung. Half of each group then received a detailed and specific set of instructions on ways to cut down or quit smoking—for example, carry gum in the pocket that usually contains cigarettes, don't sit over coffee with friends who always smoke at such times, and the like. The subjects were contacted regularly to follow their smoking frequency. At the end of three months, the group that had seen the high-arousal message and received instructions on how to quit was smoking least, whereas the group that had the same high-arousal message but no instructions was smoking most (but still less than an untreated control group). If this finding generalizes to education and action on nuclear issues, then it is necessary both to present a powerful portrayal of what nuclear weapons can do—as in Jonathan Schell's book *The Fate of the Earth,* or the BBC documentary film *The War Game*—and to provide fairly immediate and specific instructions for action in a situation structured to make that first step successful, as I've argued here. There are lots of opportunities for research on the design of nuclear education programs. However, these programs will never be conducted on a large scale without pressure from many ordinary citizens organized locally as a part of the growing peace movement.

There is a fair amount of pure laboratory research with animal subjects that is decidedly favorable to the approach to peace activism that I'm advocating. It may seem odd to support an approach to peace activism in humans living in complex social settings with data from pigeons pecking keys while isolated in operant chambers, but in fact there are a number of situations in which common laws seem to apply. For example, human signal-detection performance in the laboratory is well described by a version of Herrnstein's (1970) matching law, which was originally based on the study of continuous choice behavior in pigeons. (See Davison & Tustin, 1978, and Nevin, 1981, 1984, for extrapolations of matching to signal-detection and related situations.) Recently, signal-detection analyses have been suggested for several instances of human social behavior (Martin & Rovira, 1981). Thus, other findings with animals may also bear on human behavior in complex settings. For example, Schneider (1973) and others have reported that frequent small food reinforcers are more effective for pigeons in choice situations than occasional large reinforcers summing to the same total food access—a result that is entirely consistent with the "small wins" notion.

My own work with several colleagues and students (Nevin, 1974, 1979; Nevin, Mandell, & Atak, 1983) has examined intermittently reinforced performances of rats and pigeons, and has shown that the more frequently the reinforcement is given, the more persistently responding continues when conditions change—for example, when alternative sources of food are made available, deprivation conditions are altered, the response is punished, or the reinforcer is discontinued. I have referred to this sort of persistence in the face of some challenge to responding as "behavioral momentum," which seems particularly apt in the present connection. The arms race is often described as having a life of its own, a sort of momentum that keeps it rolling along despite the fallacies of deterrence and the dangers to our species. To stop the arms race, we need the countervailing momentum of a movement that is just as deeply and complexly embedded into the fabric of this nation, and indeed of the world, as are the factors that sustain the arms race itself.

Let's recall what is needed here: research, to provide some of the ideas to guide us, and to evaluate the effectiveness of various peace-related programs; education, to set up the prerequisites for action; and instruction, modeling, shaping, and reinforcement to establish a persistent, flexible repertoire of peace activism in many, many people. But these are just the sorts of activities that we already engage in, in our laboratories, classrooms, and offices. Now, we must use our knowledge and our skills as psychologists to help in the process of building a durable, effective peace movement. No individual action will suffice, by itself; but hundreds and thousands of individual actions can change the world.

Let us work together with hope and joy for the future of humanity.

REFERENCES

Baer, D., & Sherman, J. (1964). Reinforcement control of generalized imitation in young children. *Journal of Experimental Child Psychology, 1,* 37-49.

Davison, M., & Tustin, R. D. (1978). The relation between the generalized matching law and signal-detection theory. *Journal of the Experimental Analysis of Behavior, 29,* 331-336.

Dyson, F. (1984). *Weapons and hope.* New York: Harper & Row.

Ehrlich, P., et al. (1983). Long-term biological consequences of nuclear war. *Science, 222,* 1293-1300.

Hardin, G. (1968). The tragedy of the commons. *Science, 162,* 1243-1248.

Herrnstein, R. J. (1970). On the law of effect. *Journal of the Experimental Analysis of Behavior, 13,* 243-266.

Humphrey, N. (1983). Four minutes to midnight. In *Consciousness regained.* Oxford: Oxford University Press.

Leitenberg, H. (1976). *Handbook of behavior modification and behavior therapy.* New York: Prentice-Hall.

Leventhal, H., Watts, J. C., & Pagano, F. (1967). Effects of fear and instructions on how to cope with danger. *Journal of Personality and Social Psychology, 6,* 313-321.

Martin, W. W., & Rovira, M. (1981). Signal detection theory: Its implications for social psychology. *Personality and Social Psychology Bulletin, 7,* 232-239.

Nevin, J. A. (1974). Response strength in multiple schedules. *Journal of the Experimental Analysis of Behavior, 21,* 389-408.

Nevin, J. A. (1979). Reinforcement schedules and response strength. In M.D. Zeiler & P. Harzem (Eds.), *Reinforcement and the organization of behaviour.* Chichester, England: John Wiley.

Nevin, J. A. (1981). Psychophysics and reinforcement schedules: An integration. In M.L. Commons & J. A. Nevin (Eds.), *Quantitative analyses of behavior. Vol. 1: Discriminative properties of reinforcement schedules.* Cambridge: Ballinger.

Nevin, J. A. (1984). Quantitative analyses. *Journal of the Experimental Analysis of Behavior, 42,* 421-434.

Nevin, J. A., Mandell, C., & Atak, J. R. (1983). The analysis of behavioral momentum. *Journal of the Experimental Analysis of Behavior, 39,* 49-59.

Price, C. C. (1983). The case for disarmament: Some personal reflections on the United States and disarmament. *Annals of the American Academy of Political and Social Science, 469,* 144-154.

Rachlin, H. (1974). Self-control. *Behaviorism, 2,* 94-107.

Schell, J. (1982). *The fate of the earth.* New York: Knopf.

Schelling, T. (1960). *The strategy of conflict.* Cambridge: Harvard University Press.

Schneider, J. W. (1973). Reinforcer effectiveness as a function of reinforcer rate and magnitude: A comparison of concurrent performances. *Journal of the Experimental Analysis of Behavior, 20,* 461-471.

Seligman, M. E. P. (1975). *Helplessness.* San Francisco: Freeman.

Skinner, B. F. (1938). *The behavior of organisms.* New York: Appleton-Century-Crofts.

Vassaf, G.Y.H. (1984, September). *Toward a psychology of peace: Caution in peace research.* Paper presented at the International Congress of Psychology, Acapulco, Mexico.

Wallace, M. D. (1979). Arms races and escalation: Some new evidence. In J. D. Singer (Ed.), *Explaining war: Selected papers from the correlates of war project.* Beverly Hills, CA: Sage.

Weick, K. E. (1984). Small wins: Redefining the scale of social problems. *American Psychologist, 39,* 40-49.

Wiesner, J. B., & York, H. F. (1964). National security and the nuclear test ban. *Scientific American, 211,* 27-35.

Wolfers, A. (1966) (Ed.). *The United States in a disarmed world: A study of the U.S. outline for general and complete disarmament.* Baltimore: Johns Hopkins Press.

RALPH K. WHITE   4

TEN PSYCHOLOGICAL
CONTRIBUTIONS TO THE
PREVENTION OF NUCLEAR WAR

A great many psychologists are deeply disturbed by the danger of nuclear war and are eager to do what they can, in writing and teaching, to prevent it. Few of them, though, fully realize how much their own discipline has already contributed, directly and indirectly, to an understanding of the causes of war and of psychologically appropriate ways to prevent it.

Psychologists as such have not been the only contributors. Much that is psychological has been contributed also by psychiatrists such as Robert Lifton, John Mack, and Jerome Frank, and by psychologically oriented political scientists such as Robert Jervis, Alexander George, Richard Smoke, and Ole Holsti. Taking their work into account, I summarize ten major psychological contributions in the following propositions:

PSYCHIC NUMBING

"Psychic numbing" is a major obstacle to clear, evidence-based thinking about the causes and prevention of nuclear war—but it has been greatly reduced and can be further reduced. The term is Lifton's (Lifton & Falk, 1982, chap. 10). It was initially applied by him to the absence of conscious feeling in the face of an overwhelming catastrophe, reported to him by many survivors of Hiroshima as their chief initial response to that catastrophe. He has since broadened his definition of it to include "a number of classical psychoanalytic defense mechanisms: repression, suppression, isolation, denial, undoing, reaction formation and projection, among others. But these defense mechanisms overlap greatly around the issue of feeling and not feeling. With that issue so central to our time, we do well to devote to it a single category." A follower of Harry Stack Sullivan might want to add to Lifton's list the term "selective inattention," which covers almost as much ground but without Lifton's stress on the absence of feeling.

Many others have applied similar terms to the response of millions to the threat, as distinguished from the actuality, of nuclear destruction.

For instance, the final paragraph of Jonathan Schell's immensely moving book, *The Fate of the Earth,* (1982, p. 231), speaks of an "anesthetic fog," "the final coma," "a stupor," "breaking through the layers of our denials," and "putting aside our faint-hearted excuses" for not honestly facing up to the terrible danger we actually confront.

The literature on the effectiveness or ineffectiveness of strong fear appeals is relevant here. The possibility that they might be ineffective as compared with milder fear appeals was suggested by the results of the well-known experiment by Janis and Feshbach (1953). In their experimental conditions the strong fear appeals tended to cause a defensive response, or numbing, that involved turning thoughts not only away from the danger itself but also away from the preventive action (i.e., adequate tooth-brushing) that could ward off the danger. It is true that later experiments, such as that of Howard Leventhal and his colleagues (1965) and more recently Rogers and Mewborn (1976), have usually had a different outcome. Depending on the experimental conditions, strong fear appeals have usually been as effective as mild ones, or more effective. Here it is as if a strong fear appeal were needed in order (as Schell put it) to "break through the layers of our denials" and force attention to the reality of the danger.

The attention that a great many Americans have paid to Schell's book may well be a case in point. He virtually rubs the readers' noses in the horrors that an all-out nuclear war would inflict on themselves and their children and also in the nothingness that could follow for all future generations in a planet reduced, not to an absence of all life, but to annihilation of all bird and mammal life—the establishment of "a republic of insects and grass." His imagery does not seem to have promoted numbness—quite the opposite. It seems to have contributed to the new openness of thinking and acting, in ways designed to prevent nuclear war, that became conspicuous when the nuclear freeze movement began in earnest in 1981. That movement contrasts with the numbing, non-feeling, non-thought, and non-action that characterized enormous numbers of people from perhaps the year 1946, when the initial attention-compelling effect of Hiroshima gave way to disappointment at the failure of the Baruch Plan, until roughly 1981, when constructive and effective action began to seem politically possible. Not incidentally, the psychological importance of having a clear perception of practical and effective ways to escape from danger, as the chief determinant of whether strong fear appeals are effective or ineffective, is a major finding of experiments such as that of Rogers and Mewborn (1976).

Such research has much practical importance in connection with the question of whether the "peace movement" should continue its hitherto predominant emphasis on strong fear appeals, represented for instance by films such as *The Last Epidemic* and *The Day After,* or whether it should shift its main emphasis to discussion of how best to prevent nuclear war through actions such as a no-first-use policy, a selective freeze embodying substitution of second-strike for first-strike weapons, and carefully planned unilateral initiatives. The experimental data strongly suggest that each use of a "horror film" should be immediately followed by thoughtful discussion of preventive actions such as those mentioned.

FLEXIBILITY IN NEGOTIATIONS

There is much specific evidence of a new readiness of the American people to support flexibility in negotiations on arms control. The evidence is well summarized by Daniel Yankelovich (Yankelovich & Doble, 1984, p. 33), an outstanding pollster and interpreter of poll data. He says, for instance:

> An all-out nuclear war, at present levels of weaponry, would wipe out the distinction between winners and losers. All would be losers and the loss irredeemable. This grim truth is now vividly alive for the American electorate. Moreover, for the average voter the danger is real and immediate—far more so than among elites and experts. . . . They do not know how it should be translated into day-to-day transactions with the Soviet Union to reduce the danger. But there is an impatient awareness that the old responses are not good enough.

More specifically, to summarize Yankelovich and Doble (1984)

Americans have arrived at an astonishingly high level of agreement:

- That both we and the Soviets now have an "overkill" capability, more destructive capability than we could ever need, and the ability to blow each other up several times over (90 percent) (p. 37).
- That there can be no such thing as a limited nuclear war: if either side were to use nuclear weapons, the conflict would inevitably escalate into all-out war (83 percent) (p. 37).
- 77 percent say that by the end of the decade it should be U.S. policy *not* to use nuclear weapons to respond to a conventional Soviet attack (p. 38).
- 81 percent believe it is our *current* policy to use nuclear weapons "if and only if" our adversaries use them against us first (p. 45).

Thus it is clear that the public is ready for a no-first-use policy on nuclear weapons.

It is true, and should be emphasized, that there is a very great distrust of the Soviet Union that would militate against any arms control agreement the public felt to be unequal or unverifiable. For instance, according to Yankelovich and Doble (1984, pp. 43-44),

> To achieve solid and lasting support from the electorate . . . the United States must not adopt any policy that the majority of Americans will perceive as "losing the arms race." . . . In spite of the feeling that we can never "win" the arms race, Americans are afraid we could "lose" it. Nearly six in ten (57 percent) say we must continue to develop new and better nuclear weapons so as not to lose the arms race.

Nevertheless, they generalize that "Americans are convinced that it is time for negotiations, not confrontations, with the Soviets. . . . The dominant attitude of Americans is that of 'live-and-let-live' pragmatism, not an anticommunist crusade, nor a strong desire to reform the Russians. . . . Finally, Americans are prepared—somewhat nervously— to take certain risks for peace" (pp. 44-45).

Perhaps most significant, as an indication that the public might be prepared to endorse something resembling Charles Osgood's (1962) GRIT strategy (Graduated and Reciprocated Initiatives in Tension-reduction—see the discussion below), is the fact that as long ago as April 1982 a Washington Post/ABC News national poll found an overwhelming majority (79 percent to 16 percent) agreeing with this statement: "*It doesn't matter* if the United States or the Soviet Union is ahead in nuclear weapons because both sides have more than enough to destroy each other no matter who attacks first" [emphasis added]. And, according to Yankelovich and Doble (1984, p. 46), "a 61 percent majority favors the idea of declaring a *unilateral* six-month freeze on nuclear weapons development to see if the Soviets will follow suit, even if they might take advantage of it" [their italics].

There is a major opportunity here for the American peace movement, if it understands the nature of the attitudes on which it is now able to build.

THE MIRROR IMAGE

The thinking of the Soviet leaders and public about themselves and us resembles a mirror image of our thinking about ourselves and them.

The concept of a mirror image—the same image in reverse—introduced by Urie Bronfenbrenner (1961), has been substantiated by many others who, like Bronfenbrenner, are intimately familiar with Soviet thinking (e.g., Kennan, 1982; Shulman, 1984). Although there are obviously significant differences, such as the different meaning of "democracy" in Soviet thinking, the similarity-in-reverse includes many resemblances of feeling as well as thinking and perception. On the basis of interviews with both Soviet and American children and adolescents, Mack and Snow (in press), for instance, conclude that the picture of nuclear war in Soviet minds is, if anything, more catastrophic than the picture of it in American minds—a finding that is understandable in view of the catastrophic experience of the Soviet people in World War II. And White (1984) finds much historical and contemporary evidence that the three chief war-promoting motives in the Soviet Union—exaggerated fear, macho pride, and anger—resemble the same three war-promoting motives in the United States.

A practical implication is that a humanizing of the enemy image, preferably on both sides but at least on ours, would be a basic contribution to long-term peace. Realistic empathy—not glossing over the evils of the Soviet system but mitigating the monster-image that now prevails in the West—is urgently needed (see White, 1984, chaps. 2 and 11). Or, as Jones and Nisbett (1971) might put it, we need to consider situational as well as dispositional interpretations of the behavior of the actor, when the actor is the U.S.S.R.

ARMED DETERRENCE

Armed deterrence sometimes works but, for psychological reasons, often does not. Peace activists within psychology sometimes reject armed deterrence totally. That is a refreshing, welcome change from the near-total reliance on deterrence that characterizes much military thinking and much of the thinking of the present administration in the United States. It is in line with some historical evidence, such as the failure of deterrence to prevent World War I, and some evidence within psychology such as the counterproductiveness of a mainly punitive philosophy of child rearing or of crime prevention. It is in line with the very important fact of international life that arms intended as deterrence are often misinterpreted by the adversary as preparation for aggressive war. When that occurs, it is likely to intensify an arms race and fuel the kind of malignant spiral process that now rather obviously characterizes

East-West relations. (See Chapter 3 in this volume for further evidence.)

The entire problem is highly complex and is now the subject of much thinking and debate by sophisticated students of international affairs. The conditions that determine whether armed deterrence will work or will not work are by no means fully clear. What is clear however is that neither a simplistic prodeterrence nor a simplistic antideterrence approach fits the facts of psychology or of history. The best work has probably been done by psychologically oriented political scientists such as Robert Jervis (1976), Alexander George and Richard Smoke (1974), and Richard Lebow (1981).On the whole their thinking is "revisionist" in that it sharply challenges the prevailing, nearly total reliance on threats of armed force to keep the peace. Their conclusion, however, is by no means total rejection of deterrence.

On the side of at least some kinds of armed deterrence are such facts as these:

- Experienced parents are in fair agreement that with many children "firmness of limits" is a needed supplement to love and fairness.
- Experienced negotiators are in fair agreement that firmness often is needed, along with fairness; and the experimental evidence (e.g., Pruitt, 1981) and other systematic studies (Fisher & Ury, 1981; Walton & McKersie, 1965; Zartman, 1977) tend to bear them out. Pruitt's chief generalization is that integrative problem-solving is best served by a combination of firmness on ends and flexibility on means.
- Morton Deutsch's (1973) experiments on strategies for inducing co-operation, though they strongly favor a "nonpunitive" approach as compared with a punitive or threatening form of deterrence, lead also to an emphatic rejection of a "turn the other cheek" philosophy.
- In Robert Axelrod's (1984) computerized tournament comparing various strategies for dealing with the Prisoner's Dilemma game, Anatol Rapoport's "tit-for-tat" strategy—which can be characterized also as retaliation without escalation—did amazingly well.
- Historians are in fair agreement that the absence of effective deterrence of Hitler, Mussolini, and the Japanese during the years 1935-1941 was a major factor in permitting World War II to occur.
- The relative absence of Soviet aggression during the years 1951-1978 can be plausibly attributed to Western firmness, (e.g., in connection with Korea, Berlin, Cuba, and Vietnam, backed by unquestioned nuclear superiority during most of that period.
- The fact that the West did not intervene to protect Hungary in 1956 or Czechoslovakia in 1968, though many felt that the provocation was great, can be plausibly attributed mainly to the strength of the Soviet

army and to Western fears of another big war. In those cases we ourselves were probably deterred.

• Few respected students of international affairs favor total unilateral elimination of all nuclear weapons, including second-strike weapons, and few would oppose maintenance of at least the amount of conventional strength the West now has in Western Europe.

On the side of the argument opposed to a deterrence strategy, the key points in addition to those already mentioned, include:

• There is a grotesque amount of nuclear overkill capability now on both sides of the East-West conflict— excessive nuclear deterrence. There is a strong case that each side should reduce its nuclear weapons, especially first-strike nuclear weapons—bilaterally by agreement if possible, but unilaterally if necessary—to a small fraction of what they are now (White, 1984, pp. 80-86, 340-342.)

• There is much historical evidence that the years 1935-1941, which set the stage for World War II, were not typical of the way in which twentieth-century wars have usually started. The usual way has been a two-sided spiral process, with much aggressive action on both sides (seldom seen as aggressive by the "actor"). Examples include World War I, the Arab-Israeli series of wars, the Greek-Turkish conflict, the Vietnam war, the India-Pakistan conflict, the Iran-Iraq conflict, the Argentine-British war over the Malvinas/Falkland Islands, *and* the East-West conflict—at least during the years since 1953, when Stalin died. Although the behavior of the Soviet Union under Stalin, especially during the years 1944-1951 (including the takeover of Eastern Europe and the Korean War), was one-sidedly aggressive and did have a resemblance to Hitler's career of conquest, the same can hardly be said about Soviet behavior since Stalin's death. (For elaboration, see White, 1984, pp. 232-247.)

The last point raises a psychological question: *Why* do hardliners in the United States rely so heavily on the Munich analogy and assume that "the lesson of history" teaches us that a hard line is *the* way to get peace? Again psychological experiments can provide part of the answer. Tversky and Kahneman (1973) have developed the concept of psychological "availability" as a reason why some things come to mind readily and others do not. World War II and Stalin's aggressions since 1944 are within the personal experience of most of the decision makers on both sides of the present East-West conflict. These have been vivid and highly salient experiences for most of them. The experiments supporting the concept of availability suggest that that is one reason for the hard-liners' selective attention to what is neither the common way for wars to start nor the pattern that most resembles what has been happening between the U.S. and the U.S.S.R. since the death of Stalin.

HOSTILE INTERACTION

The great villain in the background of a possible nuclear war is not a person or a nation but a process—the process that Morton Deutsch (1983) calls the malignant process of hostile interaction.

Sane and intelligent people, once they are enmeshed in a pathological social process, engage in actions which seem to them completely rational and necessary but which a detached, objective observer would readily identify as contributing to the perpetuation and intensification of a vicious cycle of interactions. We have all seen this happen in married couples or in parent-adolescent relations when the individual people are otherwise decent and rational. . . . So this can happen with nations: otherwise sane, intelligent leaders of the superpowers have allowed their nations to become involved in a malignant process which is driving them to engage in actions and reactions that are steadily increasing the chances of nuclear war—an outcome no one wants. In such a process, both sides are right in coming to believe that the other is hostile and malevolent: the interactions and attitudes which develop in those involved in such a process provide ample justification for such beliefs. (1983, pp. 3-5)

This is one of the bridging concepts that justify, in some degree, a unified view of all social conflict, from the interaction of two individuals up to the interaction of two superpowers. Common characteristics, as Deutsch points out, can be discovered on all of those levels, including, for instance:

- Communication between the conflicting parties is unreliable and impoverished.
- The view is stimulated that the solution of the conflict can only be imposed by one side or the other by means of superior force, deception, or cleverness.
- A suspicious, hostile attitude develops that increases the sensitivity to differences and threats while minimizing the awareness of similarities.

Like realistic empathy with an opponent, an awareness of the nature of this malignant process may promote conflict resolution by directly combating the Good Guys-Bad Guys conception of the nature of the conflict. Underlying that conception there is an implicit assumption that some person or persons (on just one side) must be "to blame" for it.

Deutsch's concept has the psychological advantage that no person or persons need to be given most of the blame. Most of it can fall on an impersonal process, with the result that an empathic, two-sided approach to resolution becomes more possible. Individuals can project the blame, but onto a process, not mainly onto the adversary. And understanding of the process can lead them to ask whether in themselves, as in the adversary, the process may have brought out the worst that is in them.

REVERSING THE SPIRAL PROCESS

It may be possible, by the strategy called GRIT (Charles Osgood's (1962) Graduated and Reciprocated Initiatives in Tension-reduction), to reverse the present malignant spiral process. An urgent question is: Can the imperative need to reduce the present grotesque amount of nuclear overkill, on both sides, be more quickly satisfied by the force of example or by the hitherto extremely unsatisfactory process of arms control negotiation, with military-minded people playing a large role on both sides?

Charles Osgood (1962) argued that it can be better done by the force of example, if the nation setting the example does it in the right way. Just as the arms race itself proceeds by a kind of automatic self-reinforcing process, a reverse movement, once started, could achieve the same kind of momentum.

Osgood's arresting metaphor was that of two men on the opposite sides of a seesaw over an abyss (1962, p. 86-87):

John and Ivan stand facing each other near the middle, but on opposite sides, of a long, rigid, neatly balanced seesaw. This seesaw is balanced on a point that juts out over a bottomless abyss. As either of these two husky men takes a step on his side away from the center, the other must quickly compensate with an equal step outward on his side, or the balance will be destroyed. The farther out they move, the greater the unbalancing effect of each unilateral step, and the more agile and quick to react both John and Ivan must be to keep the precarious equilibrium.

To make the situation even worse, both of these men realize full well that this teetering board must have some limit, . . . dropping them both down to destruction. So both John and Ivan are frightened. Yet neither is willing to admit his own fear because his opponent might take advantage of him.

One reasonable solution immediately presents itself. Let both of them agree to walk slowly and carefully back toward the center of the teetering board in unison. To reach such an agreement they must trust each other. But the whole trouble is that these two husky men do *not* trust each other; each believes the other to be irrational enough to destroy them both unless he himself preserves the balance.

But now let us suppose that, during a quiet period in their strife, it occurs to one of these men that perhaps the other is really just as frightened as he himself is. If this were so, he would also welcome some way of escaping from this intolerable situation. So this man decides to gamble a little on his new insight. Loudly he calls out, "I am taking a small step *toward* you when I count to ten!" The other man, rather than risk having the precarious balance upset, also takes a small, tentative step forward at the count of ten. Whereupon the first announces another larger step forward as the count is made. Thus John and Ivan gradually work their ways back to safety by a series of self-initiated, but reciprocated, steps—very much as they had originally moved out against each other.

Applying this analogy to the nuclear arms race, Osgood paid much attention to the need for national security. With that in mind, he proposed certain guidelines as to the right way to do it. Three of them are as follows:

Unilateral initiatives must not reduce our capacity to inflict unacceptable nuclear retaliation on an opponent should we be attacked. (p. 89)

(That requirement should now be easy to meet, given the ability of a nuclear arsenal that is only a small fraction of our present one to "inflict unacceptable nuclear retaliation.")

Unilateral initiatives must not cripple our capacities to meet aggression by conventional weapons with appropriately graded conventional military responses. (p. 92)

Unilateral initiatives must be graduated in risk according to the degree of reciprocation obtained from opponents. (p. 94)

Skeptical hard-liners may question whether any such strategy could be accepted by the American public, but the evidence cited by Yankelovich, above, gives at least a partial answer to that objection. A skeptic may also question whether if it were done it would work, in the sense that it would have an effect on the other side. Amitai Etzioni (1970) has answered that question to a considerable extent, by describing how President Kennedy adopted a strategy similar to GRIT after the Cuban missile crisis. It clearly worked.

MACHO PRIDE

Macho pride is a major motive behind the actions that lead to war. Probably the chief person emphasizing this is the psychiatrist/psychologist Jerome Frank, who brings together the psychiatric concept of narcissism and the emphasis of many political scientists on national power as the chief goal of the major nations in their foreign policy. While granting that, in an anarchic world, power is necessarily wanted as a means to security, Frank (in press) stresses also the tendency to value power as an end in itself and as a way of compensating for the essential insignificance of every human individual in the immensity of the universe. In supporting this argument he quotes the anthropologist Andrew Schmookler (1984) on the role of competition for power in social evolution, the psychologist Robert White (1959) on the concept of competence-motivation, and the psychoanalyst Erich Fromm (1973) on the nature of narcissism as a factor in "the anatomy of human destructiveness."

Ralph White (1984) presents a similar emphasis, offering much evidence of the importance of "macho pride" in both the United States and the U.S.S.R., but also demonstrating that as a cause of war in the twentieth century, exaggerated fear has been even more important. Both Frank and White regard these two motives as *the* most important ones in the background of war.

The idea that pride is of great importance in international conflict has practical relevance in several contexts. One consequence is the proposition that maintaining at least equality with, if not superiority to, one's chief rival in the arms race satisfies the need for macho pride as much as it serves the need for security. Therefore, other sources of pride must be found (e.g., pride in leadership in the cause of peace) if the more macho kind of pride involved in military superiority is to be mitigated. Another consequence is that in a crisis it may be important to offer the opponent a "face-saving way out," as Kennedy did in the Cuban missile crisis. Still another implication may be that the United States should not gratuitously affront the Soviet Union's pride in its new status as a superpower by, for instance, trying to exclude it from the peacemaking process in the Middle East, or by substituting inflammatory rhetoric for normal diplomatic courtesy.

MISPERCEPTIONS

Unconsciously motivated misperceptions (denial, rationalization, projection, selective inattention), along with more strictly "cognitive" factors in misperception (such as the influence of preexisting beliefs on present perceptions), are potent causes of the actions that lead to war. Examples of unconsciously motivated distortions in the context of the East-West conflict (ones that help to perpetuate the ubiquitous Good Guys-Bad Guys picture) include the following:

- Soviet denial of any responsibility for the present parlous state of the world.
- American denial of any responsibility for the present parlous state of the world.
- The Soviets' projection of all guilt for the present parlous state of the world onto American "imperialism."
- The Americans' projection of all guilt onto "Communist aggression."
- American selective inattention to the abundant evidence that, largely because of their huge losses in World War II, the Soviet people and their leaders hate and fear nuclear war at least as much as we do.
- Soviet selective inattention to the abundant evidence that most of the people in Afghanistan hate and fear the Soviet troops supporting the government of Babrak Karmal.
- The Soviets' rationalization of their invasion of Afghanistan (perhaps actually motivated mainly by macho pride, or by balance-of-power considerations) as selfless aid offered to a fraternal ally threatened by insurrection, disintegration, and potential foreign conquest.
- The Americans' initial rationalization of their intervention in Vietnam (perhaps actually motivated mainly by macho pride, or by balance-of-power considerations involving the domino theory) as aid generously given to the beleaguered South Vietnamese, threatened by the Viet Cong insurrection and an invasion from the North. (Note: Having a much freer society, the Americans were able to discuss and somewhat revise their perception of Vietnam. The Soviets apparently have not revised their perception of Afghanistan.)

Examples of "cognitive" factors in misperception include the following:

- The momentum of the Communist belief that the "capitalism" of the United States and Western Europe necessarily involves unmitigated exploitation of the working class.
- The momentum of the American belief that Soviet society remains essentially the same as it was under Stalin.

- The momentum of the prenuclear belief that having at least parity in weapons, if not superiority, is an essential basis for peace. That belief has some factual basis when applied to conventional weapons; it has much less basis when applied to nuclear weapons. *One* nuclear-armed submarine can destroy a hundred Soviet—or American—cities.
- The momentum of the belief—which had some validity in the pre-Sputnik period—that threatening first use of nuclear weapons and deploying weapons designed for first use makes a net contribution to peace.
- The tendency in both the United States and the U.S.S.R. to make only "dispositional" (bad-guy) attributions, rather than situational attributions in explaining the behavior of their adversaries.
- The tendency in both the United States and the U.S.S.R. to see the present conflict as essentially like World War II, with their adversaries in the role of Hitler and themselves in the role of Hitler's victims—partly because World War II is cognitively the most "available" model from which to draw "the lesson of history."

IMPAIRED RATIONALITY IN A CRISIS

Emotional stress often impairs rational, realistic thinking in war-crisis situations. The political scientist Ole Holsti (1972), reviewing evidence from both psychological experiments and history, has presented what is probably the most systematic marshalling of evidence in favor of this proposition in his book *Crisis Escalation War*. (The ambiguous title means the type of war that results from escalation of a crisis.)

Holsti is one of several (e.g., Allison, 1971; George & Smoke, 1974; Janis & Mann, 1977; Jervis, 1976; Lebow, 1981; Simon, 1957; White, 1984) who have stressed the importance of misperception or in other ways challenged the model of "rational man" that had previously been widely accepted, especially by political scientists such as Hans Morgenthau. Attention to the special difficulties of being rational in a crisis situation is one element in that critique.

For instance, Holsti (1972, pp. 12-16) says:

Most research findings indicate a curvilinear relation between stress and the performance of individuals and groups. A moderate level of anxiety can be beneficial, but at higher levels it disrupts decision processes. On the basis of a series of experiments, Birch (1945) determined that intermediate—rather than high or low—motivation was most conducive to the efficient solution of problems requiring both high and low insight. A related finding (Janis, 1958) is that persons with moderate fear were better able to cope with the problems arising from major surgery than were those with high or low fear. . . . Postman and Bruner (1948) concluded: "Perceptual behavior is disrupted [in severe stress], becomes less well controlled than under normal conditions, and hence is less adaptive. The major dimensions of perceptual function are affected: selection of percepts from a complex field becomes less adequate and sense is less well differentiated from nonsense; there is maladaptive accentuation in the direction of aggression and escape; untested hypotheses are fixated recklessly.

[Also] the capabilities which may be enhanced by moderate-to-high stress tend to have limited relevance in formulating foreign policy, whereas the skills which are inhibited under these conditions are usually crucial for such complex tasks.

War-crises, Holsti argues, call for especially complex types of thinking; and at least two typical characteristics of war-crises—time pressure and information overload—are especially inimical to the more complex forms of thought, including recognition of alternative behavior options and adequate evaluation of the probable consequences of the more promising ones.

In a concluding chapter Holsti draws a considerable number of practical psychological conclusions from his analysis, such as the need for "vigorous probing from multiple perspectives, not merely from the view of the prevailing conventional wisdom," the desirability of "devil's advocates," the need to be aware of the special blindspots typical of military advisers, the need for special "sensitivity to the adversary's frame of reference" (i.e., the importance of realistic empathy), the frequent need to allow the adversary a face-saving escape route, and the need to "slow the pace of crisis events." There is a noteworthy convergence here with the recommendations of others, including those of Janis (1973) on avoidance of "groupthink" and those of Lebow (1981) on the danger of premature "cognitive closure" in crisis politics. The special relevance of all this to the danger of accidental nuclear war, when there is hair-trigger readiness and a policy of launch on warning, is obvious. It is a significant aspect of the case against superfast nuclear missiles such as the Pershing II.

INTEGRATIVE BARGAINING

Integrative bargaining and problem solving call for both firmness on ends and flexibility on means. The full meaning of integrative bargaining includes much more than is suggested by the main title of the book by

Fisher and Ury (1981), *Getting to YES*—merely reaching agreement that could, in a war crisis or tense pre-war negotiation, stave off violence. Integrative bargaining also includes Fisher and Ury's subtitle: "Negotiating Agreement Without Giving In"—integrating, and largely satisfying, the *primary* goals of each of the conflicting parties. That outcome can ordinarily be achieved only if each displays what Pruitt has called "firmness on ends" (including "selfish" ends) along with flexibility on means.

The values as well as the goals of both sides need to be appreciated. Conflicts can often be mitigated by appealing to values that are, at least in theory, held by both sides (what Fisher and Ury call "principled" bargaining), and by being willing to make concessions at the outset that are in line with genuine adherence to principles. In addition to these principles, many other useful findings have emerged from the somewhat new body of systematic research on negotiation and mediation represented, for instance, by Dean Pruitt's *Negotiation Behavior* (1981). (See Chapter 6 in the present volume for an extended discussion of this area.)

The attempt to combine firmness with flexibility, and to judge wisely where one ends and the other begins, is not an easy task. The two principles are to some extent psychologically in conflict. The process of combining them even has some resemblance to what Marxists call "dialectical" thinking; incorporating apparent opposites in a higher synthesis. Yet the effort to do so is probably essential if we want peace.

CONCLUSION

It is interesting to note in how many contexts the need to combine apparent opposites has cropped up, even in this brief treatment of ten contributions. For instance, in combating psychic numbing, we need to continue emphasizing the ultimate horrors of nuclear war, as well as adding a new stress on how the danger of those horrors can be minimized. The recommendations stemming from Deutsch's experiments on inducing cooperation combine an avoidance of punitive deterrence with stout defense of what is rightfully one's own and a complete rejection of "turning the other cheek." Yankelovich's suggestions as to how our leaders can win "solid and lasting support from the electorate" combine unwillingness to "lose the arms race" with renunciation of any desire to "win" it. Jervis finds explanatory value in both the "spiral model" and the "deterrence model," with a rational choice between them depending mainly on the nature of the adversary.

Osgood proposes initiatives in tension-reduction, even unilateral initiatives, but with careful attention to our basic security interests at the same time, including maintenance of an invulnerable second-strike capability and adequate conventional forces.

The practical consequences of the above reasoning can be summed up most concisely by saying that, to prevent any big war—including any nuclear war—each side needs *both* certain kinds of armed deterrence *and* great, sustained, intelligent efforts to reduce the tension in the East-West conflict that has been increasing so alarmingly in recent years. The key words are deterrence and tension-reduction—combined—but with primary emphasis on tension-reduction.[1]

NOTE

1. This is also the chief practical conclusion of a book of readings, *Psychology and the Prevention of War* (in press), initiated by the American Psychological Association's Board of Social and Ethical Responsibility for Psychologists (BSERP), sponsored by the Society for the Psychological Study of Social Issues (SPSSI), published by the New York University Press, and edited by Ralph White in collaboration with Morton Deutsch and Herbert Kelman.

REFERENCES

Allison, G. T. (1971). *Essence of decision: Explaining the Cuban missile crisis.* Boston: Little, Brown.

Axelrod, R. (1984). *The evolution of cooperation.* New York: Basic Books.

Birch, H. G. (1945). Motivational factors in insightful problem-solving. *Journal of Comparative Psychology, 37,* 295-317.

Bronfenbrenner, U. (1961). The mirror image in Soviet-American relations. *Journal of Social Issues, 17* (3), 45-56.

Deutsch, M. (1973). *The resolution of conflict: Constructive and destructive processes.* New Haven, CT: Yale University Press.

Deutsch, M. (1983). The prevention of World War III: A psychological perspective. *Journal of Political Psychology, 4,* 3-31.

Etzioni, A. (1970). The Kennedy experiment. In E. I. Megargee & J. E. Hokanson (Eds.), *The dynamics of aggression: Individual, group and international analyses.* New York: Harper & Row.

Fisher, R., & Ury, W. (1981). *Getting to YES: Negotiating agreement without giving in.* Boston: Houghton Mifflin.

Frank, J. (in press). Introduction to section entitled "Two war-related motives: Fear and pride." In R. K. White (Ed.), *Psychology and the prevention of nuclear war.* New York: New York University Press.

Fromm, E. (1973). *The anatomy of human destructiveness.* New York: Holt, Rinehart & Winston.

George, A. L., & Smoke, R. (1974). *Deterrence in American foreign policy: Theory and practice.* New York: Columbia University Press.

Holsti, O. (1972). *Crisis escalation war.* Montreal & London: McGill-Queen's University Press.

Janis, I. L. (1958). *Psychological stress.* New York: John Wiley.

Janis, I. L., (1973). *Victims of groupthink.* Boston: Houghton Mifflin.

Janis, I. L., & Feshbach, S. (1953). Effects of fear-arousing communications. *Journal of Abnormal and Social Psychology, 48,* 78-92.

Janis, I. L., & Mann, L. (1977). *Decision-making: A psychological analysis of conflict, choice and commitment.* New York: Free Press.

Jervis, R., (1976). *Perception and misperception in international politics.* Princeton, NJ: Princeton University Press.

Jones, E. E., & Nisbett, R. (1971). *The actor and the observer: Divergent perceptions of the causes of behavior.* Morristown, NJ: General Learning Press.

Kennan, G. (1982). *The nuclear delusion: Soviet-American relations in the atomic age.* New York: Pantheon.

Lebow, R. N. (1981). *Between peace and war: The nature of international crisis.* Baltimore: The Johns Hopkins University Press.

Leventhal, H., Singer, R., & Jones, S. (1965). Effects of fear and specificity of recommendation upon attitudes and behavior. *Journal of Personality and Social Psychology, 2,* 20-29.

Lifton, R. J., & Falk, R. (1982). *Indefensible weapons: The political and psychological case against nuclearism.* New York: Basic Books.

Mack, J., & Snow, R. (in press). Interviews with American and Soviet children and adolescents. In R. K. White (Ed.), *Psychology and the prevention of nuclear war.* New York: New York University Press.

Osgood, C. E. (1962). *An alternative to war or surrender.* Urbana: University of Illinois Press.

Postman, L., & Bruner, J. S. (1948). Perception under stress. *Psychological Review, 55,* 322.

Pruitt, D. G. (1981). *Negotiation behavior.* New York: Academic Press.

Rogers, R. W., & Mewborn, C. R. (1976). Fear appeals and attitude change: Effects of a threat's noxiousness, probability of occurrence, and the efficacy of coping responses. *Journal of Personality and Social Psychology, 34,* 54-61.

Schell, J. (1982). *The fate of the earth.* New York: Knopf.

Schmookler, A. B. (1984). *The parable of the tribes: The problem of power in social evolution.* Berkeley: University of California Press.

Shulman, M. (1984, April). What the Russians really want. *Harper's Magazine,* pp. 63-71.

Simon, H. (1957). *Models of man.* New York: John Wiley.

Sullivan, H. S. (1953). *Interpersonal theory of psychiatry.* New York: Norton.

Tversky, A., & Kahneman, D. (1973). Availability: a heuristic for judging frequency and probability. *Cognitive Psychology, 5,* 207-232.

Walton, R. E., & McKersie, R. B. (1965). *A behavioral theory of labor negotiations.* New York: McGraw-Hill.

White, R. K. (1984). *Fearful warriors: A psychological profile of U.S.-Soviet relations.* New York: Free Press.

White, R. W. (1959). Motivation reconsidered: The concept of competence. *Psychological Review, 66,* 297-330.

Yankelovich, D., & Doble, J. (1984). The public mood: Nuclear weapons and the U.S.S.R. *Foreign Affairs, 63,* 33-46.

Zartman, I. W. (1977). Negotiation as a joint decision-making process. *Journal of Conflict Resolution, 21,* 619-638.

IRVING L. JANIS   5

INTERNATIONAL CRISIS MANAGEMENT IN THE NUCLEAR AGE

During the past few years, large numbers of people have become aware of the enormous disparity between what needs to be done to avert the danger of nuclear war, according to sensible commentators, and what is actually being done by political leaders in Washington, Moscow, and other national capitals. Among the sensible commentators are prominent ex-statesmen who have held high leadership positions in the United States government—men like McGeorge Bundy, George Kennan, and Robert McNamara. They repeatedly call attention to the danger that the nuclear arms race will end in a nuclear holocaust that will destroy our entire civilization (see, for example, Bundy, Kennan, McNamara, & Smith, 1982; Kennan, 1982). And they, along with many other former governmental leaders, repeatedly urge a number of fundamental steps toward reducing the danger—a nuclear freeze as a first step toward working out comprehensive disarmament agreements, the development of an international system for controlling nuclear weapons and for negotiating disputes, the full implementation of antinuclear proliferation treaties, and the reorientation of technological research. The technological reorientation they recommend involves moving away from developing more destructive weapons toward constructing effective safety devices to reduce the chances of accidental nuclear explosions, misreadings of monitored radar screens, and inadvertent launching of nuclear missiles.

But, as we all know, these sensible recommendations continue to be ignored. Year after year the nuclear arms race has continued to accelerate, not just at the increasing pace of the Reagan administration but also during the Carter administration and all the preceding administrations since the end of World War II.

So the big question that confronts us is: Where lies our hope for survival? One common answer repeatedly given by government

AUTHOR'S NOTE: This chapter includes material from my forthcoming book *Crisis Management and Mismanagement in the Nuclear Age* (in preparation). The research described in this chapter is supported by grant SES-821351 from the National Science Foundation.

spokesmen is that we can rely upon deterrence. But deterrence from mutually assured destruction does not seem to offer any real hope for the long run. Leading scientists and experts on international relations have become increasingly critical of deterrence theory (see George & Smoke, 1974; Gottfried, Bethe, Garwin, Lebow, Gayler, Sagan, & Weisskopf, 1984; Jervis, Lebow, & Stein, 1985; Lebow, 1981; Morgan, 1977). Many of them argue that sooner or later the thousands of poised nuclear missiles are very likely to be released, either as a result of human error or as a result of deliberate decisions during an international crisis, at a time when one or another group of national leaders believe that their own country is about to be attacked and that they can somehow cut down on the amount of destruction by launching their own missiles first.

FAINT RAYS OF HOPE

So where lies our hope? Let me give you my personal answer. Like most other psychologists and social scientists concerned about the arms race, I am not optimistic. But I think I can discern a few faint rays of hope that might gradually be augmented and combined to become a brilliant beam. One of those faint rays is the spread of pro-peace movements that have arisen in America and in many European countries. Those movements at the very least provide some political incentives to help induce policymakers in their respective countries to take meaningful steps toward disarmament and control of nuclear weapons.

Another very faint ray of hope has to do with the reality-testing capabilities of the policymakers themselves. If the dangers of an all-out nuclear war are as horrendous as practically everyone I know thinks they are, then national leaders in the United States, the Soviet Union, and all the other countries that have nuclear weapons—or are about to have them—ought to become highly motivated to take preliminary steps to lessen those dangers. Of course, they might go in the direction of planning to win a nuclear war by preemptive strike strategy designed to prevent the enemy from launching a full-scale nuclear attack. But that option could become less and less attractive, especially if Paul Ehrlich, Carl Sagan, and the numerous other scientists who collaborated with them are correct in the analysis they published in December 1983 in *Science*, forecasting a hitherto unsuspected consequence of extensive nuclear explosions. According to their forecasts, even a limited nuclear war involving only a few hundred of the tens of thousands of existing nuclear warheads would lead to many months and possibly a year or more of subzero temperatures throughout the entire earth (Ehrlich, Sagan, Kennedy, & Roberts, 1984; Turco, Toon, Ackerman, Pollack, & Sagan, 1983). This prolonged "nuclear winter" would freeze all water supplies and destroy almost all food supplies, which might lead to the extinction of all human life. If those forecasts turn out to be based on sound assumptions and come to be accepted by the scientific community, policymakers will realize that launching a nuclear strike will be completely suicidal even if the enemy does not retaliate at all. If so, they may become strongly motivated to move toward genuine arms control and to favor negotiation procedures for handling international conflicts.

At present, when practically none of the fundamental steps to control nuclear weapons and to prevent international disputes from escalating into all-out war are being taken, there is still another slight ray of hope left, it seems to me. That third ray of hope has to do with conflict management. The top policymakers of the major nuclear powers show many signs of being highly motivated to avoid miscalculations and erroneous assumptions in making crucial decisions, especially in crises where there is a relatively high risk of inadvertent outbreak of nuclear war. Isn't it realistic, therefore, to expect policymakers to be in the market for improving their decision-making procedures in order to become more efficient crisis managers?

Now, you will notice that each of the three rays of hope I have mentioned involve attitude change, decision making, and behavioral change. They involve overcoming psychological resistances to new courses of action, avoiding misperceptions, and preventing various other sources of error that make for maladaptive behavior. These are topics that fall squarely within the domain of social psychological theory and research. It seems to me that social psychologists can offer a little something to strengthen each of these very faint rays of hope, to help magnify them perhaps to such an extent that they could become a dependable beam to dispel the bleak gloominess of the future as so many of us now view it.

RESEARCH ON INTERNATIONAL CRISES

A few years ago I came to the conclusion that social psychologists, along with other behavioral and social scientists, should give top priority to research problems that have some potentiality for contributing useful guidelines for preventing nuclear war. And I began redirecting my own research to concentrate on problems of crisis management in international conflicts—to focus on that third faint ray of hope. The main questions I am trying to answer are: What are the major psychological sources of error that give rise to ill-conceived policy decisions during international crises? What are the major situational factors that are determinants of each of the sources of error?

At present I am working on intensive case studies of about two dozen major international crises faced by the United States government since the end of World War II. This research includes comparative analyses, using the approach elaborated by Alexander George and Richard Smoke (1974) in their applications of the "focused comparison" method. The main hypotheses are formulated in terms of testable relationships between independent and dependent variables, which are derived from previously formulated theoretical models that specify causal sequences giving rise to one or another type of error in decision making. I am also trying to discern new causal sequences suggested by case studies of defective decision making that cannot be fitted to known sequences. Later on in this project, I plan to carry out systematic correlational analyses, using fairly large samples in order to test whatever hypotheses survive after the first series of comparative case studies and also to test any new ones that emerge.

As a strong proponent of the experimental method for testing hypotheses about causal relationships, I am keenly aware of the shortcomings of case studies and correlational analyses based on historical narratives and archival documents. But despite all the methodological difficulties, it should be possible to obtain some valuable evidence (see Oskamp, 1984; Tetlock, 1983). By developing empirically-based theory to elucidate the conditions under which misjudgments or miscalculations are made by national leaders in situations of crisis, I expect this research to provide some useful guidelines for policymakers who want to avoid gross errors when making crucial decisions about momentous issues.

One of the first requirements essential for starting to carry out research on defective policymaking is to specify criteria that can be used as dependent variables. In my earlier research (Janis, 1972; Janis & Mann, 1977), I have reviewed the extensive literature on decision making and extracted seven major criteria to use in judging whether a decision made by a person or group is of high versus low quality. Such judgments pertain to the problem-solving procedures that lead up to the act of commitment to a final choice (see Etzioni, 1968; Maier, 1967; Simon, 1957; Taylor, 1965; Wilensky, 1967; Young, 1966). As applied to decision-making groups, the seven procedural criteria or requirements are as follows: The group (1) canvases a wide range of policy alternatives; (2) takes account of a broad range of objectives to be fulfilled and the values implicated by the choice; (3) carefully weighs whatever is found out about the costs or drawbacks and the uncertain risks of negative consequences, as well as the positive consequences, that could flow from each alternative; (4) intensively searches for new information relevant for further evaluation of the policy alternatives; (5) conscientiously takes account of any new information or expert judgment to which the members are exposed, even when the information or judgment does not support the course of action they initially prefer; (6) reexamines the positive and negative consequences of the known alternatives, including those originally regarded as unacceptable, before making a final choice; and (7) makes detailed recommendations or provisions for implementing the chosen policy, with special attention to contingency plans that might be required if various known risks were to materialize.

These criteria or requirements can be used to judge the quality of decision making activities even when the outcome of the decision is too complex or too ambiguous to be evaluated as successful or unsuccessful. Although systematic data are not yet available on this point, it seems plausible to assume that when national leaders make consequential policy decisions, their failures to meet the criteria are symptoms of defective decision making that increase the chances of undesirable outcomes, such as unintended military escalation. In order to assess the frequency and intensity of such symptoms displayed by members of a policy-planning group for any given decision, it is necessary to examine the available records and memoirs bearing on the group's formal and informal meetings.

So far in my research I have been using the seven criteria for assessing the quality of decision making in an impressionistic way by making qualitative clinical judgments based on the available case materials. In a comparative study that I have just started in collaboration with Greg Herek, we are using a systematic rating procedure for each of the seven criteria and separate rating procedures for short-term and long-term outcomes. This study is designed to investigate the assumption that the outcomes are often partly determined by the quality of decision-making procedures. In subsequent studies I plan to check further on the expected relationship by obtaining ratings of the seven criteria from trained research assistants who are kept as blind as possible with regard to the outcome of the decisions and all other variables under investigation. The ratings will be used to select examples for intensive case studies focusing on psychological sources of error that lead to poorly worked out decisions.

GROUPTHINK AS A SOURCE
OF DEFECTIVE DECISION MAKING

One of the theoretical models of defective decision making that I am examining in my present research is derived from my prior research on fiascoes resulting from foreign policy decisions made by top-level governmental advisory groups (Janis, 1972, 1982). In that earlier research, I called attention to a concurrence-seeking tendency among moderately or highly cohesive groups, which I refer to as "groupthink." When this tendency is dominant, the members use their collective cognitive resources to develop rationalizations in line with shared illusions about the invulnerability of their organization or nation and display other symptoms of concurrence seeking (referred to as "the groupthink syndrome").

A number of historic fiascoes appear to have been products of defective decision making on the part of misguided government leaders who obtained social support from their in-groups of advisors. My analysis of case studies of historic fiascoes suggests that among the groups of policy advisors dominated by "groupthink" were: President Harry S Truman's advisory group, whose members supported the decision to escalate the Korean war in 1950 despite firm warnings by the Chinese Communist government that United States entry into North Korea would be met with armed resistance from the Chinese; President John F. Kennedy's advisory group, whose members supported the decision to launch the Bay of Pigs invasion of Cuba in May 1961 despite the availability of information indicating that it would be an unsuccessful venture and would damage the United States' relations with other countries; and President Lyndon B. Johnson's "Tuesday luncheon group," whose members supported the decision to escalate the war in Vietnam during the mid-1960s despite intelligence reports and other information indicating that this course of action would not defeat the Viet Cong or the North Vietnamese and would entail unfavorable political consequences within the United States.

In all these "groupthink"-dominated groups, there were strong internal pressures toward uniformity, which inclined the members to avoid raising controversial issues, even in their own minds, or calling a halt to soft-headed thinking, even when they were keenly aware that the group was moving toward an ill-conceived course of action. "In the months after the Bay of Pigs," Arthur Schlesinger, Jr., wrote in *A Thousand Days* (1965, p. 258), "I bitterly reproached myself for having kept so silent during those crucial discussions in the cabinet room. . . . I can only explain my failure to do more than raise a few timid questions by reporting that one's impulse to blow the whistle on this nonsense was simply undone by the circumstances of the discussion." Schlesinger adds, "Had one senior advisor opposed the adventure, I believe that Kennedy would have canceled it. No one spoke against it. . . . Everyone around him thought he had the Midas touch and could not lose. Despite himself, even this dispassionate and skeptical man may have been affected by the soaring euphoria of the new day" (p. 259).

Eight main *symptoms of groupthink* run through the case studies (Janis, 1972, 1982). Each symptom can be identified by a variety of indicators, derived from historical records, observers' accounts of conversations, and participants' memoirs. The eight symptoms of groupthink are as follows:

(1) An illusion of invulnerability, shared by most or all the members, which creates excessive optimism and encourages taking extreme risks;

(2) An unquestioned belief in the group's inherent morality, inclining the members to ignore the ethical or moral consequences of their decision;

(3) Collective efforts to rationalize in order to discount warnings that might lead the members to reconsider their assumptions before they commit (or recommit) themselves to a policy decision;

(4) Stereotyped views of rivals and enemies as too evil to warrant genuine attempts to negotiate, or as too weak and stupid to counter whatever risky attempts are made to defeat their purposes;

(5) Self-censorship of deviations from the apparent group consensus, reflecting each member's inclination to minimize to himself or herself the importance of doubts and counterarguments;

(6) A shared illusion of unanimity concerning judgments conforming to the majority view (partly resulting from self-censorship of deviations, augmented by the false assumption that silence means consent);

(7) Direct pressure on any member who expresses strong arguments against any of the group's stereotypes, illusions, or commitments, making clear that this type of dissent is contrary to what is expected of all loyal members;

(8) The emergence of self-appointed mindguards—members who protect the group from adverse information that might shatter their shared complacency about the effectiveness and morality of their decisions.

Taking account of prior research findings on group dynamics, I have formulated a set of hypotheses concerning the *antecedent conditions that foster concurrence seeking* on the basis of inferences from my case studies of groupthink and from comparative case studies of well worked out decisions made by similar groups whose members made realistic appraisals of the consequences. One of these counterpoint case studies is of the main decision made by the Kennedy adminis- tration during the Cuban missile crisis in October 1962. Another deals with the hardheaded way that planning committees in the Truman administration evolved the Marshall Plan in 1947. These two case studies indicate that policymaking groups do not always suffer the adverse consequences of group processes, that the quality of the group's decision making activities depends upon current conditions that influence the group atmosphere, including leadership practices.

My main hypotheses concerning the causes and consequences of concurrence seeking are summarized in Figure 5.1. This chart is a condensed representation of the causal sequence that links defective decision making with a set of antecedent conditions (involving a cohesive group of decision makers in an organization characterized by certain types of structural faults when the members are exposed to certain types of provocative situations).

In order to determine whether the groupthink hypothesis can help to account for any given policy fiasco, it is necessary to examine all the available evidence to determine whether the entire pattern represented in Figure 5.1 is present. It does not suffice merely to see if a few of the symptoms can be detected. Rather, in order to conclude that group- think affected the decision-making process, one must ascertain that practically all the symptoms were manifested and that the main antecedent conditions and the expected immediate consequences (the symptoms of defective decision making) were also present.

Not all cohesive groups suffer from groupthink, though all may be vulnerable from time to time (Janis, 1972, 1982). A cohesive group of competent people is not only characterized by high commitment to the group's decisions and conscientious implementation but is also gener- ally capable of making better decisions than any individual in the group who works on the problem alone (see Hatvany & Gladstein, 1982; Steiner, 1982). And yet the advantages of having policy decisions made by a cohesive group are often lost when the leader and the members are subjected to stresses that generate a strong need for unanimity. The striving for concurrence fosters lack of vigilance, unwarranted opti- mism, sloganistic thinking, and reliance on shared rationalizations that bolster the least objectionable alternative (see Janis & Mann, 1977). That alternative is often the one urged by the leader of the policymaking group at the outset of the group's deliberations about a strategic

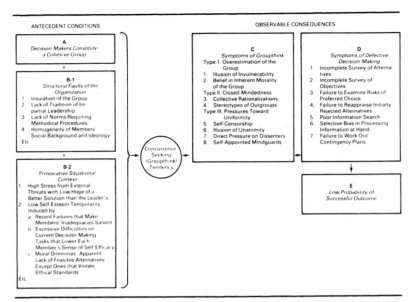

Figure 5.1 **Theoretical analysis of groupthink based on comparisons of high-quality with low-quality decisions by policymaking groups.** From *Groupthink: Psychological Studies of Policy Decisions and Fiascoes* by I. L. Janis, 1982, Boston: Houghton Mifflin. Copyright 1982 by Houghton Mifflin. Reprinted by permission.

decision. When groupthink remains dominant throughout all the meetings, the leader's initial biases are likely to remain uncorrected despite the availability of impressive evidence against them.

In order to prevent groupthink, I have suggested a set of interrelated recommendations. In my book on groupthink, I discuss in detail ten prescriptive hypotheses that involve counteracting the conditions that foster groupthink (Janis, 1982):

(1) Information about the causes and consequences of groupthink given to policymakers well before the onset of a crisis will have a beneficial deterring effect, if presented in a way that is neither unduly optimistic nor pessimistic.

(2) The leader, when assigning a policy-planning mission to a group, should be impartial instead of stating preferences and expectations at the outset. This practice is likely to be effective, however, only if the leader consistently allows the conferees the opportunity to develop an atmosphere of open inquiry and to explore impartially a wide range of policy alternatives.

(3) The leader of a policy-forming group at the outset should assign the role of critical evaluator to each member, encouraging the group to give high priority to airing objections and doubts. This practice will not

be successful, however, unless it is reinforced by the leader's acceptance of criticism of his or her own judgments in order to discourage the members from soft-pedaling their disagreements.

(4) At every meeting devoted to evaluating policy alternatives, one or more members should be assigned the role of devil's advocate. In order to avoid domesticating and neutralizing the devil's advocates, however, the group leader will have to give each of them an unambiguous assignment to present the opposing arguments as cleverly and convincingly as he or she can, as a good lawyer would, challenging the testimony of those advocating the majority position.

(5) One or more outside experts or qualified colleagues within the organization who are not core members of the policy-planning group should be present at each meeting on a staggered basis and should be encouraged to challenge the views of the core members.

(6) Each member of the policy-planning group should discuss periodically the group's deliberations with trusted associates in his or her own unit of the organization and report back their reactions.

(7) Whenever the policy issue involves relations with a rival organization or out-group, a sizable block of time (perhaps an entire session) should be spent surveying all warning signals from the rivals and constructing alternative scenarios of the rival's intentions.

(8) After reaching a preliminary consensus about what seems to be the best policy alternative, the policy-planning group should hold a "second chance" meeting at which every member is expected to express as vividly as he or she can all residual doubts and to rethink the entire issue before making a definitive choice.

(9) Throughout the period when the feasibility and effectiveness of policy alternatives are being surveyed, the policy-planning group should from time to time divide into two or more subgroups to meet separately, under different chairpersons, and then come together to hammer out their differences.

(10) The organization should routinely follow the administrative practice of setting up several independent policy-planning and evaluation groups to work on the same policy question, each carrying out its deliberations under a different chairperson.

All of these and related prescriptive hypotheses, such as the procedures recommended by A. George (1980) for ensuring "multiple advocacy" must be validated by systematic social psychological research before they can be applied with any confidence. The first five recommendations could be applied even when time is so limited that only a few emergency policy-planning meetings can be held, but the last five require a fair amount of extra time and would also be costly in terms of requiring added effort on the part of high-level personnel. All ten of the proposed remedies may prove to have other drawbacks, including undesirable side effects such as alienating the chief executive from key advisors. Nevertheless, these prescriptive hypotheses appear sufficiently promising to warrant the trouble and expense of being tested as potentially useful means for counteracting groupthink. Research on these hypotheses, which has already been started by investigators using laboratory experiments and systematic field studies, can contribute to our basic theoretical understanding of group decision-making processes as well as to practical guidelines for crisis management (see Courtwright, 1978; Flowers, 1977; Fodor & Smith, 1982; Janis, 1982, pp. 302-308; Tetlock, 1983). Many of the antigroupthink procedures might also prove to be helpful for counteracting initial biases of the members, preventing pluralistic ignorance, and eliminating other sources of error that can arise independently of groupthink.

DEFECTIVE PATTERNS OF COPING WITH STRESS

Another conceptual model I am using in my research on sources of error in international crises pertains to patterns of coping with the stresses of decision making. In my collaborative work with Leon Mann (*Decision Making*, 1977), the groupthink syndrome is treated as a special case of one particular defective coping pattern—defensive avoidance. Our work focused on a major problem that requires theoretical analysis and empirical research: Under what conditions does stress have favorable versus unfavorable effects on the quality of decision making? Our conflict-theory analysis attempted to answer this question as well as broader questions concerning the conditions under which people will use sound decision-making procedures to avoid arriving at ill-conceived choices that they soon regret. We described, on the basis of the extensive research on psychological stress, the different ways people deal with stress when they are making vital decisions. When a person is preoccupied with a decisional conflict, the main sources of stress include fear of suffering from the known losses that will be entailed by whichever alternative is chosen, worry about unknown things that could go wrong when vital consequences are at stake, concern about making a fool of oneself in the eyes of others, and losing self-esteem if the decision works out badly. Vital decisions often involve conflicting values, which make the decision maker realize that any choice he or she makes will require sacrificing ideals. As a result, the decision maker's anticipatory anxiety, shame, or guilt is increased, which adds to the level of stress.

In assuming that stress itself is frequently a major cause of errors in decision making, we do not deny the influence of other common causes, such as ignorance, defective use of analogies, prejudice, and bureaucratic politics. We maintain, however, that a major reason for many ill-conceived and poorly implemented decisions has to do with the motivational consequences of decisional conflict, including attempts to ward off the stresses generated by agonizingly difficult choices.

Our analysis deals with five basic *patterns of coping* with any threat or opportunity requiring a person to make a vital choice. These patterns were derived mainly from an analysis of the research literature on psychological stress bearing on how people react to warnings that urge protective action to avert disasters.

The five coping patterns are as follows:

(1) Unconflicted adherence (or inertia): The decision maker complacently decides to continue whatever he or she has been doing, ignoring information about the risks.

(2) Unconflicted change: The decision maker uncritically adopts whichever new course of action is most salient or most strongly recommended, without making any contingency plans and without psychological preparation for setbacks.

(3) Defensive avoidance: The decision maker evades the conflict by procrastinating, shifting responsibility to someone else, or constructing wishful rationalizations that bolster the least objectionable alternative, minimizing the expected unfavorable consequences and remaining selectively inattentive to corrective information. (This pattern usually seems to be dominant among the members of a policy-planning group when they display the symptoms of groupthink).

(4) Hypervigilance: The decision maker in a panic-like state searches frantically for a way out of the dilemma, rapidly shifting back and forth between alternatives, and impulsively seizes upon a hastily contrived solution that seems to promise immediate relief. He or she overlooks the full range of consequences of the choice because of emotional excitement, repetitive thinking, and cognitive constriction (manifested by reduction in immediate memory span and simplistic ideas).

(5) Vigilance: The decision maker searches painstakingly for relevant information, assimilates information in an unbiased manner, and appraises alternatives carefully before making a choice.

Although the first two patterns are occasionally adaptive in saving time, effort, and emotional wear and tear—especially for routine or minor decisions—they often lead to defective decisions when decision makers must make a choice that has serious consequences for themselves or for their organization or nation. Similarly, defensive avoidance and hypervigilance may occasionally be adaptive in certain extreme situations, but generally reduce the decision makers' chances of averting serious losses. Consequently, all four are regarded as defective patterns of decision making in major crises or whenever important values are at stake. The fifth pattern, vigilance, although occasionally maladaptive if danger is imminent and a split-second response is required, generally facilitates a problem-solving approach that meets the main criteria for sound decision making.

Among the main questions we addressed were: What are the conditions that make for vigilance? How do they differ from those that make for each of the four defective coping patterns? Preliminary answers to these questions are presented in Figure 5.2, which is a schematic summary of the Janis and Mann (1977) conflict model of decision making. This model, based on the research literature on psychological stress, specifies the psychological conditions that mediate the five coping patterns and the level of stress that accompanies them.

Our analysis of the pertinent research literature (Janis & Mann, 1977, Chap. 3) indicates that the coping patterns are determined by the presence or absence of three conditions: (1) awareness of serious risks for whichever alternative is chosen (i.e., arousal of conflict), (2) hope or optimism about finding a better alternative, and (3) belief that there is adequate time in which to search and deliberate before a decision is required. Although there may be marked individual differences in preference for one or another of the coping patterns, all five patterns are assumed to be in the repertoire of every person when he or she functions as a decision maker. In different circumstances the same person will use different coping patterns depending on which of the three crucial conditions are present or absent.

In our review of social psychological studies bearing on premature closure, postdecisional regret, and a number of other aspects of decisional behavior (Janis & Mann, 1977, chaps. 4-12), we call attention to scattered findings consistent with predictions about the behavioral consequences of vigilant versus nonvigilant coping patterns, from which we conclude that our theoretical analysis is plausible. We have also done some social psychological experiments that were designed to test prescriptive hypotheses derived from our conflict model. These include studies of the effectiveness of a balance sheet procedure, stress inoculation, and a number of other interventions that counteract the beliefs and perceptions specified in Figure 5.2 as being responsible for defective coping patterns. The most effective interventions can probably be incorporated into standard operating procedures to be followed by policymakers in order to promote a vigilant problem-solving approach to international crises. Some of the standard operating procedures, such as the balance sheet, which requires systematic listing of pros and cons for each available alternative, might also help to

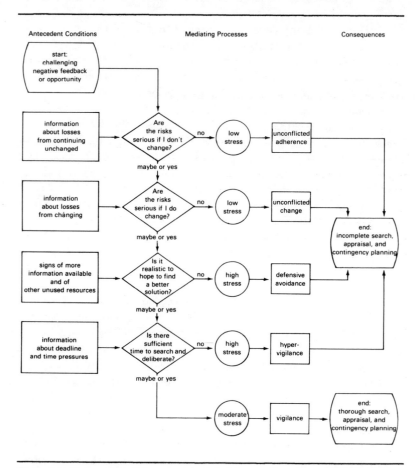

Figure 5.2   The conflict-theory model of decision making. From *Decision-Making: A Psychological Analysis of Conflict, Choice and Commitment* by I. L. Janis & L. Mann, 1977, New York: Free Press. Copyright 1977 by Free Press. Adapted by permission.

prevent other common sources of error—for example, reliance on stereotypes of opponents, the availability heuristic, oversimplified decision rules, and other cognitive shortcuts that people use to deal with complicated issues. These various types of cognitive errors are likely to increase if the person's motivational state is not conducive to vigilant problem solving. A great deal of difficult mental work is required to engage in sustained critical thinking and to avoid lapsing into defensive avoidance, which involves wishful thinking and premature closure.

HIGH EMOTIONAL AROUSAL:
HYPERVIGILANCE AND RAGE

Emotional overreactions to international crises are very worrisome during the nuclear age—especially because of the short delivery times for nuclear missiles, which place top policymakers under extreme time pressure. In a panic-like state of hypervigilance, policymakers could make serious errors by misinterpreting unexpected warning signals and acting impulsively in implementing whatever plans for protective action are most salient. If the strategic doctrine of counterforce and notions about prevailing in a nuclear war are salient (with the expectation that if you don't use your nuclear weapons you will soon lose them), the chances are much greater that momentary reactions of hypervigilance on the part of the top-level policymakers will lead to releasing the nuclear weapons. You will recall that a key factor making for hypervigilance is perceived lack of time to arrive at a satisfactory solution to a crisis. It follows from this analysis that high priority should be given to providing a realistic basis for lengthening the perceived time between the occurrence of a serious threat and a required protective response. But, of course, technological developments are going just the other way. Already, according to recent official reports, delivery times for direct transoceanic missiles to reach United States cities are down to 30 minutes and it is estimated that submarine-launched missiles could reach Washington in only 10 minutes.

If the psychological factor of time pressure leading to hypervigilant reactions were to be taken seriously, counteracting technological developments that shorten attack time would undoubtedly become an important agenda item in arms control negotiations. It might be as important to freeze technological developments that shorten delivery time of missiles as it is to freeze the manufacture of nuclear warheads.

In a few case studies of international crises involving time pressure, I have noticed that under conditions of high stress, some top-level policymakers display symptoms of high emotional arousal that have all the characteristic features of hypervigilance. Others in the policymaking group, who also react to the same danger situation with strong emotional arousal, display a pattern of rage. These alternative emotional reactions appear to illustrate the well-known textbook proposition that high emotional arousal in response to signs of danger can give rise to either flight or fight.

Examples of these two types of emotional reactions can be discerned among the top U.S. policymakers who dealt with the crisis that arose in 1956 when Britain, France, and Israel invaded Egypt in response to the

Egyptian president's taking control of the Suez Canal and illegally closing it to Israeli ships. For example, Finer (1964) asserts that many top policymakers within the U.S. State Department were "terrified" because of indirect Soviet threats to launch nuclear missiles to attack London and Paris if England and France did not immediately withdraw from Egypt. As a result, their recommendation to President Eisenhower was that "Britain, France, Israel must be brought to heel immediately." According to a U.S. State Department official, "one high-ranking official of the State Department . . . could not conceal his alarm. 'We must stop this before we are all burned to a crisp!' he exclaimed at a staff meeting after Russia had sent threatening notes to Britain and France. His reaction [was] based on fear" (Murphy, 1964, p. 391). Several sources indicate that hypervigilance was limited to a few State Department officials and that other policymakers, particularly President Eisenhower, displayed a different emotional reaction. The President, who was noted for his calmness in the face of crises, in this instance is described as having been "personally thwarted"; he "reacted with fury and insisted the United States go to the [U.N.] Security Council immediately and stop [England, France, and Israel from continuing] the invasion" (Parmet, 1972, p. 485). The President was "shocked," according to Sherman Adams, his White House chief of staff, by the dangerously destabilizing military action taken by England and France without giving him any prior warning, at a time just before election day when he was campaigning for reelection (Adams, 1961, p. 256). "Outside of his illnesses," Adams asserts, "that was the worst week that Eisenhower experienced in all the years that I worked with him in the White House" (p. 256). Adams refers to Eisenhower's "hurt feelings" and describes him as "wrought up . . . over the turn of events" (p. 260). Guhin (1972, p. 291) also characterizes Eisenhower as "irritated by the whole affair" and as having personally taken the initiative in the harsh, punitive actions taken by the U.S. government against its main allies. Guhin quotes Abba Eban, Israel's Ambassador to Washington, as having noted that President Eisenhower "was in a mood of someone betrayed" (p. 292).

Some of the main behavioral consequences of rage are similar to those of hypervigilance in that the state of high emotional arousal makes for loss of cognitive efficiency, overlooking of important objectives, and failure to work out adequate solutions to complex problems. In the case of the Suez crisis of 1956, President Eisenhower, in a "wrought-up" state, took the lead in putting extreme pressure, accompanied by severe economic threats, on England and France to give up their plan to take over the Suez canal, forcing them to pull out of Egypt immediately. He gave his allies no opportunity to save face, thereby inflicting on them such a stinging defeat that the governments in London and Paris promptly fell. At the U.N., the United States voted to censure England and France in a way that was unnecessarily humiliating. During the following weeks, the U.S. government delayed giving urgently needed oil supplies to aid the two countries when they were suffering from a severe oil shortage as a result of the closing of the Suez canal. This harsh handling undoubtedly contributed to the French government's decision to become detached from NATO and seriously impaired the United States' relations with England as well as France.

USING THE MODUS OPERANDI APPROACH TO EXTRACT "LESSONS OF HISTORY"

Can intensive case studies like the ones I have just cited illuminate psychological sources of error in policymaking, and can they provide at least some low-level evidence that cannot be dismissed as mere anecdotes? I think they can, but to do so it is necessary to make use of recent methodological refinements designed to improve the value of case study research. Michael Scriven (1976) has described a methodological approach that I believe can be applied fruitfully in research on defective policy decisions by national leaders. He has analyzed in detail the logic of the coroner who investigates the probable cause of death of each individual case brought to the morgue, using nonexperimental evidence to draw fairly dependable inferences about the causal sequences. He describes the coroner's "modus operandi" approach, which is also used by many detectives, historians, structural engineering troubleshooters, and aeronautics specialists who investigate the probable causes of death and injury in air crashes. All of these various types of investigators have found ways of determining the probable cause of undesirable events with fairly high certainty even though the data available to them do not come from controlled experiments or even quasi-experiments.

Basically, the approach involves formulating all the known causal sequences that might account for the observed outcome—whether it be a death, a crime, or a large-scale disaster—and then attempting to find out which of them appears to be implicated. This requires careful scrutiny of every shred of evidence that might provide telltale signs indicating the step-by-step ways in which each of the alternative causes is most likely to operate. Thus, the modus operandi approach involves looking for a particular configuration that corresponds to a known causal chain. Working backwards from the observed effect, the investigator watches for a pattern of indicators of mediating processes that connect antecedent conditions with the observed outcome.

Should the approach recommended by Scriven be taken seriously in the fields of research bearing on decision making in international crises? I believe that it should be, particularly when working on research problems that cannot be investigated by means of controlled experiments. Essentially the same modus operandi approach used by the coroner can be used, it seems to me, to determine the probable causes of disastrous decisions by governmental policymakers that can lead to huge numbers of deaths and other severe losses to the nation. With regard to the central problems with which I have been concerned— sources of error in dealing with international crises—we already know a fair amount about quite a few of the causal sequences involving cognitive, affective, and affiliative constraints on effective problem solving and these should be formulated much more explicitly than has been done so far.

One well-known sequence that gives rise to defective problem solving by executives involves unproductive power struggles that occur when a decision-making group is composed of competing factions engaged in internecine warfare (Halperin, 1974). Other affiliative constraints that contribute to errors in decision making involve overdependence of the members of the group on the leader. The most familiar one occurs when a powerful, autocratic leader induces conformity to his or her idiosyncratic position, stifling all dissent, skepticism, and cautionary information from the members by making it clear that anyone who does not completely go along with the leader's foregone conclusions will be fired or subjected to other punitive recriminations (Argyris, 1965; Katz & Kahn, 1966). The groupthink syndrome (Janis, 1982) and the various coping patterns described by Janis and Mann (1977), such as hypervigilance and defensive avoidance, which I described earlier, are less familiar sources of error whose modus operandi (summarized in Figures 5.1 and 5.2) require further investigation.

In line with Scriven's (1976) recommendations, my research on international crises attempts to specify as fully as possible each of the causal sequences that are major sources of error. In this research I am trying to focus on whatever faint clues can be discerned concerning such sources of error as bureaucratic politics, misperceptions arising from cognitive consistency strivings, misuse of analogies, oversimplified decision rules, faulty heuristics used to estimate probable outcomes, and stereotypes of opponents or other out-groups, as well as groupthink and the various defective coping patterns that interfere with effective problem solving. It seems to me that intensive case studies are needed initially, incorporating the modus operandi approach in order to specify step-by-step sequences that link antecedent conditions (such as structural features of the organization, design, and composition of the decision-making group, and norms of the organization affecting leadership practices) with the quality of decision-making procedures used in arriving at strategic decisions. A series of such case studies could help us to formulate descriptive hypotheses concerning the conditions under which each psychological source of error is most likely and least likely to occur.

For purposes of investigating sources of error in strategic decision making, I have begun to work out analytic flow charts showing the antecedent conditions, the telltale signs of the mediating processes, and the specific effects on quality of decision making of each of the known sources of error (one example of such a causal sequence is presented below). Once the error-sequence charts are available for a variety of cognitive and motivational sources of error, it should be possible for policy analysts as well as social scientists to use them whenever they are analyzing any major policy failure. Such charts should help investigators and practitioners to extract more valid "lessons of history" than can be inferred on the basis of the impressionistic analyses now being used. In some instances, as I mentioned earlier, more than one causal sequence may be found to play a contributory role as sources of error. In other instances, we can expect to find that the list of causal sequences is incomplete because none of them fit the case at hand, which can lead to the discovery of causal sequences that have not yet been explicated.

THE "UNSQUEAKY WHEEL TRAP"

Recently I encountered an example of a causal sequence involving serious defects in implementation planning, which I had never previously encountered in any of my prior research or in the social science literature. The case study deals with the decision by President Carter and his advisors in April 1980 that led to the ill-fated attempt to use military force to rescue the American hostages in Iran, which the news media called a fiasco comparable to the Bay of Pigs.

Government spokesmen claimed that it was all a matter of unforeseeable accidents and bad luck that helicopter failures forced the military commander to abort the entire mission on the desert sands of Iran hundreds of miles from Teheran. Some informed critics, however, say that the plan was ill-conceived. I tried to find out whether symptoms of defective decision making could be discerned in the White House deliberations that ended with presidential approval of the military rescue mission. So far as the present evidence goes, I find that no dependable answer can be given as to how many of the seven symptoms were present because details about the secret meetings in which the rescue mission was planned and approved have not yet been released and the bits of testimony available at present are somewhat contradictory. But I think that I have learned something important about one specific type of defect in planning the mission.

My major source of information is the memoirs of Zbigniew Brzezinski (1983), the President's National Security Advisor, who for many months had been urging President Carter to restore America's honor by launching a military attack rather than continuing to try to negotiate. Contrary to the reports of governmental investigative committees, Brzezinski conveys an image of the decision as having been very carefully worked out, with full exploration of the alternatives. But his overall claim that the rescue mission was thoroughly worked out is contradicted to some extent by his own detailed account of how it failed. From what he says, it is apparent that the major risks of the first crucial phase of the rescue plan—the rendezvous and refueling of the U.S. aircraft in the Iranian desert—had hardly been examined at all by President Carter and his key advisors. For example, Brzezinski acknowledges that "my concern over the possible failure of the mission did not pertain to something like what finally happened—its early abortion—but rather to . . . its execution in Teheran" (p. 488).

Brzezinski's memoirs make it clear that the top policymakers in the White House group had not envisaged the possibility that the mission might have to be aborted either because several of the helicopters might malfunction or that the mission might be compromised as a result of being observed by Iranians in passing vehicles on the nearby road. Apparently, certain of the crucial implementation plans were not examined carefully enough by Brzezinski and others in the President's advisory group. A high-level military review group set up by the Joint Chiefs of Staff to investigate what went wrong concluded that the flaws could have been corrected if the small secret circle of planners had asked for their plan to be reviewed by qualified experts within the government (Shaw, 1980). For example, arrangements could have been made to carry out a weather reconnaissance flight in advance of the helicopter flights, and more helicopters could have been added to the mission. The same report also faults the planners for having failed to arrange to have the desert rendezvous "fully rehearsed" in advance and also for having neglected to set up an identifiable on-scene command post with adequate communication and control in the event of unanticipated difficulties (Middleton, 1981, p. 112). If these additional implementation and contingency plans had been worked out, the chances of failures requiring that the mission be aborted, as well as the chances of a disaster, such as the accidental crash of U.S. aircraft in which eight men were killed, might have been considerably reduced.

From the available accounts, I surmise that a major reason that questions about the risks of the first phase of the mission were not raised within the top-level planning group is because the most obvious risks of the rescue mission were in the later phases—the enormous chances of the invading U.S. forces being detected and attacked when they approached Teheran, of the hostages being killed before their would-be rescuers could get to them, and of U.S. aircraft being shot down as they attempted to depart from Teheran. Evidently, as the old saying goes, it is the squeaky wheels that get the oil; any unsqueaky wheel is neglected. When grappling with a complicated multistage plan, policymakers are likely to focus their implementation and contingency planning on the steps that pose the most obvious risks. Perhaps there is a contrast effect whereby the least risky steps tend to be labeled as safe and easy to handle—"that's not where our troubles will be."

The main point is that even if decision makers are quite vigilant in their approach to the problems of working out or checking up on a feasible plan that takes account of the risks, their tendency may be to focus their information search, appraisals, and implementation planning entirely upon the steps that are known from the outset to be fraught with danger, the "squeaky wheels." If so, they will tend to overlook the more subtle or hidden risks in any relatively nondangerous or routine step in the plan. This is what I refer to as "the unsqueaky wheel trap." Perhaps the tendency to neglect the unsqueaky wheel could be counteracted if policymakers were to assume that every wheel is potentially squeaky and could lead to failure if one complacently assumes that it will be trouble-free.

In another case study, I have encountered what appears to be another clear-cut example of the "unsqueaky wheel trap." During almost the entire first half of 1950, numerous warnings indicating that North Korea was getting ready to attack South Korea were ignored by President Truman, Secretary of State Acheson, and other top leaders in the administration. At that time, their planning for Asia was geared entirely to the contingency of a general war. The squeaky wheels were Formosa and the China civil war, which were the trouble spots that threatened to embroil the United States in a clash with Communist China and possibly with the Soviet Union; the Korean peninsula, which was seen as having little strategic value for the United States in the event of a general war, apparently was an unsqueaky wheel (Paige, 1968; George & Smoke, 1974; Truman, 1956). In a well-documented and insightful analysis of the failure of the Truman administration to assess the policy issues posed by the neglected warnings, George and Smoke (1974) point out that the American policymakers lost the opportunity to take steps in advance to cushion the effects of a North Korean attack in such a way that they might have been able to avoid military intervention when the North Korean attack was launched; they also lost the opportunity to try to deter the attack entirely by strengthening their commitment to South Korea. The authors comment that *"A costly and tragic war through miscalculation might then have been avoided"* (p. 164, italics added). The costly and tragic consequences of that war included the deaths of over 33,600 American soldiers. Among the large number of casualties were about 14,000 soldiers sent to the aid of South Korea by America's allies, more than 1,500,000 Chinese soldiers, at least 1,360,000 North and South Korean soldiers, and an even larger number of Korean civilians, for a total of well over four million people seriously injured or killed (Paige, 1968, pp. 3-4).

The unsqueaky wheel trap is an example of the type of finding that can be extracted from case study research that focuses on the conditions under which erroneous policy decisions are made when international crises develop. This line of research is not yet far enough along, however, to answer the crucial question for crisis management in the nuclear age when threatening events occur, such as those similar to the onset of the Korean war: Can it contribute useful guidelines for preventing a far more costly and far more tragic war in the future?

CONCLUSION

I have suggested that close analytical study of decision making in international conflict situations can elucidate desirable and defective patterns shown by high-level national groups in responding to crises. Given that experimental research is impossible in this arena, the most feasible research technique is to use the "modus operandi" approach to analyze the apparent causal sequences of events and processes that are prominent in cases of major historical fiascoes or successes, and thus to attempt to provide procedural guidelines for policymakers.

From case-study material about major international crises, even including ones where the eventual outcomes were ambiguous, it is possible to identify seven criteria or requirements for good decision-making procedures (see Figure 5.1). Similarly, five patterns that groups and individuals use to cope with the stress of decision making can be discerned, of which four are usually undesirable and counterproductive. Only the pattern termed "vigilance" is apt to lead to competent planning (see Figure 5.2).

The concurrence-seeking tendency called "groupthink" is an example of a defective type of decision-making process that has been found in a number of historical fiascoes. This chapter has briefly summarized its key symptoms or characteristics and the antecedent conditions that are likely to produce groupthink. It has also suggested ten prescriptions for preventing groupthink that policymakers can use to try to improve the quality of their group decisions.

In addition to groupthink, other causal sequences that often lead to defective problem solving are power struggles within groups, over-dependence of group members on an autocratic leader, and the "unsqueaky wheel trap." All of these patterns need further research on their crucial antecedent conditions, mediating processes, and typical consequences.

REFERENCES

Adams, S. (1961). *Firsthand report: The story of the Eisenhower administration.* New York: Harper.

Argyris, C. (1965). *Organization and innovation.* Homewood, IL: Irwin & Dorsey.

Brzezinski, Z. (1983). *Power and principle: Memoirs of the national security advisor.* New York: Farrar, Straus, Giroux.

Bundy, M. G., Kennan, G. F., McNamara, R. S., & Smith, G. (1982, Spring). Nuclear weapons and the Atlantic Alliance. *Foreign Affairs, 60,* 753-768.

Courtwright, J. A. (1978). A laboratory investigation of groupthink. *Communication Monographs, 45,* 229-246.

Ehrlich, P. R., Harte, J., Harwell, M. A., Raven, P. H., Sagan, C., Woodwell, G. M., Berry, J., Ayensu, E. S., Ehrlich, A. H., Eisner, T., Gould, S. J., Grover, H. D., Herrera, R., May, R. M., Mayr, E., McKay, C. P., Mooney, H. A., Myers, N., Pimentel, D., & Teal, J. M. (1983). Long-term biological consequences of nuclear war. *Science, 222,* 1293-1300.

Ehrlich, P. R., Sagan, C., Kennedy, D., & Roberts, W. O. (1984). *The cold and the dark: The world after nuclear war.* New York: Norton.

Etzioni, A. (1968). *The active society.* New York: Free Press.

Finer, H. (1964). *Dulles over Suez: The theory and practice of his diplomacy.* Chicago: Quadrangle.

Flowers, M. (1977). A laboratory test of Janis' groupthink analysis. *Journal of Personality and Social Psychology, 35,* 888-896.

Fodor, E. M., & Smith, T. (1982). The power motive as an influence on group decision making. *Journal of Personality and Social Psychology, 42,* 178-185.

George, A. (1980). *Presidential decisionmaking in foreign policy: The effective use of information and advice.* Boulder, CO: Westview.

George, A., & Smoke, R. (1974). *Deterrence in American foreign policy: Theory and practice.* New York: Columbia University Press.

Gottfried, K., Bethe, H., Garwin, R., Lebow, R. N., Gayler, N., Sagan, C., & Weisskopf, V. (1984). *Anti-satellite weapons and ballistic missile defense.* New York: Random House.

Guhin, M. A. (1972). *John Foster Dulles: A statesman and his times.* New York: Columbia University Press.

Halperin, M. H. (1974). *Bureaucratic politics and foreign policy.* Washington, DC: The Brookings Institution.

Hatvany, N. G., & Gladstein, D. (1982). A perspective on group decision making. In D. A. Nadler, M. L. Tushman, & N. Hatvany (Eds.), *Approaches to managing organizational behavior.* Boston: Little, Brown.

Janis, I. L. (1972). *Victims of groupthink.* Boston: Houghton Mifflin.

Janis, I. L., (1982). *Groupthink: Psychological studies of policy decisions and fiascoes* (Revised ed.). Boston: Houghton Mifflin.

Janis, I. L., & Mann, L. (1977). *Decision-making: A psychological analysis of conflict, choice and commitment.* New York: Free Press.

Jervis, R., Lebow, R. N., & Stein, J. G. (1985). *Psychology and deterrence.* Baltimore: Johns Hopkins University Press.

Katz, D., & Kahn, R. L. (1966). *The social psychology of organizations.* New York: John Wiley.

Kennan, G. I. (1982). *The nuclear delusion: Soviet-American relations in the atomic age.* New York: Pantheon.

Lebow, R. N. (1981). *Between peace and war: The nature of international crisis.* Baltimore: Johns Hopkins University Press.

Maier, N. (1967). Group problem solving. *Psychological Review, 74,* 239-249.

Middleton, D. (1981, May 17). Going the military route. *New York Times Magazine.*

Morgan, P. (1977). *Deterrence: A conceptual framework.* Beverly Hills, CA: Sage.

Murphy, R. (1964). *Diplomat among warriors.* Garden City, NY: Doubleday.

Oskamp, S. (1984). *Applied social psychology.* Englewood Cliffs, NJ: Prentice-Hall.

Paige, G. D. (1968). *The Korean decision: June 24-30, 1950.* New York: Free Press.

Parmet, H. S. (1982). *Eisenhower and the American crusades.* New York: Macmillan.

Schlesinger, A., Jr. (1965). *A thousand days.* Boston: Houghton Mifflin.

Scriven, M. (1976). Maximizing the power of causal investigations: The modus operandi method. In G. V. Glass (Ed.), *Evaluation studies review annual* (Vol. 1). Beverly Hills, CA: Sage.

Shaw, G. (1980, August 24). Secrecy, ill luck cited in failure of Iran rescue raid. *Los Angeles Times,* pp. 1, 18.

Simon, H. A. (1957). *Administrative behavior: A study of decision-making processes in administrative organizations* (2nd ed.) New York: Macmillan.

Steiner, I. (1982). Heuristic models of groupthink. In H. Brandstetter, J. H. Davis, & G. Stocker-Kreichgauer (Eds.), *Contemporary problems in group decision-making.* New York: Academic Press.

Taylor, D. W. (1965). Decision making and problem solving. In J. March (Ed.), *Handbook of organizations.* Chicago: Rand McNally.

Tetlock, P. E. (1983). Psychological research on foreign policy: A methodological overview. In L. Wheeler (Ed.), *Review of personality and social psychology* (Vol. 4). Beverly Hills, CA: Sage.

Truman, H. S. (1956). *Memoirs: Years of trials and hope* (Vol. II). Garden City, NY: Doubleday.

Turco, R. P., Toon, O. B., Ackerman, T. P., Pollack, J. B., & Sagan, C. (1983). Nuclear winter: Global consequences of multiple nuclear explosions. *Science, 222,* 1283-1292.

Wilensky, H. L. (1967). *Organizational intelligence.* New York: Basic Books.

Young, S. (1966). *Management: A systems analysis.* Glenview, IL: Scott, Foresman.

PETER J. CARNEVALE

6

MEDIATION OF INTERNATIONAL DISPUTES

The day before the invasion occurred, in a telephone conversation with President Leopoldo Galtieri of Argentina, President Ronald Reagan tried to prevent the Argentine invasion of the British-held Falkland Islands ("Las Malvinas" to the Argentines). On April 2, 1982, Argentine forces attacked, producing a strong British military reaction—the dispatching of a naval armada—and also producing a highly publicized effort by Secretary of State Alexander Haig to mediate the dispute (Freedman, 1982; Purcell, 1982). It also stimulated a more discreet effort at mediation by President Lopez Portillo of Mexico (Duran, 1984). The British fleet reached the islands twenty-eight days after the invasion, and Secretary Haig announced that his mediation effort had failed. Although appearing neutral during the mediation effort, the United States subsequently, and openly, supported Britain—providing intelligence, fuel, and missiles. On June 14, after approximately 1000 Argentine and 250 British deaths, the Argentine garrison surrendered to the British forces.

When an international conflict occurs, nations that are external to it have three general options: (a) ignore it, (b) join one side against the other, or (c) attempt to facilitate its resolution. If the latter option is chosen, one approach is *mediation*, a form of conflict intervention that attempts to facilitate voluntary agreements through negotiation. Sometimes parties to a dispute request mediation, but they are under no obligation to accept it when it is offered (Pruitt, 1981; Rubin, 1980; Touval, 1982; Young, 1967).

International conflicts often involve mediation, and international mediation raises some general questions that social psychologists can help answer. Why do nations act to mediate disputes between other nations? When are they likely to intervene as mediators, and what determines the character of the mediation effort? What strategies and tactics are available to international mediators and when are they used?

AUTHOR'S NOTE: I wish to thank Stuart Oskamp, Dean G. Pruitt, Cindy Fobian, and two anonymous reviewers for their helpful comments on an earlier version of this manuscript.

87

Under what circumstances does mediation facilitate agreement—or hinder it?

The purpose of this chapter is to introduce the topic of international mediation, and to offer some answers to the above questions. The central thesis of this chapter is that social psychology can contribute to understanding mediation, and that more social psychologists should become involved in this area. At the outset, readers should be aware that international mediation involves complexities and nuances that make the application of social psychological ideas highly possible but far from complete. One reason for this is that empirical research on mediation is so scarce.

There are, however, many rich, descriptive and theoretical studies of international negotiation and mediation that this chapter benefits from. These include negotiation studies by Druckman (1983), Gulliver (1979), Ikle (1964), Kelman (1965), Pruitt (1981), Snyder and Diesing (1977), and Zartman (1977); and studies of international mediation by Berman and Johnson (1977), Campbell (1976), Frei (1976), Jackson (1952), Rubin (1981), Touval (1975, 1982), Touval and Zartman (in press), Young (1967, 1970) and Zartman & Berman (1982), to name just a few. Much of this literature involves generalizations based on case analyses of actual negotiations and mediations. A noteworthy example is the book by Campbell (1976), which presents firsthand recollections by the actual participants of the 1954 United States and British mediation of the dispute between Yugoslavia and Italy. This was a territorial and ethnic dispute that involved the city of Trieste and surrounding area, and the mediation of it is considered by many to have been highly successful (Campbell, 1976; Touval, 1975).

OVERVIEW OF INTERNATIONAL MEDIATION

The mediator role is only one of several conflict intervention roles that international actors can assume. There are at least four others, which generally do not involve as much participation in the interaction between the parties: (a) *good offices*, which entail the least involvement, simply providing an opportunity for the parties to negotiate, such as a place for them to meet; (b) *special envoy*, who conveys a message from one party to the other; (c) *intermediary*, who carries messages back and forth between the parties; and (d) *conciliation*, which involves efforts to change the parties' images and attitudes about one another (Pruitt & Rubin, in press; Touval, 1982; Young, 1967).

International mediators are often the official representatives of nations, groups of nations, or international organizations. Ralph Bunche in 1948 and 1949 represented the United Nations, as well as the United States, in mediating the Arab-Israeli conflict (Touval, 1982). Representatives of regional groups such as the Organization of American States and the Organization of African Unity attempt mediation, as do representatives of international organizations such as the International Committee of the Red Cross and the American Friends Service Committee (Berman & Johnson, 1977).

The intervention role of private individuals in international disputes is often informal, behind the scenes, and usually does not make headlines. Private individuals often are conduits of information and sources of advice when regular channels of communication are blocked, as the French lawyer Christian Bourguet was during the Iranian hostage crisis. Cyrus Eaton, the millionaire industrialist, spent time and money trying to foster positive relations between the United States and other countries such as the Soviet Union and Cuba. He did this in meetings with the leaders of these nations and also by hosting international conferences (Berman & Johnson, 1977). As another example, Herbert Kelman has engaged in problem-solving workshops with Israeli and Palestinian citizens in an attempt to reduce adversarial sentiments between these peoples (see Kelman, 1977).

When mediators represent nations, they have at their disposal the economic and political support of the nation that they represent. In his mediation of the Middle East conflict from 1973-1975, Secretary of State Henry Kissinger wielded considerable clout as the representative of the United States (Rubin, 1981). Mediators who are representatives of organizations will only be effective to the extent that their organization is viewed by the parties as legitimate. Pruitt and Rubin (in press) note that the Iranians were unresponsive during the hostage crisis to the intervention efforts of Kurt Waldheim, the United Nations Secretary-General, because they believed that he represented an illegitimate organization. However, the proposition that perceived legitimacy of mediators is an important source of their influence has not been examined empirically.

Strategies of Mediation

As a rule, mediators state their goal as the abatement of conflict, but in international contexts their agenda often includes the protection or enhancement of their own political or economic interests (Touval, 1982;

Touval & Zartman, in press). Social psychologists who study mediation discuss the strategies and tactics that are available to mediators and the circumstances in which they are likely to be followed and be successful (Pruitt, 1981; Pruitt & Rubin, in press; Rubin, 1980). Mediators of international disputes can follow any of four general strategies:

(1) *Entice a party to yield.* The mediator can compensate a party for making or agreeing to a proposal.
(2) *Pressure a party to yield.* These methods include making threats (e.g., to join one side against the other) and persuasive arguments, and may involve deception.
(3) *Seek coordinated movement* between the parties in order to achieve an alternative that is mutually acceptable. This may involve the development of integrative outcomes such as novel solutions reconciling divergent interests.
(4) *Delay mediation or withdraw it.* This has the effect of making parties who want mediation more receptive to it.

These strategies are not incompatible and to some extent may be used in combination or successively. As an example, mediation may be withdrawn with the expectation that after some period of time it will be resumed with a greater prospect of seeking coordinated movement; or a mediator may promise a reward that turns a previously unacceptable proposal into an attractive one that is mutually acceptable. The third strategy, seeking coordinated movement, is the most complex and requires the most effort on the part of the mediator; it has a wide range of tactics associated with it. The tactics associated with each strategy, and the circumstances in which they are likely to be found, are examined in some detail later.

International mediators typically are not indifferent to the possible outcomes of negotiation. Indeed, international mediation is often pursued to protect or enhance mediators' interests (Touval, 1982). This idea is worth elaboration; it contradicts the common conception of mediators as "neutral" and "disinterested" and leads to an analysis of the motives of mediators and parties in international conflict.

MOTIVATIONAL ASPECTS OF MEDIATION

There are five related topics that are particularly interesting: (a) the motives that mediators have for entry into disputes, (b) the motives that disputants have for seeking mediation, (c) the factors that make mediation and mediators acceptable to the parties, (d) the behavior of biased mediators, and (e) aspects of international mediation that differ in comparison to mediation in labor-management and judicial contexts.

Mediator Motivation To Enter International Disputes

Although international mediators may state that their goal is the abatement of conflict, this does not mean that they are indifferent to the possible outcomes of the dispute. In fact, they usually have much at stake, and this is the main reason for their intervention. Touval (1982) and Touval and Zartman (in press) find the motives for international mediation in the language of power politics. They argue that political objectives determine the occurrence, conduct, and scope of international mediation. Their analysis is consistent with the perspective in international relations that international actors are power maximizing, conforming to the rational-pursuit-of-self-interest model, or "Realpolitik" (see Holsti, 1984).

The power-politics perspective assumes international actors are motivated by cost-benefit calculations and act to maximize benefits and minimize costs. For instance, mediators of international disputes are motivated by defensive or offensive interests that serve to maintain or enhance their international standing (Touval, 1975, 1982). As the professed defender of the free world, the United States often is compelled to mediate out of fear that otherwise the dispute will provide an opportunity for Soviet involvement (Pruitt, 1983; Touval & Zartman, in press).

When asked by the press in June 1970 what his goals were in the Middle East mediation effort, Kissinger responded that the United States was "trying to expel Soviet military presence" (Kalb & Kalb, 1974, p. 193). Mediators have defensive goals when they intervene in conflicts that threaten their interests, and offensive goals when they intervene in conflicts that present opportunities for them to extend their influence (Touval, 1975; Touval & Zartman, in press). Many international conflicts involve both types of goals.

The 1954 mediation by the United States and Britain of the Trieste dispute between Yugoslavia and Italy was an example of mediation motivated by offensive concerns. The Western powers wanted to move closer to Yugoslavia, a nation that was then lessening its ties to the Soviet Union (Campbell, 1976; Touval, 1975). Similarly, the Soviet Union sought to enhance its relationship with Pakistan while maintaining its ties with India when it mediated the 1966 dispute between India and Pakistan (Touval & Zartman, in press). Mexico initiated mediation efforts in the Falkland Islands crisis in part to improve its ties to the United States (Duran, 1984).

Many international organizations have charters that require them to mediate for defensive reasons. The Organization of American States, the Organization of African Unity, and the Arab League often send representatives to mediate disputes between members in order to reduce the likelihood of external intervention (Touval & Zartman, in press). Kissinger's mediation efforts in the Middle East had both defensive and offensive elements: He was as interested in the reduction of Soviet influence as he was in the enhancement of Western interests, such as the sale of American technology (Sheehan, 1976).

Care should be exercised not to overextend this cost-benefit analysis of mediation. Some cases perhaps are best understood in light of humanitarian motives, for example, the Pope's 1980 mediation of the Argentina/Chile dispute over the Beagle Channel.

The Parties' Desire for Mediation

Depending on the circumstances, negotiators may be more or less receptive to mediation or eager for it. Sometimes, negotiators for the parties request mediation. Generally, negotiators desire mediation when they believe that they will be better off with a mediator's involvement than without it (Pruitt, 1981). The desire for mediation often signals a desire for coordination, and thus negotiators who are motivated to end their dispute are often receptive to it (Pruitt & Rubin, in press). LaTour, Houlden, Walker, and Thibaut (1976) suggest that negotiators are particularly receptive to conflict intervention—especially strong forms of it—when they are in high-conflict situations and do not have much time to negotiate.

A mediator can help reduce the image costs of making concessions (Young, 1970), an idea that has also been suggested in a laboratory study by Bartunek, Benton, and Keys (1975). These authors found that negotiators wanted mediation most, and were most receptive to it, when they were highly accountable to a constituent and thus had higher image-management concerns.

Other factors may enhance the perceived value of mediation and thus a negotiator's desire for it. These include the belief that the mediator may be able to reinforce the other's compliance with an agreement (Touval & Zartman, in press), and that the mediator will provide benefits for making or agreeing to proposals (Rubin, 1981). Pruitt (1983) suggests that mediation will be sought if it is felt that the mediator has the capacity to influence one's opponent.

Determinants of Mediator Acceptability

Acceptability of the mediator is crucial for mediation (Young, 1967, 1970). It is derived from the parties' belief that the mediator is *able and willing* to facilitate an acceptable outcome. It is constantly tested throughout negotiation, and mediators must constantly reassure parties that favorable outcomes are forthcoming (Touval, 1975). The mediator is constrained by the need for acceptance: "The intermediary must be very careful in his efforts to persuade the parties to modify their position, lest he jeopardize his acceptability as an intermediary" (Touval, 1975, p. 54).

Touval (1975, 1982) argues that international mediators do not need to be impartial in order to be accepted by the parties, and cites examples where biased mediators could be credited with successfully resolving disputes. For example, Somalia in 1965 requested mediation from Tanzanian President Nyerere in its dispute with Kenya despite Nyerere's pro-Kenyan sympathies (Touval, 1975).

Pruitt (1983) distinguishes two types of mediator bias: explicit support of one side's position, and being more closely allied in general with one side. Pruitt argues that only the former type makes it difficult to mediate; for example, it became infeasible for Secretary of State Haig to mediate the Falkland Islands crisis when the United States declared support of Britain and imposed economic sanctions on Argentina.

The point is that mediators' impartiality is not so important as long as their acceptability is preserved—that is, as long as the parties believe the mediator will be useful to facilitate an acceptable outcome. As Touval and Zartman (in press) put it, "There is no necessary relation between past partiality and future usefulness." This is also suggested in a laboratory study by Brookmire and Sistrunk (1980), who report that perceived mediator ability has greater impact on negotiators than mediator impartiality.

Pruitt (1983) suggests that mediators who have rare characteristics, such as access to one party and the capacity to influence them, are likely to be preferred over those who are neutral and do not have these characteristics. In addition, a biased third party may be accepted as mediator for the simple reason that no other mediator is available. The United States accepted the mediation of Algeria for the hostage crisis with Iran because Algeria offered access to Khomeini and the possibility of influencing him.

Knowing that mediators have certain kinds of interests, even if they are more closely allied to one's opponent, may add to their credibility; it may reinforce the belief that they want a settlement, and one that is mutually acceptable. There is evidence the United States was aware that Algeria, hardly an ally in the recent past, was interested in establishing closer ties with the West; hence, the perception of its sincerity in achieving an outcome acceptable to the United States was enhanced. There are two points here: (1) mediators' obvious concern for a lasting settlement may compensate for their friendship with one side, and (2) friendship with the side that is more difficult or must concede more can make settlement more likely (this latter point is also made by Kressel, 1982).

These points suggest that more powerful countries are more likely to be sought as mediators and will be more effective. An empirical study of international mediation cases between 1960 and 1974 by Frei (1976) supports this. A negotiator, even a disfavored one, may accept mediation by a powerful mediator out of a desire to form a relationship with or receive rewards from the mediator; negotiators may also believe that the powerful mediator will be better able to influence their opponent. Count Folke Bernadotte failed in his mediation of the Arab-Israeli conflict in large part because he did not have the resources to influence the parties (Touval, 1982). These points also suggest that disputes involving powerful countries will be more desirable to mediate than disputes involving weak countries, because the mediator has more to gain by helping powerful countries.

The Behavior of Biased Mediators

It is possible to apply notions of distributive justice to the behavior of mediators. Deutsch (1975) has argued that equality is of greater concern when rapport and positive social relationships are important, such as when people want to have extended interactions with one another. These ideas suggest that mediators can put aside any biases they may have in order to facilitate an agreement and preserve the relationship between the parties—especially when they expect to have long term dealings with the parties. In such circumstances, they are likely to strive for equal outcomes for the parties. Consistent with this formulation, several recent laboratory studies suggest that biased mediators put aside their biases and seek equal outcomes for negotiators when they have long-term interests with both parties and want to preserve their relationship with them (Carnevale, Fobian, & Weber, 1985).

Although quite removed from the international contexts that have been discussed above, laboratory studies can be useful because they suggest principles that are highly applicable to the international mediation context. For example, these studies may help us understand the behavior of the United States in the early stages of the dispute between Great Britain and Argentina over the Falkland Islands. Despite more substantial ties to Britain, the United States presented a neutral front and attempted to mediate the dispute. This was done in part to preserve relations with both sides (Smith, 1983).

In the Carnevale et al. studies (1985), all of the subjects were assigned the role of mediator in a simulated international negotiation. Their task was to "facilitate an agreement between two negotiators." The bargaining task consisted of a list of letters from "A" to "U" with a number next to each letter. The subjects were told that the numbers represented monetary payoffs, and if there was to be an agreement, the negotiators would have to agree on one letter.

The subjects (mediators) were shown the negotiators' lists and could see that the payoff values for the two negotiators were negatively correlated; also, they were told that neither negotiator could see the other's payoffs. The mediators were also given a list showing their own payoffs, which were positively correlated with one negotiator's payoffs (and thus negatively correlated with the other's). The mediators thus were biased and were aware of it.

On each round of the negotiation, the negotiators made their bid, and the mediator (subject) was then asked to make a nonbinding recommendation to the negotiators for a point at which he or she felt the negotiators should settle. (The negotiators were not actual people, but rather were preprogrammed responses.) The major dependent variable was the extent to which the mediators made recommendations that maximized their own gains versus equalizing the negotiator's outcomes.

In one study, the independent variable was whether or not the mediator expected any future negotiations. Some mediators were led to believe that there would be only one negotiation, whereas others were led to believe there would be five negotiations—and that the negotiators could deem them unacceptable and exclude them from the future negotiations if they wanted.

In the latter case, when the mediators expected possible participation in future negotiations, they were more likely to equalize outcomes between the negotiators (i.e., they gave themselves less in their recommendations) than when they expected that there would be only one negotiation. Unbiased (control) mediators were not influenced by the expectation of future negotiations. The data support the idea that biased mediators act less partially and are more likely to seek equal outcomes for negotiators when they have future relations with the negotiators to consider. There was also evidence that mediators prefer to make recommendations that *appear* to equalize outcomes between negotiators, even if they do not actually do so.

Noteworthy Aspects of International Mediation

There are several noteworthy aspects of international mediation that become salient when it is compared to mediation in labor-management and judicial contexts (which Pruitt, 1983, refers to as "traditional" mediation). These include the reasons for the mediator's involvement and the basis of the mediator's influence.

Unlike traditional mediation, international mediation does not operate under constraints that are enforceable by higher authorities (Ikle, 1964). A consequence of this is that international mediators, unlike mediators in judicial and labor-management contexts, have as much stake in the outcome of the conflict as the negotiators—and this is a main reason why they become involved. Smith (1983, p. 3) elaborates this point: "There is no important motivation for international mediation outside the mediator's interests in his relationship with the adversaries, and in the particulars of the agreement; there is in effect no international society which can enforce role requirements." In traditional mediation contexts, by contrast, mediator rewards are detached from the outcome of the dispute and there is no significant relationship between the parties and the mediator apart from the role requirements of the current situation.

Another noteworthy aspect of international mediation is the basis of the mediator's influence (Smith, 1983; Touval, 1975). In traditional contexts a mediator's proposal is compelling because it is made by an ostensibly disinterested party whose only interest is settlement. Simmel (1964) went so far as to assert that parties are open to mediators' suggestions only if mediators are seen as impartial. This assertion may be too strong for even the domestic mediation contexts, because there is some evidence that biased mediators can be useful in labor-management mediation (Kressel, 1972).

Because international mediators have interests to maintain and long-term significant interactions with the parties, international mediation can be viewed as multicornered bargaining between disputants and a mediator with interests (Touval, 1982). A compelling source of mediator influence in international contexts is the prospect that the mediator will form a coalition with one of the parties; mediators are often reluctant to threaten this, however, because of their desire to remain acceptable to both parties (Touval, 1975, 1982). In traditional mediation contexts, role requirements and the sanctions of higher authorities prevent coalitions between the mediator and either party. In some limited ways, mediators of labor-management disputes may threaten to form a coalition (for instance, by exposing the other side to the press), but they cannot do this with the impunity found in international contexts.

An interesting implication of this difference is that the mediation of interpersonal and intraorganizational disputes may have more in common with international mediation than with mediation in labor-management and judicial contexts (Pruitt, personal communication).

STRATEGIES AND TACTICS OF MEDIATION

Mediators can do many things to break stalemates and foster agreement between negotiators. The several general strategies that mediators can follow, mentioned earlier in this chapter, have specific tactics associated with them. The tactics all are aimed at the abatement of conflict and the protection or enhancement of the mediator's interests.

Strategy 1:
Entice a Negotiator To Yield

Mediators are often able to move toward agreement by rewarding the parties for cooperativeness. For example, a mediator can reward a party's concession by praising them privately, or publicly in the news media (Wall, 1981).

A mediator can offer or provide benefits, which often are economic and military assistance. President Carter promised tremendous economic and military assistance to both Israel and Egypt at the Camp David talks, leading Rubin (1981, p. 27) to say "In some sense it can be argued that the 1978 Camp David agreement was made possible by the involuntary generosity of the American taxpayer."

In order for this to be an effective strategy, the mediator must have the resources that the negotiators desire. The mediator must search for clues as to what is valuable to the parties. Also, it is useful for the mediator to distinguish between negotiator intransigence due to the opponent and intransigence due to the expectation of receiving compensation from the mediator, and to guard against the latter. Furthermore, as suggested by Touval and Zartman (in press), the mediator faces the dilemma that a benefit given to one party may produce firmness on the part of the other unless some benefit is given to the second party as well; in these cases the benefit may be transferred secretly (see Pruitt, 1981, chap. 5, for an interesting discussion of variables relevant to compensation schemes).

Strategy 2:
Pressure a Negotiator To Yield

Mediators can often exert considerable pressure on the parties to make a proposal, agree to a proposal, or act in some other way that the mediator wants. This pressure may take the form of persuasive arguments or of withheld benefits, such as delayed shipments of economic goods. In order for pressure to be successful, the mediator must have the resources to exercise it and be aware of what will be effective with the parties.

Another way a mediator may induce pressure is by threatening to take sides in a dispute, especially if mediation fails. Purcell (1982) argues that President Reagan could have prevented escalation in the Falkland Islands crisis between Argentina and Britain had he stated, prior to Argentina's invasion, that the United States would support the British. The desire by the United States to appear "even-handed" may have added to the conflict. However a mediator must exercise caution in threatening to join one side as it may alienate the other (Touval, 1975). A mediator's desire to preserve her or his own nation's interests may place her or him "between a rock and a hard place."

Strategy 3:
Seek Coordination Between the Parties

Mediators have a wide array of tactics to move parties toward a mutually acceptable agreement (Rubin, 1981). They may formulate proposals, restructure the issues and relationships, and control communications and images, among other things. These tactics are discussed in turn.

Formulate proposals. The mediator may formulate and recommend proposals for the parties' consideration; in order to do this, the mediator must uncover the negotiators' interests and concerns. Creative thinking on the part of the mediator may be required in order to reconcile divergent interests and develop integrative solutions (Pruitt, 1981; Touval & Zartman, in press). Integrative solutions may be entirely novel or may involve combinations of issues such as trade-offs. Integrative solutions often require information search about values and priorities; it seems that mediators are probably better at this than negotiators because they often can get this information more easily, are not distracted by commitments, and can be more objective about it. There is, however, no research that allows us to evaluate this generalization.

A mediator's proposal may encourage flexibility by leading the negotiators to believe that acceptable solutions are in fact possible. A mediator's suggestion is often influential because it creates a focal point of attention (Schelling, 1960, p. 214).

Restructure the issues and relationship. A mediator can create superordinate goals (Sherif & Sherif, 1969) by stressing the existence of a common enemy or a common interest. Kissinger, for example, stressed the threat of Soviet expansion in the Middle East.

Social psychological research has consistently shown that negotiators do better when they consider multiple issues as a set rather than sequentially (Kelley, 1966; Pruitt, 1981). This allows bargainers a greater opportunity to see and make trade-offs among the issues, which often leads to the most optimal outcomes. A mediator may be able to focus the parties' attention on the set of issues and away from sequential consideration of the issues (LaTour et al., 1976).

Introducing new issues or concerns may facilitate concession making: "Redefining the issues and enlarging the field of concern to include items which can be traded against each other are often the keys to a mediator's success in persuading the disputants that it is rational for them to take a conciliatory approach" (Touval & Zartman, in press). A mediator may engage in piecemeal mediation—restructuring the agenda so that issues that are easy to settle are dealt with first. This produces momentum, a belief that progress is being made and that future progress is likely (Pruitt, 1981).

A mediator may be able to create a deadlock, which has the effect of making the negotiators especially receptive to mediation (Pruitt, 1981). One way of doing this is through power balancing—creating circumstances in which the parties see themselves as having equal power. As Touval and Zartman (in press) put it "Stalemate is necessary to mediation, just as mediation is necessary to overcome stalemate." Kissinger did this in the Middle East when he prevented Israel from destroying the Egyptian Third Army at the end of the 1973 war (Pruitt, 1981; Touval, 1982). Negotiators who believe they can overwhelm an opponent are less inclined to accept mediation; and it may not be in the mediator's best interest for one side to be a victor (Touval, 1982).

Control communications and images. A mediator can often influence negotiations by controlling the communications between negotiators and hence the images that they have of one another and one another's proposals. Mediators can serve as a mechanism of "indirect communication" (Pruitt, 1981).

Negotiators may be less concerned about "saving face" when a mediator is present (Bartunek et al., 1975). Mediators can take responsibility for concessions, eliminating the negotiators' concern about looking weak, thus preventing the other's expectation that further concessions will be forthcoming (Pruitt, 1981; Young, 1970). Mediators can aid in a negotiator's retreat from a previous but now unattractive position. Pruitt and Johnson (1970) found that the presence of a mediator meant that negotiators were more likely to make concessions, and were less likely to view their concessions as indicating weakness.

Mediators often are able to have separate meetings with each party, providing a number of advantages to the mediation effort. Keeping the parties separate may reduce their impression-management concerns (Carnevale, Pruitt, & Seilheimer, 1981). Kissinger is famous for his "shuttle diplomacy" in the Middle East and his insistence on keeping the parties separate (Sheehan, 1976); labor mediators also make extensive use of separate caucuses (Carnevale & Pegnetter, in press). Separate meetings can make the mediation effort more manageable for the mediator, who may otherwise be overwhelmed by the dynamics of joint meetings. Separate meetings also allow the mediator to test a proposal on one side without having the other hear it. A mediator's proposal that is more acceptable to one party than the other, if presented in a joint session, may induce the one who likes it to adopt it in a hard stance (Pruitt, 1983).

A mediator may also use humor to lighten the atmosphere and make the parties more receptive to mediation attempts, as Kissinger did (Sheehan, 1976). The use of humor also has information processing consequences; it leads negotiators to see issues in a different light—a light that makes integrative agreements more likely (Carnevale & Isen, in press).

A mediator may be effective in reducing conflict spirals. As Simmel (1964, p. 147) put it many years ago,

> The (mediator) shows each party the claims and arguments of the other; they thus lose the tone of subjective passion which usually provokes the same tone on the part of the adversary. . . . Thus this circle that is fatal to all reconciliation is avoided: the vehemence of the one no longer provokes that of the other, which in turn intensifies that of the first, and so forth, until the whole relationship breaks down.

Strategy 4:
Delay or Withdraw from Mediation

One of the mediator's major sources of power is the negotiators' belief that they need and want mediation. A mediator may exploit this power by delaying or withdrawing mediation or threatening to do so. This imposes time pressure on the parties, which can facilitate concession making (Pruitt, 1981). At Camp David President Carter threatened to withdraw if agreement was not reached by a specific date (Pruitt, 1981).

Negotiators who see themselves in a deadlock, in a "hurting stalemate" (Touval & Zartman, in press), are especially receptive to mediation; it is then that the costs of disagreement seem highest and their motivation to listen to the mediator is greatest. Thus, mediation may be more effective if delayed until the later stages of negotiation, when the parties have made concessions and negotiations have stalled (Pruitt, 1981). This is corroborated by the experience of labor mediators, who generally favor late as opposed to early entry in negotiations (Kressel, 1972).

A mediator might be inclined to withdraw for purposes of self-protection. International mediators take the risk that a subgroup of one or both parties may become disaffected and resent the mediation effort. For example, the Swedish ambassador to the United Nations, Count Folke Bernadotte, mediator of the Arab-Israel conflict, was assassinated by Israeli extremists in September, 1948 (Touval, 1982).

THE SUCCESS OF MEDIATION

In considering the impact that mediation has on negotiation, there are two important issues: (a) under what circumstances mediation is likely to be successful or unsuccessful, and (b) what is meant by "success."

Contingent Effectiveness

Mediation may be most effective when the negotiators have a moderate interest in settling or the situation has a moderate degree of integrative potential. When the situation is zero-sum—i.e., where one party gains exactly the same amount as the other loses—mediation efforts may not be successful (Smith, 1983). When the situation involves interests that can be easily reconciled, "even the most bumbling fool can't hurt" (Pruitt, 1983, p. 2). The present author was once told by a professional labor mediator about a case in which the parties had come to agreement *despite* that mediator's bungled intervention. Thus, caution should be exercised in attributing too much importance to the role of mediator; aspects of the situation and the disputants may be more important than anything about the mediator.

The Falkland Islands crisis may have been one in which no mediator could have been successful (Pruitt, 1983). A key problem was Argentina's firm position that the sovereignty issue be settled in their favor as a precondition for negotiations, whereas Britain looked at this issue as the focus of negotiations (Purcell, 1982).

Mediation tactics that are effective when conflict intensity is low may have no impact, or may make things worse, when conflict intensity is high (Rubin, 1980). For example, Erickson, Holmes, Frey, Walker, and Thibaut (1974) suggest that helping the parties identify their points of contention may facilitate agreement when conflict intensity is low, but may exacerbate conflict when its intensity is high. Research by Carnevale et al. (1981) suggests that separating the parties may be more effective when conflict intensity is high than when it is low.

Further evidence that mediation tactics may be more or less effective in different circumstances can be found in a recent study of professional labor mediators in England by Hiltrop (in press). He reports that mediator tactics are particularly effective when the parties are motivated to settle, as during a strike; moreover, the use of aggressive mediator tactics was positively associated with settlement in nonsalary disputes, but was negatively associated with settlement in salary disputes.

The Criteria of Success

In order to judge the success of mediation, it probably is best to focus on the objectives of mediation. In some cases, this may be difficult to do. Is the goal of mediation the elimination of conflict and the establishment of harmonious relations? If so, how long should the relations be harmonious for the mediation to be considered a success? Kissinger has been criticized for seeking short-term solutions to long-term problems in the Middle East (Fisher, 1981).

If the objective of mediation is to create the conditions for the parties' own problem solving—a goal in labor-management mediation—then Kissinger's efforts can not be viewed as successful (Kochan, 1981). Pruitt and Rubin (in press) endorse this objective: "Like the dodo, the roc, and the auk, an effective third party should be able to render himself or herself obsolete and extinct." A different perspective is presented by Touval and Zartman (in press) who stress the satisfaction of *the mediator's* interests as the criterion of successful mediation.

CONCLUDING COMMENT

Few social psychological studies have examined what mediators do and the reasons for their doing it. Two recent exceptions to this are the scholarly and highly useful treatments of mediator behavior organized by social psychologists and sponsored by SPSSI: Rubin's (1981) collection of interdisciplinary essays on Secretary of State Kissinger's activities in the Middle East from 1973 to 1975, and the collection by Kressel and Pruitt (in press) on mediation in general.

Social psychological methods and ideas can contribute to understanding international mediation and the behavior of international mediators. Studies mentioned in this chapter illustrate the importance of impression management (Pruitt & Johnson, 1970) and distributive justice notions (Carnevale et al., 1985) in understanding mediator recommendations. Social psychological studies on impression management suggest the circumstances in which negotiators are receptive to mediation (Bartunek et al., 1975), and circumstances in which certain tactics are likely to be effective (Carnevale et al., 1981).

The social psychological notion that behavior is often contingent on context is highly useful for understanding not only what mediators are likely to attempt, but also the situations where their actions are likely to be successful (Carnevale & Pegnetter, in press; Hiltrop, in press). This is the approach that Frei (1976) has taken in his empirical research on international mediation. It seems likely that a contingency model of mediator success is apt to be most useful. Certain mediation tactics are likely to lead to agreements, or improved relations, under some circumstances and not others; and mediation in some circumstances may even lead to worse relations (Pruitt & Rubin, in press; Rubin, 1980).

Many of the ideas expressed in this chapter about international mediation seem to have more general applicability, but their validity in other contexts such as mediation of interpersonal and intra-organizational disputes has not been explored. However, there is an area of tremendous potential here. International mediation provides a fascinating context concerning which social psychologists should have much to contribute.

REFERENCES

Bartunek, J., Benton, A., & Keys, C. (1975). Third party intervention and the behavior of group representatives. *Journal of Conflict Resolution, 19*, 532-557.

Berman, M., & Johnson, J. E. (Eds.). (1977). *Unofficial diplomats*. New York: Columbia University Press.

Brookmire, D., & Sistrunk, F. (1980). The effects of perceived ability and impartiality of mediators and time pressure on negotiation. *Journal of Conflict Resolution, 24*, 311-327.

Campbell, J. C. (1976). *Successful negotiation: Trieste 1954*. Princeton, NJ: Princeton University Press.

Carnevale, P. J., Fobian, C. S., & Weber, K. (1985). *Factors that affect the recommendations of biased mediators*. Manuscript submitted for publication.

Carnevale, P. J., & Isen, A. M. (1986). The influence of positive affect and visual access on the development of integrative solutions in bilateral negotiation. *Organizational Behavior and Human Decision Processes, 35.*

Carnevale, P. J., & Pegnetter, R. (in press). The selection of mediation tactics in public-sector disputes: A contingency analysis. *Journal of Social Issues.*

Carnevale, P. J., Pruitt, D. G., & Seilheimer, S. (1981). Looking and competing: Effects of accountability and visual access on integrative bargaining. *Journal of Personality and Social Psychology, 40*, 111-120.

Deutsch, M. (1975). "Equity," "equality," and "need": What determines which value will be used as the basis of distributive justice? *Journal of Social Issues, 31*, 181-189.

Druckman, D. (1983). Social psychology and international negotiations: Processes and influences. In R. Kidd & L. Saks (Eds.), *Advances in applied social psychology* (Vol. 2). Hillsdale, NJ: Lawrence Erlbaum.

Duran, E. (1984). Mexico and the South-Atlantic conflict: Solidarity or ambiguity? *International Affairs, 60*, 221-232.

Erickson, B., Holmes, J. G., Frey, R., Walker, L., & Thibaut, J. (1974). Functions of a third party in the resolution of conflict: The role of a judge in pretrial conferences. *Journal of Personality and Social Psychology, 30*, 293-306.

Fisher, R. (1981). Playing the wrong game? In J. Rubin (Ed.), *Dynamics of third party intervention: Kissinger in the Middle East*. New York: Praeger.

Freedman, L. (1982). The war of the Falkland Islands, 1982. *Foreign Affairs, 61*, 196-210.

Frei, D. (1976). Conditions affecting the effectiveness of international mediation. *Peace Science Society (International), 26*, 67-84.

Gulliver, P. H. (1979). *Disputes and negotiations: A cross-cultural perspective*. New York: Academic Press.

Hiltrop, J. M. (in press). Mediator behavior and the settlement of collective bargaining disputes in Britain. *Journal of Social Issues.*

Holsti, K. J. (1984). Along the road to international theory. *International Journal, 39*, 337-365.

Ikle, F. C. (1964). *How nations negotiate*. New York: Harper & Row.

Jackson, E. (1952). *Meeting of minds: A way to peace through mediation*. New York: McGraw-Hill.

Kalb, M., & Kalb, B. (1974). *Kissinger*. Boston: Little, Brown.

Kelley, H. H. (1966). A classroom study of dilemmas in interpersonal bargaining. In K. Archibald (Ed.), *Strategic interaction and conflict*. Berkeley: Institute of International Studies, University of California.

Kelman, H. C. (Ed.). (1965). *International behavior: A social-psychological analysis*. New York: Holt.

Kelman, H. C. (1977). The problem-solving workshop in conflict reduction. In M. Berman & J. E. Johnson (Eds.), *Unofficial diplomats*. New York: Columbia University Press.

Kochan, T. A. (1981). Step-by-step in the Middle East from the perspective of the labor mediation process. In J. Rubin (Ed.), *Dynamics of third party intervention: Kissinger in the Middle East*. New York: Praeger.

Kressel, K. (1972). *Labor mediation: An exploratory survey*. Albany, NY: Association of Labor Mediation Agencies.

Kressel, K., & Pruitt, D. G. (Eds.). (in press). Mediation of disputes. *Journal of Social Issues.*

LaTour, S., Houlden, P., Walker, L., & Thibaut, J. (1976). Some determinants of preference for modes of conflict resolution. *Journal of Conflict Resolution, 20,* 319-356.

Pruitt, D. G. (1981). *Negotiation behavior.* New York: Academic Press.

Pruitt, D. G. (1983, July). *Negotation and mediation in the Falklands crisis.* Paper presented at the meeting of the International Society of Political Psychology, St. Catherine's College, Oxford University, England.

Pruitt, D. G., & Johnson, D. F. (1970). Mediation as an aid to face saving in negotiation. *Journal of Personality and Social Psychology, 14,* 239-246.

Pruitt, D. G., & Rubin, J. Z. (in press). *Social conflict: Escalation, stalemate, and settlement.* New York: Addison-Wesley.

Purcell, S. K. (1982). War and debt in South America. *Foreign Affairs, 61,* 660-674.

Rubin, J. Z. (1980). Experimental research on third-party intervention in conflict: Toward some generalizations. *Psychological Bulletin, 87,* 379-391.

Rubin, J. Z. (Ed.). (1981). *Dynamics of third party intervention: Kissinger in the Middle East.* New York: Praeger.

Schelling, T. C. (1960). *The strategy of conflict.* Cambridge, MA: Harvard University Press.

Sheehan, E. R. F. (1976). How Kissinger did it: Step by step in the Middle East. *Foreign Policy, 22,* 3-70.

Sherif, M., & Sherif, C. W. (1969). *Social psychology.* New York: Harper & Row.

Simmel, G. (1964). *The sociology of Georg Simmel.* (K. H. Wolff, Trans. & Ed.). Glencoe, IL: Free Press. (original work published 1908)

Smith, W. P. (1983, July). *Concealing mediator bias: The Falkland Islands case.* Paper presented at meeting of the International Society of Political Psychology, St. Catherine's College, Oxford University, England.

Snyder, G. H., & Diesing, P. (1977). *Conflict among nations.* Princeton, NJ: Princeton University Press.

Touval, S. (1975). Biased intermediaries: Theoretical and historical considerations. *Jerusalem Journal of International Relations, 1,* 51-69.

Touval, S. (1982). *The peace brokers: Mediators in the Arab-Israeli conflict.* Princeton, NJ: Princeton University Press.

Touval, S., & Zartman, I. W. (in press). International mediation: Conflict resolution and power politics. *Journal of Social Issues.*

Wall, J. (1981). Mediation: An analysis, review, and proposed research. *Journal of Conflict Resolution, 25,* 157-180.

Young, O. R. (1967). *The intermediaries: Third parties in international crises.* Princeton, NJ: Princeton University Press.

Young, O. R. (1970). Intermediaries: Additional thoughts on third parties. *Journal of Conflict Resolution, 16,* 51-65.

Zartman, I. W. (1977). Negotiation as a joint decision-making process. *Journal of Conflict Resolution, 21,* 619-638.

Zartman, I. W., & Berman, M. R. (1982). *The practical negotiator.* New Haven, CT: Yale University Press.

SEYMOUR FESHBACH
ELIZABETH KANDEL
FRANK HAIST

7

ATTITUDES TOWARD
NUCLEAR ARMAMENT POLICIES:
An Example of Social Research
in Behalf of Social Advocacy

This chapter emerges from an effort to apply the methods of behavioral science to further the general goal of peace and, more specifically, to further a particular advocacy goal—namely, the adoption of nuclear disarmament or moratorium policies. The studies that we implemented reflect the view that it is possible to carry out objective behavioral research that bears on an advocacy objective, and that such research can also contribute to the basic behavioral literature as well.

There are few behavioral scientists, even the "purest" of basic researchers, who would contest the appropriateness of carrying out social research that may contribute to the formation and implementation of sound social policy. When the social scientist evaluates the effectiveness of an educational enrichment program to help Congress determine the wisdom of allocating funds for this program (Coulson, 1978), or compares the utility of different approaches to the treatment of chronic alcoholics (Armor, Polich, & Stambul, 1978), the primary questions revolve around the adequacy of evaluation and the implications to be drawn from the study. Little question is raised as to whether one should be engaged in such research, although scientists may differ as to the value they place on applied or policy research relative to other kinds of research endeavors.

SOCIAL ADVOCACY BY SCIENTISTS

The situation in regard to advocacy is more ambiguous. Advocacy of a particular social policy is perceived by some psychologists as incompatible with the objective, dispassionate stance of the scientist except under certain conditions. One such permissible advocacy situation is when the social policy involved pertains to the welfare of the science—for example, funding for research and training. An advocacy role in that instance is seen to be appropriate on the part of the scientist, indeed to be a definite responsibility. Thus, the Board of Scientific Affairs of the American Psychological Association (APA) recently recommended that the APA restrict itself to advocating "positions that are beneficial to its members as scientific and professional psychologists, supplying documentation and arguments that can be summoned legitimately to support these views" (American Psychological Association, 1983). We maintain that this recommendation is too restrictive. In addition, we point out that it rests upon value judgments—namely, that whatever serves the welfare of the science enhances the welfare of the larger community (generally, but not always, true), or that the welfare of the science supersedes that of the larger community.

A second advocacy situation that is generally perceived as acceptable is advocacy of a social policy clearly based on theory and data that are widely accepted in the scientific community. For example, there would be a scientifically legitimate basis, apart from other grounds, for opposing proposals to sterilize criminals, predicated on the assumption that criminality is primarily inherited.

However, we contend that scientists, and psychologists in particular, have a broader role in the advocacy arena. The rationale for this role, in our view, is the responsibility of psychologists as professionals to speak out on social issues, including issues that are not primarily psychological in nature. We begin with the simple observation that we cannot avoid political-moral issues or social policy statements, whether as individual psychologists or as an organization. For example, if an organization is holding a meeting, and if a picket line appears at the hotel or convention center (as has happened at APA meetings), a decision would have to be made—as an organization or as individuals—about whether to cross it. If we are asked not to meet in a non-ERA state (as has occurred), then we must make a moral choice, and that choice constitutes a form of advocacy; the choice not to make a choice is still a choice. The existentialists have shown us that our daily lives are replete with choices, whether or not we are conscious of these choices, and many of these choices have social policy or advocacy implications.

There is an equally important reason why we must become involved in social advocacy that does not rest on a solid scientific base. Psychology is a profession that is devoted to the advancement of knowledge about human experience and behavior, to dissemination of that knowledge, and to application of that knowledge for reducing human distress and enhancing human growth and functioning. As a profession, we have the responsibility to advance these goals that pertain to the discovery and dissemination of knowledge, and to the reduction of human suffering and the improvement of human welfare. These goals not only have a component related to *psychological* knowledge, procedures, and problems. They also have a general component entailing important *social values*—the value of scientific inquiry and the value of reducing human suffering and enhancing human welfare—regardless of whether the suffering or welfare entails predominantly physical, psychological, or social elements. In brief, we share values that extend beyond our specific psychological skills and aims.

These values have social advocacy consequences; because we are concerned with human suffering and human welfare, we are likely to be people-oriented rather than object- or property-oriented. That does not mean that we must be political Democrats. There are many people, holding different political views, who share these same values. They differ politically because political affiliations entail other values as well. In addition, there are legitimate bases for disagreement as to how these values may be best achieved—whether through a reduction in taxes or an increase in taxes, whether through increased government regulations or through decreased government involvement.

The point is, however, that there are certain social issues that are consonant with our values as psychologists and professionals; and when these issues arise, it is appropriate for, indeed incumbent upon, the profession to support a particular advocacy position. The abolition of slavery would have been an example of such a position; more contemporary examples are the elimination of racism and the accomplishment of full equality for women. Support for these social actions derives not from our scientific knowledge (e.g., of the psychological effects of being compelled to sit in the rear of the bus, or attending a segregated school, or being subtly discriminated against in hiring, promotion, and salary); it arises, rather, from the values that we share as psychologists and enlightened professionals.

The phrase "enlightened professionals" raises another dimension of our training that bears on our role regarding social advocacy. As professionals, we have been provided by society with unusual opportunities for the development of a range of competencies. We are trained to be analytic, logical, and sensitive to the degree of empirical and rational support for a particular recommended action. We have special skills in evaluating evidence, recognizing possible sources of bias, and discriminating values from facts. Just because we have these skills, it does not necessarily follow that we must apply them. However, it is our position that we have a responsibility, as a profession, to do so. We have a responsibility to foster intellectual discussion and analyses of significant social issues. When these analyses clarify the facts and social values entailed, and where particular social actions are likely to maximize our professional values, then we should become advocates of those social actions.

Let us move from these general points to consideration of a specific contemporary social issue that has ramifications extending beyond the competence of psychologists as scientists—but an issue, in our view, that should engage us as professionals. We refer to nuclear arms policies.

There are many ways in which psychologists can contribute to the formulation of nuclear arms policies, ranging from social advocacy to more traditional research. Studies of bargaining (Carnevale, Pruitt, & Seilheimer, 1981; Stech & McClintock, 1981) of the effects of stereotyping and mutual misperception (Oskamp, 1965, 1977; Skrypnek & Snyder, 1982), of the effectiveness of small group interaction procedures in promoting greater understanding and reducing conflict (Kelman, 1972) are all germane (or should be!) to the formulation and implementation of nuclear arms policies. Many other examples can be cited of research efforts by psychologists that are relevant to the cause of peace. So far an advocacy position has not been engaged. But social events may move rapidly, and advocacy issues may intrude or become germane. The nuclear moratorium is one such issue. A nuclear moratorium is the focal issue for the peace movement in the United States. How shall the psychology profession react to it?

SOCIAL ADVOCACY BY PROFESSIONAL ORGANIZATIONS

Different considerations enter into the question of advocacy by the psychology profession as an organization and by psychologists as individual scientists. The rationale for a nuclear moratorium does not rest on psychological evidence. Yet, like the war in Vietnam, the issue is one that engages our moral and intellectual sensibilities as professionals. And so the American Psychological Association may be urged by some of its members to take an official stance on this question. A typical procedure of the association in such circumstances is, after extensive review of the question, to have its elected council vote on a resolution for a nuclear arms moratorium. If the majority of council members vote in favor of the resolution, advocacy of a nuclear moratorium receives the official imprimatur of the profession.

This procedure is faulty from several perspectives. A mere majority may be more reflective of political sentiment than of professional sentiment. If the association is to take an advocacy position on controversial issues and represent the position of its membership, then a substantial majority should be required for passage. But, more important, the passing of resolutions, despite the conflict and passion that debate over such resolutions frequently engender, is a minor contribution to the cause being advocated. Although resolutions may carry moral force and convey the judgment and support of a major professional organization, they also run the danger of being little more than empty gestures. Psychology as a profession can, and in our judgment should, do more in the advocacy arena. And, even where the issue is not fundamentally a psychological one, psychology can draw upon its talents and insights to make a significant contribution to the advocated cause.

For example, the American Psychological Association could use some of its resources and leadership skills to enlist the cooperation of other scientific and professional societies in conducting an evaluation of nuclear arms policies. Why should the American Psychological Association, American Medical Association, and American Sociological Association, and so on, become involved in such activities when this is not their special province and the government has so many experts available to it? In our judgment they should do so because of the overriding importance of the issue, because government analyses are subject to all kinds of political constraints, and because government analyses can be insensitive to value issues that may matter a good deal to psychologists and to the community at large. For example, we may value children more than those who establish nuclear arms policies; we may value human lives more; we may value territory and power less, and so on. But apart from these values that may determine our policy preference, we can make a major social contribution by fostering a free and systematic analysis of a major social policy issue. How much more effective it would be if a nuclear moratorium resolution by the American Psychological Association had the support of a "white paper" that would be available for public distribution and citation! And if the consequences of the review were not supportive of a moratorium, so be it. At least we would have stimulated and helped clarify discussion of a fundamental social issue.

Clearly, the American Psychological Association does not have the financial or personnel resources to conduct analyses of every major social issue. We always have to allocate funds judiciously, and we must choose our social issues carefully. In a like manner, even where the costs of systematic analysis are not involved, and only a vote is required, we must be judicious about the issues on which we take a public position, particularly when there is no strong empirical basis for a recommendation. We will lose credibility as a profession if we diffuse our social advocacy too much. As individual psychologists, we have a much greater choice as to the social issues in which we decide to invest our energies. When the profession speaks as a whole, it should address only those social issues that are central to the larger community, and even there it must be selective. When we speak as a profession, we must, of course, always be clear in stating the degree of scientific support for a particular advocacy statement.

How should we proceed in regard to those social positions that do not rest on specific psychological competencies? In a few selected instances, we might initiate the formal analytic study that we suggested above. In other cases, we could follow the current procedure, which entails a review by APA Boards and a vote by the APA Council of Representatives. An additional procedure that, we think, would strengthen our voice would be to determine the views of the membership. This could be implemented inexpensively and rapidly through a stratified random sampling and mail survey. One might then adopt some advocacy criterion—for instance, 70 percent of the members replying should support a particular social policy—before the Council or Board of Directors could express APA support of that policy. At the very least, a survey would provide useful information to the Council and the Board of Directors and serve as a guide in their discussion of social policy recommendations.

Summary. We have argued that we cannot avoid social advocacy choices, and that as psychologists and professionals, we have special responsibilities and a special role in regard to social advocacy. At the same time, we have suggested that we should select our social issues judiciously and that, when a recommended social policy is not rooted in psychological evidence or does not involve needed psychological services, we might survey a random sample of the membership and be guided by membership views in making policy recommendations.

RESEARCH ON THE THREAT OF NUCLEAR WAR

As individual psychologists, we can sometimes combine our advocacy interests with our research skills. To cite one example, we can engage in scholarly research that is intended to foster a nuclear moratorium policy. Although a nuclear moratorium and nuclear disarmament were the specific points of departure for the studies to be reported here, our overriding concern is the threat of nuclear war. A major challenge for behavioral scientists is the development and implementation of research programs that may help in some degree, however small, to reduce that threat. This is not to minimize the importance of political and military considerations in nuclear armament policies. However, the behavioral sciences, as they have already begun to demonstrate, can make a significant contribution to our understanding of the nuclear war threat and of how we might productively respond to diminish that threat. (See any of the preceding chapters in this volume for more details.)

There has been considerable clinical and research interest in the psychological effects of the nuclear war threat, particularly on children and youth (Bartlett, Byrnes, & Martin, 1980; Beardslee & Mack, 1982; Escalona, 1982; Schwebel, 1982). The social psychological reciprocity between the effects of threat and the perception of the "enemy," and how these in turn influence nuclear armament policies, are additional questions that have been addressed by behavioral scientists (Bronfenbrenner, 1961; Mack, 1982; Bennett & Dando, 1983; Frank, 1982). And behavioral theory and research on negotiations and conflict resolution has direct relevance to nuclear arms policies and agreements (Intriligator, 1982; Osgood, 1962, 1981; Pruitt, 1981; Rubin, 1982; Wagner, 1982).

Our Approach

Our own involvement in nuclear arms issues research stems from the nuclear disarmament referendum that was on the November 1982 California ballot. The senior author of this chapter was particularly interested in the factors that deter individuals from supporting nuclear disarmament programs and from voting for the nuclear moratorium. Why were they hesitant, resistant, or opposed? It was this question that provided the focus for the studies to be described here. We felt that through providing a deeper and more comprehensive understanding of the sources of resistance to nuclear disarmament policies, we might be able to facilitate the development of approaches that would be responsive to the needs and perspectives of people opposed to or remote from the nuclear disarmament effort.

It is evident that the way the research question was formulated implied an advocacy position; that is, we did not assume an indifferent stance on the question of support for nuclear armament versus support for nuclear moratorium and disarmament programs. Rather, we were interested in understanding the sources of resistance and opposition to nuclear moratorium and related disarmament proposals. However, we do not believe that the advocacy role need in any way diminish the validity and utility of data yielded by the research studies that have been motivated by this advocacy position. The methodology of the behavioral sciences provides safeguards against the distorting tendencies of investigator biases and motivations. Further, when researchers explicitly state their advocacy position, readers can more readily take account of possible experimenter bias in evaluating the interpretation of the research findings.

Methodology of Our First Study

As an initial step in exploring the basis for resistance and opposition to nuclear disarmament efforts, we interviewed college students and, on the basis of their responses, we developed a structured questionnaire. The questionnaire tapped attitudes toward nuclear armament and disarmament policies and some factors that might be related to these attitudes, including anxieties about the possibility of nuclear warfare, opinions of the Soviet Union, assessments of the consequences of nuclear warfare, and the values placed upon the losses entailed in a nuclear conflict.

The questionnaire consisted of 28 items, 8 introductory ones with a multiple choice format, and 20 others with a dichotomous Agree-Disagree format. Eighty UCLA students, 45 males and 35 females, completed this initial questionnaire. Of these students, 60 percent were freshmen with most of the rest being sophomores. The sample was not intended to be representative of California voters, and the response distributions might be expected to vary markedly with the nature of the population being assessed. However, the absolute frequencies, that is, the marginals for each item, were for the most part of secondary interest. Our primary focus was on the items or factors correlated with attitudes toward a nuclear moratorium and nuclear disarmament policies. (It may be noted that a more recent study, employing a revised version of the questionnaire with a random sample of the community of Muncie, Indiana [White & Feshbach, 1984], yielded data comparable to the present findings.)

Results

Although the marginal statistics have limited inferential value, they do provide descriptive information of interest concerning the attitudes and values of the sample. The respondents were about equally divided regarding the nuclear moratorium, 56 percent being in favor, and 44 percent opposed (in this regard differing from the Muncie sample, who were supportive of a moratorium); 30 percent of the students were opposed to using nuclear weapons under any circumstances. However, there were still nine individuals, or 11 percent of the sample, who were in favor of a first strike, and 15 percent indicated agreement with the following statement: "If we could wipe out the Soviet Union, and be sure they wouldn't retaliate, we should do it." One wonders about the extent to which such views are held by decision-making power groups in the United States, and their counterparts in the Soviet Union. No less disturbing were the 26 percent who, when asked, "Assuming Soviet threats, what is the largest number of probable casualties the U.S. should be willing to accept in order to engage in a nuclear war?" indicated a willingness to accept 25 to 50 million or more casualties. Although it is reassuring that the majority of respondents were opposed to accepting the much lower figure of 5 million casualties, one wonders again about the opinion of national decision makers on such issues.

The descriptive data indicated that even on items with really extreme choices, there was considerable variability in people's responses and a meaningful pattern in their attitudes. Analysis of the 20 dichotomous items, which addressed attitudes and opinions that might be linked to support for or opposition to a nuclear moratorium, showed that 3 items were negligibly correlated with the others; but the remaining 17 yielded an alpha coefficient of internal consistency of .80, indicating that these items were assessing a coherent dimension involving the degree of support for or opposition to nuclear armaments. The content of these items ranged from perceptions of the motivation of the Soviet Union, to feelings about entrusting nuclear arms policies to government experts, to opinions regarding survival of the individual and of political democracy in a nuclear war (see Table 7.1 for examples).

The relationship of sex to this dimension and to support for a nuclear moratorium, somewhat surprisingly, was no more than marginally significant on some items. On the pro-nuclear scale, with a possible range from 0 to 17, the mean for the males was 6.9, and for the females 5.6, a nonsignificant difference. Similarly, 53 percent of the men in comparison to 60 percent of the women supported the nuclear moratorium. On the individual items, only the following two items displayed a sex difference significant at the .10 level: 91 percent of the females in comparison to 72 percent of the males disagreed with the statement "Talk about ourselves dying or becoming sick or blind as a result of exposure to a nuclear blast is largely sentimental and is basically irrelevant to the nuclear war issue." And 24 percent of the

TABLE 7.1
Examples of Items on the Attitudes Toward Nuclear Armament Scale

(2) There is really nothing that individuals can do to prevent a nuclear war.

(5) A nuclear moratorium now would give the Soviets a nuclear advantage.

(6) The Soviets are basically out to conquer and control the world.

(7) It's not the whole or necessarily the basic reason but, to some extent, the pressure for a nuclear moratorium is a reflection of a lack of guts.

(12) With careful planning, although there will be many casualties, it will be possible for the U.S. civilization to survive a nuclear war.

(16) If we could wipe out the Soviet Union, and be sure they wouldn't be able to retaliate, we should do it.

(19) People who support the nuclear moratorium movement are either stupid, ignorant, or unpatriotic.

(21) The more nuclear weapons and the bigger nuclear weapons we have, the safer we are.

males in comparison to only 6 percent of the females agreed that "People who support the nuclear moratorium are either ignorant, stupid or unpatriotic."

Correlates of Nuclear Moratorium Attitudes

Turning to a more detailed examination of correlates of the nuclear moratorium question, we found, as might be expected, a sharp and highly significant difference ($p < .0001$) between the proponents and opponents of the nuclear moratorium on the nuclear armament attitude scale, the means being 4.9 versus 7.9, respectively. More interesting were the items that were the most and least discriminating. Proponents of a nuclear moratorium did not indicate more anxiety about a possible nuclear war than opponents; and they shared similar opinions on the likely outcome of a nuclear conflict and on the number of casualties they are willing to tolerate. They both disagreed with the notion that people who oppose nuclear armaments lack courage, and they did not differ on who should have access to bomb shelters during a nuclear conflict.

Proponents and opponents of a nuclear moratorium did differ, as would be expected, on willingness to use nuclear weapons and in their estimates of the relative nuclear strength of the United States and the Soviet Union. The opponents felt that the United States needs more nuclear arms; that the nuclear arms negotiations are complex matters, so that nuclear arms policies should be entrusted to government experts (71 percent of opponents versus 33 percent of proponents), and that it is important for the United States to be the most powerful nation in the world (62 percent versus 35 percent).

The differences between opponents and proponents of a nuclear moratorium extended to more remote topics as well: 32 percent of the opponents versus 10 percent of the proponents responded that animal death or injury is largely a sentimental and irrelevant matter—a tough-minded versus tender-minded difference. Also, although the two groups did not differ in their estimates of nuclear casualties, or in how many casualties they were willing to accept, the opponents placed greater emphasis than the nuclear moratorium supporters on the likelihood that there would also be survivors of a nuclear conflict. Finally, although these two groups only differed marginally in their estimates of Soviet intentions, they differed significantly in their expressed willingness to wipe out the Soviet Union (29 percent of opponents versus 4 percent of proponents).

Advocacy Implications

The results of this initial study have some advocacy implications for supporters of a nuclear moratorium and a nuclear disarmament policy. They suggest that media materials focusing on the dire consequences of nuclear warfare may not be very useful in influencing attitudes toward nuclear arms policies (though of course they might have other useful functions, such as engaging nuclear moratorium supporters in action programs). The results also indicate that anxiety, at least overt anxiety, is not an important mediator of attitudes toward nuclear arms policies. Rather, they suggest that the persuasive focus of moratorium proponents should be on the issue of implications of a nuclear arms race for United States power. Furthermore there should be greater emphasis on the facts that there are important differences between the armament views of various experts and that experts can be affected by economic and political considerations.

The findings of this first survey encouraged us to pursue the investigation of individual difference factors mediating attitudes toward nuclear disarmament/armament policies. Apart from any advocacy contribution that such research might make, the examination of differences in these attitudes can help to clarify the nature of public perceptions of nuclear arms policies, and thus it provides one mechanism by which research can contribute to the nuclear disarmament discussion and the formation of a sensible, publicly understood, and consensual nuclear arms policy.

OUR SECOND STUDY

One factor that is relevant to nuclear armament policy attitudes is the amount of information that individuals have concerning nuclear arms policies. From the perspective of a nuclear disarmament/moratorium advocate, one might anticipate that high information about nuclear armament matters would be associated with antiarmament attitudes. However, this expectation is not theoretically compelling. A pro-armament advocate might well predict an opposite correlation. In any case, the relation is of empirical interest and merits exploration.

In addition to the variable of information, our second study examined the relationship of the value placed on children to nuclear armament attitudes. One of the serious concerns of many individuals involved in nuclear disarmament activities, including behavioral scientists, is the psychological impact upon children of the threat of nuclear war. As in the case of information, there is no necessary theoretical relationship between the extent to which one values children and one's position on nuclear arms policies. Advocates of a major nuclear arms buildup who believe that the United States should be the dominant world power undoubtedly feel that such a policy is in the best interests of both children and adults. Nevertheless, a nuclear arms buildup and arms race are symbolically if not actually associated with the threat of nuclear war, and the diminution of such tensions is a very important concern of people who value children. Also, people who value children highly are likely to be less sanguine about the state of the world as a place for children following a nuclear war than are individuals who value children less. Consequently, in contrast to the uncertainty of the relationship between information and nuclear armament attitudes, a negative correlation was anticipated between the value placed on children and the degree of support for a nuclear armament buildup.

Method

For this second study, a child value scale, a nuclear armament information test, and the nuclear armament attitude scale were administered to 138 UCLA students registered in summer session courses in 1983. Of this group, 23 did not complete the information test, leaving a sample of 115 for analyses involving the information measure.

The information test consisted of 18 items, 13 multiple choice and 5 true-false. The items tapped knowledge of the Cruise and Pershing missiles, the MX and ICBMs, and explicit nuclear arms policies of the U.S. and U.S.S.R. (see Table 7.2 for examples). The Children's Value

TABLE 7.2
**Examples of Items on the Nuclear Armament Information
and Value of Children Scales**

Nuclear Armament Information Scale

(1) The chief concern of the U.S.S.R. with the U.S.-made Pershing II missile is its:

A) destructive 400 kiloton warhead.
B) the ten warhead capability.
C) the time it takes for the missile to reach its target.

(4) Who has made a commitment to not use a "first-strike"?

A) U.S.
B) U.S.S.R.
C) neither
D) both

(7) The U.S.S.R. relies mainly on its _____ as primary defense.

A) ICBM ground-based system.
B) Submarine-based system.
C) Air launched system (airplanes).
D) There is about an equal reliance on all three above.

(8) The U.S. relies mainly on its _____ as primary defense.

A) ICBM ground-based system.
B) Submarine-based system.
C) Air launched system (airplanes).
D) There is about an equal reliance on all three above.

(9) The largest missile in either the U.S. or the U.S.S.R. arsenal contains:

A) three warheads.
B) five warheads.
C) ten warheads.
D) fifteen warheads.

(11) The United States Arms-Control director is   True   False
Kenneth Adelman.

(12) The MX Missile is an aspect of President Reagan's   True   False
plans to modernize the U.S. land-based missile force.

(13) The Soviets are far ahead of the U.S. in cruise   True   False
missile technology.

(18) NATO employs a(n):

A) arms-reduction strategy.
B) deterrent strategy.
C) pacifist strategy.

(continued)

TABLE 7.2 Continued

Value of Children Scale

(All items are rated strongly agree, agree, neutral,
disagree, or strongly disagree.)

(3) I feel that our society should spend more on education than it currently does.

(5) While it is necessary to do so, it is a great deal of trouble to raise a child, and it holds few rewards.

(6) I enjoy being with children.

(12) I feel that there should be quality daycare available to all working parents, free of charge or at a very reasonable rate.

(14) I feel that all children should be entitled to a free, high quality education.

(17) I feel that our government currently does not allot enough resources for the general care of our children.

(23) I find young children's dependence and need for me as an adult gratifying and pleasing.

Scale initially consisted of 26 items, two of which were eliminated. The largest group of items dealt with resources for children, assessing degree of support for funding to meet children's educational, health, recreational, and related needs. The other items assessed liking for children and related beliefs about children (see Table 7.2 for examples).

Almost all of the Children's Value Scale items were interrelated, as reflected in an alpha of .82 for the total scale. A factor analysis yielded one principal factor plus several additional factors. The major factor was clearly a "resource" dimension, 11 of the resource items loading substantially on this factor. The alpha for the 14 resource items was .84. The second factor included the items about children's need for love and affection, and the few items tapping desires to have children and enjoyment of children loaded on another factor. For simplicity, these two sets of items were combined to yield an "Affection" scale, although it was recognized that the alpha coefficient of internal reliability for the combined set of 10 items was only .65.

Results

Our principal interest was in the relationship of the child value scales and of the nuclear armament information index to nuclear armament attitudes, but first we will consider several other aspects of the data. As in our first study, no significant sex differences were obtained on any of the scales. Both males and females expressed positive attitudes toward children and were equally supportive of spending public resources on children.

Both males and females averaged approximately 7 correct responses out of the 18 items on the information scale. These information scores were quite low, particularly considering that guessing also contributed to the number correct (5 items were True-False, and all but one of the others had four or fewer alternatives; thus a score of 5.7 would be expected on the basis of chance factors alone). Most students were not aware of the unique properties of the Pershing II missiles, or the Soviet SS-20, or the American MX. They tended to have only a vague idea about Soviet and U.S. nuclear armament policies, and the particular concerns of Soviet and U.S. disarmament negotiations.

The errors that were made were also revealing. Thus, in response to the question "Who has made a commitment to not use a 'first strike'?" 11 percent of the students failed to give any answer, 40 percent indicated that neither the United States nor the Soviet Union has made such a commitment, 30 percent asserted that both have, 12 percent indicated that only the United States has, and a mere 7 percent were aware that only the Soviet Union has made a "no-first-strike" commitment. The errors in response to this and other questions suggest that the respondents tended to exaggerate Soviet power and intransigence, and underestimated that of the United States. It might be expected that Soviet respondents would have analogous ("mirror image") distortions of United States and Soviet power and behavior, perceiving the Soviets as weaker and more flexible than they actually are, and the United States as stronger and more militant than we actually are (see Bronfenbrenner, 1961). It would be interesting, although probably not politically feasible, to determine whether Soviet students do in fact display these distortions in information regarding nuclear armament/disarmament issues.

Data on the relationship of nuclear information and children's value to nuclear armament attitudes are presented in Table 7.3. It can be seen that information was inversely related to pro-armament attitudes; that is, the more accurate information respondents have concerning nuclear armament issues, the less likely they are to favor a nuclear armament buildup. A similar inverse relationship held for the value placed on children. Whether the value was based on affection toward children, or on willingness to expend resources to benefit children, the more respondents valued children, the more they were opposed to augmenting nuclear armaments. The joint combination of nuclear

TABLE 7.3
Intercorrelations Among Value Placed on Children,
Amount of Information Regarding Nuclear Armament Issues,
and Attitudes Toward Nuclear Armament/Disarmament

Scale	Child value (overall)	Child value (resources)	Child value (affection)	Nuclear arms information
Child value (overall)				
Child value (resources)	.89***			
Child value (affection)	.76***	.37***		
Nuclear arms information	−.11	−.11	−.08	
Nuclear armament attitude	−.20*	−.16*	−.17*	−.23**

*p < .05; **p < .01; ***p < .001.

information and children's value in predicting nuclear armament attitudes resulted in a multiple R of .36.

Implications

The relationship between the value placed on children and attitudes toward nuclear armament issues, while not large, was in accordance with our expectations. Though one might argue that there is a common "liberal-conservative" factor influencing the response to the nuclear arms attitude scale and the child value scale, this argument does not apply to the child value measure based on affection toward and enjoyment of children, which is not related in any obvious way to differences in political ideology.

The inverse relationship found between information and pro-nuclear-armament attitudes is encouraging for nuclear disarmament and moratorium advocates. Though this relationship was not derived from any theoretical hypotheses, it does make theoretical sense, given the type of distortions that were noted in information errors. Because these distortions tended to underestimate the nuclear resources of the United States vis-à-vis the Soviet Union, and to exaggerate the inflexibility and militancy of Soviet nuclear policies, one might anticipate that people who had little information and made many errors would be more fearful of Soviet power and would be more supportive of increasing the nuclear arsenal of the United States.

As an alternative interpretation of the relationship between information and nuclear attitudes, it might be contended that there is a curvilinear relationship, such that students with some information are more disarmament-oriented than those with very little information, whereas students with a great deal of information are more concerned about Soviet power and thus more supportive of the United States increasing nuclear armaments. To evaluate this possibility, the nuclear armament attitudes of the 12 students who obtained the highest scores on the information measure (12 or more correct responses; mean correct = 12.8) were compared to those of the rest of the sample (less than 12 correct; mean correct = 6.7). The mean pro-nuclear attitude score for the 12 high-information students was 4.1, in comparison to the mean of 6.5 for the other students, a difference significant at the .01 level. Thus, the students who were the most informed about nuclear armament matters were also the most favorably disposed toward disarmament/moratorium policies.

One cannot infer from these findings that the dissemination of information concerning nuclear armaments will necessarily foster pro-disarmament attitudes. Certainly there are many informed experts who would obtain high scores on our pro-nuclear armament scale. An extensive analysis of the dynamics entailed in the nuclear images and judgments of policymakers and of ordinary members of the community is provided in a recently edited publication by Fiske, Fischhoff, and Milburn (1983). To the insights provided by that volume, we would like to add the importance of analyzing values of policymakers that may influence the international options they deem feasible or acceptable.

One of these values, as suggested by the present data, is the value of children. Are the values of policymakers with regard to the importance of children representative of those of the larger community? Have these values been articulated so that they become identifiable elements in their risk-times-value decision equations? More generally, to what extent have any of the values that influence the decisions of nuclear arms policymakers been identified and made explicit? In addition, the decision-making context is important. We know from analyses of group decision making (Janis, 1972) and risk-taking (Burnstein, 1983) that under many circumstances groups tend to make riskier decisions than individuals. Consciousness of relevant values becomes especially important under these circumstances.

RESEARCH FOR ADVOCACY

The behavioral sciences can make a major contribution to the debate over nuclear armament/disarmament policies through identifying and assessing the values that are explicitly or implicitly engaged when making nuclear arms decisions. We need to have a clear idea of the relative value our leaders place on human life—such as the numbers and kinds of casualties they are willing to tolerate (our own citizens, children, those of other combatants and of nonparticipant nations)—versus the importance of other values such as territory, international power, political freedom, economic resources, the treasures of the past, the obligations to future generations.

Analysis of the values influencing the judgments of our policymakers and, where possible, those of the Soviets as well, is an appropriate and useful undertaking regardless of the particular policy position that we happen to support. Although these efforts may be stimulated by particular advocacy motivations, they also provide a basis for more informed discussion of nuclear armament alternatives. And if research should demonstrate that being informed about nuclear issues and being clear regarding the relevant value considerations leads to the view that nuclear war can better be avoided through some alternative to the policy we favored, then we must be open to that alternative. The overriding goal is the prevention of nuclear war. Advocacy-based research can help foster that goal as long as it remains governed by the canons of scientific objectivity.

At a fundamental level, advocacy-based research is little different than basic, applied, or policy-oriented research if it is guided by academic, scholarly values and procedures. Students of decision-making policies (Janis, 1972), of negotiation strategies (Rubin, 1982), of attitude change and mutual misperception (Kelman, 1972; Oskamp, 1977), of United States and Soviet relations (White, 1984) may contribute to the nuclear moratorium movement even if their research was not directly oriented toward that topic. For example, specific research findings may improve negotiation procedures, which facilitate compromise international agreements, which in turn may lead to a nuclear moratorium. In addition, theoretical analyses of extant social-psychological data can provide a more substantive basis for achieving a nuclear moratorium (White, 1984); and, as we suggested above, organizations such as the American Psychological Association and other scientific and professional associations could cooperate in conducting thoroughgoing reviews of present nuclear armament policies. In this arena, the ultimate value and consideration should be the avoidance of nuclear conflict. And there are many ways in which psychologists can contribute to that goal, whether they strive toward reducing resistance to the adoption of a nuclear moratorium, increasing our understanding of the Soviet Union, providing our negotiators with more effective bargaining procedures, or studying how the peace movement can increase its political power.

REFERENCES

American Psychological Association. (1983, February 2). *Memorandum: Limits of advocacy* (Enclosure 15). Washington, DC: Author.

Armor, D. J., Polich, J. M., & Stambul, H. B. (1978). *Alcoholism and treatment.* New York: John Wiley.

Bartlett, G. S., Byrnes, L., & Martin, J. L. (1980, September). *Reaction of adolescents to the emergency at Three Mile Island.* Paper presented at meeting of the American Psychological Association, Montreal.

Beardslee, W., & Mack, J. E. (1982). The impact on children and adolescents of nuclear developments. In *Psychological aspects of nuclear developments* (Task Force Report #20, pp. 64-93). Washington, DC: American Psychological Association.

Bennett, P. G., & Dando, M. R. (1983, February 17). The arms race: Is it just a mistake? *New Scientist,* pp. 432-435.

Bronfenbrenner, U. (1961). The mirror image in Soviet-American relations: A social psychologist's report. *Journal of Social Issues, 17*(3), 45-56.

Burnstein, E. (1983). Persuasion as argument processing. In M. Brandstatter, J. H. Davis, & G. Stocker-Kreichgauer (Eds.), *Group decision processes.* London: Academic Press.

Carnevale, P.J.D., Pruitt, D. G., & Seilheimer, S. D. (1981). Looking and competing: Accountability and visual access in integrative bargaining. *Journal of Personality and Social Psychology, 40,* 111-120.

Coulson, J. E. (1978). National evaluation of the Emergency School Aid Act (ESAA): A review of methodological issues. *Journal of Educational Statistics, 3,* 1-60.

Escalona, S. K. (1982). Growing up with the threat of nuclear war: Some indirect effects on personality development. *American Journal of Orthopsychiatry, 52,* 600-607.

Fiske, S. T., Fischhoff, B., & Milburn, M. A. (Eds.). (1983). Images of nuclear war. *Journal of Social Issues, 39*(1), 1-180.

Frank, J. D. (1982). *Sanity and survival: Psychological aspects of war and peace* (2nd ed.). New York: Random House.

Intriligator, M. D. (1982). Research on conflict theory. *Journal of Conflict Resolution, 26,* 307-327.

Janis, I. L. (1972). *Victims of groupthink: A psychological study of foreign-policy decisions and fiascoes.* Boston: Houghton Mifflin.

Kelman, H. C. (1972). The problem-solving workshop in conflict resolution. In L. L. Merritt (Ed.), *Communication in international politics.* Urbana: University of Illinois Press.

Mack, J. E. (1982). The perception of U.S. Soviet intentions and other psychological dimensions of the nuclear arms race. *American Journal of Orthopsychiatry, 52,* 590-599.

Osgood, C. E. (1962). *An alternative to war or surrender.* Urbana: University of Illinois Press.

Osgood, C. E. (1981). Psycho-social dynamics and the prospects for mankind. In E. Laszlo & D. Keys (Eds.), *Disarmament: The human factor* (pp. 73-91). New York: Pergamon.

Oskamp, S. (1965). Attitudes toward U.S. and Russian actions: A double standard. *Psychological Reports, 16,* 43-46.

Oskamp, S. (1977). *Attitudes and opinions.* Englewood Cliffs, NJ: Prentice-Hall.

Pruitt, D. G. (1981). *Negotiation behavior.* New York: Academic Press.

Rubin, J. Z. (1982). *Dynamics of third party intervention: Kissinger in the Middle East.* New York: Praeger.

Schwebel, M. (1982). Effects of the nuclear war threat on children and teenagers: Implications for professionals. *American Journal of Orthopsychiatry, 52,* 608-618.

Skrypnek, B. J., & Snyder, M. (1982). On the self-perpetuating nature of stereotypes about women and men. *Journal of Experimental Social Psychology, 18,* 277-291.

Stech, F., & McClintock, C. G. (1981). The effects of communication timing on duopoly bargaining outcomes. *Journal of Personality and Social Psychology, 40,* 664-674.

Wagner, R. H. (1982). Deterrence and bargaining. *Journal of Conflict Resolution, 26,* 329-358.

White, M., & Feshbach, S. (1984, August). *Individual differences in attitudes towards nuclear armament policies: Some psychological and social policy considerations.* Paper presented at meeting of the American Psychological Association, Toronto.

White, R. K. (1984). *Fearful warriors: A psychological profile of U.S.-Soviet relations.* New York: Free Press.

STUART OSKAMP
JEANNE C. KING
SHAWN M. BURN
ALISON M. KONRAD
JOHN A. POLLARD
MICHAEL A. WHITE

8

THE MEDIA
AND NUCLEAR WAR:
Fallout from
TV's *The Day After*

The mass media in our society both reflect public opinion and help to shape it. An outstanding example of the media's potential effects on public opinion was the November 20, 1983 television program about nuclear war, *The Day After*—a media event of a unique sort. Even before it was shown, it aroused widespread fears about how it would affect children and other impressionable viewers, and it created extensive political controversy between antinuclear and pro-armaments activists ("Nightmare Comes Home," 1983). Cover stories in national newsmagazines trumpeted that

> [the program] will reach out and detonate a thermonuclear apocalypse in our communal psyche. . . . The very idea of what television can do may never be the same. ("TV's Nuclear Nightmare," 1983, p. 66)

The program attracted a huge viewing audience, estimated at 100 million people who watched it in 46 percent of America's TV households. That was the twelfth largest viewing audience of all time for a U.S. TV program, and the second largest audience ever for a movie on TV ("Fallout," 1983; Kaatz, 1984). A survey study by a major advertising agency concluded:

> In the history of television, no single program ever created so much controversy for such an amount of time by so many people at so many levels of society as *The Day After*. By the time it actually aired, many

AUTHORS' NOTE: We are grateful to the many instructors who assisted in the data collection and to Lyn Macbride, Vera Dunwoody-Miller, Anita Kantak, and Aaron Cohen, who helped in the early phases of the research.

people felt they had already lived through it. (J. Walter Thompson, 1983, p. 6).

Psychologists, too, were strongly affected by the program and responded in typical fashion, by doing research and writing papers. At the 1984 American Psychological Association convention there were 14 papers on *The Day After* and at least as many more on related nuclear war issues. Research articles on public opinion about nuclear war, children's fears of nuclear war, and psychological aspects of United States-Soviet relations soon appeared in journals ranging from scholarly to popular (Klineberg, 1984; Moyer, 1985; Plous & Zimbardo, 1984; Yudkin, 1984). Research on *The Day After* was even done in other nations (Gunter & Wober, in press).

A group of us at Claremont Graduate School also became fascinated with the research possibilities. Because the publicity and printed viewer's guide materials were widely distributed more than a month before the program was shown, we saw a chance to do a pretest-posttest study on a nuclear catastrophe—an unprecedented, perhaps never to be repeated opportunity! Hence, after some careful planning we conducted a multiple-group quasi-experiment with a large sample of respondents.

OTHER RESEARCH FINDINGS

Before describing our study and its results in detail, we will summarize some findings from other studies of *The Day After* as a background and comparison for our findings.

After the intense buildup for the program, some commentators saw the film itself as anticlimactic and disappointing. Within days after the program was shown, some instant-analysis polls claimed that it had had little or no effect on viewers' attitudes (Schneider, 1983), and the White House was reported to be vastly relieved that it had not converted viewers to an antinuclear stance. Two studies proclaiming these negative results received national publicity.

The ABC Study

One study was done by ABC, the network that produced and broadcast *The Day After*. It was a telephone interview, conducted on the two days following the program, with a national probability sample of 1921 respondents including 288 children from age 10 to 18.

Instead of asking content-oriented questions about the issues involved in the program, the ABC study asked several items about the program's appropriateness for children, attitudes toward the program's advertisers, the ABC network, the "Viewpoint" panel discussion moderated by Ted Koppel that followed the program, and toward rebroadcasting the program here and abroad. The network's concerns can be easily inferred from their summary of the study's major findings:

The Day After audience was large and diverse.

The Day After was evaluated favorably, and ABC was praised for presenting the program.

Attitudes toward ABC changed in a positive direction as the result of *The Day After.*

Very few viewers of *The Day After* perceived the film in terms of political overtones or negative effects on children.

While most viewers had no change in their attitudes toward advertisers, favorable reactions to the sponsors outweighed the negative reactions by better than 3 to 1. (ABC, undated, p. 1)

Perhaps the most fascinating thing about this network study was that it carefully sought to avoid any responses about the political issues involved and reported that "the overwhelming majority of *The Day After* viewers did *not* evaluate it as a political film (97%)" (ABC, undated, p. 8). However, to reach this conclusion, ABC did not ask directly about the message of the film, but instead obtained this figure from answers to the question:

What was your overall reaction to *The Day After.* . . . did you think this program was. . . excellent, very good, good, fair, or poor?

Why do you feel that way?

In answer to that follow-up question, the following kinds of answers were tabulated:

General presentation (e. g., good acting, well produced)	48%
Increased awareness of nuclear war/the tragedy of war	27%
Thought provoking	11%
Made a statement/had an important message	6%
Other	8%

Of the 6 percent who said the program had a message, 3 percent responded in "general terms," whereas only 1 percent made pro-nuclear comments and 2 percent made antinuclear comments. ABC asked no questions about attitude change as a result of the program, except attitudes toward the network and the advertisers. Thus, by avoiding asking about its message, ABC concluded that the movie was nonpolitical.

The Adams et al. Study

The other instant-analysis study was a commercial survey conducted under the supervision of William C. Adams of George Washington University. In it, a nationwide random sample of 510 intended viewers of the progam was interviewed by telephone in the one-and-a-half hours immediately before it began, and a separate nationwide random sample of 418 actual viewers was interviewed in the hour immediately after it ended (Adams et al., 1984). The margin of error for the pretest-posttest difference for such sample sizes would be about ±7 percent.

The survey asked eight questions, tapping attitudes on: (1) U.S. defense spending, (2) a bilateral nuclear freeze, (3) unilateral U.S. nuclear disarmament, (4) likelihood of a full-scale nuclear war within ten years, (5) likelihood of a nuclear war if Reagan or Mondale were President, (6) the respondent's chances of living through a nuclear war, (7) whether there is nothing one can do to influence war or peace, and (8) whether the program would be (was) politically fair or mainly propaganda.

Adams et al.'s report concluded that there were practically no pretest-posttest changes among their respondents. In fact, two of their eight items showed changes large enough to be significant, though neither of these was directly related to the program's message. After the program, more viewers thought the film was politically fair than had expected it to be (good news for ABC!), and somewhat fewer viewers thought that Reagan would be more likely than Mondale to get us into a nuclear war (though still nearly twice as many as thought Mondale would be more likely to do so). Support for a bilateral nuclear freeze was very high (over 75 percent) on both occasions—almost exactly the same percentage shown in a series of polls by the *Los Angeles Times* (Schneider, 1983). There were also no noticeable changes in viewers' opinions on U.S. defense spending or unilateral U.S. nuclear disarmament, nor on their estimates of the likelihood of a nuclear war, their own chances of living through one, or whether they could do anything to influence war or peace.

Although Adams et al.'s sample of viewers was apparently a representative one, there are several reasons to doubt their conclusion of no change in viewers: (1) Their respondents were called within minutes after the program (most of them were called during the course of the immediately following "Viewpoint" panel discussion, which was watched by about three-quarters of *The Day After* viewers—Adams et al., 1984). Thus there may be a question as to whether the program's contents had had a chance to register fully, particularly as the "Viewpoint" discussion added considerable factual information that could augment the impact of *The Day After* program itself on viewers' attitudes.

(2) It is possible that more changes would have been found if more questions had been asked that were relevant to the specific focus of the program, for such results have been found in past media research (Elliott & Schenck-Hamlin, 1979; Kaid, Towers, & Myers, 1981; Robinson, 1976).

(3) The program may have caused some viewers' attitudes to shift in one direction (e.g., antinuclear) and other viewers to change in the opposite direction, so that the net effect of these offsetting changes was negligible. Such a result would be consistent with ABC's clear intention that the program not have any political message that could be perceived as one-sided.

(4) Even if there were minimal changes in a national cross section of viewers, there might be larger attitude changes in particular population subgroups. For instance, this might be especially true of students and other young viewers whose attitudes about nuclear war were less crystallized and more open to change than the average citizen's. (However, Adams et al. reported that their viewers under age 30 did not change more than older viewers.)

(5) It is likely that the prebroadcast respondents were not a true unexposed control group, because their attitudes may already have been markedly influenced by all the publicity and controversy in the weeks before the program. Such an effect would be consistent with the anticipatory attitude changes that have been found in many laboratory studies of persuasive communication (Cialdini & Petty, 1981). Several findings of the present study are relevant to these alternate explanations of Adams et al.'s findings.

More Comprehensive Studies

In contrast to commerical studies, which are sometimes conducted and reported in a few days, more thorough academic survey studies tend to take much longer to carry out and report. The papers on *The Day After* that were presented at the 1984 American Psychological

Association meeting (summarized by Oskamp, 1984) took a more complete and careful look at the question of the program's effects, studying them with a variety of theoretical viewpoints, research designs, and measurement techniques.

The majority of these studies gave written questionnaires to college students, though others ranged widely from laboratory experiments to surveys of high school and elementary school children or of representative samples of adults in the community. They all had large groups of participants, ranging from 157 to more than 1000. The percentage of respondents who had watched the program ranged from 61 percent to 96 percent in the various studies, with a median of 77 percent. Most of the studies gave pretests and posttests to the same sample of respondents, but a majority included posttest-only groups to avoid sensitization of these respondents due to pretesting. Four studies gave delayed posttests as well, to check on longer lasting attitude changes, and six obtained some measures of respondents' behavioral intentions or commitment to taking actions related in some way to the nuclear arms race. All of the studies investigated some aspect of attitude change; however, the measures that each used and the nature of their findings were highly varied.

All of these studies reported at least some indications of attitude change following *The Day After.* The findings of several suggest that there really were important effects of *The Day After,* and that one or more of the five alternative explanations mentioned above may account for the limited changes found in Adams et al.'s (1984) study. Further discussion of the findings of these studies is saved for the final section of this chapter.

THE CLAREMONT STUDY—METHOD

In our study eight main questions were investigated: (1) What kinds of people chose to watch or not to watch the program? (2) What were the nuclear war attitudes of our student respondents? (3) Did they change their attitudes following the program? (4) Did our pretesting sensitize viewers and cause different attitude changes than in non-pretested viewers? (5) What kinds of people changed the most? (6) Did any attitude change persist more than a few days? (7) Did any behavioral intentions or commitments result from the program? (8) What differences were found between our college students and our adult, professional respondents?

The research design was a quasi-experimental one, in which the viewing decision was up to the respondents and viewing took place in their own natural settings (usually with one to three close friends or family members), so we could not control how much or what they viewed. Because most of those who viewed *The Day After* also watched some or all of the immediately following "Viewpoint" panel discussion, the two programs were considered as a single event. In our analyses, as in all pre-post designs, the effects of the program were combined with those of any other events that occurred in the interval between pretest and posttest, especially the media publicity about the program. Thus we were studying the program and its byproducts as a total "media event."

Subjects

The respondents in this study were primarily college students, 607 of whom took written questionnaires during class sessions in five quite different southern California colleges: two small private colleges, a junior college, a state university, and a branch of the University of California system. In addition, an older comparison group was provided by 56 research psychologists and engineers in Southern California who were working on various government projects (mostly defense-related). Most of this report concentrates on the large group of college student respondents, but the final section of results analyzes differences between the students and the adult professionals.

Most respondents took the pretest in the week before the program and the posttest the week after it (N = 298 plus 46 professionals). However, the quasi-experimental research design included some groups of students who received no pretest (N = 65), and others who received an additional delayed posttest two weeks after the first posttest (the latest possible date at which they could still be contacted as a group—N = 98).

Questionnaire

Somewhat different versions of the questionnaire were used for the pretest, posttest, and delayed posttest. All three versions contained the same 18 questions about nuclear war issues, such as attitudes toward various aspects of the arms race, the respondent's concern about the likelihood of a nuclear war, and expectations about specific results if a nuclear war were to occur. In addition, the pretest had questions about whether respondents had heard of the upcoming *The Day After* program and their intentions of watching it. The main posttest form had questions about their demographic characteristics, about conditions of watching *The Day After* and affective and cognitive reactions to it, and about commitment to subsequent action. Because all respondents who took the delayed posttest had earlier taken the main posttest, the delayed posttest omitted the demographic items and questions about reactions to the program. Completion of each questionnaire typically took about 20 minutes.

RESULTS

Who Watched the Program?

Before *The Day After* was broadcast, we didn't anticipate the huge size of its viewing audience, and we feared that only a small proportion of our students might watch the program, thus weakening our tests of attitude changes. Consequently, we urged the students to watch the program, and a few of our classes were assigned to watch it. As a result, 86 percent of the posttest student respondents watched the program. However, even among our adult professionals, who were not so influenced, 72 percent of the posttest respondents were viewers. Of course, among the nonviewers, some were prevented from watching by work, church meetings, or other regular activities, rather than by their own choice.

Though viewing or nonviewing was thus not entirely voluntary, it was still of interest to know what kinds of people watched the program or did not do so. We investigated 16 demographic and personal character-istics of the students in relation to a 3-point scale of viewing (none, partial, or full viewing of the program). All of these relationships were relatively low ($r < .20$), but some were significant for our large group of students. On the average, groups who were slightly more likely to be viewers included men, U.S. citizens, whites, sophomores and above, veterans, and employed students. Thus, in general, viewers were slightly more likely to be from those groups who had broader life experience and who may have been more interested in the subject of war.

General Nuclear War Attitudes

In studying nuclear war attitudes, we first wanted to know how similar our student participants' views were to national public opinion on nuclear war issues. A rough indication of similarity was provided by their responses to four questions on topics that have been asked in

TABLE 8.1
Attitudes of College Student Viewers and Nonviewers
Following Showing of *The Day After* Compared with
Representative Samples of Adults in 1982

Item	Sample	Response (% yes)
I am very worried about the possibility of a nuclear war.	1982 adult sample	28
	College viewers	57
	College nonviewers	40
I am in favor of both sides halting the production of nuclear weapons.	1982 adult sample	74
	College viewers	80
	College nonviewers	70
The Soviets are leading in the nuclear arms race.	1982 adult sample	41
	College viewers	29
	College nonviewers	25
I favor using nuclear weapons on the Soviet Union if its conventional forces invade Europe.	1982 adult sample	28
	College viewers	5
	College nonviewers	2

various large and representative public opinion polls ("A Hard Look," 1983; Kramer, Kalick, & Milburn, 1983). These questions were on our posttest questionnaire as we were not yet aware of these national data when constructing the pretest form. Thus the TV program may have somewhat influenced the respondents' answers, but presumably that would be less true for nonviewers of the program. The comparative results for college viewers, nonviewers, and a representative adult sample are displayed in Table 8.1.

Table 8.1 shows that, in comparison to representative samples of the United States population in 1982, our college students were substantially more worried about the chances of a nuclear war, about equally in favor of a bilateral freeze on nuclear weapon production, somewhat less inclined to think that Russia was ahead in the nuclear arms race, and markedly less willing to use nuclear weapons first, even in response to a Russian invasion of Europe. It is possible that the U.S. population had changed some of its views since 1982 in such a way as to diminish these differences, but it also seems likely that these items are ones on which college students tended to be more extreme than adults.

Next we looked descriptively at the responses of our students on 18 questions related to nuclear war and international relations—very interesting indications of their attitudes. Here are the mean posttest responses of viewers and nonviewers combined (as well as the medians when they differed noticeably from the means due to skewed distributions of responses):

(1) They thought or worried about the possibility of a nuclear war between once a week and once a month.

(2) They thought there was a 29 percent chance of a nuclear war involving the United States occurring during the next 5 years (median = 22 percent).

(3) There was a 55 percent chance of such a war occurring in the next 50 years (median = 49 percent).

(4) If such a war occurred, it would destroy civilization, but some people would survive.

(5) In the year following the beginning of such a war, they thought that 175 million of the United States' 230 million people would die (median = 194 million). (In addition, they felt 40 million would be injured; median = 29 million.)

(6) Thus they estimated that only 16 million of the people in the United States would be *neither* dead nor injured—that is, about 7 percent of the population (median = one-third of a million, or less than 0.2 percent of the population).

(7) They estimated that the chances of getting needed medical treatment would be only 18 percent (median = 9 percent).

(8) They estimated that the chances of social chaos, such as looting, mob violence, and a breakdown of order would be 76 percent (median = 89 percent).

(9) They estimated that their personal chances of survival would be 21 percent (median = 7 percent).

(10) On average, they felt it was slightly likely that a future nonnuclear conflict anywhere in the world would escalate into a nuclear war (70 percent said "likely" to some degree, whereas 30 percent said "unlikely" to some degree).

(11) They felt it was fairly unlikely that any nuclear war could be limited in scope (i.e., that only a small number of nuclear weapons would be used).

(12) They thought that the U.S. government's current civil defense measures would be quite ineffective in preventing deaths and injuries in a nuclear war.

(13) Given the current Russian level of armaments, 30 percent of them favored decreasing the number of U.S. nuclear weapons in the next few years, whereas 47 percent favored maintaining the present number, and 23 percent favored increasing the number.

(14) They were quite favorable toward the idea of signing an arms control treaty with Russia to substantially reduce both nations' number of nuclear weapons.

(15) They were almost evenly divided pro and con toward the current administration's proposed increases in the U.S. Defense Department budget.

(16) They were a trifle more favorable than unfavorable toward the use of U.S. troops in Grenada a few months earlier.

(17) A total of 51 percent thought there were some specific actions that people could take to increase their chances of *surviving* a future nuclear war. Nearly 40 percent of the *yes* answers specified going to a rural area or leaving the country.

(18) A total of 65 percent of them thought there were some specific actions that people could take to help *prevent* a future nuclear war. Nearly two-thirds of the *yes* answers specified working for arms control or engaging in political protest.

To summarize these responses, our students did worry about the possibility of a nuclear war, but not too frequently, and they thought there was about a fifty-fifty chance of one occurring in their lifetime, quite possibly escalating from a nonnuclear conflict. If one did occur, they expected that civil defense measures would be ineffective and that the war would destroy civilization, kill or injure over 90 percent of the U.S. population, and cause widespread social chaos. They favored a bilateral arms control treaty, but unilaterally they were only willing to make small reductions in U.S. nuclear arms. They were divided in their attitudes toward increasing the U.S. defense budget and using U.S. troops in places like Grenada, as well as toward whether it was possible to increase one's chances of surviving a nuclear war, but they were a bit more optimistic about the possibility of taking steps to prevent a future nuclear war.

Changes Following the Program

Next we asked whether viewing the program had affected our students' attitudes, and if so, how? Based on past psychological research and theories (e.g., Fiske, Pratto, & Pavelchak, 1983), we expected that a highly vivid presentation of nuclear war and its consequences would increase the availability of viewer's images of war, modify their cognitive beliefs and attitudes toward war, and possibly also change their relevant behavior and feelings of personal efficacy regarding war. The specific prior publicity about the program led us to expect that viewers would undergo the following sorts of changes: increased worry about nuclear war, increased estimates of the chances of their own death, of the amount of destruction and disruptive social consequences of nuclear war, increased estimates of the likelihood of a nuclear war, greater favorability to arms control, greater opposition to nuclear weapons increases and other U.S. military actions, and so on.

In addition to examining the 18 relevant attitude items separately, we combined items that were empirically correlated on both the pretest and the posttest into scales. Six items (numbers 4, 5, 6, 7, 9, and 11) with average intercorrelations of .40 were combined into a scale measuring the *seriousness of consequences* of nuclear war (alpha coefficient of internal consistency = .80), and three items (numbers 2, 3, and 10) with average intercorrelations of .54 were combined into a scale indicating the *likelihood* of nuclear war (alpha coefficient = .78). The scales were constructed to give each item equal weight, using standard scores based on the means and standard deviations for the entire pretest student sample.

The analysis of changes was based on the student respondents who had taken both the pretest and posttest. It utilized a two-way analysis of variance: repeated measures before and after the program crossed with three levels of viewing (37 nonviewers, 34 partial viewers who watched less than two hours of the program, and 221 full viewers). Thus, this analysis yielded main effects for change during this period of time and for the level of viewing, as well as interactions between these two variables. The results are shown in Table 8.2.

The data in Table 8.2 demonstrate that there were many changes in students' attitudes about nuclear war during the period surrounding the showing of *The Day After*—eight of the items and the seriousness scale showed highly significant changes during this period of time, and one other item approached significance. By contrast, as expected, none of the items or scales showed significant main effects for the level of viewing (there was no reason for viewers' attitudes to be more extreme at *both* the pretest and posttest). There were also no significant interaction effects. However, this absence was probably due in part to the small size of the nonviewer and partial viewer groups, for the table footnote shows that there were six variables that displayed trends toward significance and in which simple effects t-tests showed that viewers who watched the whole program changed to a highly significant degree (p < .001).

Thus, the attitudes of both *The Day After* viewers *and* nonviewers changed significantly and substantially on about half of our items and on the seriousness scale; and on six variables the viewers changed significantly though the nonviewers did not. We interpret these results to mean that *The Day After* program and all the media publicity and controversy that surrounded it had a pronounced effect on our students *and that they affected the small proportion of students who didn't watch the program (only 13 percent of these respondents) very nearly as much as those who watched it.*

Moreover, all of these changes except one were in the direction that we expected on an a priori basis (e.g., increased worry about nuclear war, more disastrous estimates of its consequences, increased expectations of social chaos, decreased chances of survival or of getting needed medical treatment if one did survive, decreased belief in the effectiveness of civil defense measures, etc.). The one directional finding that we didn't predict (item 17) was an increased number of respondents saying that there *were* specific actions that people could take to increase their chances of surviving a nuclear war (pretest 41 percent, posttest 53 percent). In view of the number of survivors shown in the film and particularly the survival of the farm family in their basement retreat, our students' change in this direction seems understandable. However, note that they nevertheless displayed a large increase in their posttest estimates of casualties, saying that many more millions of people would die in a nuclear war and fewer millions of people would survive uninjured than they had said before the program.

Did Pretesting Contribute to the Changes?

The fourth issue that we investigated was whether pretesting our respondents before the program might have sensitized them to it and consequently either magnified or diminished its effects. This question was addressed by comparing the responses of a posttest-only group at a large state university ($N = 48$) with the posttest responses of pretested classes at the same school. On the same list of 18 questions and 2 scales, there were no significant t-test differences between the pretested groups and the posttest-only group. Thus it seems safe to conclude that being exposed to the pretesting did not cause any noticeable changes in the respondents' posttest answers.

Who Changed the Most?

Next we asked which particular kinds of people changed most as a result of watching *The Day After*. Here we used several dependent variables to measure different types of changes.

New information. The first variable was a question asking what new information (if any) respondents had learned from the program. We

TABLE 8.2
Pretest and Posttest Attitudes of Student Respondents and ANOVA Results for Significance of Pre-Post Changes and Level of Viewing *The Day After*

Item and Range of Scores	Pretest Mean (N = 298)	Posttest Mean (N = 298)	Significance of Pre-Post Change	Significance of Level of Viewing	Significance of Interaction
(1) Worry about nuclear war (1-7)	3.26	3.68	.002	ns	ns[a]
(2) Chance of nuclear war in 5 years (0-100)	27.93	30.41	ns	ns	ns
(3) Chance of nuclear war in 50 years (0-100)	55.66	55.06	ns	ns	ns
(4) Seriousness of nuclear war consequences (1-7)	5.13	5.28	ns	ns	ns
(5) Millions of U.S. dead in nuclear war (0-230)	150	174	.0001	ns	ns[a]
(6) Millions of U.S. *noninjured*	29.5	16.9	.0001	ns	ns
(7) Chances of getting needed medical treatment (0-100)	25.0	17.5	.0001	ns	ns[a]
(8) Chances of social chaos (0-100)	70.0	78.6	.003	ns	ns
(9) Personal chances of survival (0-100)	29.4	21.5	.005	ns	ns[a]
(10) Likelihood of nonnuclear conflict escalating (1-6)	3.96	4.03	ns	ns	ns

Item					
(11) Likelihood of nuclear war remaining limited (1-6)	2.73	2.37	ns	ns	.09[a]
(12) Effectiveness of current U.S. civil defense measures (1-6)	2.49	2.12	.003	ns	ns
(13) Favor decreasing the number of U.S. nuclear weapons (1-3)	1.88	2.05	.10	ns	ns
(14) Favor signing arms control treaty with Russia (1-6)	4.81	4.87	ns	ns	ns
(15) Favor proposed increases in U.S. Defense Dept. budget (1-6)	3.59	3.42	ns	ns	ns
(16) Favor recent use of United States troops in Grenada (1-6)	3.85	3.84	ns	ns	ns
(17) Think some specific actions can increase chances of *surviving* future nuclear war (1 = no, 2 = yes)	1.41	1.53	.005	ns	ns
(18) Think some specific actions can help *prevent* a future nuclear war (1 = no, 2 = yes)	1.67	1.62	ns	ns	ns
(19) Seriousness scale (standard score)	.03	.29	.0001	ns	.09[a]
(20) Likelihood scale (standard score)	.00	.07	ns	ns	ns

NOTE: On all items, higher scores indicate greater amounts of the attitude in the direction indicated by the item stem.
a. Simple effects tests for full viewers of the program showed change (p < .001).

classified responses on a 3-point scale (none; incidental facts, such as ICBMs having a 30-minute flight time; more central facts about nuclear effects, chances of survival, etc.), and we investigated 16 demographic and personal characteristics of viewers as related to the information gain they reported. Of the 16 personal variables there were two that displayed a significant relationship to information gain and six others that showed nonsignificant trends, but which contributed to a meaningful picture of the amount of learning from the program by particular groups of viewers. On the average, men reported learning less central information than women (means 1.75 versus 2.32; $F = 29.13$, $df = 1, 293$, $p < .0001$); and college graduates and upperclassmen reported learning less than underclassmen (means 1.78 versus 1.85 versus 2.18; $F = 3.81$, $df = 2, 286$, $p < .03$). The nonsignificant trends showed that the following groups (many of them quite small groups) reported learning less information from the program: students who were 20 or older; those with children; veterans of the armed forces; members of organizations concerned with peace, war, or national defense issues; those who were *not* politically neutral; and those who reported being not at all religious. Several of these results, such as those for men, older students, and veterans, were opposite to the findings on the characteristics of viewers—that is, the same groups who were more likely to watch the program were less likely to say that they had learned much from it.

The highly significant gender difference in the amount of information gain may be related to the occasional findings in the literature on social influence that each sex is more easily influenced on sex-typed topics that are the province of the opposite sex (Sistrunk & McDavid, 1971; Cacioppo & Petty, 1980; Feldman-Summers, Montano, Kasprzyk, & Wagner, 1980). Because knowledge about war is traditionally a male sex-typed topic, it is not surprising that women should report learning more about it from the program. The other significant difference and trends all fit together in portraying the viewers who reported learning most from the program as being the youngest, least experienced, and least politically involved students (similar to past findings by Him-melweit, Oppenheim, & Vince, 1958). These viewers who were most open to new information were probably still in the process of attitude formation about many aspects of international affairs and nuclear war.

Self-reported attitude change. A second variable was self-reported attitude change on a question that asked respondents whether seeing *The Day After* had changed any of their attitudes or feelings. Here we classified responses into three categories (no attitude change; dysphoric affective attitude change, such as greater fear, realization of the drastic effects of nuclear war, or worry over its likelihood; and action-oriented attitude change, such as a desire to get more information or participate in relevant actions).

The results here were somewhat similar to those for learning new information. Only two of the 16 personal variables showed significant differences, and gender again displayed by far the strongest relationships. There were more men than women in the no-change group (63 percent to 42 percent) and more women than men in the affective change group (47 percent to 31 percent). The other significant variable was religious affiliation, with fewer Protestants (44 percent) and Catholics (41 percent) being in the no-change group, when compared with Jewish, other, and respondents with no religious affiliation. The Protestants and Catholics were overrepresented in the affective-change group (41 percent and 50 percent, respectively).

Pre-post attitude differences. A third way of measuring changes was an empirical comparison of respondents' differences between their pretest and posttest responses. Here we focused just on the two multi-item scales that indicated the seriousness and the likelihood of nuclear war. Again we related them to the 16 demographic and personal characteristics of respondents, and again we found only a few significant relationships.

For change in the seriousness scale, degree of religiousness was significant beyond the .01 level, with respondents who were not all religious increasing slightly on seriousness of nuclear war consequences, those who were slightly or moderately religious increasing more, and those who were very or extremely religious increasing most. The only other relationship here was a trend for students who were also employed to increase their view of the seriousness of nuclear war consequences somewhat more than nonemployed students.

For change in the likelihood scale, gender was again a significant correlate, with men increasing slightly in their estimates of the likelihood of nuclear war whereas women decreased somewhat. Similarly, religiousness was again significant, with respondents who were not all religious increasing in their estimates of the likelihood of nuclear war, those who were slightly or moderately religious decreasing slightly, and those who were very or extremely religious decreasing more. Thus, women and religious students tended to see nuclear war as less likely after the program; but paradoxically, as mentioned above, religious students increased in their view of the seriousness of nuclear war's consequences, and women reported increasing in their negative affective reactions to nuclear war.

Persistence of Changes

At this point in our analysis we felt able to assert that *The Day After* had indeed affected our college student respondents. However, a very important issue was how long these attitude changes lasted. To investigate this issue, we examined the subgroup of 98 students who were tested in the week after the program and given another, delayed posttest two weeks after that. Due to the academic semester schedule, this was the latest that we could retest them, but we felt that it was better to investigate a three-week delay than not to consider the issue at all. Here we looked at the same 18 items on which the changes for the total pre-post student group were reported above. The mean scores for significant items and for the two scales are shown in Table 8.3.

Examination of the pretest and initial posttest means in Table 8.3 shows that they quite closely paralleled the results for the total pre-post student group displayed in Table 8.2, indicating that this subgroup was generally similar to the total student group. Likewise, the table shows that their significant pretest-posttest differences were similar to the larger student group, 10 of the 18 items plus the seriousness scale displaying significant changes.

The important question of persistence of these attitude changes was first addressed by t-test comparisons of pretest versus delayed posttest responses on the items that had shown initial posttest changes. As Table 8.3 indicates, three of the initially significant items no longer were significant on the delayed posttest, though two of the them were still beyond the .10 level (items 9 and 10). These items on which changes decayed were estimates of the chances of social chaos, personal survival, and the likelihood of a nonnuclear conflict escalating into a nuclear war. The other seven significant items and the seriousness scale all retained a significant amount of change at the time of the delayed posttest. Thus, nearly three weeks after the program, these respondents still showed significant changes in their views about the seriousness of nuclear war, worry about nuclear war, beliefs about how many people would die and how many would emerge uninjured, estimates of the chances of getting needed medical treatment, the likelihood of a nuclear war remaining limited, the ineffectiveness of U.S. civil defense measures, and decreased favorability toward proposed increases in the U.S. defense budget. Moreover, three of these variables displayed no decay or even an increased amount of change from the initial posttest to the delayed posttest, and one additional item that was initially nonsignificant became significant at the delayed

TABLE 8.3

Comparison of Pretest Attitudes with Initial and Delayed Posttest Attitudes and Significance of Linear and Quadratic Trends for Days 1, 8, and 22

Item and Range of Scores	Pretest Mean	Initial Posttest Mean	Delayed Posttest Mean	Significance of Linear Trend	Significance of Quadratic Trend
(1) Worry about nuclear war (1-7)	2.76	3.26***	3.39***	***	**
(5) Millions of U.S. dead in nuclear war (0-230)	135	178 ***	168 ***	S	S
(6) Millions of U.S. *noninjured*	37.6	20.7 ***	20.8 ***	S	S
(7) Chances of getting needed medical treatment (0-100)	30.5	17.6 ***	20.5 **	S	S
(8) Chances of social chaos (0-100)	66.7	79.4 **	72.1	ns	***
(9) Personal chances of survival (0-100)	27.0	21.8 *	22.6	S	S
(10) Likelihood of nonnuclear conflict escalating (1-6)	3.55	3.85*	3.79	ns	*
(11) Likelihood of nuclear war remaining limited (1-6)	2.79	2.34**	2.44*	S	S
(12) Effectiveness of current U.S. civil defense measures (1-6)	2.44	2.00**	2.18*	ns	***

(continued)

TABLE 8.3 Continued

Item and Range of Scores	Pretest Mean	Initial Posttest Mean	Delayed Posttest Mean	Significance of Linear Trend	Significance of Quadratic Trend
(15) Favor proposed increases in U.S. Defense Dept. budget (1-6)	3.74	3.48*	3.48*	*	ns
(17) Think some specific actions can increase chances of *surviving* future nuclear war (1 = no, 2 = yes)	1.39	1.50	1.37	ns	*
(18) Think some specific actions can help *prevent* a future nuclear war (1 = no, 2 = yes)	1.63	1.52	1.37***	***	ns
(19) Seriousness scale (standard score)	.03	.33***	.33***	***	***
(20) Likelihood scale (standard score)	−.07	.08	.00	ns	ns

NOTE: Ns for tests range from 53 to 62. On all items, higher scores indicate greater amounts of the attitude in the direction indicated by the item stem; S = items included in Seriousness scale (item trend analyses not computed).
* p < .05; ** p < .01; *** p < .001; ns = nonsignificant.

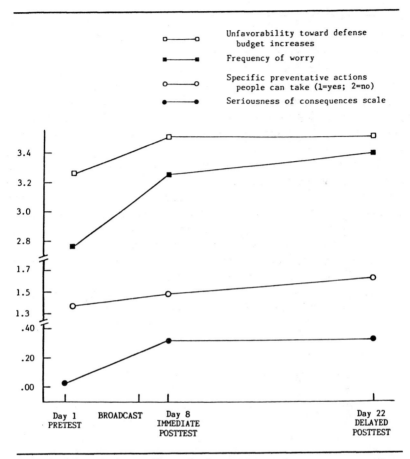

Figure 8.1 Attitude changes that persisted.

posttest (a decrease in belief that some specific actions can help prevent a future nuclear war).

Trend analysis. To estimate more precisely the amount of attitude change as a function of the actual periods of time between the three measurement points, we also performed a trend analysis on the likelihood and seriousness scales and the other seven items not included in the seriousness scale that were shown in Table 8.3 The significance levels are also displayed in Table 8.3, and the results are depicted graphically in Figures 8.1 and 8.2. (Note that in Figures 8.1 and 8.2 the direction of scoring of three items—defense increases, preventive actions, and civil defense—is reversed from that in Table 8.3 in order to show the parallelism of the results.) The trend analysis showed

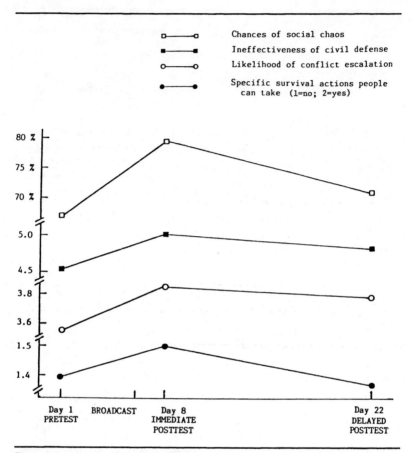

Figure 8.2 Attitude changes that decayed.

significant linear components for the four variables that had displayed no decay (the seriousness scale, worry about nuclear war, reduced favorability toward increases in the U.S. defense budget, and pessimism about people's actions helping to prevent nuclear war). This finding indicates that these attitudes and fears were persisting strongly rather than diminishing. The other four items displayed significant quadratic components, indicating some drop-off, and most of these were ones where the amount of change at the delayed posttest, shown in Table 8.3, was no longer significant.

The two items that showed an increased amount of change at the delayed posttest were particularly interesting because they both indicate a substantial delayed reaction of increasing pessimism about future nuclear wars. They were:

(1) increased worry about the possibility of a nuclear war occurring, and
(18) decreased belief that some specific actions can help prevent a future nuclear war.

In general, the above results concerning attitude change and persistence demonstrate that there was a substantial and significant initial attitude change on about half of our items about nuclear war, and that most of these items retained a large and significant portion of their changes for a period of nearly three weeks after the showing of the program *The Day After*.

Were There Any Behavioral Changes?

Another important issue in our study was whether these attitude changes would be extended to the behavioral level. Because we could not follow up our respondents over a long time period, the only practical way to investigate this issue was to obtain measures of their behavioral commitment and behavioral intentions. We did this with several questions, as follows.

Following questions 17 and 18 (what actions could help one to survive or to prevent a future nuclear war), we asked: "Which of the actions you listed in the preceding two questions have you taken, or do you intend to take?" Though some of the answers described past actions, most of them reflected future behavioral intentions. On the posttest, 40 percent of the respondents wrote down one or more such actions. Comparison of the posttest responses with the pretest for all students, both viewers and nonviewers, showed no change in intentions to take war-survival actions but a marginally significant increase in intentions to take war-prevention actions (from 25 percent to 31 percent, $p < .10$). On the latter item, viewers of the program showed a significant increase ($p < .01$) whereas nonviewers had a nonsignificant decrease.

In addition to those behavioral intention items, we included two items on the posttest questionnaire that gave respondents a chance to make behavioral commitments. One item allowed them to check that they would like their name and address to be placed on the mailing list of several organizations that were either pro-nuclear armaments or anti-nuclear armaments, or on both sets of mailing lists. The second, weaker, commitment item allowed respondents to check that they would like to receive a list of the above organizations' names and addresses for their own information (again, either pro- or antinuclear organizations, or both). Both items required the respondents to fill in their names and addresses on the previously anonymous questionnaire, and of course we were ethically bound to fulfill their requests and did so soon thereafter.

Although 75 percent of the posttest respondents said no to the offer of being placed on either set of mailing lists, 2 percent did request to be on the pro-nuclear mailing lists, 15 percent requested to be on the antinuclear mailing lists, and 8 percent asked to be on both sets. The offer to receive the list of organizations' names and addresses was accepted by a somewhat larger (and substantially overlapping) group of respondents: 3 percent requested the pro-nuclear organization list, 19 percent requested the antinuclear organization list, and 11 percent requested both. Although these actions do not guarantee dedicated long-term commitment, it nevertheless seems rather impressive that 17 percent of the respondents would ask to be put on the mailing lists of organizations active on nuclear armaments issues, and that 15 percent of them chose the antinuclear side. (Those who asked to be on the mailing lists of both sides, it seems, may have been more interested in obtaining information than in becoming more involved in partisan activities.)

Interestingly, these behavioral commitment actions were related to having seen *The Day After*, but they were not confined to viewers (26 percent of viewers and 12 percent of nonviewers requested to be placed on the mailing lists; 35 percent of viewers and 16 percent of nonviewers asked to receive the lists). That is, viewers of the program were about twice as likely to make these commitments as were nonviewers. Respondents who made either of the *antinuclear* commitments were significantly different from the nonrequesters in the following ways: They were more worried about the possibility of nuclear war, favored larger decreases in U.S. nuclear weapons, more opposed to increases in the U.S. defense budget and to U.S. troops in Grenada, more favorable to signing an arms control treaty with Russia, more liberal politically, more likely to belong to organizations concerned with issues of peace and war, and believed more strongly that personal actions could help prevent a future nuclear war—a consistent and meaningful pattern of relationships. There were too few respondents who asked for the pro-nuclear information to allow empirical comparisons. Respondents who asked for *both sets* of information were significantly characterized by only a few of these same variables—more worry about nuclear war, belief that personal actions could help prevent a nuclear war, and higher levels of membership in peace/war organizations—but in addition they were more likely to be somewhat older, to be married, and to have children.

How Did Professionals Differ from Student Respondents?

A final issue for our research was to investigate differences between our 56 professionals (engineers and research psychologists) and our college student respondents. The professionals were not a representative group of adults, but their high educational level and their vocational areas made them a reasonable comparison group for the student respondents. However, because of the limited size of the professional group, some analyses could not be conducted, and the significance levels would be expected to be lower than for the large group of students.

The professionals' nuclear war attitudes displayed some similarities and some differences from the students. On the four public opinion issues listed in Table 8.1, they answered as follows:

Very worried about the possibility of a nuclear war	42% yes
Favor both sides halting the production of nuclear weapons	86% yes
The Soviets are leading in the nuclear arms race	16% yes
Favor using nuclear weapons on the U.S.S.R. if it invades Europe	0% yes

Thus they were considerably more "dovish" than the 1982 representative adult sample, but not greatly different from our student respondents—somewhat less worried about future nuclear war, slightly more favorable to halting production of nuclear weapons, and a little less convinced that Russia was leading the nuclear arms race. On the item regarding worry about a nuclear war, there was a huge difference between the professionals who viewed the program and those who did not (53 percent of the viewers versus 18 percent of the nonviewers reported such fears).

Larger differences were found between the professionals and students on many of the 18 more specific attitude items that were listed in Table 8.2.[1] In comparison to the students, the professionals predicted a lower chance of nuclear war (Q2 and Q3 and likelihood scale), less serious consequences from such a war (Q4 and seriousness scale), fewer millions of U.S. dead and more millions of U.S. uninjured (Q5 and

Q6), lower likelihood of a nonnuclear conflict escalating and more likelihood of a nuclear war remaining limited (Q10 and Q11), even less effectiveness of U.S. civil defense measures (Q12), and they more strongly favored signing an arms control treaty with Russia (Q14). In view of the fact that most of these professionals were working in defense-related positions, their attitudes see more "dovish" than might be expected, though somewhat less so than the students'.

There were also some important differences in the findings for professionals and students on the significance tests displayed in Table 8.2. The professionals had absolutely no significant changes between their pretest and posttest mean responses, whereas the students had many. Moreover, although the students had no significant main effects for the three viewing levels, the professionals had two significant ones (the likelihood scale and Q10, about a nonnuclear conflict escalating) and several trends that probably would be significant for larger Ns (Q2, Q3, Q5, and Q14—the level of viewing tests for professionals compared only nonviewers and full viewers, due to the tiny number of partial viewers). Finally, the interaction effects for professionals showed one significant item (Q11, likelihood of a nuclear war remaining limited) and one that approached significance (the likelihood scale), whereas the students had two variables that approached significance and four other interaction trends in which the viewers changed to a highly significant degree.

Careful consideration of these patterns of significant findings suggests a very interesting interpretation. The professionals' lack of change from pretest to posttest indicates that their attitudes were relatively firm and were not much changed by either *The Day After* program or all the media attention that it attracted. Their near lack of significant interaction effects between level of viewing and change over time reinforces this interpretation—viewers changed very little as a result of watching the program. The several significant differences and trends for the two levels of viewing cannot be due to the effects of viewing the program, because watching the program could not cause a difference in the *pretest* as well as the posttest. Thus these differences for professionals suggest that people with different attitudes self-selected whether they would be viewers or not, and their subsequent viewing did not markedly change their already established attitudes. On several of these items the viewers held more pessimistic attitudes about the nuclear war than the nonviewers, but on Q5 they were more optimistic about the number of dead, and on Q14 they were less favorable toward signing an arms control treaty with Russia.

This analysis of the professionals' responses suggests that they chose to view or not view *The Day After* largely on the basis of their previously held attitudes, and that viewing barely affected their attitudes, whereas the student sample was much more influenced by the program and all the hoopla that surrounded it. This finding is consistent with our previous interpretations that the least knowledgeable and least experienced viewers were generally most influenced by the program.

DISCUSSION

Although some news reports have concluded that *The Day After* did not have any major effects on its audience (e.g., Adams et al., 1984), all of the studies summarized by Oskamp (1984) reported some indications of attitude change following the program, and other media polls have reported some large attitude changes (e.g., McFadden, 1983). Moreover, most of the studies that reported relatively weaker effects can be seen, on close analysis, to have investigated a limited set of variables or ones that were not directly relevant to the program's content. This is consistent with past communication research findings showing that effects are generally confined to issues that are the specific focus of a program (Kaid, Towers, & Myers, 1981; Robinson, 1976). Findings of the studies with more complete analyses suggest that *The Day After* as a total media event really did have important effects on U.S. citizens' attitudes and behavioral intentions. As a case in point, our study of college students showed that they displayed substantial attitude changes on a variety of different topics. Furthermore, there were a number of variables in our study and in others (e.g., Feldman & Sigelman, in press; Pavelchak & Schofield, 1984) on which viewers changed more than nonviewers.

A crucial fact that the deprecatory research reports have failed to take into account is that the media attention to the nuclear war issues in *The Day After* was so pervasive that it affected *both viewers and nonviewers* to almost the same degree on many measures (see Table 8.2 above; also Feldman & Sigelman, in press; Gutierres et al., 1984; Pavelchak & Schofield, 1984). For instance, Adams et al.'s (1984) pretest, intended-viewer sample had undoubtedly already been influenced by the publicity concerning nuclear war issues that preceded the program. Similarly, some conventional pre-post studies that used nonviewers as a control group have failed to find significant differences because their supposedly untreated control-group members were actually much affected by the publicity and controversy surrounding *The Day After*, even if they didn't watch it. Thus, in effect, such studies become single-group studies and, as such, they are subject to validity threats from other historical events that occurred in the pretest-posttest interval. However, in the case of *The Day After*, there does not seem to have been any powerful contemporaneous event other than all the media publicity concerning the program.

Another factor that could have diminished the apparent effect of the program (as indicated by posttest responses) is the very high audience expectations induced by all the preprogram media hype. Ehrlichman and Kobasa (1984) found that respondents' anticipations were more extreme than their reactions to the film when they actually saw it. In another poll 80 percent of viewers said that the devastation shown in the movie was less severe than the results of a real nuclear war would be (Sussman, 1983).

Almost all of the students' attitude changes found in our study were in the expected directions, such as increased worry about nuclear war, more disastrous estimates of its consequences, increased expectations of social chaos, decreased belief in the effectiveness of civil defense measures, and so on. One of our subsidiary analyses demonstrated that the pretest given to most of our respondents was not responsible for the attitude changes that they displayed. Other analyses showed meaningful patterns in the characteristics of viewers who said they learned the most from the program and viewers who displayed the most resulting attitude change.

Perhaps our most important finding was that many of the students' attitude changes that were evident a few days after the program persisted at least until the time of our delayed posttest two weeks later. These persisting significant changes included greater worry about nuclear war, beliefs about how many people would die and the seriousness of consequences of a nuclear war, estimates of the chances of getting needed medical treatment, the likelihood of a nuclear war remaining limited, the ineffectiveness of U.S. civil defense measures, and less favorability toward proposed increases in the U.S. defense budget. Furthermore, several of these variables displayed no decay or even an increased amount of change from the initial posttest to the delayed posttest (see Table 8.3 and Figure 8.1). This conclusion of the persistence of effects of *The Day After* is supported by similar findings by Pavelchak and Schofield (1984) and by continuing attitude changes found over a 12-week follow-up period by Gutierres et al. (1984).

Another important analysis showed that substantial minorities of *The Day After* viewers (but significantly smaller percentages of nonviewers) stated behavioral intentions or made behavioral commitments that were in keeping with their attitudes concerning nuclear war. Similar findings have been reported by several other studies of *The Day After* (Brown, 1984; Ehrlichman & Kobasa, 1984; Pavelchak & Schofield, 1984; Wolf, Gregory, & Stephan, 1984). Not surprisingly, our students who requested that their names be placed on the mailing lists of antinuclear organizations were high in worry about nuclear war, dissatisfaction with some current U.S. defense policies, favorability to signing an arms control treaty, and belief that personal actions could help prevent a future nuclear war. The conclusions of much past research on effects of fear-arousing communications suggest that even more viewers would probably have exhibited behavior in line with such attitudes if the program had contained specific, detailed recommendations of actions that would be effective in reducing their fear (Leventhal, 1970).

Although the findings for our college students showed substantial and persisting attitude changes resulting from *The Day After*, it is possible that the results of studies such as Adams et al.'s (1984) might be partly due to adult viewers displaying little or no attitude changes. Past research on attitude formation and persuasion processes indicates that young people are apt to have less information, less rigid attitudes, and to be more susceptible to influence than most adults. However, it should be noted that the survey study of *The Day After* by Cross and Saxe (1984), using a representative sample of adult Bostonians, found a substantial number of self-reported attitude changes, indicating that adults, too—particularly senior citizens—were strongly influenced by the program and all the surrounding publicity. Nevertheless, based on the evidence from our sample of professionals in comparison with our college students, it seems very possible that attitude changes following the program were greater for younger viewers or those currently in college, whereas adults might be less easily influenced, more cynical, or already more knowledgeable about nuclear war. Even if that is true, however, the impact of such a program can still be very great, for college-age youth make up a large, vocal, and influential part of our population.

In considering media effects, it is well to keep in mind that corporations will often spend many millions of dollars for advertising just to increase their market share of a product by 1 percent or 2 percent. Similarly, if only a miniscule 1 percent of the viewers of *The*

Day After changed their attitudes afterwards, that would still be *one million* people who were affected—enough people to have a great effect on current affairs if they all acted in concert. However, it seems likely that many more than that number were deeply affected by this unprecedented media event, which has been reported to be the most controversial TV program ever shown (J. Walter Thompson, 1983). Fiske, Pratto, and Pavelchak (1983) have found that the concreteness of people's images of nuclear war is positively related to their degree of antinuclear activity. Thus, graphic programs such as *The Day After* can play a crucial role in exposing the public to some of the concrete realities of abstract war-and-peace issues and helping to shape their attitudes and behavioral commitments.

Epilogue

To illustrate that conclusion, let us give our respondents the last words. Here are a few of their written comments about the effects of the program:

> Previously the possibility of nuclear war never crossed my mind much. The movie helped to clear a lot of the fuzziness I had surrounding such things as the effects of nuclear war.

> I realize it is an ever growing issue and threat in my life every day.

> My reaction to the movie was one of terror and surprise. . . . I feel that this film is something that everyone in every country should see. If they see it, they may take more drastic measures to prevent future nuclear war.

> I realized what a horrifying event a nuclear war would be. For the first time, I actually thought about the reality of the whole issue. The devastation of human life and the destruction of all civilization is all we have to gain by engaging in such a frightening affair. Yet, the most terrifying thought I came to grips with is a decision I made. I don't want to survive a nuclear war. . .

NOTE

1. Readers who want a table of pretest and posttest means and significance test results for the professionals can request one from the senior author.

9

THE SOCIAL PSYCHOLOGY OF U.S. PRESIDENTIAL EFFECTIVENESS

Presidential performance is constantly being evaluated, and our nation's leaders are constantly being classified as effective or ineffective. In our society, "president-watching" is not only a full-time activity but a crucial one, for the U.S. presidency has become—in the words of John F. Kennedy—the "center of the play of pressure, interest, and idea in the nation" (quoted in Sorensen, 1963, p. xi). We are all aware that one irrational act by the president can lead to the destruction of each and every one of us, as well as civilization as we know it.

For more than that sole reason, the presidency is a matter of national concern. Over the span of the last 50 years, Franklin D. Roosevelt is the only president who would be considered by both the general populace and experts as having been a generally effective leader. We have seen a deterioration in the president's performance, or at least the *evaluation* of performance, virtually president by president, from Truman and Eisenhower on down to Nixon and Carter. No president since Eisenhower has served two full terms. The presidency is in trouble. What are scholars doing about it?

The study of U.S. presidential effectiveness should be a broadly interdisciplinary topic, but in the past its investigation has been left almost entirely to political scientists and historians. The application of *psychological* concepts in this area seems quite justified; ironically, one of the most widely known books on the presidency written by a political scientist, James David Barber's *The Presidential Character* (1977), relies almost entirely upon personality characteristics in its attempt to explain behavior in the White House.

But we can go beyond personality and other internal characteristics of the incumbent (such as values, stage of moral development, and assumptions about human nature) as we catalogue those psychological concepts applicable to an assessment of presidential effectiveness. The body of literature from group dynamics and organizational behavior on

AUTHOR'S NOTE: I wish to thank the following for their comments on earlier drafts: Barbara Kellerman, Robert L. Lineberry, Gary McCullough, Jeffrey Z. Rubin, William Tuttle, Phillip Kissam, and Tom Bryder.

communication networks and the functions of leaders, for example, can be used—with some caution. Likewise, there are many psychological aspects of the situation (such as perceived threat from abroad, media distrust, presence of an electoral "mandate") that contribute to a president's relative success. Yet, psychologists have almost entirely avoided the systematic study of the presidency. (An exception is Edwin Hollander's address at the 1983 APA convention.)

I find this a curious situation, for which this chapter is a modest attempt to begin a remedy. If we, as psychologists, sincerely want to follow Miller's (1969) admonition to "give psychology away," we must make efforts to apply our concepts to real-world phenomena that have previously been the exclusive "turf" of other disciplines. Although recognizing that the job of the U.S. president is far more complex than that of, for instance, the army platoon leaders in the Ohio State Leadership Study or Fred Fiedler's basketball team captains—from whom findings are often generalized—we must not be reluctant to examine the utility of research-based concepts and findings for understanding the presidency.

I believe that it was my experience as an administrator (a department chairperson for five years) that propelled my interest in presidential effectiveness. No, I have not yet succumbed to grandiose thoughts that a psychology department chairperson out in the "heartland of America" faces the breadth, enormity, and seriousness of challenges facing our country's chief executive. Still, there are basic dilemmas common to all executive and leadership positions, and for many of us these conflicts are not easy resolved. Decisions must be made as to the allocation of finite amounts of time and effort between system maintenance and task accomplishment (Kessel, 1983b). If your secretary calls in to say she wants to stay home because of a sick child, and if that day you need to have a proposal typed before a 5:00 p.m. deadline, how do you respond? Which need takes precedence? You may say that this example is far removed from the choice facing the president, but even at that lofty level, similar dilemmas occur. Zbigniew Brzezinski, in his account of his years as President Carter's national security adviser (1983, p. 282), tells of a time when Carter wanted him to go on a delicate mission to Egypt. This would conflict with Brzezinski's son's confirmation. He writes, "Carter, with real feeling, offered to attend the religious ceremony in my place" (1983, p. 282). Only after much agonizing on everybody's part was some kind of resolution achieved. Brzezinski went to Egypt on schedule and Carter sent a handwritten note to the youngster, telling him that his father had to go on the sensitive overseas trip and hoping that the note from the president would partly substitute for his father's absence from the confirmation ceremony.

Some of us may assume that presidents are vastly more concerned with their images as successful leaders than they are with being liked by their staff, but in truth, most recent presidents have had great difficulty in firing—or even disciplining—certain associates (Truman with General Harry Vaughan, Eisenhower with Sherman Adams, Carter with Bert Lance, Reagan with David Stockman and Edwin Meese), even after the associate's questionable behavior had been so publicized that a continuation of White House service would jeopardize the effectiveness of the president in achieving his goals for the nation.

A second major dilemma for every administrator or leader who is confronted with stimulus overload (and what leader isn't?) is whether to focus on the details or on the broad policy issues. The unrelenting paper flow, demanding attention from *someone,* never stops, but those administrators who do stop to process everything themselves never are able to develop or implement long-range policies. The contrasting orientations of our two most recent presidents are instructive here. Jimmy Carter, it is said, began his administration by telling his staff, "I'll take care of everything [that is, all paperwork] the same day it comes in"; he religiously read every line of every document that crossed his desk. Carter even went so far as to check the arithmetic in budget documents (Quirk, 1983). For a while he was reviewing the daily reservation list for the White House tennis court. Why was Carter not more effective as president? One explanation is that he was never able to identify, or at least implement, broad priorities and goals. One of his former speechwriters, James Fallows (1979), wrote:

> I started to wonder about the difference between a good man and an inspiring man; about why Jimmy Carter, who would surely outshine most other leaders in the judgment of the Lord, had so much trouble generating excitement, not only in the nation but even among members of his own staff. One explanation is that Carter has not given us an *idea* to follow. . . . I came to think that Carter believes fifty things, but no one thing. (p. 42, italics in original)

This is no surprise, for Jimmy Carter chose to submerge himself in detail (Quirk, 1983). Ronald Reagan, in contrast, is ideologically clear and consistent. As a result of giving thousands of speeches (or the same speech thousands of times) Reagan has articulated in his own mind an ideological stance on important issues. And he sees his role as elucidating programmatic policies—such as reduced government intervention, tax cuts, and increased spending for defense—which are left to others to implement. As the detailed analysis by Kessel (1983b) shows, Reagan has selected top aides who share his conservative yet pragmatic position on policies.

In summary, it is a working assumption of this chapter that the job of the U.S. presidency, although vitally important and exceedingly complex, is in many senses like any other executive position. The job can be analyzed into identifiable tasks; effectiveness on each of those tasks can be assessed to some degree, and contributions to effectiveness from both the person and the environment can be identified.

APPROACHES TO THE PRESIDENCY
THROUGH POLITICAL SCIENCE

I mentioned previously that the scientific study of presidential effectiveness has been left almost entirely to political science and history. But some political scientists (R. L. Lineberry, personal communication, June 13, 1983; Pika, 1981-1982; Kessel, 1983b) consider the literature dealing with the presidency to be among the weakest in their discipline. Ironically, one of the reasons for this is the problem of the small sample size (Prindle, 1983). Much of the most impressive work in modern political science deals with large numbers—voters, countries, census tracts, members of Congress, for example. With an *n* of only 1 at a time and only 40 presidents over the span of 200 years, it is hard to generalize. Second, much of the presidency has been hidden from view, even to the most talented researchers (R. L. Lineberry, personal communication, June 13, 1983). Of course, this limitation is changing—particularly as a result of the Freedom of Information Act— partly because of the more intense scrutiny by the media and by scholars, and partly because of the rush to publish "show-and-tell" books by insiders. Every ex-president from Truman on (with the exception of Kennedy) has published his memoirs, and Nixon has done so, some would say, ad nauseam. Books by presidential aides— Sherman Adams, Califano, McPherson, Valenti, Ehrlichman, Haldeman, Dean, Hartmann, Nessen, Jordan, Brzezinski, Vance, Powell, and others—have become a cottage industry. Although as a group— like most memoirs and autobiographies—these slant strongly in a self-serving direction, they still can provide informative perspectives on decision making.

A third reason for the recent low status of studies of the presidency is, to some observers (Edwards, 1979; Pika, 1982; Prindle, 1983), that the topic is theoretically impoverished and hence has not yet been adequately conceptualized; there is not even agreement as to what questions to ask. Of course, there are agreed-upon classics in the field, such as Richard Neustadt's (1960) *Presidential Power*, that seek to explain the presidency from a conceptual viewpoint. And Stephen Hess's *Organizing the Presidency* (1976) is considered to be a very useful analysis of the president's—any president's—deterioration in effectiveness over the length of his time in office.

But political scientists have also made several attempts to classify every president on one or two personality dimensions. It may be questioned whether these crude classifications contribute very much to our understanding. For example, Stoessinger (1979) has labeled recent presidents as either rigid crusaders or flexible pragmatists. No one denies Stoessinger's claim that an officeholder's personality can play a very important role in influencing national reactions to events; had a less rigid, less messianic person than Woodrow Wilson been president in 1919-1920, compromises would doubtless have been negotiated so that the League of Nations covenant could have been ratified by the U.S. Senate. But such a conception fails to give enough recognition to the specific conditions under which a person operates and to acknowledge these as equally important determinants of presidential success. It also overlooks the fact that there are presidents like Reagan who can be crusaders on some issues and pragmatists on others.

Certainly the most widely quoted of such efforts is the classification by Barber (1977) of recent presidents on two personality dimensions: active-passive and positive-negative. Such a 2 × 2 classification of variables is not unfamiliar to social psychologists! Barber has provided detailed, useful descriptions of each president's psychological development, relating the above dimensions to how well the president does in office. But Barber has decided to force each president into one of those four cells, at times with less than satisfying consequences. For Barber, the active-positive combination clearly makes for the most effective presidents (FDR and JFK were both active-positives), and prior to Carter's inauguration Barber proclaimed Carter to be an active-positive. Although Carter's administration is too recent to judge his effectiveness adequately, the early returns indicate that Carter will not rank near Roosevelt nor Kennedy in accomplishments.

Although criticisms of the sophistication of scholarship on the presidency within political science may have been justified, there is now a resurgence of interest, along with the use of new conceptualizations and more rigorous methods. Contemporary scholars including George Edwards, Stephen Wayne, John Kessel, and Stephen Hess have led this movement. Among political scientists, the conceptualization that comes closest to what I am advocating is that by Glenn Paige (1977). His work is not specifically on the president but on political leadership in general. Paige identifies six concepts that he sees as interacting to lead to effective or ineffective leadership. These are *personality, role, organization, task, values,* and *setting.*

WHAT DOES SOCIAL PSYCHOLOGY HAVE TO OFFER?

Like Paige, social psychology chooses to focus on behavior and emphasizes that behavior is a function of the interaction between the person and the situation. A U.S. president's effectiveness is a result of how his personality and skills interact with the domestic and international conditions he faces. Some presidents may benefit from the situation: There may be strong majorities in Congress favoring their platform; there may be, in the *Zeitgeist,* a desire to respect the wishes of a suddenly dead hero, such as Lyndon Johnson experienced in his first year of office, thus permitting the congressional passage of extensive and revolutionary social legislation.

But other presidents may run into streaks of bad luck, just as the rest of us do; they may face strong situational constraints on their effectiveness—balance of payment deficits, suspicious media, or aggressive enemies abroad or even in their own Executive Branch.

In focusing on the interaction between the officeholder and the situation, social psychology acts to avoid the *fundamental attribution error* (Heider, 1958)—that is, the tendency for people in general, including the media and some scholars—to blame the deterioration of the presidency on the personal character or skills of recent incumbents. The common wisdom seems to be saying that contemporary candidates are not capable enough to handle the job. For instance, Jimmy Carter was, in the view of Hodgson (1980), the sixth consecutive president who failed to achieve most of his major goals.

Are such observers placing too much emphasis on the person? When we contrast recent presidents with the seemingly superhuman Roosevelt, we should recall two things. First, when Roosevelt was initially elected in 1932, he did not presage the greatness that was to follow. Walter Lippmann, that sage observer, described the newly elected president as a charming but shallow person and an intellectual lightweight. Roosevelt is now considered one of the three most effective presidents of all time, but we need to acknowledge that it was situational factors combined with his magnificent personal qualities that led to his greatness as president. It was a fortuitous match of presidential style and the needs of the country (Bratton, 1983). In both of the major challenges to Roosevelt's leadership—the Great Depression and World War II—many aspects of the situation facilitated the possibility of effectiveness. There was national sentiment to do something drastic about the economy when he took office; his radical measures, such as the bank closing, might at another time have led to overwhelming protests by the media and the electorate. In actuality, Roosevelt's effectiveness waned sharply after his first term in office; his court-packing scheme and the failure to reduce unemployment significantly (until the war came along) are evidence that even Roosevelt was not able to maintain his effectiveness consistently throughout his presidency.

Rather than the faults of the person holding the presidency, perhaps it is the increased complexity of the job that is the major cause of the decline in presidential effectiveness over the last 50 years. The nature of the president's responsibilities and their demands on him have increased a hundredfold in this century. Compare a contemporary president's challenges with the tasks of Woodrow Wilson's time. According to the chief usher at the White House, the activities of the president then were quite limited; before World War I started, President Wilson "worked but three or four hours a day and spent much of his time happily and quietly sitting around with his family" (quoted by Hess, 1979, p. 1).

We sometimes fail to recognize the prodigious growth of the modern presidency (Hess, 1976, p. 9). Roosevelt began with a White House staff of 37 people, 9 of whom were of professional rank; recent presidents have had as many as 600. There was no Executive Office staff when Roosevelt became president—it was established in 1939, and now many thousands work for agencies and commissions based in the Executive Office Building. We have, in the past 40 years, witnessed a "bureaucratization" of the presidency. Although at first glance the provision of a large support staff might be seen as easing the president's burden, the opposite is actually true. As Quirk (1983, p. 6) notes, "the larger the government has become, the more complex its policies, and the more sophisticated and numerous the people who analyze them, the more presidents have become dependent, massively and inevitably, on the judgments of others" and the more impossible the president's job has become.

Related to the above is the president's increasing suspicion of the "permanent government," leading him to create offices and agencies under White House supervision. Roosevelt and Kennedy particularly contributed to this proliferation as a result of their impatience and distrust of the slow-moving bureaucracy. Concurrent with the growth of administrative size is the rising influence of White House staff members as presidential advisers, with a corresponding decline in the role of the Cabinet in generating legislation and policy.

The president has become a manager.

But these are not the only kinds of constraints. The role of the media has become accentuated, so that anyone within the range of a television set or a news magazine can be an instant expert on the president's actions. In the nineteenth century "most Americans had only the vaguest idea what their president looked like. Today everyone can 'see' the president practically every day" (Donovan, 1981, p. 122). His every act is highlighted, and the more information available, the less effective the president seems. The emergence of "single-issue" interest groups, with their own vehicles for publication, has strengthened this phenomenon.

The increased criticism of the president that I have described is correlated with a general reduction in trust in government, as revealed in Gallup and Harris polls. In 1958, when an adult sample was asked, "Do you trust the government to do what is right?" 75 percent answered "always" or "most of the time." By 1976, these responses were chosen by only 32 percent. Funderburk (1982, p. 113) attributes one of the causes of the change to "public dissatisfaction with the performance of government and political leaders in specific policy areas"; here the media play a role, for instance, in informing people of Carter's inability to curb inflation, or the impact on people in "South Succotash" of Reagan's cutbacks in delivery of social services. And of course another cause of the decreased trust is the revelations of misconduct by recent presidents (Nixon's Watergate cover-up, Johnson's lying about troop needs in Vietnam, Kennedy's sexual activities while in the White House). The decrease in trust in government doubtless is also caused by factors beyond the performance of public officials, including the increased impersonalization of our society.

At another level, situational constraints limit the degree of presidential effectiveness currently attainable. The massive buildup of nuclear weapons makes any foreign policy decision more important—and more controversial. The recent state of the economy has also contributed to the deterioration of presidential effectiveness. For example, from 1960 to 1984, the national debt increased from $290 billion to $1585 billion (or $1.585 trillion). The deficit for 1984 alone (the year ending September 30, 1984) was approximately $190 billion, and fiscal 1984 was the fifteenth year in a row that the government operated in the red. The interest payments are so high—$148 billion in 1984—and so much of the president's budget allocations are already committed through entitle-ment payments, that there is little that any president can do to reduce this deficit—even if the defense budget were not increased. Likewise, our international balance of payments deficit has increased in a positively accelerated fashion, from around $15 billion five years ago to about $130 billion in 1984, further constraining what any president can do with the economy.

Although all of this paints a depressing picture, awareness of it may cause observers to reduce their tendency to attribute presidential ineffectiveness solely to the incumbent.

There is a second contribution that a social-psychological approach can make. By focusing on the nature of leadership functions, it can break the job of the presidency down into more specific tasks. The analysis of discrete tasks contrasts with the predominant tendency to make global evaluations of the effectiveness of any president. I hypothesize that presidents are differentially effective with respect to the discrete tasks of the presidency. It may well be that the outcome of this analysis will document Hodgson's (1980) conclusion that the presidency has become a job so complex as to be unmanageable.

APPLICATIONS OF CONTINGENCY THEORY TO THE PRESIDENCY

Social psychology also has theoretical concepts that can be applied to understanding the presidency. The most prominent approach to leadership in social psychology is called "contingency theory," for it emphasizes that a given leader's effectiveness is contingent on the degree to which his or her skills and values are congruent with aspects of the work situation. This theory, developed by Fiedler (1964, 1967, 1978) of the University of Washington, proposes that no one person can be an effective leader in *every* setting or in every group. This proposition provides the fundamental structure for this chapter, although I am extending its application. Previous research on the theory has been based on small work groups, but I am hypothesizing that the contingent quality of the leader's effectiveness is especially salient for the U.S. presidency, because the job involves so many tasks, each requiring different (and often mutually incompatible) traits and skills.

Hence, the purpose of this project is not to test the specifics of Fiedler's theory, but rather to employ its basic contingency notion and its emphasis on the interaction of situational and personal qualities in an attempt to understand the nature and determinants of U.S. presidential effectiveness. In doing so, I recognize some of the problems in applying the theory to the presidency. Effectiveness here is much more than a matter of high productivity (the criterion used in many of the tests of Fiedler's theory with small groups). Another problem is that every modern president was or is a low-LPC leader, to use Fiedler's term, in the sense that he is task-oriented. (Yet some—and only some—also possess high-LPC qualities; that is, they receive satisfactions from the relationships with co-workers.) Different definitions of the situation, of personal qualities, and of effectiveness must be used when studying each task that is a part of the presidency.

Effectiveness, as it is used here, deals with what the president is able to accomplish (Prindle, 1983). More specific questions about effectiveness cover a variety of aspects: Does the president seek and obtain a second term? Does he aid his party in its quest for election to Congress and governorships? Is he able to control events—in Congress, in the economy, in relations with other nations? Can he inspire a nation? Can he articulate and implement the highest moral principles present in American society? Does he identify priorities and initiate rather than react? The political scientist David Prindle (1983) has identified ways of operationalizing answers to at least some of these measures of effectiveness.

A JOB ANALYSIS OF THE PRESIDENCY

Admittedly the presidency possesses a complicated job description. How do we subdivide the nature of presidential leadership? Are there agreed-upon dimensions that will assist us in refining the challenge of understanding presidential effectiveness?

The early group dynamics literature promoted two main qualities that distinguished between successful and unsuccessful leaders of small groups. These were labeled *initiating structure* and *consideration*. Note that these are similar to Fiedler's two types: one deals with the accomplishment of tasks, the other with the maintenance of positive relationships between members of the group (Shaw, 1981).

Within the political science literature, three aspects of political leadership often appear; Barber (1968) identified these as *rhetoric* ("verbal dramatization"), *business* (attention to administrative detail), and *interpersonal relations* (interpersonal persuasion, especially in an intimate, face-to-face context). Another conception from political science is Tucker's (1981) emphasis on three major activities of the political leader: the diagnostic function, the remedial function, and the function in which consensus support is mobilized.

It follows from contingency theory that a given occupant of the presidency might be more effective in one of these aspects and less so in another. In fact, the small group literature indicates that within a group, it is common for the person who provides group maintenance functions to be different from the one who keeps the group headed toward its task.

But given the complexity of the job of the president, it seems appropriate to propose more than two or three dimensions by which to describe presidential behavior and evaluate its effectiveness. What other conceptions do political scientists and historians have to offer? Cronin (1975) finds so many ill-defined roles that he concludes it is impossible to specify a catalogue of presidential duties. Others have posited an unmanageable number of criteria. Bailey (1966), in a book entitled *Presidential Greatness*, first identifies 100 measures of presidential success and then collapses them into 43 final criteria.

Other political scientists have provided lists of duties. Clinton Rossiter (1960), in his influential book on the American presidency, lists ten duties: chief of state, chief executive, commander in chief, chief diplomat, chief legislator, chief of party, voice of the people, protector of the peace, manager of prosperity, and world leader. In offering this political taxonomy, Rossiter is almost apologetic for his "piecemeal analysis" because he wishes to emphasize the "seamless unity" of the office, "an office whose power and prestige are something more than the arithmetical total of all its functions" (1960, p. 31). After asserting that each of these functions feeds upon the others, Rossiter also acknowledges that several of these functions are in competition, not only for time and energy but in the sense that they lead to conflicting behaviors.

Taking the analyses of leadership functions from the group dynamics and organizational behavior literature and giving them specificity from the taxonomies of political scientists and historians, my model offers ten task dimensions for analyzing U.S. presidential effectiveness (see Table 9.1). These dimensions partially overlap with Rossiter's list, but they are more behavioral and operational in structure.

If space permitted, I would offer, for each dimension, some examples from recent presidents that reflect the interaction between the president's personality and the situation, and then one or more social-psychological conceptualizations that may describe the effectiveness of the president on that task. However, I will limit my examples to three of these tasks.

TABLE 9.1
Ten Presidential Tasks

Situational Influences	*Personal Influences*
(1) Persuading the nation	
The constituency of Congress	Willingness to use the resources available (media appearances, press conferences, national trips)
The crisis level in the country	
National atmosphere regarding status quo or change	Skilled communicator, persuader
Media's liking for the president	Ability to inspire confidence
	Social influence mechanisms (use of rationality vs. irrationality and direct vs. indirect influence)
(2) Providing moral leadership	
National needs	Values (extent of decency, courage, honesty)
Responsiveness of the citizenry	
Congruence of values between the citizenry and the president	Moral judgment level
	His view of the presidency
	Willingness to express unpopular truths
(3) Appearing "presidential"	
Cynicism level in the citizenry	Appearance
Media support or hostility toward president	Voice qualities
	Manner/style: charm, gusto, buoyancy
	Enjoyment of the office
(4) Identifying goals and priorities	
Was electoral mandate present?	Values
Conflict level in the country	Past experience in government, leadership, and administration
Presence of single-issue groups	
	Possess "big picture" vs. a detailed orientation
	Willingness to delegate
(5) Maintaining the on-going activities of the Executive Branch	
Upper-level personnel in the Executive Branch (their quality, experience, sympathy with president's goals)	Interests in bureaucracy per se
	Concern with detail and routine
	Tolerance for frustration
Budget status	Persistence

(continued)

TABLE 9.1 Continued

Situational Influences	*Personal Influences*

(6) Getting domestic legislation passed

Constituency of Congress	Past experience in Congress
Degree of election mandate	Delegation of responsibility to liaison
Crisis-level in the country	Communication skills and social influence mechanisms (see 1)
Conflict, divisiveness, and presence of single-issue groups	Willingness to ask for help
Quality and relevant experience-level of congressional liaison staff	Energy level
Length of time in office, including "election year" syndrome	Willingness to negotiate and compromise
	Political sensitivity/awareness

(7) Determining and conducting foreign policy

International crisis-level (economically and militarily)	Values and goals regarding foreign policy
Goals held by other nations	Importance given to foreign policy
Quality of staff advice	Delegates or serves as one's own secretary of state
Intransigence or "hard-line" nature of foreign leaders	Preference for economic, diplomatic, or military "solutions"
	Assumptions about human nature

(8) Managing the White House staff

Quality of White House staff	Organizational style (formalistic, competitive, or collegial)
Size of staff	Task-oriented vs. relationship oriented (or LPC score)
Cohesiveness of staff, including mechanisms for conflict-resolution	Needs for nurturance and loyalty, self-esteem, feelings of self-confidence

(9) Crisis decision making

Nature, frequency, and severity of crisis	Ability to process information and make decisions
Intransigence of the other side	Sensitivity-awareness (i.e., judgments about evidence brought by advisers)
Quality of staff advice	Ability to avoid "groupthink"
	Conflict/confrontation style
	Patience; tolerance of ambiguity

(continued)

TABLE 9.1 Continued

Situational Influences	*Personal Influences*
(10) Providing political party leadership	
Intra-party conflict (within president's own party)	Interest level in political activity
	Being a party "pol" vs. an outsider
Strength of opposing party	(i.e., "history" within the party)

Foreign Policy

One of the most important of the tasks is task 7, determining and conducting foreign policy. It has been estimated by former White House advisers that a president spends from half to two-thirds of his time on foreign policy or national security deliberations (Cronin, 1975, p. 13). Of course, this may reflect a situational cause, such as a foreign-affairs crisis (the military takeover in Poland, or the Iran-Iraq war), or it may result from the personality of a president who values diplomacy as his most crucial activity. John F. Kennedy was fond of saying that the difference between domestic and foreign policy was that between a bill being defeated and a country being wiped out (quoted in Cronin, 1975, p. 13). And Richard Nixon once said, "I've always thought this country could run itself domestically—without a president; all you need is a competent Cabinet to run the country at home. You need a president for foreign policy; no secretary of state is really important; the president makes foreign policy" (quoted in White, 1969, p. 147).

Despite Nixon's claim, one distinction with regard to presidents and their foreign policy activities is whether they acted as their own foreign secretary or whether they delegated those decisions to the secretary of state. Roosevelt was so accustomed to making decisions himself that he didn't even inform Secretary of State Cordell Hull about his first meeting with Churchill in August 1941 (whence came the Atlantic Charter) until it was almost over.

At first it is hard to understand why Kennedy chose the courtly Dean Rusk, a southern gentleman but a member of the Eastern Establishment, as his secretary of state. Certainly they were not close; Kennedy always referred to him as "Secretary Rusk"—never, even in private, as "Dean" (Wills, 1982, p. 172). But it soon became apparent that Kennedy intended to handle foreign policy himself, or at least from within the White House, and Rusk's job was only to supervise the State Department's traditional duties. In fact, Rusk soon became the butt of jokes by "the best and the brightest" occupants of the White House; it was reported, in a condescending manner, that Rusk actually *liked* to attend committee meetings (Wills, 1982, p. 166).

In contrast was Eisenhower's reliance on John Foster Dulles, his original secretary of state, not only in carrying out policy but in establishing it. For example, in response to the Suez crisis of 1956, Eisenhower opposed the use of force over the Suez Canal, even as a last resort. But "by hinting that the United States did not rule out force if all other methods failed, the secretary of state had already gone beyond the wishes of his president" (Stoessinger, 1979, pp. 116-117). Yet, as indicated before, Eisenhower wanted to be freed of routine activities— and more. His heart attack in September 1955 was triggered, he claimed, when he was repeatedly interrupted on the golf links by "unnecessary" phone calls from the State Department (quoted in Stoessinger, 1979, p. 98). Eisenhower dealt only reluctantly even with problems of high-level foreign policy.

When Johnson suddenly became president, he felt quite inexperienced in foreign policy and hence relied on people he had inherited from Kennedy—including, especially, Dean Rusk, who remained secretary of state.

One social-psychological way to conceptualize the president's behavior regarding foreign policy is the distinction between "tender-minded" and "tough-minded" orientations (Wrightsman, 1964). The tender-minded person incorporates moral considerations into his or her policies; such individuals may be idealists who view the values of nations as being in ultimate harmony with each other, or they may view communism as immoral (John Foster Dulles once said, "Bolshevism was a product of the Devil, but God would wear out the Bolsheviks in the long run," quoted in Stoessinger, 1979, p. 98). On the other hand, the tough-minded person is a cold realist. His or her motivations are basically power-oriented. For example, Richard Nixon exemplified a tough-minded stance when he initiated steps to recognize mainland China. Despite his avowed hatred of communism, he realized the practical necessities. In contrast, Roosevelt's policy at the end of World War II—demanding "unconditional surrender"—reflected a moral position that probably stood in the way of reasonable action. Stoessinger sees it as follows:

Even though his chiefs of staff had urged him to modify the doctrine, Roosevelt insisted on it [unconditional surrender] to the end. It probably hardened the resistance of the German people, discouraged the opposition against Hitler inside the [German] armed forces, and quite possibly prolonged the war. The policy also prevented Roosevelt from saving Jews from the gas ovens of Auschwitz because such an initiative would have forced him to negotiate with Hitler. (Stoessinger, 1979, pp. 45-46).

A different way of conceptualizing a president's effectiveness with regard to foreign policy is to examine his world view. Is he an isolationist? If he is an internationalist, does he reflect a view that encourages cultural diversity between nations, or is his perspective essentially an ethnocentric one? Along these lines, Scott (1960) identified eight distinct goals in foreign policy: pacifism, cultural development, humanitarianism, coexistence, religiousness, independence (i.e., autonomy and neutrality), power, and nationalism. Scott developed an attitude scale to measure these 25 years ago, but little has been done with it since. A content analysis of a president's public statements—such as Hermann's (1983) recent analysis of President Reagan's statements in interviews and public debates—could be implemented to determine which of Scott's values were emphasized.

Managing a Staff

In considering task 8, managing the White House staff, we shift to a different kind of presidential responsibility. Here we refer to the way in which the president organizes his own working staff, his decision-making style, and his relationship with his closest aides. Again two aspects, although related, seem separable, one being the emotional relationship between the president and his aides and the second being the organizational chart or flow of information used in decision making.

With regard to the first aspect, Funderburk (1982, pp. 171-172) notes the conflict between the need for loyalty and the need for openness to new ideas:

> The tendency of presidents to use their assistants as sources of emotional support is easily understandable. The presidency is a high-pressure job and is inevitably frustrating. The key to the president's relationship with his assistants is balancing his demands for *loyalty* with *receptivity* to new information and ideas. This has proven particularly difficult for insecure personalities who, when threatened by having their ideas challenged, equate independent thinking with disloyalty. This eliminates the give-and-take necessary for the careful scrutiny of ideas in the decision-making process. (italics in the original)

Although I am not completely in agreement with them, numerous observers (Barber, 1977; Kearns, 1976; Funderburk, 1982) have considered Presidents Kennedy and Johnson to be polar opposites in the above respects. Kennedy was described as being self-assured and confident in his dealings with his advisers. He enjoyed the give and take of heated discussions. Johnson was said to overwhelm others so as to assure himself that he was in control. It is claimed that he did not really seek an exchange of ideas, but simply a reaffirmation of his own wisdom. There is no question that Johnson demanded subservience, and his conception of a loyal subordinate was extreme—"I want him to kiss my ass in Macy's window at high noon and tell me it smells like roses" (quoted in Halberstam, 1972, p. 34). Did these so-called polar opposite traits affect the quality of their decisions? In some important decisions, the answer seems to be "yes." In responding to the Cuban missile crisis, Kennedy took steps to build in corrective mechanisms so that proposed responses would be reevaluated and "groupthink" would not occur (Janis, 1972). In contrast, with regard to the decision to escalate U.S. troop shipments to Vietnam, Johnson coerced his advisers to comply with his preliminary decision; "open" discussions had as their real purpose the legitimizing of "a previously selected opinion by creating the illusion that other views were being considered" (Berman, 1982, p. 112).

With regard to the other management aspect, organization of the White House staff, it is again striking to note the tremendous diversity in procedures from one president to another. As Hess (1976, p. 3) says, "A president chooses the degree of tidiness or chaos that best supports his work habits." Some prefer much communication; others, less. Similarly, each president receives advice in a way that he finds congenial. Some prefer large meetings; some, small; some, none at all. Kessel (1983a, 1983b), comparing the two most recent presidencies and basing his conclusions on interviews with over 80 percent of the respective professional staffs, found that "the principal difference was that there was simply more communication in the Reagan White House, and the principal reason for that was the group of central coordinators" (1983b, p. 17). Carter's White House was organized around specialists, but their activities were, at best, only loosely coordinated by Hamilton Jordan, the chief of staff. Reagan's top-level aides know that he abhors conflict within the organization, and they work hard to reconcile everything from contrasting policy recommendations to bruised egos. Despite the conflict between the conservatives and the pragmatists for Reagan's ear, early in the Reagan administration there evolved a daily meeting of chief advisers; often consensus recommendations to the president were hammered out at these meetings.

Johnson (1974) has contrasted, as a conceptual system for organizing these diverse procedures, three basic formats, which he called formalistic, competitive, and collegial. Eisenhower, Nixon, and certainly Reagan reflect a formalistic approach. Emphasis is on *order* and *analysis*. Staff conflict is discouraged; "open expressions of . . . competition, bargaining, and hostility [are] taboo" (Johnson, 1974, p. 4). A formalistic approach collects information and funnels it to the top of the pyramid—or, in Reagan's case, to a four-person team; ultimately, the president is presented a sheet of paper containing summaries of the pros and cons and the options on each issue. (A maxim of the Eisenhower administration was, "If a proposition can't be stated on one page, it isn't even worth saying.") As Funderburk (1982, p. 176) notes, any president who uses this structure must be comfortable with delegating power to others, for there is a broad reliance on staff and consultants, especially on a chief of staff who coordinates the flow of information. In Reagan's administration, a troika initially served as joint chiefs of staff; later the foreign affairs adviser (first William P. Clark, then Robert McFarlane) was added. Nearly all the information that reached Reagan filtered through these men (Church, 1981). Opposition by any of these four men to a proposal was, in the opinion of other Reagan staff members, "enough to kill it" (Kessel, 1983b, p. 23).

In the case of Eisenhower, the delegation of responsibilities served to create elaborate buffer zones between the president and his department heads. But Eisenhower was shrewder than most casual observers gave him credit for being (Greenstein, 1983). Because he delegated decisions, executive branch blunders were blamed less often on the president. James Hagerty, Eisenhower's press secretary, later recalled, "President Eisenhower would say, 'Do it this way.' I would say, 'If I go to that press conference and say what you want me to say, I would get hell.' With that, he would smile, get up, and walk around the desk, pat me on the back, and say, 'My boy, better you than me' " (quoted in Hoxie, 1971, p. 4). But this structure had its advantages for the staff, too. Eisenhower's appointees had considerable latitude to act, yet they knew the outer limits of their responsibilities. That is one reason why Eisenhower's Cabinet appointees stayed in office longer than those of any other president.

Quarrelling and bitterness were mostly absent in Eisenhower's staff for another reason; his Cabinet was exceedingly homogeneous. (So was President Ford's.) Eisenhower tended to select people who had successfully administered large organizations and thus ended up with people of similar experience, perspective, and temperament. As the social-psychological literature indicates, groups that are homogeneous in traits and abilities are compatible but tend to be low in creative and imaginative proposals (Shaw, 1981). And so it was with Eisenhower's administration.

There is a similar degree of homogeneity in the Reagan White House staff. Kessel (1983b) has used a cluster analysis to look at the relative similarity of policy attitudes between members of the Reagan senior staff. This group of 39 persons agreed with each other more than did Nixon's staff, and their contrast with Carter's staff was striking. One of the strengths of Reagan's staff is that each of the "Big Four" (as of July 1984) has different skills: James Baker is a superb problem solver, Michael Deaver an effective ameliorator of potential discord, Edwin Meese a synthesizer of policy options, and William Clark a trusted conduit of foreign policy information (Kessel, 1983b, p. 36). Note also how quickly Reagan dispatched those who could not be team players (Richard Allen, Alexander Haig).

In sharp contrast to Eisenhower's and Reagan's style is the competitive managerial style of Franklin Roosevelt, who deliberately sought involvement and controversy. Roosevelt characteristically gave two or more persons or committees overlapping responsibilities, so that they might come to him with different recommendations. He would also go outside government to find persons who could provide different perspectives (Quirk, 1983). Jurisdictional boundaries were ambiguous; one of the Cabinet secretaries, Henry Stimson, spoke of the "inherently disorderly nature of the Roosevelt administration." Roosevelt gave the impression that he wasn't aware of the turmoil he created in his staff; he kept saying, "I have to have a happy ship." But could he *not* have been aware? Harold Ickes, another Cabinet secretary, once told him, "You are a wonderful person but you are one of the most difficult men to work with that I have ever known." Roosevelt asked, "Because I get too hard at times?" "No," Ickes replied, "you never get too hard, but you won't talk frankly even with people who are loyal to you and of whose loyalty you are fully convinced. You keep your cards close up against your belly. You never put them on the table" (quoted in Schlesinger, 1958). Ickes added that Roosevelt took all this frank talk in a perfectly friendly manner.

Perhaps he had to, because he considered it essential that an unlaundered flow of information come to him and only to him. Roosevelt had a consuming passion for information and control (Quirk, 1983). Here we have what group dynamics would label the classic wheel-type communication network (Shaw, 1981), with a number of independent parties each communicating only with the central person. No wonder there were multitudinous staff dissatisfactions that were described as "nerve wracking and positively demoralizing" (Quirk, 1983, p. 3).

Any managerial style is more effective in reaching some goals than others. Roosevelt's style was much more useful in attacking the economic crisis of 1933 than it was in carrying out the war effort of 1941-1945. "When the New Deal groped its way toward economic solutions that had never before been considered within government's province, the heady clash of ideas and the heavy emphasis on experimentation proved to be highly productive" (Hess, 1976, p. 42). But the massive war effort required organization and efficiency instead; Roosevelt was not able to adapt to a sufficient degree, and his management of the war effort was less effective. Here again is an illustration of the interaction of personal and situational determinants of success.

The third kind of managerial style, called by Johnson (1974) a collegial approach, strives to avoid the limitations of each of the previous ones:

> The managerial thrust is toward building a team of colleagues who work together to staff out problems and generate solutions which, ideally, fuse the strongest elements of divergent points of view. By virtue of encouraging subordinates to work together, this approach recognizes the existence, and in fact the merit, of conflict. The emphasis, however, is not on the win-lose interplay among competing individuals or ideas but rather on treating conflicting viewpoints as a resource. The collegial approach has as its principal strength the potential for forging solutions that are both substantively sound and politically doable, having taken the strongest arguments of all sides into account. Its greatest limitation stems from its dependence on people working together. (Johnson, 1974, p. 7)

John F. Kennedy adopted the collegial pattern for his administration but soon found it not completely free of problems, especially for covert decision making, such as the Bay of Pigs attack on Cuba. In fact, no structure is foolproof; each has its own clear advantages and limitations. Unless check-back procedures are employed, the collegial approach is subject to predecision "groupthink," but the formalistic system is so hierarchical that creative solutions are not likely to survive the staffing process. Although the competitive procedure generates many ideas—including many creative ones—the toll in staff morale may lead to frequent personnel turnovers and hence less experienced decision makers in the future. Perhaps most important is that the chosen system be congenial with the president's own personality and the situation, including the nature of the problems to be solved and the quality of the staff.

Crisis Decision Making

The person-situation interaction is also salient when we consider presidential responses to crises. A crisis is defined as a specific action taken by another country, largely or completely unexpected by the United States, causing either death to citizens of the United States, or danger to them, or threat to the territory, property, or goals of the United States. This action requires some kind of decision by the president, even if the decision is *not* to respond.

Crises can differ in their severity. An ongoing study by two students (Gary McCullough and David Christy) and myself is attempting to identify the determinants of the severity of a crisis. We have selected at least one crisis faced by each of the nine most recent presidents. How aggressively did the president respond to the crisis? Which options did he choose? Is it characteristic of some presidents—as is feared of Reagan—to impose only military "solutions" to crises? What goals did the president seek—reparation, apology, retaliation, punishment, humiliation of the other? To try to answer such questions we have described 55 different responses to crises that we are currently Thurstone-scaling. A basic hypothesis is that the aggressiveness of the president's response is correlated with the severity of the crisis. But through regression techniques we also plan to identify those presidential responses that are outliers, those cases in which the president's response was *more benign or aggressive* than the severity of the crisis would have warranted. This is a means by which each president's unique personal contribution can be identified and assessed.

RECOMMENDATIONS BASED ON A SOCIAL-PSYCHOLOGICAL ANALYSIS

All in all, the president faces a situation that makes effectiveness almost impossible. There is a paradox here: The "office has at once too much power and too little" (Hodgson, 1980, p. 44). There is power to change the nature of the office, to broaden its impact, and yet there are obstacles to the achievement of goals—constitutional obstacles and bureaucratic ones. Nixon tried to free himself from the accepted constitutional constraints on presidential freedom of action, and he was worse than ineffective; Carter "tried to keep his office scrupulously within its constitutional limits" (Hodgson, 1980, p. 49) and was impotent. The president's task has become progressively more difficult. What can be done? Can anything give? From our list of 10 task dimensions can any be redefined, curtailed, or discarded? Are some more important than others? Of course, they subjectively differ in importance, and presidents spend their greatest time and effort on differing tasks. Any overall judgment of presidential effectiveness needs to reflect a weighting of the tasks, based on the perceived importance of each at a given time as judged by experts, and the president's commitment to that task in a given term of office.

Some presidents probably spend too much time on foreign policy; at least delegation of foreign policy, within general value-oriented guidelines, needs to be explored. President Truman had his Secretary of State James F. Byrnes serve as an "assistant president" for international affairs. During the last half of 1945 Byrnes for the most part ran foreign policy, with Truman content to exercise only minimal supervision from the White House (Messer, 1982). The arrangement worked—for a while, at least—because the two men agreed on the tactics to be used in dealing with the Soviet Union.

More generally, pressure could be relieved from the president and the White House staff by returning the responsibility for initiating legislation to the departments of the Executive Branch. President Reagan appears to be doing this to some extent; he willingly shares power with the Cabinet, whose members he feels he can trust. On another front, nomination and election campaigns could be shortened, thereby reducing the time and effort incumbents spend in political party leadership.

Some recent proposals for reform seem implausible and psychologically and politically unlikely. For example, Sorensen (1984), in an effort to dislodge the gridlock in Washington policymaking, has proposed a one-term presidency, with the vice-president from the other party, and the Cabinet and the White House staff equally divided between the parties. However, party realignment on ideological grounds seems more likely than these proposed reforms.

Something needs to be done. President Carter's press secretary, Jody Powell, told the New York Times, "If people keep getting told that their leadership is poor, or ineffective, and that they don't have any real choices, you'll see a steady erosion in the legitimacy of government. That's going to have a real impact on anybody's ability to govern" (quoted by Griffith, 1980, p. 98). Although President Reagan's actions in

his first term and his overwhelming reelection have somewhat damp-
ened concern over the effectiveness of the presidency, the complexity
of the job remains, and the tensions centered on its unmanageable
aspects will surface again—probably before the next presidential
election.

REFERENCES

Bailey, T. A. (1966). *Presidential greatness: The image and the man from George Washington to the present.* New York: Appleton-Century-Crofts.

Barber, J. D. (1968). Classifying and predicting presidential styles: Two weak experiments. *Journal of Social Issues, 24*(3), 51-80.

Barber, J. D. (1977). *The presidential character* (2nd ed.). Englewood Cliffs, NJ: Prentice-Hall.

Berman, L. (1982). *Planning a tragedy: The Americanization of the war in Vietnam.* New York: Norton.

Bratton, D. L. (1983). The rating of presidents. *Presidential Studies Quarterly, 13,* 400-404.

Brzezinski, Z. (1983). *Power and principle.* New York: Farrar, Strauss, & Giroux.

Church, G. J. (1981, December 14). The president's men. *Time,* pp. 16-22.

Cronin, T. E. (1975). *The state of the presidency.* Boston: Little, Brown.

Donovan, H. (1981, November 9). Fluctuations on the presidential exchange. *Time,* pp. 121-122.

Edwards, G. C., III. (1979). *The quantitative study of the presidency.* Paper presented at the meeting of the American Political Science Association, Washington, DC.

Fallows, J. (1979, May). The passionless presidency. *Atlantic,* pp. 33-48.

Fiedler, F. E. (1964). A contingency model of leadership effectiveness. In L. Berkowitz (Ed.), *Advances in experimental social psychology* (Vol. 1). New York: Academic Press.

Fiedler, F. E. (1967). *A theory of leadership effectiveness.* New York: McGraw-Hill.

Fiedler, F. E. (1978). The contingency model and the dynamics of the leadership process. In L. Berkowitz (Ed.), *Advances in experimental social psychology* (Vol. 11). New York: Academic Press.

Funderburk, C. (1982). *Presidents and politics: The limits of power.* Monterey, CA: Brooks/Cole.

Greenstein, F. (1983). *The hidden-hand presidency: Eisenhower as leader.* New York: Basic Book.

Griffith, T. (1980, November 17). Newswatch: Pirandello would have been lost. *Time,* p. 98.

Halberstam, D. (1972). *The best and the brightest.* New York: Random House.

Heider, F. (1958). *The psychology of interpersonal relations.* New York: John Wiley.

Hermann, M. G. (1983, Spring). *Assessing personality at a distance: A profile of Ronald Reagan* (Quarterly Report, Mershon Center, Vol. 7, No. 6). Columbus: Ohio State University.

Hess, S. (1976). *Organizing the presidency.* Washington, DC: Brookings Institution.

Hodgson, G. (1980). *All things to all men: The false promise of the modern American presidency.* New York: Simon & Schuster.

Hollander, E. P. (1983, August). *Paradoxes of presidential leadership: Party, popularity, promise, performance . . . and more.* Paper presented at the meeting of the American Psychological Association, Anaheim, CA.

Hoxie, R. G. (Ed.). (1971). *The White House: Organization and operations.* New York: Center for the Study of the Presidency.

Janis, I. L. (1972). *Victims of groupthink.* Boston: Houghton Mifflin.

Johnson, R. T. (1974). *Managing the White House.* New York: Harper & Row.

Kearns, D. (1976). *Lyndon Johnson and the American dream.* New York: Harper & Row.

Kessel, J. H. (1983a). The structures of the Carter White House. *American Journal of Political Science, 27,* 431-463.

Kessel, J. H. (1983b). *The structures of the Reagan White House.* Paper presented at the meeting of the American Political Science Association, Chicago.

Messer, R. L. (1982). *The end of an alliance: James F. Byrnes, Roosevelt, Truman, and the origins of the Cold War.* Chapel Hill: University of North Carolina Press.

Miller, G. A. (1969). Psychology as a means of promoting human welfare. *American Psychologist, 24,* 1063-1075.

Neustadt, R. E. (1960). *Presidential power: The politics of leadership.* New York: John Wiley.

Paige, G. D. (1977). *The scientific study of political leadership.* New York: Free Press.

Pika, J. A. (1981-1982). Moving beyond the Oval Office: Problems in studying the presidency. *Congress and the Presidency, 9*(Winter), 17-36.

Prindle, D. F. (1983). *Toward a comparative science of the presidency.* Paper presented at the meeting of the American Political Science Association, Chicago.

Quirk, P. J. (1983). *Presidential competence.* Columbus: Ohio State University, unpublished manuscript.

Rossiter, C. (1960). *The American presidency* (2nd ed.). New York: Harcourt, Brace, & World.

Schlesinger, A. M., Jr. (1958). *The coming of the New Deal.* Boston: Houghton Mifflin.

Scott, W. A. (1960). International ideology and interpersonal ideology. *Public Opinion Quarterly, 24,* 419-435.

Shaw, M. E. (1981). *Group dynamics: The psychology of small group behavior* (3rd ed.). New York: McGraw-Hill.

Sorenson, T. C. (1963). *Decision making in the White House.* New York: Columbia University Press.

Sorensen, T. C. (1984). *A different kind of presidency.* New York: Harper & Row.

Stoessinger, J. G. (1979). *Crusaders and pragmatists: Movers of modern American foreign policy.* New York: Norton.

Tucker, R. (1981). *Politics as leadership.* Columbia: University of Missouri Press.

White, T. H. (1969). *The making of the president, 1968.* Boston: Atheneum.

Wills, G. (1982). *The Kennedy imprisonment: A meditation on power.* Boston: Little, Brown.

Wrightsman, L. S. (1964). Tender- and tough-minded interpretations of government policies. *American Behavioral Scientist, 7*(8), 7-8.

ARIEL MERARI
NEHEMIA FRIEDLAND

10

SOCIAL PSYCHOLOGICAL
ASPECTS OF
POLITICAL TERRORISM

As a social and political phenomenon, terrorism is undoubtedly older than recorded history. The use of assassinations, bombings, and other forms of violence to achieve political ends did not start in this century. Yet, since 1968, terrorism has increasingly attracted public attention worldwide. (Among the many definitions of political terrorism that have been suggested (see Schmid, 1984), the one employed in this chapter is the systematic utilization of actual or threatened violence by nonstate groups, aimed to achieve political objectives.)

Several reasons may explain this sudden interest. Among them is the fact that, although it is doubtful that domestic (intrastate) terrorism has grown much recently, there has been a marked rise since 1968 in international terrorism, defined as an incident of terrorism involving more than one country in any possible way. Official U.S. statistics tally 142 international terrorist incidents in 1968 and 760 in 1980 (U.S. Central Intelligence Agency, 1981); 794 such incidents reportedly occurred in 1982 (U.S. Department of State, 1983). Another explanation is the growing lethality of terriorism. In the words of a Rand Corporation report: "1983 was the bloodiest year yet for terrorist activity, with 720 fatalities and 963 injuries. . . . Since 1977, the number of international terrorist incidents resulting in fatalities has increased each year. . . . Terrorists seem to be less and less reluctant to inflict casualties, demonstrating an increased willingness to kill" (Cordes et al., 1984, pp. 6-7). According to the same source, among incidents with fatalities, the share of those with multiple fatalities increased from 33 percent in 1982 to 59 percent in 1983. Last, terrorism is increasingly being used by states as a tool of foreign policy. Whatever the reason, it seems that political terrorism as a phenomenon is currently at the center of political, media, and, increasingly, academic interest.

References to terrorism can be found in the writings of psychiatrists, sociologists, criminologists, political scientists, and historians. Social psychologists, on the other hand, have shown little interest in the topic. This chapter examines social psychology's potential contribution to the study of terrorism and to the development of means to cope with it.

The student of terrorism has to overcome three major obstacles: a scarcity of data, the heterogeneity of the phenomenon, and the ambiguity surrounding its causes. These are discussed in the first section of this chapter. The second and third sections define a role for social psychology by portraying terrorism as a sophisticated form of psychological warfare. As such, terrorism employs fear induction to maximize its attitudinal impact on target publics. A social psychological analysis of determinants of this impact is presented in the fourth section. The fifth section evaluates the potential contribution of social psychology to designing procedures whereby target publics' ability to withstand this impact can be bolstered.

TERRORISM: HETEROGENEITY AND AMBIGUITY

The subject of terrorism does not lend itself easily to research. In the first place, although several academic, government, and commercially run data bases routinely document international terrorist events, data on the larger group of domestic terrorist incidents are lacking. Second, contrary to the loose common usage of the term "terrorism," the phenomenon it denotes is not uniform. Terrorist groups vary greatly in size, from less than a score of members to thousands, as well as in national composition and cultural background. Responsibility for international terrorist incidents that took place in 1982 was claimed by 125 different organizations (as compared to 61 in 1970), of 75 different nationalities (U.S. Department of State, 1983). The number and diversity of terrorist groups involved in domestic terrorism is considerably greater. Data on 500-odd groups, active during the last decade, have been compiled by the Jaffee Center for Strategic Studies at Tel Aviv University.

The declared motivations of terrorist groups are rather diverse. Some are nationalistic, others are separatist. Social ideologies from the extreme right to the extreme left are well represented among present-day terrorist groups: A variety of neo-Nazis and neo-Fascists can be found on one side and a plethora of Leninist, Maoist, Trotskyist, and anarchist groups on the other.

Among religious terrorist groups are ones formed by Catholics, Protestants, Jews, Shi'ite Moslems, and Sunnite Moslems. Other terrorist groups have a racial motivation: white, black, or red. To further complicate the picture, quite often a terrorist group's credo is a composite one (though most present-day separatist groups espouse a leftist ideology), and some groups have changed ideology in midcourse (e.g., the Colombian M-19, that started as a right-wing-oriented, populist movement and turned to Marxism). In sum, as a social, political, and psychological phenomenon, terrorism is very heterogenous, and there is no sound, a priori reason to assume much in common between different terrorist groups (e.g., the anarchist German Revolutionary Cells and the Argentinian populist Montoneros).

The heterogeneity of terrorism might be responsible for the current failure to formulate a coherent, well-grounded theory of its causes. Explanations of the phenomenon range from in-depth psychological analyses of individual terrorists to general sociopolitical interpretations. The former, which have been primarily undertaken by psychiatrists, psychologists, and criminologists, sought to chart the "terroristic personality" and to determine the dynamics that turn an individual into a terrorist (e.g., Hacker, 1976, 1980; Kellen, 1979). Such clinically oriented analyses have typically been carried out on a small number of cases, and their conclusions are frequently overgeneralized. Moreover, even if it were possible to identify some common attributes of the terrorist personality, transformation of such information into an explanation would be hindered by its predictive irreversibility. That is, the fact that terrorists share certain characteristics or traits by no means implies that any person who has these traits is bound to become a terrorist. This kind of irreversibility also limits the usefulness of statistical profiles of the "typical" terrorist, such as Jenkins's (1982) conclusion that the typical terrorist is male, in his early twenties, single, from a middle- to upper-class urban family, well educated, and has some university training.

An alternative approach depicts terrorism as a group phenomenon (e.g., Turk, 1982). It primarily derives from theories and studies of social destabilization (e.g., Lipset, 1960; Davies, 1962, 1973; Johnson, 1966; Huntington, 1968; Gurr, 1970, 1973; Muller, 1979; Monti, 1980). Yet, identification of correlates of destabilization goes only part way toward the explanation of terrorism: The process whereby destabilization generates terrorism remains undetermined. Moreover, destabilization theories rely quite heavily on "blockade" or frustration-aggression hypotheses, or on assumed gaps between expectations and their fulfillment. It is therefore somewhat difficult to reconcile such theories with the recent proliferation of terrorism in democracies or with the fact that terrorists are not necessarily underprivileged. (For a more extensive criticism of frustration-aggression theories of terrorism see, for instance, Schmid, 1984, pp. 161-166.)

TERRORISM AS PSYCHOLOGICAL WARFARE

The great diversity of terrorism and the ambiguity surrounding its cause notwithstanding, terrorists of all nationalities, races, religions, and ideological or political leanings employ the same tactics and strategy. All of them wage a sophisticated form of psychological warfare. That is, by bearing on target publics' emotions and attitudes, terrorists create an impact that disproportionally exceeds the physical consequences of their action. Clearly, on a national scale, such consequences are negligible. According to the U.S. Department of State (1983), in the 10-year period from 1973-1982, international terrorism around the globe resulted in the death of 3509 persons. As a manifestation of a severe international or national problem, this figure is quite small, considering that in the United States alone, the annual death toll in road accidents is approximately 45,000. To illustrate this point further, one of the deadliest terrorist incidents in history was the October 23, 1983 suicidal car-bomb attack on the U.S. Marine headquarters in Beirut, in which 241 American soldiers were killed. This event instigated vocal criticism of the U.S. administration by politicians and the media, and was arguably a precipitating factor in the ultimate decision to evacuate United States troups from Lebanon. Thus, the death of several hundred men, in a single incident, had a profound effect on a superpower policy in a critical region and, quite possibly, on the fate of Lebanon as a state.

The preceding example points to the essence of terrorist tactics, which is to drawing authorities into public, widely exposed confrontations, and let the public judge their course and pass the verdict on their outcome. A successful terrorist incident is one that maneuvers authorities into "no win" situations. Consider the contrast, for instance, with a criminal kidnap case, where the kidnapper will often strive to maximize the amount of ransom extorted. The sophisticated political terrorist, on the other hand, might minimize the ransom demands, such that authorities' refusal to concede would be perceived as unduly intransigent, whereas a concession, albeit trivial, could nevertheless be construed as capitulation. From this line of reasoning, terrorism can be seen as "the indirect strategy that wins or loses only in terms of how you respond to it. . . . Terrorism wins only if you respond to it in the way the terrorists want you to; which means that its fate is in your hands and not in theirs" (Fromkin, 1975, p. 697).

WHAT CAN SOCIAL PSYCHOLOGY CONTRIBUTE?

Our portrayal of terrorism gives rise to some doubts about the feasibility of eradicating it. The multiplicity of causes espoused by terrorists and uncertainty about the dynamics that turn individuals into terrorists make it difficult, if not impossible, to follow the advice that lasting solutions to problems require the uprooting of their antecedents. As regards terrorism, a root treatment would necessitate removal of the terrorists' political motivation—a solution to their grievances. Such a treatment, however, is impossible in many cases where terrorism, as argued by Ferracuti, "is a fantasy war, real only in the mind of the terrorist" (1982, p. 137). Moreover, accepting the claims of one group might infuriate another segment of the population. For instance, a negotiated settlement between the British government and the Catholic IRA would almost certainly unleash Protestant terrorism in Ulster. In retrospect, it can be shown that terrorism ceased when its perpetrators gained full power (the FLN in Algeria or Mau-Mau in Kenya) or when they were forcefully crushed (the SLA in California or the Second of June movement in West Germany). We do not recall any instance in which a violent subversive group halted its activity in the context of a mutually agreed-upon compromise with authorities.

The difficulty of addressing the root causes of terrorism does not preclude a potentially more promising attempt to cope with its consequences. In terms of the analogy drawn by Brian Jenkins (1975) between terrorism and a theater, one may say that what really counts is not the activity on stage but the audience responses. Thus, the main battle against terrorism has to be fought in the arena of public opinion. Much in the same way as terrorism is an indirect strategy—a sophisticated form of psychological warfare—we hold that the response and counterstrategy ought to be largely indirect and to use psychological tactics. More specifically, we propose that the core of an effective containment strategy consists of denying terrorists the most essential condition for their success: namely, a responsive and excitable public.

This proposition highlights the potential contribution of social psychologists to the struggle against terrorism. The challenge is twofold: First, social psychological methods should be harnessed to investigate factors that determine the potency of terrorism's effect on public opinion. Identification and understanding of such factors is an indispensible prerequisite for assessment and prediction of the impacts of terrorism. Second, social psychologists should formulate principles and devise means for bolstering public resistance to the attitudinal effects of terrorism. In the following sections we offer some preliminary observations that are based on our own research studies and firsthand practical experience with certain aspects of the response to political terrorism. We hope that these observations will stimulate other social psychologists to join the effort.

FACTORS INFLUENCING PUBLIC ATTITUDES TOWARD TERRORISM

Though definitions of terrorism vary, all stress the induction of fear and intimidation as the means used by terrorists to effect political change: for example, "coercive intimidation" (Wilkinson, 1977, p. 48); "putting the public in fear" (Mickolus, 1980, p. 295); "Terrorism is aimed at the people watching. Fear is the intended effect, not the byproduct of terrorism" (Jenkins, 1975, p. 1).

These definitions pose two key, fundamental questions to the student of terrorism. One, is terrorism an effective means of political influence? Two, is the extent of attitude and behavior change induced by terrorists linearly related to the intensity of fear elicited by their actions? That is, should we accept the intuitively compelling assumption that the more severe and threatening the terrorists' assault, the greater the target's willingness to give in?

Historical precedents show that the above questions cannot be answered in the affirmative. The number of cases in which political change can be unequivocally attributed to terroristic activity is rather small. Furthermore, most of those cases were in the category of anticolonial struggle (e.g., the Jewish groups in Palestine, EOKA in Cyprus, and Mau-Mau in Kenya against the British, the FLN in Algeria against the French, and FRELIMO in Mozambique against the Portuguese). That is, in all these cases, terrorists fought against a foreign rule and occupying forces. On the other hand, domestic terrorism, in which the insurgents rose against people in their own country, has been largely unsuccessful. Although most terroristic activity in the last half of the century may be categorized as domestic, in only six instances did terrorists carry out successful campaigns that overturned existing regimes in their native countries (Cuba, Nicaragua, Cambodia, Laos, Iran, and Rhodesia). In Europe, where scores of terrorist groups have been active, there has not been a single case of an insurgent group gaining power since the end of World War II.

This historical pattern is intriguing, for domestic terrorism appears to be more threatening both in its modus operandi and in its potential lethality than anticolonial terrorism. In the colonial situation, the typical targets are soldiers, policemen, and officials of the occupying country who are stationed in the colony, and the ruling nation's homeland is usually immune to danger. Domestic terrorism, on the other hand, is characteristically less discriminating. Ideologically motivated terrorists usually target whole classes of people associated with the regime, with ethnic or religious groups, or even just the population at large. Such randomly targeted, seemingly senseless attacks (e.g., the bombing of a railway station in Bologna, Italy, which resulted in 83 dead, or of a crowd celebrating the Munich Oktoberfest, which killed 13) turn every member of the population into a potential victim and thereby induce much fear and anxiety. Moreover, no terrorist campaign against a foreign rule compared to the lethality of domestic terrorism in El Salvador, where 8,000 to 10,000 are estimated to have died in recent years; or in Turkey, where approximately 2,000 persons were killed annually in the period preceding the 1980 coup; or in northern Ireland, where thousands have died as a result of terrorist activity since 1969. It is quite surprising, therefore, that on the whole, domestic terrorist groups have been considerably less successful than anticolonial groups in achieving their political objectives.

Empirical Evidence

Historical analyses such as this are obviously tentative. However, the possibility that—contrary to a commonly held belief—terrorism's ability to effect social or political change is not a simple, direct function of the amount of fear it induces has also been supported by empirical research. In 1979, during a period of relatively intense terroristic activity in Israel, we conducted a nationwide survey that was designed to assess Israelis' emotional and attitudinal reactions to terrorism (Friedland & Merari, 1985). The results confirmed the notion that terrorism induces fear beyond its physical significance. Although only 23 Israelis were killed and 344 were wounded in 1979 as a result of Palestinian terrorism, 93 percent of our respondents expressed "worry" or "extreme worry" about terrorism in the country. Close to three-quarters stated that they were "worried" or "extremely worried" about the possibility that they or members of their families might get hurt by terrorism.

Despite these high levels of expressed anxiety, the respondents maintained an uncompromising position vis-à-vis the terrorists' political objectives. More than 90 percent regarded terrorism as a reason to deny the PLO a representative status and to avoid political change in the areas occupied by Israel (i.e., either the establishment of an independent Palestinian state or the granting of autonomy to the Palestinian population). Furthermore, very large majorities favored the use of radical counterterrorist measures, including the demolition of houses whose owners harbored terrorists (79.5 percent support), deportation of individuals who held contacts with terrorist organizations (90 percent), imposition of curfews (87 percent), shelling of terrorist bases, even if it jeopardized civilians (75.5 percent), and assassination of terrorist leaders (92 percent).

Effects of the Intensity of Threat

Taken together, historical evidence and our survey data suggest the need to reconsider the pattern of relationship between the determinedness of a target population to adhere to its political positions and the intensity of an actual or potential terrorist assault. The already mentioned assumption that the two are linearly related might have been valid if the cost of adhering to their positions were the sole determinant of the public's resolve to resist terrorist pressure. There is reason to believe, however, that two conflicting processes shape individuals' willingness to change their attitudes and behavior as a function of the intensity of attempts to effect such change. On one hand, utilitarian considerations and the cost of resistance to change tend to produce a positive relationship between individuals' readiness to change and the intensity of raw power that is brought to bear on them. On the other hand, the perception of threats as illegitimate means of influence might promote reactance and resentment (Brehm, 1966; Friedland, 1976). As a result, reluctance to change might grow stronger as the attempts to induce such change become more persistent. (This effect is likely to be particularly potent when terrorism is employed to compel political change.)

Combined, the conflicting effects just described yield a curvilinear relationship between public steadfastness in the face of terrorism and the intensity of threat. Below a certain level of intensity, the lethal effects of terrorists' actions are too weak to compel the public to reconsider the costs and benefits of adhering to its political positions, but sufficient to arouse animosity toward terrorists and their causes. Hence, in the range of low to moderate threat intensities, terrorism might result in a radicalization of public attitudes in a direction *opposed* to the terrorists' interests. Within this range, the more severe the threat, the stronger the public's opposition. Beyond a certain threshold of suffering, however, public steadfastness is likely to erode, and then the greater the severity of terrorists' assaults, the more inclined toward concessions the public is likely to be. Cohen (in press) described this curvilinear or biphasic effect, based on interviews with officials who held high ranking positions in the British government before 1948, during the British rule in Palestine:

> To the extent that public opinion influenced British policy, it was mainly affected by the actions of the IZL and LHI [Jewish terrorist organizations in Palestine]. Terrorism influenced public opinion in two opposing directions. Initially it aroused and stimulated the public against the Zionist struggle and created disgust and weakened the support of Zionism. In a later phase, this disgust had a cumulative effect that brought about public opinion pressure to evacuate [Palestine]. The public became tired of the loss of soldiers' lives.

Importance of the Issues

The effect of the intensity of terrorism on public steadfastness interacts with two additional factors: the importance of the issues at stake, and public hopefulness. As regards the former, it is hardly necessary to assert that individuals' resistance to relinquishing their attitudes and political positions, even in the face of threats to their physical safety, is related to the importance that they assign to the contested issues. Although fear is a potent motivation, under certain circumstances individuals and collectives adhere to opinions, attitudes, and behaviors despite extreme danger. Such has been true of POWs who stood up to their captors and nations that fought "lost wars" for the sake of honor or other intangible rewards. Hence, the curvilinear function described above is, in effect, a family of functions, as shown in Figure 10.1.

Two parameters of the proposed functions are noteworthy. One, the greater the perceived importance of the issues at stake, the higher the threshold that must be reached before the cost and intensity of terrorism will start eroding public resistance. Two, the greater the perceived importance of the issues at stake, the steeper the negative

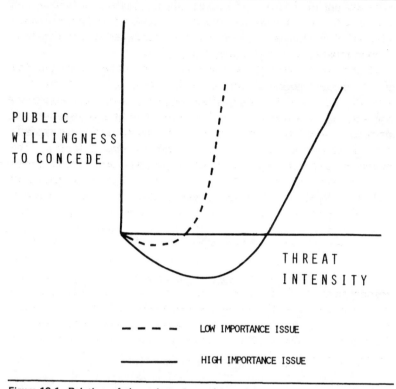

PUBLIC
WILLINGNESS
TO CONCEDE

THREAT
INTENSITY

– – – –   LOW IMPORTANCE ISSUE

—————   HIGH IMPORTANCE ISSUE

Figure 10.1 Relation of threat intensity and issue importance to public willingness to concede to terrorism.

part of the function and the more moderate its positive part. That is, antiterrorist attitudes are likely to crystallize faster and the erosion of public resistance to terrorism is likely to be slower when the issue of conflict is vitally important to the target public than when it is less important. These functions, then, can explain the seemingly self-contradictory findings that intense terrorism of the domestic kind is usually less effective than the typically less intense anticolonial terrorism, and that terrorism's success in inducing fear does not necessarily enhance the target public's willingness to concede. The hardening of Israelis' attitudes, for instance, or the finding that 94 percent of the Protestants and even 55 percent of the Catholics in Ulster advocated harsher British action against the IRA (Moxon-Browne, 1981), can be attributed to the fact that in both Israel and Ulster terrorism concerns issues of a truly existential nature for the target populations. By contrast, most modern anticolonial struggles were carried out to obtain concessions that had no immediate or direct effect on the beleaguered public. Consequently, in these cases, concessions were more readily granted, even though the intensity of terrorism was considerably lower than in most instances of domestic terrorism.

Taken to its extreme, our analysis would appear to suggest that when terrorism threatens the very existence of a nation or strives to alter the character of a society in a manner wholly unacceptable to the majority of its members, it is unlikely to prevail. After all, nations have withstood wars that claimed more lives and caused more material damage than any known or conceivable terrorist campaign. This suggestion is not entirely valid, however, as there exist two fundamental differences between conventional wars and terrorism. First, attacks on civilian populations during conventional wars are usually patterned (e.g., German air raids on Britain took place at night, against major cities) and have a specific nature (e.g., bombings). Hence, early warning is feasible and the population can be trained to take evasive action. Terrorist attacks, on the other hand, are usually more random in their timing, location, and targeting, and are considerably more varied with respect to method. In war, then, the targets of violence have a greater degree of predictability and control over their fate than in terrorist campaigns. Second, the course and dynamics of conventional wars usually enable the involved parties to form at least tentative expectations about their ending. Terrorism, on the other hand, often lacks a clear and determinable point of extinction (see Devine & Rafalko, 1982). As one Israeli official recently commented, "The public ought to become reconciled to bearing a hundred years of terrorism." Thus, a second factor that distinguishes between individuals' ability to withstand the hardships of war and their resilience in the face of terrorism may be termed "hopefulness."

Public Hopefulness

The possibility that hopefulness has a decisive effect on a public's ability to withstand terrorism was recently illustrated by the collapse of the white regime in Rhodesia. After several years of contained, albeit continuous, terrorist attacks by the ZAPU and ZANU black insurgents, the white regime decided to yield. Thus, despite the fact that by all indications the whites had enough strength to continue their struggle indefinitely, and that the very existence of a dominant white society in Rhodesia was at stake, opposition to terrorism suddenly collapsed. We would speculate that this sudden surrender resulted from the loss of hope, caused by the white regime's growing isolation in the international community and failure to see an end to its predicament.

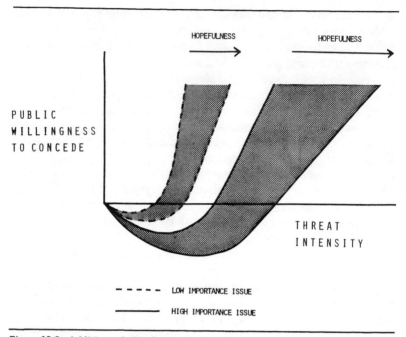

Figure 10.2 Addition of the factor of public hopefulness in explaining reactions to terrorism.

Turning back to the functions described in Figure 10.1, we propose that the position of the threshold beyond which public steadfastness will start to erode, and the rate and intensity of such erosion, are affected by the degree of hopefulness. Taking the hopefulness factor into consideration, we can enlarge our family of curves, as shown in Figure 10.2.

Our analysis of factors that determine the attitudinal impact of terrorism is clearly preliminary. A systematic investigation of these factors is sorely needed in order to arrive at a valid and comprehensive model that explains the processes whereby public opinion regarding terrorism is shaped. Such a model is an indispensable foundation for the measuring, monitoring, and prediction of public reactions to terrorism.

Prediction of Responses to Terrorism

The practical importance of this investigation can hardly be exaggerated. If public opinion is the key to terrorists' success or failure, then its constant monitoring can provide authorities with "intelligence" needed to combat terrorism. For example, it often appears that although the returns from investments in the prevention of road accidents, crime, and diseases would be considerably greater than from investments in counterterrorist action, governments are more willing to make the latter investment (Alon, 1980). Such a disproportionate investment is usually justified by "public morale" considerations, yet governments rarely bother actually to measure public morale. Thus, the monitoring of public opinion could provide valuable information for the allocation of national resources.

The intelligence that is essential for authorities' effective response to terrorism consists not only of actual public reactions but also of projections to the future. Since terrorism might plague a society for an extended period of time, authorities could benefit immensely from predictions about the long-term, cumulative effects of a drawn-out exposure to terrorism. Furthermore, decision making and policymaking could be aided by predictions of public reactions to contingencies that are currently hypothetical but have a high probability of materializing in the future. For instance, a government that seeks to implement a credible "no ransom" policy in order to stem hostage-taking tactics might be compelled to sacrifice individuals who have been taken hostage. Advance knowledge of public reaction to such an event could help the government decide whether or not to adopt the policy.

Projections into the future are of course risky, yet their importance is so great that even approximations are valuable. Several methods may be employed. The routine measurement of public attitudes can eventually provide a data base for detecting regularities of change in public opinion. These may then be extrapolated to forecast future trends. Such extraplations are at best tentative, as it is impossible to foresee all future events that might affect public reaction. On the other hand, some confidence regarding their reliability may be drawn from the fact that the characteristics of the relevant target population are unlikely to undergo rapid changes.

Surveys can also be used to present respondents with scenarios to which they are asked to respond. Our use of this procedure, as part of the nationwide survey we conducted in 1979, yielded data that attest to its usefulness. Respondents were given three barricade-and-hostage scenarios, two of which had actually occurred—the Ma'alot incident in 1974 and the Savoy Hotel incident in 1975. In both, heavy casualties were sustained in the course of rescue operations. The third was a hypothetical scenario that ruled out a military rescue operation, due to technical constraints. The respondents were asked to indicate the policies that in their view should have been implemented in the three cases, as well as their general preferences for the handling of various kinds of barricade-and-hostage situations differing in the number and type of hostages, the magnitude of terrorist demands, and the feasibility of military rescue operations. The results showed that about one-third of the public opposed any concession to terrorists' demands, the cost of hostages' lives notwithstanding. Less than 10 percent preferred always to concede so as not to jeopardize hostages. The position of the remaining 60 percent of the public depended on the specifics of the situation, with the feasibility of forceful rescue appearing to be the decisive factor. Whereas only 33 percent of the sample advocated no concessions to terrorists in the hypothetical scenario, where no military rescue was possible, 65 percent recommended this policy in the Savoy scenario and 58 percent in the Ma'alot case. It should be noted that in the latter, opting for forceful action actually led to the death of 22 high school students who were held hostage. These findings on specific scenarios were consistent with policy preferences that were expressed in response to general questions. Combined, they suggest that public steadfastness in situations where military options were available did not stem from an expectation that such options would necessarily increase the chance of saving the hostages. A majority of the public appeared willing to sustain losses in the process of an active attack on the terrorists, but would yield to some demands if military action were impossible. The number and kind of hostages appeared to have less importance as a determinant of public policy preferences. Although responses to the general questions revealed a greater importance of these factors than responses to the scenarios, we believe the latter provide a better reflection of public attitude.

The validity of public-reaction assessments can be further enhanced by increasing individuals' perceived involvement in relevant situations. We refer here to the use of experimental simulations in which individuals are asked to assume the roles of decision makers or policymakers. Such an application of the experimental method might prove fruitful in providing information on the effects of a wide variety of factors. Although simulations have sometimes been criticized on the grounds that they lack realism, our own experience and that of others (e.g., Zimbardo, 1971) suggests that a faithful reproduction of the key characteristics of a real-life situation is entirely possible.

Each of the research avenues suggested above has its shortcomings. Hence the generation of predictions about a target public's behavior must be methodologically eclectic. We believe that, despite any shortcomings, the data that such methods might yield would provide a sounder basis for decision making than the guesswork on which many decisions concerning the response to terrorism are based. From a practical point of view, such data might constitute the single most important contribution of social psychologists to combating terrorism.

ENHANCING PUBLIC RESISTANCE
TO THE IMPACTS OF TERRORISM

Social psychologists' second potential contribution to the struggle against terrorism involves planning interventions designed to bolster public resistance to the effects of terrorism. After extensive thought on this topic, we have concluded that existing social psychological knowledge offers little help here. Although social psychologists have made some headway on procedures for enhancing resistance to influence (e.g., Freedman & Sears, 1965; Haas & Grady, 1975; McGuire, 1964; McGuire & Papageorgis, 1962; Petty, Brock, & Brock, 1978; Petty & Cacioppo, 1977), their contribution is mostly limited to the inducement of cognitive resistance to persuasive arguments. Little is known, on the other hand, about ways to hinder influence attempts that are aimed at arousal of primitive motivations such as fear.

Having failed to find ready-made solutions, we attempted to design interventions that we could suggest if asked to help in enhancing the public's resistance to the impacts of terrorism. This attempt was rather frustrating, for the outcome was quite meager, and the uniqueness of our inputs as psychologists was not apparent. The following pages of discussion illustrate this predicament and indicate that the needed breakthroughs have yet to be made.

Although our analysis of factors that determine the impact of terrorism indicated that fear is just one determinant, nevertheless fear is a critical factor, and its attenuation could weaken the power wielded by terrorists.

The fear of terrorism is largely a fear of the unknown. Anxiety and apprenhension stem not only from what terrorists have already done but from unrealistic projections as to what they might be capable of doing. Faced with an ambiguous threat, such as a force that strikes at random, individuals tend to expect the worst (see Kupperman, 1977). Fear and worry are further fueled by the magnifying effect of the news media and by their depiction of terrorists as desperate, ideology-driven persons who are willing to sacrifice everything for a cause (see Netanyahu, 1979). Authors of fiction have contributed their share by weaving intricate plots suggesting that terrorists are sophisticated planners and faultless strategists (e.g., Harris, 1976; Collins & Lapierre, 1980; Mills, 1977). And governments and politicians, in an effort to justify counterterrorist acts and policies, tend at times to present terrorism in more dramatic colors than it actually warrants.

The above arguments suggest that the fear of terrorism can be considerably alleviated by making terrorism known, that is, by disseminating valid and accurate information about terrorism, terrorists, and their capabilities. This is not to suggest that terrorism should be trivialized or that its targets should be lulled into a false sense of security, for terrorism is dangerous. Yet the danger might be exacerbated if its dimensions are exaggerated. The dissemination of accurate information about terrorism might lead the public to realize that terrorism, in Jenkins's (1982, p. 13) words, "is a pain, not a mortal danger."

The main culprits in magnifying the perceived might of terrorism are doubtlessly the news media. Their role in the "theater of terrorism" has been extensively discussed elsewhere (e.g., Netanyahu, 1979; Alexander, 1979). Here it is sufficient to point out the ways in which the media serve terrorism. First, the printed space and broadcast time devoted to terrorism and terrorist incidents turn terrorism into an ever present threat in individuals' consciousness. Second, the media's technical capabilities, which allow them to convey information in real time, by word, sound, and image, force millions to experience vicariously the horrors of terrorism. Third, modern journalists provide not only news but also background and "in depth" analyses; and journalistic explanations of terrorism—which are almost invariably of a social nature—have sometimes combined with a tendency to forgive whatever is "socially explainable" to exculpate terrorism (Podhoretz, 1979). Fourth, Western journalism often adopts an adversarial position vis-à-vis authorities, and as a result, some reports of terrorist incidents have been more critical of the authorities than of the terrorists. To the extent that one of the major aims of terrorism is to discredit authorities, journalists sometimes act as valuable allies of terrorists (Netanyahu, 1979).

In principle, the damage caused by the news media could be prevented if the operating philosophy and practices of the news media were changed. It would not seem to be a gross violation of the "public's right to know" if, for instance, a terrorist incident were not reported while it was unfolding, or if the occurrence were made known without being shown. Difficulty would arise, however, in implementation of such changes, which might entail a serious infringement on the freedom of the press. As social psychologists we can only stress that a fundamental change in journalists' modus operandi might be the single most important antiterrorist remedy.

Terrorism derives much of its power from the randomness of its attacks. Terrorism, in other words, is potentially powerful because it may come to be perceived as unpredictable and uncontrollable, and thereby induce a feeling of helplessness. The power of terrorism can therefore be weakened by preventing the public from adopting a passive stance vis-à-vis terrorism; that is, by teaching the public that terrorism can be coped with actively.

Active coping with terrorism can take a variety of forms. On a most elementary level, individuals can be taught and encouraged to take certain precautionary and defensive actions that, aside from their practical utility, could also ward off feelings of helplessness. In Israel, for instance, where bombing attacks are commonplace, authorities routinely encourage the public to keep on the alert for suspicious objects and parcels found in public places, and they provide information on the various methods that terrorists can employ to plant bombs. The frequent early discovery of bombs, by civilians, has reinforced public alertness and, we believe, instilled confidence that the threat can be coped with. There is no evidence whatsoever that the planting of bombs has deterred Israelis from frequenting public places or from using public transportation, which is a popular target of bombing attacks. It should be immediately stressed, however, that in encouraging the public to beome actively involved in its own protection, one should be careful to avoid excesses. Unnecessarily exaggerated safety measures might become a burden and interfere with daily routines to a degree that could by itself be considered a small victory for terrorism. Additionally, the human tendency to rationalize action could turn such measures into fear stimulants.

Individuals' perceived control over the threats posed by terrorism derives not only from coping behaviors that they themselves are capable of undertaking. In times of stress, individuals' dependence on authorities is enhanced, and authorities' performance in dealing with terrorism becomes a yardstick by which the public assesses the likelihood that there will be an end to its ordeal.

During the last two decades, most Western governments have been notably hesitant in their response to terrorism. Many have favored the so called "flexible response" policy (see Friedland, 1983), which advocates the adoption of ad hoc responses, in accordance with conditions prevailing in each terrorist incident. The inevitable resultant inconsistency is detrimental in two important respects. Authorities might come to be regarded as inept and noncredible. The Israeli government has many times stated its opposition to dealing with terrorists; yet it traded 3500 jailed terrorists for the release of 6 Israelis held captive by the PLO and may thus have impaired its ability to inspire public trust. Second, authorities' indecisiveness might be interpreted as evidence that the problem is insurmountable. We therefore submit that the public's confidence that "something can be done" and its hope that "there is light at the end of the tunnel" have to be nurtured by authorities' adoption of clear and consistent policies regarding terrorism and by their visibly undertaking decisive counterterrorist action. Our 1979 public opinion survey, referred to above, revealed that the Israeli public strongly supported the implementation of extreme counterterrorist measures.

Underneath the desire for action, revealed by our research and that of others (see Jenkins, 1982), there lurks an elementary psychological phenomenon: namely, the helplessness-reducing or stress-reducing quality that activity, whether instrumental or not, can have in threatening situations. In our view, authorities should be better attuned to this psychological need of their constituents. Our own experience has taught us that officials and politicians entrusted with the response to terrorism often act on the basis of misconceptions of public attitudes. Thus, for instance, the worry and concern of the close relatives of kidnap victims and their understandable desire to assure the victims' release at any cost has sometimes been interpreted as the attitude of the public at large and thus led to unwise decisions. Such seems to have been the case in the Israeli government's agreement to release 76 convicted terrorists, some of them sentenced to life terms for multiple murders, in exchange for a single Israeli soldier who was held captive by a terrorist group. Our 1979 survey, conducted shortly after the exchange, showed that 81.5 percent of the public thought that the government had conceded too much in this case.

To reiterate, authorities should pay closer attention to psychological processes that could enhance the public's ability to withstand terrorism. In so doing, they might discover that their indecisiveness, which they often rationalize as "public concern," is ill-founded. Governments are frequently paralyzed by the fear that they would be damned if they energetically responded to terrorism—and in so doing impinged on the rights, freedoms, and welfare of their constituents—and would be equally damned if they tried to weather the threat passively. The dilemma is genuine, and the importance of carefully weighing the intensity and scope of counterterrorist action can hardly be exaggerated. Nevertheless, the guiding question for authorities should not be whether the public will tolerate action, but rather, how will it fare without action?

THE RELEVANCE OF SOCIAL PSYCHOLOGY

Although the present wave of political terrorism is by now 16 years old and seems to be growing, it has not yet attracted the attention and interest of mainstream social psychology or other branches of psychology. The *Psychological Abstracts* listed no reference to terrorism or to related terms such as "hostages" or "hijacking" until the end of 1981. By this criterion, official psychology only recognized the problem of terrorism in 1982, when 10 publications were listed under that heading. Meanwhile, from 1967 through October 1981, there were 19,450 listings for the subject "rats," 243 for goldfish, and 52 for seagulls. By contrast, during the aforementioned period, only 42 items were listed under "nationalism" and 32 under "political revolution."

A detailed analysis of the reasons for this apparent indifference to problems of immense social importance is beyond the scope of the present chapter. Some of the more salient reasons can nevertheless be pointed out. The traditional emphasis on individuals and small groups rather than on mass behavior, and the more recent "cognitive shift" in social psychology, have considerably restricted the truly social content of social psychology. Researchers' preference for experimental rather than observational methodologies, and their reluctance to undertake studies that do not allow complete control over variables, constitute a second reason. Also, disciplinary specialization makes it professionally inconvenient to deal with subjects that are clearly interdisciplinary, even though most, if not all, real-life phenomena cannot be readily reduced to a narrow disciplinary framework. Unfortunately, human scientists, with their embedded need for orderliness in nature, try to understand and treat societal problems using the narrow approaches of disciplines created by convenience and influenced by long-past historical circumstances.

In defense of social psychologists, we must note that the potential consumers of their knowledge—political decision makers and government officials—have not done much to entice them from the academic ivory tower by seeking their expertise. Our own experience has taught us that decision makers are better equipped to deal with tangible, technical aspects of a problem (e.g., the costs of mounting an attack against terrorists) than with its more subtle, intangible features (e.g., moods, attitudes). They would rather address immediate than long-range problems. They are usually so busy making decisions that they rarely have any time left to think about these decisions. And they are generally wary of academic advice.

The feasibility of a fruitful dialogue between social scientists and politicians is worthy of a special treatise. There is no doubt, however, that officials would be more receptive to social scientists if they could provide evidence of their usefulness. We have learned that the road to creation of such evidence is arduous, yet it can be traversed. In doing so, we have come to appreciate the wise advice of Professor Yehezkel Dror to social scientists who wish to contribute in real-life situations: Approach the task with a large stock of stoic enthusiasm.

REFERENCES

Alexander, Y. (1979). Terrorism and the media: A special issue. *Terrorism, 2,* 1-147.

Alon, H. (1980). *Countering Palestinian terrorism in Israel: Toward a policy analysis of counter-measures.* Santa Monica, CA: The Rand Corporation.

Brehm, J. W. (1966). *A theory of psychological reactance.* New York: Academic Press.

Cohen, G. (in press). *Hainu ke'kholmim* (Hebrew).

Collins, L., & Lapierre, D. (1980). *The fifth horseman.* New York: Simon & Schuster.

Cordes, B., Hoffman, B., Jenkins, B., Kellen, K., Moran, S., & Sater, W. (1984). *Trends in international terrorism, 1982 and 1983* (Report No. R-3183-SL). Santa Monica, CA: The Rand Corporation.

Davies, J. C. (1962). Toward a theory of revolution. *American Sociological Review, 27,* 5-19.

Davies, J. C. (1973). Aggression, violence, revolution, and war. In J. N. Knutsen (Ed.), *Handbook of political psychology.* San Francisco: Jossey-Bass.

Devine, P. E., & Rafalko, R. J. (1982). On terror. *The Annals of the American Academy of Political and Social Science, 463,* 39-53.

Ferracuti, F. (1982). A sociopsychiatric interpretation of terrorism. *The Annals of the American Academy of Political and Social Science, 463,* 129-149.

Freedman, J. L., & Sears, D. O. (1965). Warning, distraction, and resistance to influence. *Journal of Personality and Social Psychology, 1,* 262-266.

Friedland, N. (1976). Social influence via threats. *Journal of Experimental Social Psychology, 12,* 552-563.

Friedland, N. (1983). Hostage negotiations: Dilemmas about policy. In L. Z. Freedman & Y. Alexander (Eds.), *Perspectives on terrorism.* Wilmington, DE: Scholarly Resources.

Friedland, N., & Merari, A. (1985). *The psychological impact of terrorism: A double edged sword.* Unpublished manuscript, Tel Aviv University.

Fromkin, D. (1975). The strategy of terrorism. *Foreign Affairs, 53,* 683-698.

Gurr, T. R. (1970). *Why men rebel.* Princeton, NJ: Princeton University Press.

Gurr, T. R. (1973). The revolution—social change nexus: Some old theories and new hypotheses. *Comparative Politics,* 359-392.

Haas, R. G., & Grady, K. (1975). Temporal delay, type of forewarning and resistance to influence. *Journal of Experimental Social Psychology, 11,* 459-469.

Hacker, F. J. (1976). *Crusaders, criminals, crazies: Terror and terrorism in our time.* New York: Norton.

Hacker, F. J. (1980). Terror and terrorism: Modern growth industry and mass entertainment. *Terrorism, 4,* 163-169.

Harris, T. (1976). *Black Sunday.* New York: Bantam Books.

Huntington, S. P. (1968). *Political order in changing societies.* New Haven, CT: Yale University Press.

Jenkins, B. M. (1975). International terrorism: A new mode of conflict. In D. Carlton & C. Shaerf (Eds.), *International terrorism and world security.* London: Croom Helm.

Jenkins, B. M. (1982). Statements about terrorism. *The Annals of the American Academy of Political and Social Science, 463,* 11-23.

Johnson, C. (1966). *Revolutionary change.* Boston: Little, Brown.

Kellen, K. (1979). *Terrorists—what are they like?* Santa Monica, CA: The Rand Corporation

Kupperman, R. H. (1977). *Facing tomorrow's terrorist incident today.* Washington, DC: U.S. Department of Justice.

Lipset, S. (1960). *Political man: The social bases of politics.* Garden City, NY: Doubleday.

McGuire, W. J. (1964). Inducing resistance to persuasion: Some contemporary approaches. In L. Berkowitz (Ed.), *Advances in experimental social psychology* (Vol. 1). New York: Academic Press.

McGuire, W. J., & Papageorgis, D. (1962). Effectiveness of forewarning in developing resistance to persuasion. *Public Opinion Quarterly, 26,* 24-34.

Mickolus, E. F. (1980). *The literature of terrorism.* Westport, CT: Greenwood.

Mills, J. (1977). *The seventh power.* New York: Harcourt Brace Jovanovich.

Monti, D. J. (1980). The relation between terrorism and domestic civil disorders. *Terrorism, 4,* 123-161.

Moxon-Browne, E. (1981). The water and the fish: Public opinion and the provisional IRA in Northern Ireland. In P. Wilkinson (Ed.), *British perspectives on terrorism.* London: George Allen & Unwin.

Muller, E. N. (1979). *Aggressive political participation.* Princeton, NJ: Princeton University Press.

Netanyahu, B. (Ed.). (1979). *Terrorism and the media: Abdication of responsibility.* Jerusalem: The Jonathan Institute.

Petty, R. E., Brock, T. C., & Brock, S. (1978). Hecklers: Boon or bust for speakers? *Public Relations Journal, 34,* 10-12.

Petty, R. E., & Cacioppo, J. T. (1977). Forewarning, cognitive responding, and resistance to persuasion. *Journal of Personality and Social Psychology, 35,* 645-655.

Podhoretz, N. (1979). The subtle collusion. In B. Netanyahu (Ed.), *Terrorism and the media: Abdication of responsibility.* Jerusalem: The Jonathan Institute.

Turk, A. T. (1982). *Political criminality: The defiance and defense of authority.* Beverly Hills, CA: Sage.

Schmid, A. P. (1984). *Political terrorism.* Amsterdam: North Holland Publishing.

U.S. Central Intelligence Agency. (1981, June). *Research paper.* Washington, DC: Author.

U.S. Department of State. (1983). *Patterns of international terrorism: 1982.* Washington, DC: Government Printing Office.

Wilkinson, P. (1979). *Terrorism and the liberal state.* London: Macmillan.

Zimbardo, P. (1971). *The psychological power and pathology of imprisonment* (statement prepared for the U.S. House of Representatives Committee on the Judiciary). Unpublished paper, Stanford University.

LAURA M. DAVIDSON
ANDREW BAUM

11

IMPLICATIONS OF
POST-TRAUMATIC STRESS
FOR SOCIAL PSYCHOLOGY

One of the more profound psychobiological outcomes of stressful experience is the Post-Traumatic Stress Disorder (PTSD), recently established as an affective disorder (DSM-III; American Psychiatric Association, 1980). Post-traumatic stress has both psychological and physiological components that appear to result from stressors that are powerful enough to be considered outside the realm of normal experience. Events such as natural disasters may give rise to PTSD, although the effects are described as more severe following human-made accidents or stressors such as war, aircraft disasters, or exposure to toxic substances (DSM-III). The specific causes and nature of the disorder, however, are not well understood, and the policy implications of its sources and costs are not very clear. In this chapter, we will consider these issues in light of research on combat veterans and victims of disasters.

This chapter is divided into four sections. The first provides a brief historical perspective on post-traumatic stress, tracing the progression from interpreting symptoms as organically derived to explaining them as psychological manifestations of trauma. The second section examines PTSD in the context of the Vietnam experience. Due either to an unprecedented incidence of PTSD among Vietnam combat veterans or to unique aspects of the war there, psychological costs of serving in Vietnam have received a great deal of attention. Further, it is in the context of the Vietnam experience that many of the social aspects of PTSD were particularly relevant and many of its implications became apparent. The third part of this chapter extends discussion of war-related PTSD to instances of emotional disturbance following natural and human-made disasters. The similarities of response to stress involved in these catastrophes are striking and suggest that the syndrome may represent an extreme case of stress response. Finally,

AUTHORS' NOTE: Preparation of this chapter was facilitated by support from USUHS (C0720 and T07248). The opinions or assertions contained herein are our own and are not to be construed as official or reflecting the views of the Department of Defense or the Uniformed Services University of the Health Sciences.

policy implications are discussed. Through continued examination of the causes and costs of PTSD, we may move closer to minimizing its disruptiveness and destructiveness.

DEFINING PTSD

Although PTSD has only recently been included in common parlance, the symptoms associated with severe trauma have been of interest for a long time. In fact, Trimble (1981) has suggested that a number of the symptoms of PTSD included in the DSM-III are described in the following passage from Shakespeare's *Henry IV*, in which Lady Percy speaks to her husband, Hotspur:

Tell me, sweet lord, what is't that takes from thee
Thy stomach, pleasure, and thy golden sleep?
Why dost thou bend thine eyes upon the earth,
And start so often when thou sit'st alone?
Why hast thou lost the fresh blood in thy cheeks,
And given my treasures and my nights of thee to
Thick ey'd musing and curs'd melancholy?
In thy faint slumbers, I by thee have watch'd,
And heard thee murmur tales of iron wars.

According to his wife, Hotspur had been experiencing recurrent dreams of war. Reexperiencing the trauma through painful recollections or dreams is an essential criterion for diagnosis of PTSD, and intrusive imagery is common. A second necessary component for diagnosis of the syndrome is a numbing or reduction in responsiveness to the outside world. This withdrawal can result in social problems including decreased interest in friends and loss of social support. Along with the diminished responsiveness is a constricted affect, with anxiety and depression being the most common forms of expression. Hotspur, though not explicitly anxious or depressed, often sat alone and had been neglecting his wife. Finally, symptoms of autonomic arousal are indicative of PTSD, including hyperalertness or exaggerated startle response, difficulty in falling asleep, and impairment of concentration or memory. Hotspur exhibited at least two of these symptoms. Whether or not he actually manifested PTSD is less important than the recognition of these effects of trauma. They have been known for years, but have not been easily explained.

This example has served to outline essential features of PTSD. It is a syndrome involving what appear to be integrated, often persistent psychological and biological responses to chronic or severe stress. Its primary defining characteristic is its source, the occurrence of an event or events generally regarded as outside normal human experience. Its symptoms include intrusive thoughts or recurring dreams or images, social withdrawal, constricted affect, autonomic arousal, and numbness. The extent of co-occurrence of these symptoms is variable, but there is the possibility that they reflect independent parts of an integrated response.

EARLY PERSPECTIVES ON POST-TRAUMATIC STRESS

Physicians of the eighteenth and nineteenth centuries recognized that symptoms similar to those associated with PTSD could result from injury or accidents. Most believed that these problems were neurological in nature, even though it was often noted that these neurological problems did not occur for years following an injury. The causes of the neurological problems were thought to be organic lesions in the spinal cord or brain (Erichsen, 1882).

Many of the observations of trauma-induced symptoms derived from treatment of survivors of train accidents. With the widespread use of railways for transportation and the frequency of railroad collisions, cases of "concussion of the spine" became common (Erichsen, 1882). It was widely accepted that symptoms similar to those associated with PTSD could be caused by other types of accidents such as falls, horse accidents, or accidents in a gymnasium, but they occurred to more people at a greater frequency after railway transportation became common. Erichsen (1882) was one of the first physicians to describe the condition that often resulted from railway accidents. Consistent with the prevailing emphasis on organic causes of emotional disturbances, he felt that problems following the accident were due to changes in the molecular structure of the cord.

Others had different views. Page (1885) was unable to find any evidence of organic changes in many victims of railway accidents, and introduced the concept of "nervous shock" to describe symptoms resulting from a traumatic accident. He emphasized the importance of psychological factors in the development of symptoms after an accident and argued that the probability of developing manifestations of shock depended on certain characteristics of the accident. For example, railway accidents might cause severe reactions because of the fear and alarm associated with them. He did not entirely dismiss organic factors in the production of symptoms, however. Instead, he advocated dividing the cases into those that could be ascribed to organic causes and those that were not organic or were mainly psychological in nature.

The development of psychoanalytic theory and practice contributed to changing views of trauma and its effects. Charcot, Janet, and Freud elaborated the concept of traumatic neuroses with their investigations of hysteria. Janet (1893) introduced the concept of unconscious motivation in the formation of symptoms, and Freud (1920) believed that the symptoms of hysteria were due to repressed memories of traumatic events. For him, trauma was psychological in nature, and the consequences of trauma were often not evident for years. In discussing trauma, he focused on its impact on the ego. Real trauma occurred when the conflict caused by a stressor intruded on the ego (Freud, 1920).

These ideas had a profound impact on later conceptions of post-traumatic disorders. Theorists began to emphasize psychological factors in the etiology of the disorder that paralleled the physiological changes enumerated by Selye (1956) in describing the general adaptation syndrome (GAS). According to Selye, when an organism is exposed to a stressor, it responds in three consecutive phases—alarm, resistance, and exhaustion. Alarm involves a mobilization of bodily resources for resistance, which continues until the stressor is overcome. If adaptive abilities are not great enough or if the stressor is persistent enough, exhaustion is reached and damage is likely. Kamman (1951) and Kardiner and Speigel (1941) conceptualized post-traumatic stress in a similar fashion, noting that post-traumatic reactions occurred when the adaptive abilities of an organism were exceeded or depleted.

Although much was learned about post-traumatic disorders through study of victims of railway accidents, wars have provided the best opportunity to study the disorder. Physicians during the American Civil War observed post-traumatic symptoms, attributing them to mental and physical exhaustion, weak heart, or damage to nerves (Mitchell, Morehouse, & Keen, 1964). It was not until World War I, however, that traumatic neuroses were first observed in large numbers. The sudden emergence of relatively large numbers of these cases was probably due to a number of innovations. It was the first time that neurologists and psychiatrists were part of the military community, and there were extreme conditions present during that war that were not present during earlier ones. Accounts suggest that the introduction of modern weapons resulted in unprecedented and horrifying experiences. Soldiers remained at the front for long periods of time, living with the constant threat of sudden death caused by new and awesome weapons.

Often, instances of negative reactions were associated with heavy artillery bombardment, and the term "shell shock" (Mott, 1944) was coined to refer to post-trauma patients. In these cases it was often thought that the aberrant behaviors exhibited by soldiers were due to microstructural lesions in the central nervous system associated with the concussion of artillery explosions. It was only after a number of autopsies failed to find any evidence of organic changes that psychiatrists began to use psychoanalytic methods to understand the disorder (Kardiner & Speigel, 1941). Thus, explanations of war neuroses followed the same pattern as did those for "railway spine."

During World War II, the incidence of psychiatric casualties increased by over 300 percent from the previous World War figure (U.S. Army Medical Department, 1943). Soldiers suffering from psychiatric problems were thought to have battle or combat fatigue, and the symptoms were attributed to stress, fatigue, exposure to environmental conditions, and exposure to extreme danger (Craighill, 1966). Some physicians at this time used aggressive treatment strategies with these patients. For example, evacuation was avoided and cases were treated at the front. In addition, treatment included the use of sodium pentothal or hypnosis. Based on observations during this treatment, it was argued that the reactions occurred primarily in soldiers who were somehow psychologically predisposed to react poorly to stress (Kardiner & Speigel, 1941; Hurst, 1940; Lewy, 1940; Symonds, 1943).

PTSD AND VIETNAM

Psychogenic casualties were also common during the Korean War, and experiences with these victims furthered our knowledge of PTSD. By the 1950s the possibility of psychological damage as a result of warfare was more widely accepted. The symptoms of the syndrome were separated from those caused by exhaustion, and treatments were further refined. However, the Vietnam War has produced the greatest awareness of PTSD in the general public and has led to a great deal of research on its causes and ways to treat it. It has been debated whether this war had different effects on its survivors than did other conflicts on their survivors. Some have coined the term "Post-Vietnam Syndrome" (Shatan, 1973) to describe the psychiatric casaulties of this war, although others maintain that the consequences of serving in this war were no different from serving in any other war (Thienes-Hontos, Watson, & Kucala 1982; Renners, 1973; Borus, 1975; Starr, Henry, &

Bonner, 1973; Worthington, 1978). Statistics have been cited in support of both positions. Whether or not Vietnam produced more psychic trauma than did other wars, the outcomes of the "living-room war" have received greater scrutiny than have others, and it can be argued that it presented unique stressors for soldiers in combat.

On the surface, one would not be hard-put to find evidence of disturbances among Vietnam veterans. A number of problems, including exposure to herbicides such as Agent Orange, drug abuse, and the search for missing servicemen, are still aired regularly in the media some 12 years after the war. Many PTSD victims experience flashbacks, and some become involved in violent episodes during which they may harm themselves and others. These outbursts are covered by the media, often in sensational tones. In a sense, however, this may have led to the use of Vietnam as an attribution sink. News stories about erratic violence, such as mass murders, have often initially explained violence in terms of PTSD or Vietnam, only to report later that this was not the case. The dramatic nature of the Vietnam experience or our preoccupation with it may lead us to expect levels of resulting impairment that are out of line with reality.

Determining whether or not Vietnam had a disproportionate cost in terms of PTSD is complicated by a number of factors. One of the most troublesome is the question of who participated. Many believe the predispositions acquired prior to service in Vietnam are primarily responsible for difficulties experienced since then. This is reflected in the search for background characteristics that distinguish between PTSD sufferers and those not affected, or between those who served in Vietnam and those who did not.

A recent investigation (Card, 1983) showed that those involved in the military during the Vietnam era had similar family backgrounds and academic abilities to those who were not. This breadth of the veteran population was probably a result of the draft. Historical data were available for these subjects because of a study conducted on high school students in 1960 called Project TALENT (Wise, McLaughlin, & Steel, 1979). These subjects were surveyed again in 1974. Data collected at both times assessed such things as academic abilities, vocational and avocational interests, personalities, home life, and plans for the future.

Although there were no differences in the backgrounds of those who served in the military and those who did not, there were differences between them on some psychological variables. For example, those who served in the military were less able to manipulate their environment (Card, 1983). It is possible that many of those who were able to manipulate their environment effectively were able to avoid the draft.

More important, although background did not differentiate those who served in the military from those who did not, it did differentiate those who fought from those not involved in actual combat. The Army and the Marine Corps did much of the actual fighting, and the majority of these veterans came from poorer backgrounds (Card, 1983). They also showed lower than average academic ability.

In addition to questions as to whether demographic variables predict PTSD rates and whether Vietnam veterans constitute a cross section of the Vietnam-era soldiers, reports of the incidence of psychiatric casualties in the Vietnam War have also varied. During the war, reports indicated that the neuropsychiatric casualty rates were lower for the Vietnam War than for any other war in American history (Bourne, 1970). For instance, during 1965 and 1966, the number of soldiers hospitalized or relieved from duty was 12 per 1000 troops per year. The rate during the Korean War was 73 per 1000 troops per year, and during World War II the rates ranged from 28 to 101 per 1000 troops per year (Tiffany, 1967). The degree to which these data reflect the actual extent of distress during service in Vietnam has been questioned. However, they reveal that, at least during the early part of the war, apparent psychic costs were low.

A number of factors have been proposed as possible causes of these low rates. The 12-month rotation policy, which ensured a set, predictable period of service in Vietnam, and the nature of combat—which was often brief and allowed more time for rest—have been credited with improving morale and coping abilities (Tiffany, 1967). (However, these same factors have also been used as explanations of why reporting of PTSD symptoms has been high since the war, as discussed in the following section.) Alternatively, low reporting rates during the war may have been due to superior training or the improved capability of combat psychiatric facilities (Bourne, 1970).

These factors may well have increased soldiers' ability to withstand the threats associated with combat and thus reduced psychiatric casualties. However, it is also possible that widespread use of drugs during the Vietnam War reduced reporting by masking symptoms (Figley, 1978a). If soldiers were self-medicating to help them cope, it is possible that problems would not be reported until use of drugs ceased. For many, drug use did not cease until they returned home.

After the war ended, many mental health professionals began reporting a significant number of problems among Vietnam veterans. Some argued that the unique nature of the war was responsible for the increasing incidence of problems among Vietnam War veterans (Wilson, 1980; Figley, 1978a). Others contended that the problems seen in Vietnam War veterans were no different from those seen following other wars. Thienes-Hontos et al. (1982) compared the admission rates in the psychiatric division in ten Veterans Administration (VA) hospitals 9 to 36 months after soldiers returned from Vietnam with the rates of psychiatric admissions 7 to 36 months after Korean War veterans returned home. They examined psychiatric records for symptoms and rates of admission due to PTSD, and reported that the two groups exhibited the same number of symptoms and were comparable on the number of patients who qualified for diagnosis of PTSD. Their conclusion was that PTSD was not unique to Vietnam veterans, nor was it more common among them.

These findings suggest that PTSD is not unique to Vietnam, but they are open to a number of interpretations. Carroll (1983), for example, has argued that the exclusive focus on hospitalized patients is unfortunate because it does not adequately reflect all the veterans suffering difficulties. Because many Vietnam-era veterans feel disenfranchised and tend to shun VA programs, they may be underrepresented in the sample studied by Thienes-Hontos et al. (1982).

To some extent, differences in other reports of psychiatric casualty rates may also be attributable to methodological inconsistencies. The selection of appropriate control groups for studying Vietnam combat veterans has proven difficult. Whether investigators have or have not found unusual levels of psychological problems among Vietnam veterans has depended in part on the samples that they have chosen to study.

If one considers sampling methods, it becomes clearer why different findings may have been reported. For example, Carr (1973) compared veterans and nonveterans in terms of self-concept and perceptions of control, and found no differences on either of these two variables. However, his college sample of veterans may be a biased sample because many veterans did not attend college. In addition, there was no indication of controls for level of combat, and the veteran group was not separated into Vietnam-era veterans and veterans who had actually served in Vietnam. Borus (1975) is frequently cited in support of the hypothesis that the consequences of being in Vietnam are not long-lasting, based on a study of Vietnam veterans for evidence of disciplinary-legal problems and emotional problems 11 months after their return to the United States. He found no differences between Vietnam veterans and nonveterans. However, all of his subjects were still in the military when he collected his data. Figley (1978a) suggests that one of the reasons for these results is that release from the military was dependent on passing a variety of psychological as well as medical tests. Release from the service would be delayed until it was clear that the veteran had no need for treatment. Thus, it is possible that veterans might make certain not to report things that would delay their discharge.

Whatever the final outcome of the debate concerning psychiatric casualties may be, a number of interesting figures remain. Over nine million Americans served in the armed services during the Vietnam era. Of these, approximately four million were stationed somewhere in Indochina (Resing, 1982). Approximately 57,002 were killed in Vietnam and 303,704 more were wounded (Walker, 1981). Vietnam-era veterans exhibit a suicide rate that is 23 percent greater than non-Vietnam veterans (U.S. House of Representatives Committee on Veteran Affairs, 1979), and some authorities estimate that as many as 1.5 million veterans may be suffering from the consequences of the war (Figley, 1978a). If one also considers family members indirectly affected by the war, its impact becomes even greater.

Sources of Post-Traumatic Distress in Vietnam Veterans

Many researchers have concluded that the Vietnam War was distinct from other American wars in a number of ways, and that these unusual characteristics were in part responsible for the variety of problems that it caused. At least six major characteristics of the war that set it apart from other wars have been proposed (Figley, 1978a; Wilson, 1980). The first relates to the rotation policies that were instituted during Vietnam. After training, troops were transported separately to Vietnam, rotated frequently during their tour of duty, and given a finite term of service. Intended to reduce distress, this policy may in fact have increased it. A tour of duty was only one year, and an individual soldier's goals may have been survival for that year, rather than victory. This could have worked against group cohesiveness and identification, the development of social support, and ultimately against morale. In addition, the war was very controversial and there was no real sense of support from home. Therefore, many of the soldiers may have felt a sense of purposelessness and social isolation. When they returned home, they were often greeted with antagonism.

A third factor is that the war was longer than the Korean conflict or American involvement in the two world wars, and it was a guerilla war in which the enemy was an indigenous group, often difficult to find or distinguish from allies and civilians. There were no front lines as in previous conflicts, and the war did not advance geographically as others had. Territory was often captured just to be given up and then recaptured again. The geographical conditions made it difficult to find the enemy, and enemy attacks were highly unpredictable. Fourth the drug and alcohol problems during this war also appear to have been different from any other. The widespread substance abuse may have masked many of the symptoms, which might have improved more quickly if they had been treated immediately. Fifth, the transition between military and civilian life was frequently abrupt and allowed little time for preparation. Soldiers could find themselves fighting one day and home in the same clothes two days later (Wilson, 1980).

Finally, reports of witnessing atrocities or of participating in them were common during this war (Wilson, 1980). Cases of rape and mutilation were reported, and soldiers were sometimes required to shoot children, women, or old men. These types of killings were often repugnant and engendered more horror. Mutilations of American soldiers by the Vietcong were also reported. Veterans have recounted tales of seeing American servicemen with their genitals cut off and stuffed in their mouths. Experiences like these have probably contributed to emotional problems following the war, because these types of episodes are not forgotten. Often, terrifying scenes are relived through nightmares and flashbacks. One soldier, obsessed by visions of death, wrote poems such as the following in an attempt to purge the scenes from his memory (Hendin & Haas, 1984):

Bodies entangled in "heaps"
   Children—"Crispy crittered"
   Mutilated
   Dead

Women; young and beautiful
Old and precious—for their giving
   how cold
   broken
   fly-covered

Even dead men
   Ours and theirs—reside inside,
   rotting in my
   head.

These factors may have combined to reduce servicemen's ability to cope with the unique stressors in Vietnam, as well as those more generally associated with combat. Research suggests that combat veterans can and usually do adjust following military service (e.g.,

Holloway & Ursano, 1984). However, the loss of social supports, perceived control, and purpose that many reported in the Vietnam War may have made adjustment more difficult. The fact that soldiers in Vietnam were younger than United States soldiers in previous wars may have compounded this problem (Egendorf, Kadushin, Laufer, Rothbart, & Sloan, 1981). The typical serviceman in Vietnam was 19 years old, and interruption of identity formation processes at this age may cause emotional problems later in life (Erikson, 1968).

Consequences of Service in Vietnam

Despite differences in reports of relative incidence of PTSD following Vietnam, a number of symptoms and problems characterizing veterans have been identified. Differences in educational achievement after serving have been found (e.g., Card, 1983); Rothbart and Sloan (1981) reported that nonveterans were generally better educated and that more of them had earned college degrees. These educational differences may have affected the employment and wage-earning potential of veterans. Yankelovich (1974) noted that there was more unemployment among Vietnam veterans, and, similarly, Card (1983) found that more veterans than nonveterans had experienced at least one episode of unemployment. Card also found that the jobs held by veterans tended to be of lower prestige. Bordieri and Drehmer (in press) have reported that Vietnam veterans suffer discrimination in job seeking. Although the occupational achievements of veterans tended to be lower, veterans were reported to have earned higher mean wages in 1977 (Rothbart & Sloan, 1981). Card (1983) reported related results, finding that when Vietnam veterans first began earning money, they typically earned more than nonveterans. However, their wage changes tended to flatten out over the years, whereas nonveterans' wages continued to climb so that they surpassed the earnings of the veterans.

Another area where involvement in the war tended to have an impact was in the social experience of the veterans. One common symptom of PTSD is a decreased interest in interpersonal relationships. A number of studies have reported that Vietnam veterans experienced greater difficulty with intimate relationships (DeFazio, Rustin, & Diamond, 1975; Roberts et al., 1982; Penk et al., 1981). Others have noted that veterans more often reported having problems with alienation (Laufer et al., 1981). Penk et al. (1981) reported that experience in heavy combat was associated with more problems in getting along and also with more family problems. Card (1983) noted significant differences in marital problems between nonveterans and veterans in the first year following discharge from the armed services. She found that during this year, there was a 5 percent divorce rate among veterans but that the overall rate averaged less than 1 percent. However, by the time her subjects were 36, one-fourth of them were divorced, regardless of their previous military status.

These interpersonal problems could be aggravating the stress experienced by the veterans or could be products of this syndrome. Kadushin, Boulanger, and Martin (1981) found that veterans with positive social support systems were better off, suggesting that with high levels of social support it takes more stress for the negative consequences of stress to become apparent. It is difficult to know, however, whether veterans with more problems alienate their friends and relatives and hence have less social support, or whether the lack of social support produces more problems.

Certain behavioral manifestations of stress have also been noted among Vietnam veterans. Some veterans seem to have difficulty with authority. They are more often arrested (Yager, Laufer, & Gallops, 1984; Laufer et al., 1981) and have a higher conviction rate (Card, 1983). Veterans also appear to have more difficulty with substance abuse. Combat exposure is related to self-reported drug use (Laufer et al., 1981). In whites, heavy exposure to combat was associated with more drinking problems, whereas among blacks, exposure to combat was associated with use of drugs. Card (1983) reported that the use of drugs and alcohol was greater for veterans while they were in the service than for nonveterans, but 10 years later the rates of drug use for veterans and nonveterans were the same.

Another behavioral manifestation of PTSD often reported by researchers is sleep disturbances. Vietnam veterans more often report problems with sleep (Card, 1983; DeFazio et al., 1975; Goodwin 1980). One of the reasons for the disturbed sleep is that veterans suffering from PTSD have nightmares of troubling Vietnam experiences. One soldier reported a recurrent dream of a severed head. The head was very large and was always screaming. This veteran reported the deaths that he witnessed in Vietnam were largely because of head injuries. He was a helicopter pilot and, on one particular night when he landed, a severed head was lying right outside his door. The mouth, he reported, was open as if the man had been screaming when he died. He also saw several people beheaded by a helicopter's rotor blade, and he saw a soldier blow his head off with a rocket. Therefore, it is not surprising that bodies and heads were a recurrent theme in his dreams.

A number of self-reported symptoms of emotional distress seem to be more common among Vietnam veterans than among other groups.

Depression is one of the most common symptoms reported by veterans (Card, 1983; Strayer & Ellenhorn, 1975; Helzer, Robins, & Davis, 1973; Nace, Meyers, O'Brien, Ream, & Mintz, 1977; DeFazio et al., 1975; Fairbank, Keane, & Malloy, 1983; Blanchard, Kolb, Pallmeyer, & Gerardi, 1981). Veterans also report more feelings of guilt (Lifton, 1973; Strayer & Ellenhorn, 1975), anxiety (Card, 1983; Fairbank et al., 1983; Malloy, Fairbank, & Keane, 1983), and more physical symptoms in general (Card, 1983).

Finally, researchers have noted differences between physiological responses of Vietnam veterans who are experiencing problems and other groups of people. For example, Malloy et al. (1983) used a 2 × 3 design in order to examine the physiological responses of veterans. They assessed three groups of veterans; one group consisted of veterans who were diagnosed as having PTSD, another was composed of seemingly well-adjusted Vietnam War veterans, and the third group consisted of psychiatric patients with diagnoses other than PTSD and who had never been assigned to combat. Each group had physiological measurements taken under the neutral condition of watching a film of a family, as well as while watching combat scenes. The investigators reported greater heart rate changes to the combat situation for the PTSD group only. Blanchard et al. (1981) exposed a group of nonveteran controls to combat sounds and mental arithmetic tasks. They found that heart rate increased for both groups during the mental arithmetic task, but changed only for the PTSD group during the combat sounds.

These findings suggest that veterans suffering from PTSD may be experiencing a conditioned emotional response. That is, the sympathetic nervous system may have become programmed to respond more vigorously under conditions of external threat or to symbolic representations of trauma (Holloway & Ursano, 1984). In order to test the hypothesis that physiological changes were due to sympathetic discharge, Kolb, Burris, and Griffiths (1984) administered either propranolol or clonidine to a group of PTSD patients. Propranolol blocks receptors for adrenal hormones in the sympathetic nervous system and clonidine blocks similar receptors in brain areas where the most norepinephrine is found. Both reduce sympathetic arousal. Subjects were followed on these medications for six months. Results indicated that the patients' symptoms improved following treatment, suggesting that blocking the effects of SNS response to challenge or trauma-related stimuli helps to reduce overall symptomatology.

Some researchers have reported positive aspects of having served in the Vietnam War. The veterans that Card (1983) studied reported that their military experience was more positive than negative. Others have reported that veterans felt that serving in the war helped them to mature (Laufer et al., 1981). Most evidence, however, suggests that the negative consequences outweighed the good. Another cautionary note should be added, however. LaGuardia, Smith, Francois, and Bachman (1983) have noted that a bias may be introduced by the experimenters investigating these issues. Some researchers may expect to find emotionally scarred individuals, may be predisposed to interpret data as evidence of pathology, and may only ask questions that address pathology. LaGuardia et al. argue that if experimenters expect Vietnam veterans to be well-adjusted, subjects will respond in that way. Likewise, if the experimenter leads the veterans to believe that they should be poorly adjusted, they may respond in that way. Their findings indicated that such priming did make a difference under certain circumstances, particularly when veterans were asked to rate themselves.

In summary, research on Vietnam veterans is neither complete nor definitive. It is not yet possible to determine whether Vietnam was responsible for more or less adjustment difficulty than other wars. It is fairly clear, however, that some veterans of this war suffered prolonged consequences of their service experiences. These have included states such as social alienation, sleep disturbance, hyperresponsiveness, and emotional distress. In addition, specific characteristics of the Vietnam War have been identified that may have contributed to post-traumatic stress.

ETIOLOGY OF PTSD

As a result of these studies on Vietnam veterans, we have advanced our knowledge of post-traumatic stress states. With a better understanding of the principal signs and symptoms of these disorders, researchers have been able to propose theories of the etiology of the syndrome. There are four major factors that are thought to influence the development of post-traumatic stress disorder (Keane & Fairbank, 1983). One relates to premorbid factors. Certain characteristics that exist in a person prior to a trauma can make him or her more susceptible to post-trauma pathology. Such things as a childhood trauma, abnormal adolescent development, or preexisting personality disorder could make an individual more susceptible to developing PTSD. Hendin and Haas (1984) emphasize the importance of premorbid factors in the development of postcombat problems. They feel that precombat and combat factors interact to give meaning to specific combat experiences. Only when both time periods are adequately explored can problems be resolved.

The second factor that might be involved in the development of the syndrome is changes in physiological systems as a result of exposure to a stressor. At least two hypotheses regarding PTSD are pertinent. One suggests that people who are primarily sympathetic reactors are more likely to develop the disorder. According to de la Pena (1984), individuals suffering from PTSD report feeling better when they are on stimulants and appear to be better able to tolerate arousal-producing conditions such as combat. When these veterans returned home, however, they were unable to tolerate the relatively low levels of stimulation that now dominated their lives. Some of their symptoms may have resulted from central nervous system attempts to increase stimulation.

Another physiological explanation has been suggested by van der Kolk, Boyd, Krystal, and Greenburg (1984). These investigators compared PTSD to the animal model of inescapable shock. Inescapable shock increases norepinephrine turnover, plasma catecholamine levels, and MHPG production (Anisman, Ritch, & Sklar, 1981). Stress-induced analgesia also occurs after exposure to inescapable shock due to activation of the endogenous opioid system (Maier, Davies, & Grau, 1980). This stress-induced analgesia can be conditioned. Thus, veterans with PTSD may respond to trauma and the reexperiencing of that trauma with increased secretion of endogenous opiates. Following exposure or reexposure to the traumatic event, symptoms of opiate withdrawal can occur. Many of the symptoms of opiate withdrawal are similar to symptoms of PTSD, and the symptoms of PTSD might well be due to the withdrawal of opioids from the system.

A third factor in development of the disorder involves characteristics of the event. A number of characteristics of stressful events have been linked to traumatic pathology, including threat to life, bereavement, loss, and exposure to the grotesque (Gleser, Green, & Winget, 1981). Boulanger and Smith (1980) and Wilson and Krauss (1982) identified characteristics specific to Vietnam that made the experience more stressful. One such characteristic was the degree of participation in high-risk combat. Experiences such as seeing friends killed, participating in mutilations or atrocities, and participating in body counts may have added to stress levels.

Social support is the fourth factor thought to play a role in the development of the disorder. As has been noted, social support can buffer stress, but conditions may reduce its availability. Support systems are thought to have been influential during combat as well as at home (Figley & Leventman, 1980; Lindy, Grace, & Green, 1984). As discussed earlier, one response to chronic or severe stress is withdrawal, and social relationships often suffer. In Vietnam, this may have been exacerbated by rotation policies that reduced feelings of cohesion and establishment of group goals as superordinate ones. The result may have been a vicious cycle wherein low support levels led to increased stress and in turn were lowered further by that stress.

Holloway and Ursano (1984) have suggested several other factors in the development of PTSD, which relate to memory, social context, and metaphor. Memories are modified by subsequent experience, and what is remembered about what actually happened in a war experience will be influenced by available information, the combat community, reactions at home, and the development of each individual. The war experience might later be used to represent current troubling life experience, and the focus of the veteran's memory in the future is dependent on his present circumstances. Post-traumatic reexperiencing of the initiating trauma may be an expression of current difficulties.

Examining the signs and symptoms of PTSD in war veterans is useful in gaining a better understanding of the consequences of exposure to a variety of stressors. However, research on post-traumatic stress is not restricted to military settings. The syndrome also occurs following civilian trauma, but such traumas usually do not affect the large numbers of people that wars do. Further, the intensity of trauma experienced during war is often greater than that associated with civilian accidents. It has been noted that not everyone who undergoes a stressful experience will develop a full-blown case of PTSD. This is true of both civilian and military stressors. Further, some of the symptoms that have been linked to PTSD are common to a more general stress response. If mental disorders and healthy functioning are viewed as being polar opposites on a continuum, then a wide variety of normal and abnormal responses can be imagined. Hence, fully understanding PTSD, which is toward one end of the continuum, will make the range between it and normal functioning less difficult to comprehend. To some extent, PTSD may be thought of as a constellation of common stress symptoms, defined more by their temporal characteristics than by their uniqueness.

PTSD AND CIVILIAN EMERGENCIES

The emotional consequences of natural disasters, such as tornadoes, storms, or earthquakes, may not be as chronic as those caused by human-made disasters like war (Baum, Fleming, & Davidson, 1983). This is suggested in the DSM-III description of post-traumatic stress disorders and follows from several studies of these events (e.g., Gleser et al., 1981). However, a number of psychological symptoms have been documented following natural disasters which are similar to the symptoms that occur following war stress.

For example, many researchers have found increased negative emotional responses such as depression for up to a year following disasters. Moore (1958) and Penick, Powell, and Sick (1976) found higher levels of depression as much as a year following tornadoes, and similar psychological problems have also been documented after cyclones and floods. Cyclone Tracy, which struck Darwin, Australia, in 1974, was studied in part because of its great destructive power. Over 500 people were injured and 50 people were killed; in addition, most of the homes were destroyed and over 80 percent of the population had to be evacuated. Although Milne (1977) found that only 10 percent of the people he surveyed had emotional problems 10 months after the accident, Parker (1977) found more persistent problems 14 months later in a small sample of people, all of whom had lost their homes in the cyclone. Emotional problems were evident in 72 percent of this group—far more profound effects than in a group of randomly chosen victims who had been less severely affected. Bennet (1970) found similar results among flood victims in England, 32 percent of whom developed symptoms in the year following the disaster.

Fires have been studied as acute stressors, and results suggest that victims often develop psychological problems. Adler (1943) studied the survivors of the Cocoanut Grove fire, a nightclub fire in which almost 500 people were killed. Eleven months following the incident, Adler documented nervousness and anxiety in over one-third of the survivors. These symptoms were greater for those who had been conscious throughout the fire than for those who passed out and were rescued. In a more recent nightclub fire at the Beverly Hills Supper Club, Green (1980) documented emotional problems in 33 percent of the survivors. These problems persisted for at least 15 months following the disaster. Experiences such as handling dead bodies put survivors at a greater risk for developing symptoms of psychological distress.

One of the most widely studied disasters was the dam collapse and flood at Buffalo Creek, West Virginia. The disaster occurred when a slag dam collapsed, and it created a nonfunctional and disordered environment that was probably responsible for some of the long-term effects caused by this disaster. Two years after the event, researchers found evidence of anxiety, depression (Titchner & Kapp, 1976; Gleser et al., 1978, 1981), hostility (Gleser et al., 1981) and sleep disturbances (Gleser et al., 1981) among survivors.

Three Mile Island

Researchers have also noted stresslike symptoms of accidents involving hazardous or toxic substances. The accident at Three Mile Island (TMI) in 1979 and the subsequent cleanup activities there involved the actual or implied release of radiation and threatened the possibility of more. Research has shown that the accident itself was associated with distress (e.g., Dohrenwend, Dohrenwend, Kasl, & Warheit, 1979; Flynn, 1979) and that some problems lingered throughout the year following the accident (Bromet, 1980; Houts & Goldhaber, 1981).

Our research at TMI has suggested that stress persisted among people living near the reactor as much as 28 months after the accident (Davidson, Fleming, & Baum, 1984). Many of the problems that we found are similar to symptoms of post-traumatic stress disorder. Although none of our residents experienced the gross psychopathologies sometimes seen in soldiers following a war, some seem to be exhibiting mild forms of many of the same problems.

In this research, subjects living within five miles of the damaged reactor at TMI were compared with three different control samples, all drawn in a quasi-random fashion. One control group was drawn from a comparable area 80 miles from TMI, and its members lived at least five miles from any type of power plant.

Results indicated that people living near TMI reported experiencing more anxiety, depression, concentration problems, physical symptoms, and alienation than did control subjects. Reported problems with alienation suggested that TMI area residents might be having more interpersonal problems, and their self-reports confirmed these interpersonal problems. Low levels of social support were associated with persistent stress among TMI area residents (Fleming, Baum, Gisriel, & Gatchel, 1982), but social support mediated only certain aspects of the stress response. Higher levels of social support were associated with fewer behavioral and psychological symptoms of stress. However, social support had no influence on arousal reflected in levels of adrenal hormones or on reporting of bothersome physical symptoms such as headaches, backaches, and nausea. This could have been due to the persistence of sources of stress at TMI. The benefits of having social support may be sufficient to reduce or eliminate consequences of stress and costs of coping, but not be enough to eliminate threat and arousal related to the stressor itself. When a stressor persists, social support may not affect whether stress is experienced but may reduce the consequences of the experience.

Subjects living near TMI also reported more sleep disturbances; they had longer sleep latencies and more night wakings (Fleming & Baum, 1983). They also reported sleeping less and feeling less rested after waking. These subjects responded to a number of questions in a way that suggested that the crippled reactor still troubled them. Many of them perceived the plant as a threat, feared further radiation exposure, and were worried about possible effects of radiation on their health and on their family's health. Finally, physiological measures showed significant differences between the groups. TMI area residents had higher urinary levels of both epinephrine and norepinephrine than all the control groups. These data suggest the hyperarousability that often accompanies PTSD.

These continuing symptoms of stress were similar to those observed among the same TMI area residents 6 and 11 months earlier. They are also similar to those associated with PTSD. As stated earlier, the intensity of stress did not appear to be great, and the intensity of PTSD-like symptoms was mild. On the other hand, the symptoms were persistent, continuing long after the accident, and they can be traced to conditions similar to those that appear to cause PTSD.

More recently we have assessed the incidence of specific symptoms of post-traumatic stress in the TMI sample. Emphasis was placed on the relationship of symptoms listed among the DSM-III criteria for PTSD and more general indicators of stress. Symptoms of PTSD were assessed by the Impact of Events Scale (IES; Horowitz et al., 1979) as well as part of the Horowitz Interpersonal Problems Scale. The IES contains two subscales: a measure of avoidance of social contact and one of frequency and nature of intrusive thoughts—two dimensions that parallel DSM-III characteristics of PTSD. The Interpersonal Problems Scale also has been found to distinguish PTSD populations from other groups, specifically on items dealing with intimacy and sociability. Other self-report measures of stress that we used included the SCL-90, which provides a global self-report measure of distress as well as individual scores on a variety of specific symptom clusters such as depression and anxiety. Our physiological indicators of arousal and stress included heart rate, systolic and diastolic blood pressure, and urinary norepinephrine, epinephrine, and cortisol.

Median splits were performed on the avoidance and intrusion subscales of the IES in order to divide the TMI group into two groups: those with a number of symptoms common to PTSD and those with few. Analyses of variance were then performed using self-report and physiological measures of stress as dependent variables. Results indicated that subjects experiencing more intrusive thoughts also reported more bothersome symptoms in general as well as more somatic complaints, problems with concentration and interpersonal relations, depression, anxiety, anger, fear, and alienation. Intrusive thoughts were also associated with stress-related physiological arousal. Subjects reporting more intrusive thoughts had higher resting levels of systolic blood pressure as well as higher baseline levels of norepinephrine and cortisol. A similar pattern of results was also apparent for subjects experiencing more avoidance symptoms as well as interpersonal problems. These results indicate that subjects at TMI displaying symptoms of PTSD were also experiencing symptoms of a more general stress syndrome. Although no gross psychopathologies were evident in our sample, the defining characteristics of PTSD were present.

POLICY IMPLICATIONS

There is evidence that persistent stress-related symptoms can follow trauma, whether of military or civilian origin. We have not considered in this chapter the issue of acute, chronic, or delayed onset of PTSD, partly because of a lack of widely held explanations for this time factor. We have also not considered a wide range of other experiences that may give rise to similar problems, including victimization by a number of horrors. Regardless, chronic effects do appear in varying levels of severity for some victims of trauma. As a research issue, then, PTSD is important as an integrated syndrome associated with chronic stress or trauma, which may help us to understand response to other stressors. As a treatment issue, it provides a model for learning where and how various kinds of interventions may be best applied in protracted stress situations. These issues are being explored. However, policy implications of this syndrome have received less attention. Its very existence calls attention to neglected aspects of public policy and encourages a psychosocial perspective in approaching many public health problems.

At a basic level, the existence of this post-traumatic stress syndrome suggests a cost of war or disaster that is often overlooked. Societal planning for these events typically focuses on factors that assure success in the short run. Wars are to be won, and effort is channeled into assuring this by producing needed material and keeping soldiers in action. The wounded are treated and, if possible, sent back into combat, just as postdisaster efforts are directed toward rebuilding and regaining a sense of normalcy. Long-range psychological consequences of trauma rarely receive much attention. Whether they could be prevented if more attention were paid to them is debatable. Treatment of individual cases of PTSD and their associated long-term consequences has become a major issue. Yet, as a society, we have given little emphasis to those consequences.

The costs to society posed by PTSD are potentially formidable. Mental health services alone are costly, and much of the treatment of PTSD victims is at public expense. The associated drug and alcohol abuse also strains the system and engenders social and financial costs. Physical health may also suffer as part of this syndrome, and these costs are likely to be borne by society. Finally, the occasional outbursts of violence that have been linked to PTSD, together with the alienation and lack of involvement it engenders, represent other costs that are not ordinarily considered.

These kinds of long-term costs do not seem to be a central concern of those who make decisions about potentially traumatic events. There are general expectations that young men who go off to war will be changed by that experience, but the vast potential for long-term negative consequences of these experiences appears to have been underestimated. Current interest in psychological preparation of soldiers for combat reflects growing concern about these problems, but it is important that such costs be considered more prominently ahead of time in shaping public policy.

The reluctance to consider psychological factors in estimating costs of trauma or determining the impact of potentially traumatic events is exemplified in the recent controversy about restarting the undamaged nuclear reactor at TMI. At the time of the accident, the other reactor was off-line for maintenance. Though it did not experience any damage, it was not restarted after the accident. Plans for this restart led a citizens' group to petition the courts to require that psychological responses to possible restart be considered in the impact statement for such action. One court decision (People Against Nuclear Energy v. United States Nuclear Regulatory Commission, 1981) found for the plaintiff, ordering that psychological problems that might be caused by a restart be considered. A Supreme Court ruling (Metropolitan Edison Company et al., petitioners, v. People Against Nuclear Energy et al., 1983) overturned this decision, however, noting that the law allows only for consideration of impacts on physical health.

Though in some ways this account is an oversimplification of the legal processes that led to this decision, it points out another important aspect of post-traumatic stress. Though it is a psychiatric category, PTSD includes a composite of psychological and biological changes and is a condition that can predispose a person toward physical health problems. Stress can lead to illness by altering behavior so that it is no longer health inducing (e.g., reducing motivation to maintain good health, increasing drug and alcohol abuse), or by producing physiological changes that facilitate the development of heart disease, hypertension, atherosclerosis, and other serious illnesses (e.g., Hauss, 1973; Krantz, Glass, Contrada, & Miller, 1980; Schneiderman, 1983; Selye, 1976). Because these deleterious effects of stress often do not coincide in time with the stressor, they are frequently neglected and not linked to events that may have contributed to them.

All of this suggests that formulations of costs of war of impacts of accidents and disasters leave as unknown their long-term psychophysiological effects. One can see immediately the direct physical costs of war or disaster in number of dead or lost, and so on. The dead are buried, the wounded are treated, and the damage is restored. But it is more difficult to determine long-term costs for these events. Partly for this reason, current perspectives emphasize reaction to, rather than prevention of, these costs. Medical treatment is more oriented to treatment of symptoms than prevention of them, and, as a result, victims may not receive any attention until symptoms are detected. More attention to these problems at the outset is needed in order to help prevent debilitating chronic stress and associated societal costs.

Another aspect of this syndrome that has important implications is the social nature of some of its causes and symptoms. Social support has been of central concern to researchers interested in health for many years, but has only recently found new attention in basic psychological research. However, it has proven to be an elusive phenomenon, producing a number of inconsistent effects as well as clear and explainable findings. Few doubt that social relationships can have beneficial effects when people must deal with stress, but the nature and strength of these effects are topics of debate. Accounts of post-traumatic stress, however, provide a powerful instance of the importance and influence of social variables in resisting stress. As one leafs through reports on combat experiences, disasters, traumas associated with rape and witnessing homicides, and emergency rescue worker experience, social support emerges as a consistent and crucial theme. The effect of these traumas cannot be denied, and the role of friends, family, medical personnel, and therapists in providing a social environment in which individuals can regain a sense of normalcy cannot be underestimated. These relationships, mechanisms, and benefits need further research, but they should be increasingly factored into decision making and planning about traumatic events and emergencies.

REFERENCES

Adler, A. (1943). Neuropsychiatric complications in victims of Boston's Cocoanut Grove disaster. *Journal of the American Medical Association, 123,* 1098-1111.

American Psychiatric Association. (1980). *Diagnostic and statistical manual of mental disorders* (3rd ed.) (DSM-III). Washington, DC: Author.

Anisman, H. L., Ritch, M., & Sklar, L. S. (1981). Noradrenergic and dopaminergic interactions in escape behavior: Analysis of uncontrollable stress effect. *Psychopharmacological Bulletin, 74,* 263-268.

Bassett, J. A., & Llewellyn, L. J. (1915). *Malingering or the simulation of disease.* London: William Henemann.

Baum, A., Fleming, R., & Davidson, L. M. (1983). Natural disaster and technological catastrophe. *Environment and Behavior, 15,* 333-354.

Bennet, G. (1970). Bristol floods, 1968: Controlled survey of effects on health of local community disaster. *British Medical Journal, 3,* 454-458.

Blanchard, E. B., Kolb, L. C., Pallmeyer, T. P., & Gerardi, R. J. (1981). Psychophysiological study of post-traumatic stress disorders in Vietnam veterans. *Psychiatric Quarterly, 54,* 220-227.

Bordieri, J. E., & Drehmer, D. E. (in press). Vietnam veterans: Fighting the employment war. *Journal of Applied Social Psychology.*

Borus, J. F. (1975). The re-entry transition of Vietnam veterans. *Armed Forces and Society, 2,* 97-114.

Borus, J. F. (1977). Incidence of maladjustment in Vietnam returnees. *Archives of General Psychiatry, 30,* 554-557.

Boulanger, G., & Smith, J. R. (1980). Traumatic stress reaction scale.

Bourne, P. G. (1970). Military psychiatry and the Vietnam experience. *American Journal of Psychiatry, 127,* 481-488.

Bromet, E. (1980). *Three Mile Island: Mental health findings.* Pittsburgh: Western Psychiatric Institute and Clinic and University of Pittsburgh.

Card, J. A. (1983). *Lives after Vietnam.* Washington, DC: Heath.

Carr, R. A. (1973). *Comparison of self-concept and expectations concerning control between Vietnam-era veterans and nonveterans.* Unpublished doctoral dissertation, St. Louis University.

Carroll, E. (1983). Stress-disorder symptoms in Vietnam and Korean war veterans: A commentary on Thienes-Hontos, Watson, and Kucala. *Journal of Consulting and Clinical Psychology, 51,* 616-618.

Craighill, M. D. (1966). In R. S. Anderson, A. J. Glass, & R. J. Berinucci (Eds.), *Neuropsychiatry in World War II* (Vol. 1). Washington, DC: Government Printing Office.

Davidson, L. M., Baum, A., & Collins, D. L. (1982). Stress and control-related problems at Three Mile Island. *Journal of Applied Social Psychology, 12,* 349-359.

Davidson, L. M., Fleming, I., & Baum, A. (1984, August). *Chronic stress and Three Mile Island: The role of toxic exposure and uncertainty.* Paper presented at the meeting of the American Psychological Association, Toronto, Canada.

DeFazio, V. J., Rustin, S., & Diamond, A. (1975). Symptom development in Vietnam era veterans. *American Journal of Orthopsychiatry, 45,* 258-263.

de la Pena, A. (1984). Post-traumatic stress disorder in the Vietnam veteran: A brain-modulated compensatory information-augmenting response to information underload in the central nervous system? In B. A. van der Kolk (Ed.), *Post-traumatic stress disorder: Psychological and biological sequelae* (pp. 108-122). Washington, DC: American Psychiatric Press.

Dohrenwend, B. P., Dohrenwend, B. S., Kasl, S. V., & Warheit, G. J. (October, 1979). *Report of the task group on behavioral effects to the president's commission on the accident at Three Mile Island.* Washington, DC: U.S. Nuclear Regulatory Commission.

Egendorf, A., Kadushin, C., Laufer, R., Rothbart, G., & Sloan, L. (1981). Summary of findings. In *Legacies of Vietnam: Comparative adjustment of veterans and their peers* (Vol. 2). Washington, DC: Government Printing Office.

Erichsen, J. E. (1882). *On concussion of the spine: Nervous shock and other obscure injuries of the nervous system in their clinical and medico-legal aspect*. London: Longmans, Green & Company.

Erikson, E. H. (1968). *Identity, youth and crisis*. New York: Norton.

Fairbank, J. A., Keane, T. M., & Malloy, P. F. (1983). Some preliminary data on the psychological characteristics of Vietnam veterans with post-traumatic stress disorders. *Journal of Consulting and Clinical Psychology, 51,* 912-919.

Figley, C. R. (1978a). Psychosocial adjustment among Vietnam veterans: An overview of the research. In C. R. Figley (Ed.), *Stress disorders among Vietnam veterans* (pp. 57-70). New York: Brunner/Mazel.

Figley, C. R. (1978b). Symptoms of delayed combat stress among a college sample of Vietnam veterans. *Military Medicine, 143,* 107-110.

Figley, C., & Leventman, S. A. (1980). *Strangers at home: Vietnam veterans since the war*. New York: Praeger.

Fleming, R., & Baum, A. (1983). *Sleep disturbance at the Three Mile Island Nuclear Power Station*. Unpublished manuscript, Uniformed Services University of the Health Sciences, Bethesda.

Fleming R., Baum, A., Gisriel, M. M., & Gatchel, R. J. (1982). Mediating influences of social support on stress. *Journal of Human Stress, 8,* 14-22.

Flynn, C. B. (1979). *Three Mile Island telephone survey,* (NUREG/CR—1093). Washington, DC: U. S. Nuclear Regulatory Commission.

Freud, S. (1920). *Selected papers on hysteria* (Nervous and Mental Diseases Monograph Series, No. 4).

Gleser, G. C., Green, B. L., & Winget, C. W. (1981). *Prolonged psychosocial effects of disaster: A study of Buffalo Creek*. New York: Academic Press.

Gleser, G. C., Green, B. L., & Winget, C. W. (1978). Quantifying interview data on psychic impairment of disaster survivors. *Journal of Nervous and Mental Disease, 166,* 209-216.

Goodwin, J. (1980). The etiology of combat-related posttraumatic stress disorders. In T. Williams (Ed.), *Posttraumatic stress disorders of the Vietnam veteran: Observations and recommendations for the psychological treatment of the veteran and his family* (pp. 1-23). Cincinnati: Disabled American Veterans.

Green, B. L. (1980). *Prediction of long-term psychosocial functioning following the Beverly Hills fire*. Unpublished doctoral dissertation, University of Cincinnati.

Hauss, W. H. (1973). Tissue alterations due to experimental arteriosclerosis. In H. G. Vogel (Ed.), *Connective tissue and aging* (Int. Cong. Ser. No. 264, pp. 23-33). Amsterdam: Excerpta Medica.

Helzer, J., Robins, L., & Davis, D. (1973). *Depressive disorders in Vietnam returnees*. Unpublished manuscript.

Hendin, H., & Haas, A. P. (1984). *Wounds of war: The psychological aftermath of combat in Vietnam*. New York: Basic Books.

Holloway, H. C., & Ursano, R. J. (1984). The Vietnam veteran: Memory, social context, and metaphor. *Psychiatry, 47,* 103-108.

Horowitz, M., Wilner, N., & Alvarez, W. (1979). Impact of Event Scale: A measure of subjective stress. *Psychosomatic Medicine, 41,* 209-218.

Houts, P., & Goldhaber, M. (1981). Psychological and social effects on the population surrounding Three Mile Island after the nuclear accident on March 28, 1978. In S. Majundar (Ed.), *Energy, environment and the economy*. Harrisburg: Pennsylvania Academy of Sciences.

Hurst, A. P. (1940). *Medical diseases of war*. London: Edward Arnold.

Janet, P. (1983). *Contribution a l'etude des accidents mentaux chez les hysteriques*. Paris: Rueff et Cie.

Kadushin, C., Boulanger, G., & Martin J. (1981). Long-term stress reactions: Some causes, consequences, and naturally occurring support systems. In *Legacies of Vietnam: Comparative adjustment of veterans and their peers* (Vol. 4). Washington, DC: Government Printing Office.

Kamman, G. R. (1951). Traumatic neurosis: Compensation neurosis or attitude pathosis. *Archives of Neurology and Psychiatry, 65,* 593-601.

Kardiner, A., & Speigel, H. (1941). *War stress and neurotic illness.* London: Paul B. Hoeber.

Keane, T. M., & Fairbank, J. A. (1983). Survey analysis of combat-related stress disorders in Vietnam veterans. *American Journal of Psychiatry, 140,* 348-350.

Kolb, L. C., Burris, B. C., & Griffiths, S. (1984). Propranolol and clonidine in treatment of the chronic post-traumatic stress disorders of war. In B. van der Kolk (Ed.), *Post-traumatic stress disorder: Psychological and biological sequelae* (pp. 97-107). Washington, DC: American Psychiatric Press.

Krantz, D. S., Glass, D. C., Contrada, R. J., & Miller, N. E. (1981). Behavior and health. In National Science Foundation, *The 5-year outlook on science and technology* (Vol. 2). Washington, DC: Government Printing Office.

La Guardia, R. L., Smith, G., Francois, R., & Bachman, L. (1983). Incidence of delayed stress disorder among Vietnam era veterans: The effect of priming on response set. *American Journal of Orthopsychiatry, 53,* 18-26.

Laufer, R., Yager, T., Frey-Wouters, E., Donnellan, J., Gallops, M., & Stenbeck, K. (1981). Post-war trauma, social and psychological problems of Vietnam veterans in the aftermath of the Vietnam war. In *Legacies of Vietnam: Comparative adjustment of veterans and their peers* (Vol. 3). Washington, DC: Government Printing Office.

Lewy, E. (1940). Compensation for war neurosis. *War Medicine, 1,* 887-889.

Lifton, R. (1973). *Home from the war.* New York: Simon & Schuster.

Lindy, J. D., Grace, M. C., & Green, B. L. (1984). Building a conceptual bridge between civilian trauma and war trauma: Preliminary psychological findings from a clinical sample of Vietnam veterans. In B. van der Kolk (Ed.), *Post-traumatic stress disorder: Psychological and biological sequelae* (pp. 43-59). Washington, DC: American Psychiatric Press.

Maier, S. F., Davies, S., & Grau, J. W. (1980). Opiate antagonists and long-term analgesic reaction induced by inescapable shock in rats. *Journal of Comparative and Physiological Psychology, 94,* 1172-1183.

Malloy, P. F., Fairbank, J. A., & Keane, T. M. (1983). Validation of a multimethod assessment of post-traumatic stress disorder in Vietnam veterans. *Journal of Consulting and Clinical Psychology, 4,* 488-494.

Metropolitian Edison Company et al., petitioners, v. People Against Nuclear Energy et al., respondents. (1983). Supreme Court of the United States.

Milne, G. (1977). Cyclone Tracy: 1. Some consequences of the evacuation for adult victims. *Australian Psychologist, 121,* 39-54.

Mitchell, S. W., Morehouse, C. R., & Keen, N. S. (1964). *Gunshot wounds and other injuries of nerves.* Philadelphia: Lippincott.

Moore, H. E. (1958). Some emotional concomitants of disaster. *Mental Hygiene, 42,* 45-50.

Mott, F. (1944). *War neuroses and shell shock.* London: Oxford University Press.

Nace, E. P., Meyers, A. L., O'Brien, C. P., Ream, N., & Mintz, J. D. (1977). Depression in veterans two years after Vietnam. *American Journal of Psychiatry, 134,* 167-170.

Page, H. D. (1885). *Injuries of the spine and spinal cord without apparent mechanical lesion.* London: J. & A. Churchill.

Parker, G. (1977). Cyclone Tracy and Darwin evacuees: On the restoration of the species. *British Journal of Psychiatry, 130,* 548-555.

Penick, E. C., Powell, B. J., & Sick, W. A. (1976). Mental health problems and natural disaster: Tornado victims. *Journal of Community Psychology, 4,* 64-67.

Penk, W. E., Robinowitz, R., Roberts, R., Patterson, E. T., Dolan, M. P., & Atkins, H. G. (1981). Adjustment differences among male substance abusers varying in degree of combat experience in Vietnam. *Journal of Consulting and Clinical Psychology, 49,* 426-436.

People Against Nuclear Energy, petitioner, v. United States Nuclear Regulatory Commission, respondents; Metropolitan Edison Company et al., intervenors. (1981). Washington, DC: United States Court of Appeals.

Renners, J. A. (1973). The changing patterns of psychiatric problems in Vietnam. *Comprehensive Psychiatry, 14,* 167-181.

Resing, M. (1982). Mental health problems of Vietnam veterans. *Journal of Psychiatric Nursing and Mental Health Services, 20,* 40-43.

Roberts, W. R., Penk, W. E., Geaning, M. L., Robinowitz, R., Dolan, M. P., & Patterson, E. T. (1982). Interpersonal problems of Vietnam combat veterans with symptoms of post-traumatic stress disorder. *Journal of Abnormal Psychology, 91*, 444-450.

Rothbart, G., & Sloan, L. (1981). Educational and work careers: Men in the Vietnam generation. In *Legacies of Vietnam: Comparative adjustment of veterans and their peers* (Vol. 2). Washington, DC: Government Printing Office.

Schneiderman, N. (1983). Animal behavior models of heart disease. In D. S. Krantz, A. Baum, & J. E. Singer (Eds.), *Handbook of psychology and health: Cardiovascular disorders and behavior* (Vol. 3, pp. 19-56). Hillsdale, NJ: Lawrence Erlbaum.

Selye, H. (1956). *The stress of life.* New York: McGraw-Hill.

Selye, H. (1976). *The stress of life (2nd ed.).* New York: McGraw-Hill.

Shakespeare, W. (1966). King Henry the Fourth, Part 1. In Kittredge (Ed.), *The Kittredge Shakespeares.* Waltham, MA: Blaisdell.

Shatan, C. F. (1973). The grief of soldiers: Vietnam combat veterans' self-help movement. *American Journal of Orthopsychiatry, 43*, 440-653.

Starr, P., Henry, J., & Bonner, R. (1973). *The discarded army: Veterans after Vietnam.* New York: Charter House

Strayer, R., & Ellenhorn, L. (1975). Vietnam veterans: A study exploring adjustment pattern and attitudes. *Journal of Social Issues, 31*, 81-91.

Symonds, C. P. (1943). The human response to flying stress. *British Medical Journal, 2*, 703-708.

Thienes-Hontos, P., Watson, C. G., & Kucala, T. (1982). Stress disorder symptoms in Vietnam and Korean war veterans. *Journal of Consulting and Clinical Psychology, 50*, 558-561.

Tiffany, N. J. (1967). Mental health of army troops in Vietnam. *American Journal of Psychiatry, 123*, 1585-1586.

Titchner, J. L., & Kapp, F. T. (1976). Family and character change at Buffalo Creek. *American Journal of Psychiatry, 133*, 295-297.

Trimble, R. (1981). *Post-traumatic neurosis: From railway spine to whiplash.* New York: John Wiley.

U.S. Army Medical Department. (1943). Neuropsychiatric disease: Cause and prevention. *Bulletin of the U. S. Army Medical Department, 1*, 9-13.

U.S. House of Representatives Committee on Veteran Affairs. (1979). *Presidential review memorandum on Vietnam-era veterans.* (House Committee Print No. 388, pp. 11-33). Washington, DC: Author.

van der Kolk, B., Boyd, H., Krystal, J., & Greenburg, M. (1984). Post-traumatic stress disorder as a biologically based disorder: Implications of the animal model of inescapable shock. In B. van der Kolk (Ed.), *Post-traumatic stress disorder: Psychological and biological sequelae.* Washington, DC: American Psychiatric Press.

Walker, J. (1981). The psychological problems of Vietnam veterans. *Journal of the American Medical Association, 246*, 781-782.

Wilson, J. P. (1980, May). *Toward an understanding of post-traumatic stress disorder among Vietnam veterans.* Testimony before U. S. Senate, Washington, DC.

Wilson, J. P., & Krauss, G. E. (1982, October). *Post-traumatic stress syndromes among Vietnam veterans.* Paper presented at 25th Neuropsychiatric Institute, VA Medical Center, Coatesville, PA.

Wise, L. L., McLaughlin, D. H., & Steel, L. (1979). *The Project TALENT data bank handbook.* Palo Alto, CA: American Institute for Research.

Worthington, E. F. (1978). Demographic and pre-service variables as predictors of post-military adjustment. In I. Figley (Ed.), *Stress disorders among Vietnam veterans: Theory, research and treatment* (pp. 273-289). New York: Brunner/Mazel.

Yager, T., Laufer, R., & Gallops, M. (1984). Some problems associated with war experience in men of the Vietnam generation. *Archives of General Psychiatry, 41*, 327-333.

Yankelovich, D. A. (1974). *A study of American youth.* New York: McGraw-Hill.

KENNETH R. HAMMOND
JANET GRASSIA

12

THE COGNITIVE SIDE
OF CONFLICT:
From Theory to Resolution
of Policy Disputes

Psychologists, who have established their disciplinary domain over the study of how people think and act, should be professionally as well as individually alarmed at the persistent inability of nations to resolve international conflict and their increasing capability for engaging in it. Yet psychologists' efforts have not diminished these problems. That is because psychologists have studied mainly the psychology of disputes about who gets what. They have focused on the motivational aspects of disputes rather than their cognitive aspects. (For examples of early research, see Sherif, 1936; Osgood, 1962; Deutsch, 1973.)

As the ongoing research described in this chapter will demonstrate, people dispute many things besides differential gain, or who gets what. They also disagree about (a) the facts (what is, what was), (b) the future (what will be), (c) values (what ought to be), and (d) action (what to do). This distinction deserves to be emphasized because folklore, the media, and social scientists as well, treat nearly all disputes as if differential gain were all that mattered. It is true that disputes are likely to be *reduced* to the level of "who gets what," but that is because people fail to resolve them in their initial form, whatever that might be. In fact, however, when many of the most important disputes begin, they are of a different kind. For example, disputes between the U.S. and the U.S.S.R. are fundamentally disputes about values, as John F. Kennedy recognized:

> For the facts of the matter are that the Soviets and ourselves give wholly different meanings to the same words: war, peace, democracy and popular will. We have wholly different views of right and wrong, of what is an internal affair and what is aggression. And above all, we have wholly different concepts of where the world is and where it is going. ("Kennedy's Address," 1961)

AUTHORS' NOTE: Research described in this chapter was supported by the Engineering Psychology Programs, Office of Naval Research, contract N00014-81-C-0591, work unit NR 197-073 and contract N00014-77-C-0336, work unit NR197-038; Biomedical Research

These are cognitive differences; they have been *reduced* to who gets what because no progress has been achieved in resolving or even understanding cognitive differences, in particular the dispute about values. As a result, contention between the U.S. and the U.S.S.R. now focuses on who *gets:* who gets the "advantage" of one form or another of nuclear superiority; who gets a head start on the peculiar horrors of mutual nuclear destruction. *Everyone* agrees that the dispute has become an absurdity. Yet no one can stop it.

No one knows how to cope with disputes about values because no one has ever been taught how to do so. On the other hand, we are familiar from our childhood onward with disputes about who gets what. We are taught that quarrels are about who gets what, and we are taught how to cope: fight, wheedle, cheat, and when all else fails, "divvy up." As the memoirs of Jimmy Carter, George Kennan, and Dean Acheson—to name a few—consistently record, all of these responses to dispute can be seen in behavior at international bargaining tables.

We are convinced that our best hope for understanding and reducing conflict is, first, to shift our investigation from the motivational aspects of dispute to the underlying cognitive aspects, to the study of how people think about facts, values, and causation. We believe that Einstein was correct when he said: "The unleashed power of the atom has changed everything save our modes of thinking and we thus drift toward unparalleled catastrophe" ("Atomic Education," 1946). What we propose is a program of research to establish "new modes of thinking."

Second, we must adopt a comprehensive and scientific approach: that is, (a) devise a theory, (b) develop methods to explore the utility of the theory in the laboratory, and (c) test the theory against real problems in the world outside the laboratory. And that leads us to the principal aim of this chapter: to describe research-based efforts, initiated in 1965 (Hammond, 1965), that have increased our theoretical and practical knowledge about conflict. We shall therefore (a) outline briefly a theory of cognition (more specifically a theory of judgment), (b) show how we and our colleagues tested the value of the theory in laboratory experiments, and (c) illustrate the utility of its application to disputes outside the laboratory.

Support Program, Division of Research Resources, National Institute of Health grant RR-07013-14; National Institute of Mental Health grant 1647-36; National Institute of Mental Health grant MH16437; National Science Foundation grant BNS 76-09560; National Institute of Health grant CA 31682. Additional funds were provided by Ciba-Geigy Ltd., the Rocky Flats Monitoring Committee, the University of Colorado, and the Denver City Council.

THEORY

Social Judgment Theory (SJT; Hammond, Stewart, Brehmer, & Steinmann, 1975; see also Hammond, McClelland, & Mumpower, 1980) developed during the past two decades from basic work by Egon Brunswik (1952, 1956). It is a cognitive theory of the mental process by which individuals collect and evaluate information in order to reach a judgment—for example, a judgment about facts, or values, or the likelihood of future events. When information is certain and when there is a known formula for organizing and applying it, judgment becomes analytical thought, and the cognitive process is relatively apparent: The individual can accurately explain the judgment to himself or herself and to others by reference to the formula. However, as the nature of the problem becomes more complex—as the number of factors to be considered grows, as information becomes less certain and doubt about the outcome of the judgment increases, and when the individual has no formula or rules for reaching the judgment—the judgment process becomes increasingly obscure, difficult for the individual to describe, and very difficult for others to infer. At the extreme end of this process, judgments are intuitive; that is, based on a vague sense of "experience" and not on conscious evaluation of information. But in general judgment is "quasi-rational"; it incorporates elements of both intuition and analytical thought. (See Hammond & Brehmer, 1973; Hammond, 1982; Hammond, Hamm, Grassia, & Pearson, 1984, for further detail).

The components of the judgment process are represented in Social Judgment Theory by the Lens Model (see Figure 12.1) An explanation of this model will make clear that variability in one or more of these components can cause people's judgments to differ. The theory predicts that the more complex the problem, the greater the obscurity of the judgment process will be, and therefore, the more difficult it will be for individuals to resolve disagreements. Not only will they be unable to discover the true source of their disagreement but also they will attribute their disagreement to erroneous causes, including ill-will, hidden agendas, and the like.

Different outcomes. The outcome, the *criterion* or object of the individual's judgment, is frequently an intangible quality, a past or future event—essentially, something that cannot be directly perceived or known. And when action is taken on the basis of the judgment, it is impossible to ascertain what the outcome might have been had some other action been taken. For example, we can never know whether the Japanese would have surrendered in 1945 had Truman's scientific

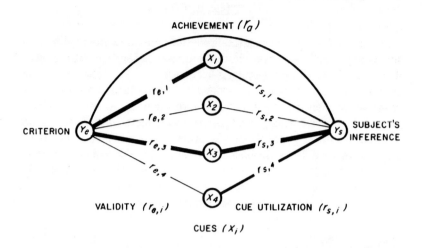

ACHIEVEMENT (r_a)

CRITERION

SUBJECT'S
INFERENCE

VALIDITY $(r_{e,i})$

CUE UTILIZATION $(r_{s,i})$

CUES (X_i)

Figure 12.1   The lens model, width of line indicating weight. From "Social judgment theory: Its use in the study of psychoactive drugs" by K. R. Hammond. In K. R. Hammond & C.R.B. Joyce (Eds.), 1975, *Psychoactive Drugs and Social Judgment: Theory and Research* (p. 73). New York: John Wiley & Sons. Copyright 1975 by John Wiley & Sons. Reprinted by permission.

advisors urged him to provide a demonstration of the power of the atomic bomb rather than to proceed directly to the bombing of Hiroshima, as they did.

Different cues. Individuals base their judgments on *cues,* hard or soft information about the criterion. For example, the judgment about a demonstration of the atomic bomb versus its actual use was based on soft information such as (a) data regarding the reliability of the mechanism (would it actually work?), (b) past experience with the Japanese government (would they capitulate even if the demonstration worked?). On the other hand, weather forecasts are based on hard data, relatively precise measurements of such phenomena as temperature and humidity. Disputes often arise because different people base their judgments on different cues, and because they may be unaware that they are in fact basing their judgments on different cues (Hammond et al., 1975).

Differential weighting of cues. The cues from which the individual draws inferences about the criterion may vary in their *ecological validity,* that is, the degree to which they are related to the criterion. The individual may weight each cue differently—that is, rely to a different extent on each cue. The weight the individual places on a cue may not match the ecological validity of the cue in relation to the criterion. In Figure 12.1, for example, the individual places relatively small weight on Cue X_1 even though it happens to be strongly related to the criterion (as illustrated by the varying thickness of the connecting lines in the figure) and thus makes less accurate judgments. Or, in the case of two individuals making judgments about the same criterion, each individual may weight the same cues differently and therefore reach different judgments that lead to a quarrel. Because persons are often unaware of the differences in the weights they attach to various cues, they may be unable to discover this source of dispute (Hammond et al., 1975). Thus, one graduate admissions committee member may weight GPA very highly and ignore letters of recommendation, whereas another may weight these cues in the reverse order in reaching his or her judgment. Such differences are not easy to detect and indeed are seldom detected unless one is alert to them.

Different functional relations between cue and judgment. The relationships between each cue and the individual's judgment may differ. Figure 12.2 displays four *function forms*, each of which describes a possible relation of cues to the judgment. Although the linear function form occurs far more often in human judgment than any of the others, others do occur. And when different individuals use different function forms for the same cue, their judgments will almost certainly differ. For example, the two faculty members on the admissions committee may have different function forms related to courses that candidates have taken in psychology. One may simply believe "more is better," that is, apply a linear function form to courses already taken in psychology. His or her colleague, on the other hand, may believe that "more is better, up to a point," that is, that there is some optimal number of previous courses in psychology and that, beyond that number, a student should have been taking courses in other departments. Because persons are rarely familiar with the concept of a function form, they rarely detect differences in them and, therefore, rarely discover the source of their dispute.

Different ways of organizing information into a judgment. All information must somehow be combined into a judgment. The manner in which the individual combines cues to reach a judgment is termed the *organizing principle.* Although an additive (or weighted average) combination of cue data is usually a powerful predictor of persons' quasi-rational judgments, it is possible for people to organize information in other ways. Even highly sophisticated persons rarely discover why their judgments disagree if the reason is that they are using

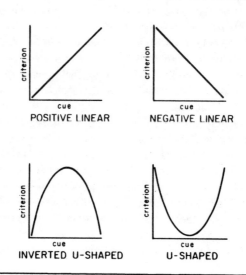

Figure 12.2   Graphic representation of positive linear, negative linear, inverted U-shaped, and U-shaped cue-criterion function forms. From "Social judgment theory: Its use in the study of psychoactive drugs" by K. R. Hammond. In K. R. Hammond & C.R.B. Joyce (Eds.), 1975, *Psychoactive Drugs and Social Judgment: Theory and Research* (p. 75). New York: John Wiley & Sons. Copyright 1975 by John Wiley & Sons. Reprinted by permission.

different organizing principles (Hammond et al., 1975). For example, the two faculty members on the admissions committee will almost certainly be organizing information about each candidate by means of an additive (or weighted average) organizing principle. But it is possible to do otherwise. One might combine information by an *interactive,* or *multiplicative* principle. That is, the rating for the letter of recommendation might be *multiplied* by the rating for the student's GPA. Even though the two faculty members might employ the same weights and function forms, use of two different organizing principles would result in far different judgments in most cases. It would be very difficult for two person untrained in judgment analysis to discover this source of their differences.

Cognitive control. Cognitive control is defined in terms of the correlation between an individual's actual judgments and the judgments he or she is predicted to make according to the mathematical model that best predicts his or her judgments. When cognitive control, or consistency in judgment, is sufficiently low, it is possible for *false disagreement* to occur; that is, two individuals' judgments may differ even though they are derived from the same cues, weights, function forms, and organizing principle simply because, with low cognitive control, they produce different judgments in response to the same data. Occasionally low cognitive control may also cause *false agreement*, that is, similarity in judgments that would have diverged had the individuals exercised their judgment with complete control (Hammond & Brehmer, 1973).

In summary, there are at least six aspects of every judgment task that can produce different judgments between two or more people: (a) different possible outcomes or criteria, (b) use of different cues, (c) attachment of different weights to the cues used, (d) use of different functional relations between cue and judgment, (e) use of different organizing principles, and (f) low cognitive control. It can be confidently predicted that few persons are aware of these potential sources of dispute. Without such knowledge, disagreement will be assigned to an unfortunate motive (greed, aggression, etc.) or to stupidity.

LABORATORY RESEARCH

Studying Conflict in the Laboratory

Social Judgment Theory (SJT) leads to the prediction that all that is necessary to cause people to disagree in their judgments is a difference among the parameters of their judgment policies, as indicated above. Differences in gain may also—and of course do—induce conflict, but they are not *necessary*. In order to test this theory, subjects have been trained in the laboratory to develop precisely the parametric differences (e.g., differences in weights, differences in function forms) that researchers predict will produce disputes. For example, in a typical experiment subject 1 is trained through repeated trials to weight cue A more than cue B, whereas subject 2 learns to weight cue B more than cue A. In addition, the function forms may be varied. Subject 1 may be trained to use cue A in a linear fashion (i.e., the greater the value of cue A, the higher subject 1's judgment should be) whereas subject 2 may learn to use cue A in a curvilinear way (the greater the value of cue A, the higher the subject's judgment up to an optimal point; beyond this point, the higher the cue value, the lower the judgment). Although subjects are trained side by side at the same table, they are kept unaware that differential training is taking place.

Thus the training conditions mimic life: through experience we gradually develop *judgment policies,* or general rules for making judgments in a variety of cases (Hammond & Brehmer, 1973). Generally we are only marginally aware of the parameters of our judgment policies, and our policies are exercised with less than complete cognitive control. And although we may have a more or less accurate view of the weights we place on different cues (usually they are inaccurate), few of us will be aware of the function forms we employ; and rarely will we be able to describe or explain the covert principle by which we organize information into a judgment because we don't know how to do so.

In the next phase of the experiment, subjects are brought together without being told of their different training and are asked to make individual judgments. Also they are asked to reach agreement on a joint judgment through the use of natural language and free discussion. The rate of reduction of their differences in initial judgments over trials is a measure of conflict reduction. (For examples, see Rappoport & Summers, 1973; Brehmer, 1976; Brehmer & Hammond, 1977.) Note that the training conditions establish precisely those differences in the parameters of judgment policies (e.g., weights and function forms) that the theory directs us to establish. In the experiment we then observe whether such cognitive differences actually lead to disputes over what the correct judgment should be, and we also observe and measure the extent and the means by which such disputes are resolved. Here again we mimic, or represent, life outside the laboratory. Not only are the training conditions representative of life outside the laboratory but so are the conditions of the conflict task, for we change the task conditions so that they are *midway* between the different bases on which each subject was trained. Therefore, if each subject listens to the other and changes accordingly, the joint judgment will be accurate. To the extent that a subject maintains the policy she or he was trained to use, the joint judgment will be off the mark. As in life, failure to heed the contributions of others is costly.

Studying Interpersonal Learning in the Laboratory

After subjects have exchanged judgments and attempted to resolve their differences, they may participate in the interpersonal learning phase of SJT research. Each subject is asked separately to look at a set of cases, and for each case, to make a judgment about the correct answer and then to *predict* what the other participant's judgment of the same case would be. Subject 1's own judgments are thus the criterion for subject 2's predictions as to what subject 1's actual judgments will be, and vice versa. The correlation between each subject's prediction of the other's judgment, and the other subject's actual judgment, provides a measure of the extent to which each subject has learned about and from the other. The ability to predict accurately the judgment of another person is a test of interpersonal understanding as well as a means of evaluating various methods of communicating each person's judgment policies (see Brehmer, 1974, 1976; Brehmer & Hammond, 1977; Holzworth, 1983).

Results of Laboratory Research (1966-1983)

Approximately 30 studies, mainly carried out by Berndt Brehmer in Sweden, show definitively that cognitive differences are not reduced by the subjects. This result has been found to be general over 12 nationalities and seven languages (English, French, Swedish, Japanese, Italian, Greek, and Czech). Differences in judgments that are caused by use of different function forms are particularly difficult to resolve because, as indicated above, persons ordinarily are unfamiliar with the concept of function form. in addition, decreases in cognitive control exacerbate disagreement when differentially trained pairs of subjects are required to make a series of joint judgments:

> Closer analysis . . . [in which we] disentangle the effects of systematic differences in cognitive systems and lack of consistency . . . leads to a surprising picture. . . . The results show that persons rapidly reduce the systematic differences between their cognitive systems . . . and that they apply virtually identical relative weight and function forms after very little experience of conflict. At the same time, however, the consistency of their systems decreases, and to such an extent that it counteracts the effects of the reduction in systematic differences. Thus, although the level of conflict remains the same, its structure changes. What started out as a conflict caused by systematic differences in how the people thought about a problem changes into a conflict caused by lack of consistency. However, the subjects have no way of knowing this; as a result the experience of disagreement is no less at the end of the series of problems than at the beginning. (Brehmer, 1980, pp. 21-22)

Not only do the subjects fail to reach agreement, but interpersonal learning is poor. Subjects are unable to predict the judgments of their partners despite repeated explanations of their judgments to one another, a result that is consistent with our argument above that persons are poor communicators of the parameters of their judgment policies (see Hammond et al., 1975; Mumpower & Hammond, 1974; Hammond & Brehmer, 1973; Brehmer & Hammond, 1977).

In addition to these laboratory studies, mainly using college students as subjects, Gillis (1979a, 1979b) investigated whether psychoactive drugs used in the treatment of psychotic patients enhanced or impaired their ability to exercise their judgment and their ability to reduce interpersonal conflict or increase interpersonal learning. Several studies made it clear that whatever other therapeutic benefits such drugs may have, the drugs commonly used to treat schizophrenia impair rather than enhance patients' cognitive abilities (see Hammond & Joyce, 1975, for additional studies).

The implications of Gillis's research go far beyond the treatment of schizophrenics. People who hold positions of great power in our society also use or are treated with drugs that might affect the central nervous system, albeit in as yet unknown ways. Examples from the recent past include Winston Churchill (Gilbert, 1983, p. 336; James, 1970, pp. 335-336) and Richard Nixon (Hersh, 1983, pp. 108-110), who were heavy users of alcohol; and Anthony Eden (Carlton, 1981, p. 428), Georges Pompidou (Altman, 1974), Leonid Brezhnev (Altman, 1982), and Yuri Andropov (Altman, 1984), who were either known or surmised to have taken medication for serious chronic illnesses. Indeed, many critical decisions may have been made by numerous world leaders (and their assistants) under the influence of alcohol or medication with unknown effects on cognitive processes. Although we cannot be sure whether we are better or worse off as a result, there are indications that at least one common psychoactive drug, alcohol, impairs subjects' ability to use complex rules in judgment (Brehmer & Almqvist, 1976). These findings, together with those from Gillis's research, suggest that the effects of drugs (whether alcohol or others) on judgment is a topic clearly in need of study. This is particularly true in view of the fact that the two superpowers are currently controlled by a number of elderly men, many of whom may be taking drugs that affect their cognitive processes, and thus their judgment, in ways that are largely unknown.

The results of laboratory research clearly show that conflict persists simply as a function of cognitive differences, even in situations where the prospect of differential rewards does not exist. That means that the conventional wisdom is wrong: *removal* of motivational differences— greed, avarice, the opportunity for differential gain—will *not* necessarily lead to conflict reduction. The subjects in our laboratory studies failed to reduce the disagreement that was obvious to them because they did not know what to communicate to one another, or how to communicate it. They were unable to describe accurately how they reached a judgment because they lacked the conceptual tools that would enable them to do so. We therefore conclude that "talking it out" will *not* lead to true conflict reduction because people do not know what to talk about. Moreover, without fundamental understanding of cognitive differences, *false* agreement, or disagreement, is likely to be the result of "talking it out," thus producing the grounds for mistrust.

Laboratory research has been extensive and representative of nonlaboratory conditions, but it merely *illustrates* the applicability of the theory. Although the theory successfully predicts and interprets the results observed, we cannot say with conviction that this theory must hold for conflict *outside* the laboratory. Therefore, we have undertaken the task of testing the theory in those circumstances.

We remind the reader that we are proceeding in a direct link from theory, to method, to laboratory test, to direct application to disputes outside the laboratory—a highly desirable order of progression.

TACKLING PROBLEMS OUTSIDE THE LABORATORY

A Technological Aid for Communicating About Judgment Policies

Our laboratory research had shown us that lay persons and even experienced negotiators do not know *what* or *how* to communicate in situations that require human judgment (Balke, Hammond, & Meyer, 1973). Therefore, our first objective was to devise a means to improve the substance and form of communication among people who disagree. POLICY, a judgment-oriented computer program, was developed to display an individual's cue weights and functional relations in pictorial form, so that if person A weights Cue 1 very high and Cue 2 very low, and if person B's weighting system is the reverse, they can see that fact clearly and thus understand why their judgments differ.

As we shall demonstrate below, this interactive graphics program (initiated in 1968) has become invaluable in the solution of disputes. Its capabilities carry great significance for international disputes, for it is now just as easy to transmit displays of weights, function forms, and other parameters of a judgment policy to computer terminals around the world as it is to transmit them to terminals in adjoining rooms. Moreover, because this display of information is largely pictorial, it is virtually language-independent, and thus it bypasses the vicissitudes of translation. Although no cross-language test has as yet been carried out, an online test of this procedure carried out between students in Australia and students in the United States was successful (Hammond, 1977).

We now present four examples of the application of the theory and its associated technology to problems outside the laboratory.

Study 1: Acquisition of Open Space—A Qualified Success

The first serious test of our work was an attempt to minimize dispute within the Open Space Board of Trustees of Boulder, Colorado, a committee charged with devising a policy for acquiring land for Boulder's open space program. The committee members had been chosen to reflect the diversity of opinion on land use in the community and included realtors, developers, and environmentalists. The following description is excerpted from the published report of that study (Steinmann, Smith, Jurdem, & Hammond, 1977, pp. 69, 80):

> Social Judgment Theory and interactive computer graphics procedures [POLICY] were used to identify cognitive sources of disagreement among members of the committee with regard to the acquisition of land for open space purposes. Making overt the differences in the relative importance of the factors underlying individual policies resulted in a reduction of the disagreement. Conflict was thus avoided in attaining a compromise policy, the concrete consequences of which were formally adopted by the committee. . . . The Board's special action to have the written report [of the procedure they had learned from us] entered into its official minutes gave an initial concrete indication that the above procedures aided the process of the Board's policy formulation, produced a satisfactory rationale for the Board's policy, and provided a useful tool for the implementation of that policy. Yet six months after the report was accepted, the authors were startled to read in the newspaper that use of the Compromise Policy and priority list had ended.

What went wrong? First, we vastly overestimated the durability of cognitive change; second, we failed to appreciate the situational determinants of behavior; and third, we lost control of the procedures we had established. Fortunately, a follow-up had been planned, and continuous observations of the board meetings had been made by independent observers who had not participated in the first part of the study. The results of these observations were clear: (a) the procedures the board members had been taught were seldom used, and (b) when used, they were often misused. The report concluded:

> The application of Social Judgment Theory to the formulation of a Compromise Policy was successful: It was found that Board members (a) considered the information they received useful, (b) formulated a Compromise Policy efficiently, (c) adopted the priorities which it provided, and in general, (d) made good use of the procedures over an extended period of time. . . . The policy that was formulated was not permanently retained, however, because of (a) incomplete understanding of what had been accomplished, (b) the lack of the continued services of a consultant, and (c) the appearance of a new Open Space Administrator unfamiliar with the procedures, who advocated a different policy. Future applications of Social Judgment Theory must place a far greater stress on educating the users than was done in the present study and must anticipate the possible need for providing continuing advisory services, if maximal benefits are to be derived from the procedures. (Steinmann et al., 1977, pp. 87-88.)

We would try not to make these mistakes again.

Study 2: The Bullet Study—Complete, Startling Success in a Dangerous Situation

In 1974 the police chief of Denver, Colorado asked the city council to approve the use of hollow-point bullets in the handguns carried by Denver police. This request was only one in a nationwide movement by police in the early 1970s to substitute the hollow-point bullet for the .38 caliber round-nosed that had been widely used for decades. Police had asserted that the hollow-point bullet was less likely to ricochet and had greater ability to make a person shot by the police incapable of shooting back. But the American Civil Liberties Union and others countered that the police were attempting to reintroduce the infamous "dum-dum" bullets used during World War I. In Denver a dispute immediately broke out and spread from the city council to the state legislature. Minority groups in particular were incensed by the issue inasmuch as they considered the use of hollow-point bullets an inhumane treatment of persons involved in altercations with the police, which during that period in Denver frequently involved members of minority groups.

The dispute grew increasingly acrimonious. Matters came to a head when a policeman was shot and killed by a robber firing hollow-point bullets. Outraged Denver police walked away from their posts, marched on the police department, and demanded from the chief of police the right to use hollow-point bullets. They continued on to the state capital and repeated their demand to the governor. The governor responded that he could not legally act on their request; but the chief of police stated that although he could not order the use of hollow-point bullets, he could not stop the police from loading their sidearms with whatever bullet they chose to use. It is the view of the researchers subsequently involved in the dispute that, had a minority group member been shot at this time by police using hollow-point bullets, riots would have erupted in Denver.

The published report of the study that our research center undertook at the request of the Denver City Council (Hammond & Adelman, 1976) explicates the confusion of social values and technical expertise that had thwarted attempts to resolve this conflict:

> From the beginning both sides focused on the question of which bullet was best for the community. As a result of focusing on bullets and their technical ballistics characteristics, legislators and city councilmen never described the social policy that should control the use of force and injury in enforcing the law; they never specified the relative importance of the societal characteristics of bullets (injury, stopping effectiveness, or ricochet). Instead, the ballistics experts assumed that function. When the legislators requested their judgment as to which bullet was "best," the ballistics experts implicitly indicated the social policy that should be employed. That is, in recommending the use of a specific bullet, they not only implicitly recommended specific degrees of injury, stopping effectiveness, and ricochet, but also recommended a social policy regarding the relative importance of these factors. In short, the legislators' function was usurped by the ballistics experts, who thus became incompetent and unauthorized legislators—incompetent because of their lack of information about the social and political context in which a choice would be made; unauthorized because they assumed a function for which they had not been elected. . . .In parallel fashion, the ballistics experts turned their scientific-technical function over to those who should have formed social policy—the legislators. When the experts presented scientific information to policy-makers about various bullets, they found themselves disputing ballistics data with legislators who preferred a different type of bullet. Thus, the legislators, none of whom were ballistics experts, in their turn served as incompetent ballistics experts in the hearings. (Hammond & Adelman, 1976, pp. 392-393)

This role reversal may have been one of the most important findings in the study; we have observed a similar reversal in every policy dispute we have studied.

Researchers began their work by imposing a "double-blind" system to separate technical judgments from value judgments. Government officials, representatives of minority groups, and the Denver police department were asked independently to judge the desirability of a set of hypothetical bullets described in terms of three attributes: stopping effectiveness, severity of injury, and threat to bystanders. Because analysis showed considerable disagreement among these participants as to the relative importance of these attributes, the city council adopted a policy under which the acceptability of a bullet would be determined by weighting the attributes equally. Next, data about the physical characteristics of 80 real and available bullets were obtained from the National Bureau of Standards. On the basis of this information, a panel of ballistics and medical experts were asked to rate these bullets on stopping effectiveness, severity of injury, and threat to bystanders. Analysis showed that the judgments of these experts closely agreed. Finally, the equal-weighting policy of the city councilmen was applied to the experts' ratings of each bullet (see Figure 12.3). Of the 80 bullets considered, a hollow-point bullet—not the one originally requested by the Denver police, however—was found to have greater stopping effectiveness and to cause less injury than the round-nosed bullet then in use by the police department. This bullet was accepted by all factions in the dispute.

In this study, *research-based* methods of conflict resolution were successfully applied to a tension-filled situation involving local politics, bitter intergroup hostility, and intense scrutiny by the media. Ten years later the solution still stands, and the work has been recognized internationally.

Study 3: Conflict Resolution for the Governor— Technical Success, Covert Implementation

For several years government officials in Colorado had debated whether to decentralize the state government in order to distribute the economic benefits of government installations and activities more widely throughout the state. In 1976 the incumbent governor made decentralization a part of his campaign platform. Upon his reelection four years later, the Office of State Planning and Budgeting (OSPB) was directed to create a decentralization plan that would meet quotas for moving various units from each department of state government from Denver to other communities in rural Colorado. All of the departments affected by this plan objected to it, and a dispute arose between those who favored decentralization, including the Governor's Office and the

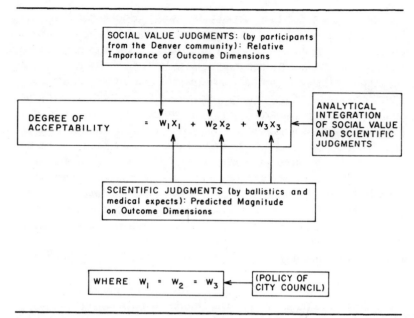

Figure 12.3 Analytical integration of social values and technical judgments. From "Science, values, and human judgment" by K. R. Hammond & L. Adelman, 1976, *Science, 194*, p. 394. Copyright 1976 by the American Association for the Advancement of Science. Adapted by permission.

OSPB, and those who opposed the idea, including cabinet heads, state employees, and others.

After a year of deadlock on this issue, the governor asked our research center to evaluate the concept of decentralization for two departments, Highways and Revenue. "The task was to (i) structure consideration of the relevant issues so that a cabinet decentralization policy could be made explicit, and (ii) analyze the effects of the application of that policy" (Adelman & Brown, 1979, p. 13). In a session with the governor we identified several goals of decentralization. These goals were then used as criteria for evaluating each proposed transfer of a governmental unit to a particular community, including (a) the unit's level of service during and after decentralization, (b) the cost of decentralization and of operation afterwards, and (c) the socioeconomic impact of the transfer on the receiving community. These goals were broken down into subgoals, which were operationalized for each proposed transfer in terms of empirical data concerning unit payroll, the growth rate of the community, and so on. As in the bullet study, it was important to separate *value* judgments, in this case concerning the relative *importance* of the decentralization goals, from factual judgments, in this case facts concerning the *impact* of decentralization on those goals. Whereas unit leaders and the staff of OSPB were the appropriate people to estimate the factual impact of decentralization (what would be), it was the responsibility of the cabinet members to determine the desirability of decentralization (what ought to be).

It turned out that the judgments of the cabinet members of 40 hypothetical decentralization cases exhibited moderate agreement on the relative importance (weights) of the decentralization goals and perfect agreement in the function forms relating those goals to the desirability of decentralization. The importance weights of the cabinet members for each goal were averaged to produce a compromise policy, and an overall desirability score for each proposed transfer was computed by applying this policy to the predicted effects of the transfer. The results of this analysis were unanimous. Not one of the 150 proposed transfers of governmental units to communities outside the Denver metro area exceeded a minimum cutoff score for desirability; in no case were the predicted socioeconomic benefits to the receiving community sufficient to compensate for deleterious effects on costs and services (Adelman & Brown, 1979). A sensitivity analysis was run to test these results for bias in the technical judgments of unit leaders and the OSPB staff about the effect of decentralization on subgoals. Even when each technical judgment was changed to be more favorable by 25 percent, the overall scores were not high enough to indicate that decentralization was desirable. The report submitted to the Governor's Office stated:

> Only the adoption of a policy that was extremely different from that expressed by the Governor and the cabinet members would result in a conclusion that it would be appropriate to decentralize units in the Departments of Revenue and Highways. (Adelman, Brown, Deane, & Marvin, 1977, pp. 4-5)

Thus, the research effort was successful; it produced a clear result that was disputed by no one. Judgment analysis again proved to be successful in eliminating persistent and apparently unresolvable conflict.

Aftermath. We sent our report to the governor and, in return for their cooperation during the study, to the various department heads and to the Colorado Association of Public Employees. We also made an appointment to present and interpret the findings to the governor in person. That never happened. We were met at the door of his office by an aide who took us aside and announced: "Good or bad, right or wrong, we are going ahead with decentralization." After this we initially assumed that, even though those who strongly opposed decentralization would be able to use our report against the governor, he would press for decentralization in order to fulfill his campaign promise. However, the report evidently posed a serious threat to the credibility of the governor's proposal, and he never mentioned decentralization again. Thus our recommendations prevailed, but our work was never acknowledged. In the process we had learned an unhappy lesson: Recognition of work well done should never be taken for granted in the political arena.

Study 4: The Rocky Flats Study—Making More Effective Use of Scientific Information

What happens when there is a conflict among experts? This was the case in the Rocky Flats study, which involved a dispute among scientists about risk.

In 1978 the Rocky Flats Monitoring Committee was created and charged with advising and informing government officials and the public as to the health and safety risks of the Rocky Flats Plant, a facility near Denver where plutonium is used to manufacture triggers for nuclear weapons. The sometimes bitter disagreements among scientists empaneled to provide the monitoring committee with information about health and safety risks of plutonium emissions from the plant prevented the committee from making any statement to its constituents for the next three years. That is, for three years the public—including people residing near the plant—was deprived of information vitally related to personal health and safety, as well as to the value of their property.

Eleven of the scientists, including epidemiologists, radiologists, and biostatisticians, participated in the Rocky Flats study. The study focused on their prediction of the risks of cancer from exposure to plutonium emissions from the plant. In the first phase of the study the scientists judged the risk of cancer for 40 hypothetical persons described in terms of six characteristics (diet, smoking habits, etc.) related to that disease. A Lens Model analysis of these judgments showed that the scientists did in fact disagree, and that their disagreement was not caused by differences in their professional backgrounds (Hammond & Marvin, 1981). The published report of the study stated:

> It became obvious that a nonretraceable process of organizing information into a judgment of risk for the hypothetical persons exposed to

radiation was being employed instead of an explicit principle derived from research findings. (Hammond, Anderson, Sutherland, & Marvin, 1984, p. 71)

That is, because it was impossible to move the Rocky Flats Plant and nearby residents to a laboratory for controlled, long-term, scientific investigation, the scientists were obliged to extrapolate from their scientific knowledge and experience to uncertain conditions outside the laboratory. They were compelled to make judgments; they could not deduce conclusions rigorously and thus in retraceable form from experimental data, as scientists ordinarily do in laboratory experiments. Rather, they expressed judgments, and thus were unable to trace out explicitly the parameters of the judgment policy employed. (See Hammond, 1978, for a discussion of the barriers to extrapolating laboratory findings for policy purposes; see also Hammond, Mumpower, Dennis, Fitch, & Crumpacker, 1983.)

The five scientists who disagreed most deeply were asked to participate in a second phase of the study. The goal was to assist them in developing a mutually acceptable formula for predicting risk of lung cancer by helping them to explicate their judgment policies and then to substantiate them.

Such a method would not include subjective weighting of variables. Instead, each variable to be included would have to be defended by a specific reference to directly related studies. Furthermore, each scientist's suggestion for each step of the process would be checked by the other four scientists; differences would be settled by reference to the relevant literature. (Hammond et al., 1984, pp. 71-72)

This method led to agreement among the scientists; and the explicit organizing principle they produced ultimately led to development of tables whereby the probability of lung cancer for a person of a certain age and smoking habits could be assessed. The scientists were then able to coauthor a report of this work for the Rocky Flats Monitoring Committee (Anderson et al., 1981).

Settling this dispute was an important test of our theory and methods a new and demanding context. We were attempting to assist scientists to think about their own areas of expertise in a new way. We certainly were not confident that such an effort would be accepted. The fact that it was leads us to believe that our methods can be used to increase the effective use of scientific information in public policymaking.

DISCUSSION

What do these four examples teach us? In the Open Space study we learned that we *could* reduce conflict in the real world, but that we cannot simply help policymakers reduce their disputes and then leave them with the policy they have worked out. The approach we asked them to take was so different from the conventional one that they should have been assisted in the application of the policy. The bullet study taught us that we could be *completely* successful, even under the most demanding circumstances of "hot" conflict, if we controlled the entire process right to the end. That lesson about control was repeated in the decentralization study. We carried out our work successfully but incompletely; as a consequence our recommendations were implemented covertly, by inaction rather than action. The Rocky Flats study taught us that our methods could be very successful in reducing disputes about facts as well as values, and even among sharply disagreeing scientists. In short, the conclusions reached from theoretical and empirical research about the cognitive side of conflict have stood up to tests outside the laboratory. Success in conflict resolution was achieved in all cases; failure in implementation occurred when we lost control of the process.

Our approach to conflict resolution is unique in two ways. Other efforts to reduce conflict have almost always been based on the assumption that it is differential gain that must be negotiated; we approach the problem entirely from the standpoint of resolving cognitive differences, with no reference whatever to who gets what. Other efforts are still based on the assumption that "mediation is an 'art' unsuited to systematic analysis" (Kochan & Jick, 1978, p. 209). But we have shown, on the contrary, that conflict resolution can be achieved when it is based on a theoretical framework that can be tested in the laboratory and then applied outside the laboratory to the problem for which it was intended. When we combine these two aspects of our approach—the focus on how we think, rather than what we want, and the emphasis on learning from scientific research rather than relying on myth—we see hope that it may indeed be possible to respond to Einstein's warning ("Atomic Education," 1964) that unless we change "our modes of thinking" we shall "drift toward unparalleled castastrophe."

REFERENCES

Adelman, L., & Brown, C. (1979). *The use of judgment analysis in resolving public policy disputes* (Technical Report No. 220). Boulder: University of Colorado, Institute of Behavioral Science, Center for Research on Judgment and Policy.

Adelman, L., Brown, C., Deane, D., & Marvin, B. (1977). *Report to the Governor regarding the decentralization of the executive branch of the State of Colorado* (Technical Report No. 206). Boulder: University of Colorado, Institute of Behavioral Science, Center for Research on Judgment and Policy.

Altman, L. K. (1974, April 4). Political leaders' health: Should the public know? *The New York Times,* p. 16.

Altman, L. K. (1982, November 13). Serious ailments plagued Brezhnev. *The New York Times,* p. 5.

Altman, L. K. (1984, February 11). U.S. doctors believe Andropov had failing kidney when he took office. *The New York Times,* p. 6.

Anderson, B. F., Hammond, K. R., Berg, J., Hamman, R., Johnson, C., Marine, W., & Sutherland, J. (1981). *Second report to the Rocky Flats Monitoring Committee concerning scientists' judgments of cancer risk* (Technical Report No. 233). Boulder: University of Colorado, Center for Research on Judgment and Policy.

Atomic education urged by Einstein. (1946, May 25). *The New York Times,* p. 13.

Balke, W. M., Hammond, K. R., & Meyer, G. D. (1973). An alternative approach to labor-management relations. *Administrative Science Quarterly, 18,* 311-327.

Brehmer, B. (1974). Policy conflict, policy consistency, and interpersonal understanding. *Scandinavian Journal of Psychology, 15,* 273-276.

Brehmer, B. (1976). Social judgment theory and the analysis of interpersonal conflict. *Psychological Bulletin, 83,* 985-1003.

Brehmer, B. (1980). Probabilistic functionalism in the laboratory: Learning and interpersonal (cognitive) learning. In K. R. Hammond & N. E. Wascoe (Eds.), *Realizations of Brunswik's representative design* (pp. 13-24). San Francisco: Jossey-Bass.

Brehmer, B., & Almqvist, K. (1976). *Effects of alcohol in subjects' ability to use functional rules* (Umea Psychological Reports No. 109). Umea, Sweden: University of Umea, Department of Psychology.

Brehmer, B., & Hammond, K. R. (1977). Cognitive factors in interpersonal conflict. In D. Druckman (Ed.), *Negotiations: Social-psychological perspectives* (pp. 79-103). Beverly Hills, CA: Sage.

Brehmer, B., & Hammond, K. R. (1973). Cognitive sources of interpersonal conflict: Analysis of interactions between linear and nonlinear cognitive systems. *Organizational Behavior and Human Performance, 10,* 290-313.

Brunswik, E. (1952). The conceptual framework of psychology. In *International encyclopedia of unified science* (Vol. 1, No. 10). Chicago: University of Chicago Press.

Brunswik, E. (1956). *Perception and the representative design of psychological experiments* (2nd ed.). Berkeley: University of California Press.

Carlton, D. (1981). *Anthony Eden: A biography.* London: Penguin.

Deutsch, M. (1973). *The resolution of conflict: Constructive and destructive processes.* New Haven: Yale University Press.

Gilbert, M. (1983). *Winston S. Churchill. Vol. 6: Finest hour 1939-1941.* Boston: Houghton Mifflin.

Gillis, J. S. (1979a). Antipsychotic drugs and conflict resolution: A study of the comparative effects of trifluoperazine, haloperidol, and thioridazine. *Research Communications in Psychology, Psychiatry, and Behavior, 4,* 3-20.

Gillis, J. S. (1979b). Antipsychotic drugs and interpersonal learning: A five-year progress report. In R. Shulman (Ed.), *Sociopharmacology.* Dordrecht, Holland: Reidel.

Hammond, K. R. (1965). New directions in research on conflict resolution. *Journal of Social Issues, 21,* 44-66.

Hammond, K. R. (1977, February). Facilitation of interpersonal learning and conflict reduction by on-line communication. *Proceedings of the Society for General Systems Research.*

Hammond, K. R. (1978). Toward increasing competence of thought in public policy formation. In K. R. Hammond (Ed.), *Judgment and decision in public policy formation* (pp. 11-32). Boulder: Westview.

Hammond, K. R. (1982). *Unification of theory and research in judgment and decision making.* Unpublished manuscript, University of Colorado at Boulder, Center for Research on Judgment and Policy.

Hammond, K. R., & Adelman, L. (1976). Science, values, and human judgment. *Science, 194,* 389-396.

Hammond, K. R., Anderson, B. F., Sutherland, J., & Marvin, B. (1984). Improving scientists' judgments of risk. *Risk Analysis, 4*(1), 69-78.

Hammond, K. R., & Brehmer, B. (1973). Quasi-rationality and distrust: Implications for international conflict. In L. Rappoport & D. Summers (Eds.), *Human judgment and social interaction* (pp. 338-391). New York: Holt, Rinehart & Winston.

Hammond, K. R., Hamm, R. M., Grassia, J., & Pearson, T. (1984). *The relative efficacy of intuitive and analytical cognition: A second direct comparison* (Technical Report No. 252). Boulder: University of Colorado, Center for Research on Judgment and Policy.

Hammond, K. R., & Joyce, C.R.B. (1975). *Psychoactive drugs and social judgment: Theory and research.* New York: John Wiley.

Hammond, K. R., & Marvin, B. A. (1981). *Report to the Rocky Flats Monitoring Committee concerning scientists' judgments of cancer risk* (Technical Report No. 232). Boulder: University of Colorado, Institute for Behavioral Science, Center for Research on Judgment and Policy.

Hammond, K. R., McClelland, G. H., & Mumpower, J. (1980). *Human judgment and decision making: Theories, methods, and procedures.* New York: Praeger.

Hammond, K. R., Mumpower, J., Dennis, R. L., Fitch, S., & Crumpacker, W. (1983). Fundamental obstacles to the use of scientific information in public policy making. *Technological Forecasting and Social Change, 24,* 287-297.

Hammond, K. R., Stewart, T. R. Brehmer, B., & Steinmann, D. O. (1975). Social judgment theory. In M. F. Kaplan & S. Schwartz (Eds.), *Human judgment and decision processes* (pp. 271-312). New York: Academic Press.

Hersh, S. M. (1983). *The price of power: Kissinger in the Nixon White House.* New York: Summit.

Holzworth, J. (1983). Intervention in a cognitive conflict. *Organizational Behavior and Human Performance, 32,* 216-231.

James, R. R. (1970). *Churchill: A study in failure, 1900-1939.* New York: World.

Kennedy's address to the nation on his talk in Europe. (1961, June 7). *The New York Times,* p. 16.

Kochan, T. A., & Jick, T. (1978). The public sector mediation process: A theory and empirical examination. *Journal of Conflict Resolution, 22,* 209-240.

Mumpower, J. L., & Hammond, K. R. (1974). Entangled task dimensions: An impediment to interpersonal learning. *Organizational Behavior and Human Performance, 11,* 377-389.

Osgood, C. (1962). Graduated unilateral initiatives for peace. In Q. Wright, W. Evan, & M. Deutsch (Eds.), *Preventing World War III: Some proposals* (pp. 161-177). New York: Simon & Schuster.

Rappoport, L., & Summers, D. A. (1973). *Human judgment and social interaction.* New York: Holt, Rinehart & Winston.

Sherif, M. (1936). *Psychology of social norms.* New York: Harper.

Steinmann, D. O., Smith, T. H., Jurdem, L. G., & Hammond, K. R. (1977). Application of social judgment theory in policy formation: An example. *Journal of Applied Behavioral Science, 13,* 69-88.

LEONARD SAXE
DENISE DOUGHERTY

13

TECHNOLOGY ASSESSMENT AND CONGRESSIONAL USE OF SOCIAL PSYCHOLOGY:
Making Complexity Understandable

Six blocks south of the U.S. Capitol, at the edge of an area of Washington, D.C., which was "gentrified" in the late 1970s, is a modern office building. Typical of Washington, the building's motif is colonial and its facade, which suggests that it houses a bank, indicates that it is not an important building. A careful observer, however, will note on the building's roof (in addition to a set of solar collectors) a large American flag. A person venturing into the structure would discover that its floors are patrolled by U.S. Capitol police and that government offices occupy almost all of its space. The building is the home of the Office of Technology Assessment (OTA), smallest of four support agencies of the U.S. Congress.

OTA was established by Congress in 1972 to help legislative policymakers anticipate and plan for the consequences of technological change and to examine how technology affects peoples' lives (Arnstein, 1977; Gibbons, 1984; Wood, 1982). The agency is responsible to Congress, rather than the Executive Branch, and is overseen by the Technology Assessment Board (TAB), a bipartisan group of six members of the House of Representatives and six members of the Senate. By statute, OTA functions with a staff of less than 150 people, but draws upon thousands of consultants and advisors from academia, industry, and the public. OTA has now operated for over a decade and during its short history has conducted over 200 major studies, published 500+ reports, and tesified before hundreds of Congressional committees. Although it is difficult to measure precisely OTA's impact, it has influenced countless pieces of legislation and, probably, the direction of scientific and technological development. OTA is an interesting and important experiment in the use of science to assist public policymaking.

The concept of technology assessment was first articulated by Congressman Emilio Daddario, and arose from policymakers' concerns about the effects of unbridled technology (see Arnstein, 1977). Although it may not be obvious how technology assessment relates to psychology, in fact, a broad range of social scientific knowledge is esstential to the conduct of technology assessments. OTA explicitly defines technology assessment as the exploration of physical, biological, economic, social, and political impacts that result from applications of scientific knowledge. This view of technology provides a great potential for social scientists, and in particular psychologists, to contribute to its analysis. This chapter describes a number of efforts to utilize social science, particularly social psychology, in the development of OTA's policy analyses. Although the present analysis is based on the specific circumstances of OTA, it has a number of implications for the application of psychology more generally.

The work described in this chapter primarily concerns health problems and, more particularly, efforts to develop mental health policy and policy about psychology-based interventions. The examples are drawn from the authors' experiences during the past five years, working both as internal and external staff to Congress. The issues described range from how to make reimbursement decisions for psychotherapy and alcoholism treatment, to the use and validity of polygraph tests. Despite the specific content focus of this work, our sense is that the issues are not particularistic. The issues illustrate both the problems and potential of using a social psychological perspective (see Saxe, 1983) in efforts to understand and ameliorate social problems. Congress is, in some sense, the ultimate consumer of applied research and, as such, provides a litmus test of our abilities to utilize psychology in the service of the larger social good.

This discussion is intended to be nonparticularistic not only in its analysis of problems, but also in its assessment of appropriate models for understanding the policy influence process. We suggest that application of social psychology to legislative problems involves use of knowledge-driven, as well as problem-driven theory and research (see Masters, 1984). In addition, we argue that application is an educative process rather than a problem-solving set of techniques. This analysis has implications both for how social psychologists approach the conduct of applied research and how social psychology itself is conducted.

TECHNOLOGY ASSESSMENT

Jerome Frank (1966), in his presidential address to the Society for the Psychological Study of Social Issues (SPSSI) almost 20 years ago, called the "headlong rush of technology and science" the outstanding characteristic of our times. Although he recognized the beneficial effects of "galloping technology," Frank was apprehensive about the ways in which technology was remaking the world. Technology, according to Frank, was creating new strains of "social diseases" and was exacerbating problems of "unemployment, urbanization, racial and international tensions, war, and overpopulation" (p. 193). What was true in the mid-1960s is probably even more true in the 1980s and the prescience of Frank's analysis is remarkable.

One might expect a social scientist and SPSSI leader to express concern about the effects of technology. Interestingly, at about the same time, members of the U.S. Congress were articulating similar concerns. In the language of the 1972 act that created the Office of Technology Assessment, technological applications were seen to be large and growing in scale, "increasingly extensive, pervasive, and critical in the impact, beneficial and adverse, on the natural and social environment." Congress wanted to ensure that, to the fullest extent possible, the consequences of technological application would be anticipated, understood, and considered in determining public policy.

One of the most interesting aspects of the development of OTA was the fact that it was conceptualized by legislators, rather than by the scientific community. To be sure, many scientists were expressing concerns about uncontrolled technology, yet their models for how to understand these effects were not directly responsive to the needs of policymakers. For example, evaluation research was developing as a subdiscipline in psychology, but its focus, on the improvement of specific programs, was somewhat different than that of technology assessment advocates. In fact, there has been a long-standing debate within the evaluation field about whether it is decision driven or research driven. Particularly for the U.S. Congress, the notion of assessment of concrete technologies was far more attractive, if not more far-reaching, than evaluation research. Despite different labels, however, there are many similarities between evaluation research and technology assessment.

The idea of technology assessment is also similar to the concept of social experimentation (see Riecken & Boruch, 1974), developed by researchers (many of whom are social psychologists) to describe how to analyze and evaluate policy initiatives. Although one view of social experimentation is that it involves collaboration between policymakers and researchers (Saxe & Fine, 1981), the term clearly emphasizes the scientific side of the enterprise. As Koppel (1979) has noted, the logic of the experimental model is only one of a number of perspectives that need to be included in a technology assessment.

The closest current research model to technology assessment is probably meta-analysis. In recent years, there has been increased interest in using systematic quantitative procedures to summarize and assess the meaning of multiple investigations. A set of methods has been developed (see Glass, McGaw, & Smith, 1981; Rosenthal, 1978) to quantify the conclusions of studies and statistically combine results. Although the emphasis in most discussions of meta-analytic techniques has been on quantitative procedures, in fact the thrust of such methods is to organize bodies of research evidence in order to develop inferences about current knowledge. In this sense, its task parallels technology assessment.

Methods

We have said a good deal about what technology assessment methods are not, but what they are is a bit more difficult to describe. Even at OTA, where many technology assessments have been conducted and where an effort has been made to describe these procedures (e.g., Wood, 1982), it is clear that there are many options. At OTA, an assessment typically begins through consultation with congressional committees. Most studies are conducted at the request of these committees, usually as a result of discussions with OTA staff about feasibility.

Development of a study approach and methodology is done by OTA staff preparing a project proposal. Although not as elaborate as proposals that researchers might prepare for unsolicited research funding, these proposals describe the rationale and logic of the assessment, its implications, and the staff and budget required. Proposals are reviewed internally and ultimately by the Technology Assessment Board (TAB). Although it is rare that requests developed into proposals are rejected by TAB, the process of consulting with TAB often has a significant impact on the scope of the project.

An important structure at OTA, perhaps its most unique feature, is the use of advisory panels. At the top of the advisory hierarchy is the Technology Assessment Advisory Council (TAAC), which functions to advise OTA on overall strategy, both for choosing areas on which to concentrate resources and for conducting assessments. Its members are leading scientists and academicians. The OTA health program, for which we have conducted our assessments, has a parallel advisory committee, composed of physicians and other health and social scientists. Each project also has an advisory panel, with anywhere from

6 to 20 members. Formal advisory committees are supplemented by workshops, and large numbers of other reviewers (often "stakeholders") are asked to comment on draft reports.

Once a project is approved, a staff selected, and an advisory panel constituted, there are a number of models for how the assessment is conducted. In almost all cases, the emphasis is on making sense of already collected data, and therefore literature reviews and methods for synthesizing research results are relied upon. In some cases, cost-benefit analyses are conducted, surveys or interviews performed, or computer models developed. The methods typically depend on the nature of the problem and the resources available to the study team. When in-house resources are not available (as is often the case), elements of a project are contracted out to scholars and researchers in academia and industry.

Although the emphasis on evaluating currently available evidence probably makes OTA analyses unique, they are also unusual in what is done with the information. Throughout the development of a report, staff are in contact with leading researchers and stakeholders. This occurs though the advisory panel, contractors, and contact with congressional staff (principally, professional committee staff). There may, in addition, be assistance provided by the other congressional support agencies: the Congressional Research Service (CRS), General Accounting Office (GAO), and Congressional Budget Office (CBO).

An additional feature of OTA assessments concerns the way in which reports are written and reviewed. Although the project staff will have substantial input from the panel and others, it is the staff's responsibility to develop the report. With larger studies, an overall report will be written and supplemented by monograph-length case studies. The key word in guiding development of reports is "even-handedness." Analysts are expected to integrate information from various sources and to remain as unbiased as possible. Where controversy exists, it is expected that it will be described so that readers of policy can understand the nature of the conflict.

In all cases, reports go through an extensive review and revision process. Internally, various staff members participate in the review of a project. This review is supplemented by outside reviews, from members of the advisory panel, stakeholders, and others identified during development of the study as having important information about the problem being studied. Usually, several dozen reviewers are involved; in the studies described below, it was over 50 in each case. Once a report is finalized, it is edited by an in-house publication staff and presented both to the OTA director and to the board for review. Reports such as case studies do not require board approval and are published after the director has reviewed them.

Publication of reports involves making copies available to each member of Congress and, through the Government Printing Office (GPO), to the public. In some cases, OTA reports are republished commercially as books or, more typically, become journal articles or monographs. Many studies are released either through the requesting committee or through a press conference.

ASSESSMENTS OF SOCIAL TECHNOLOGY

The above describes the typical procedures for conducting technology assessments. There are considerable variations, however, and the best means of demonstrating how a technology assessment proceeds, and its social psychological implications, is to describe a number of specific assessment projects. As noted earlier, the projects to be described reflect a relatively narrow substantive range. Nevertheless, they illustrate both how social psychology can contribute to public policy development and how such work can affect research and theorizing in psychology. Described below are three projects, each of which—by standards of technology assessment—is small. In two cases, the projects were part of larger assessment efforts. The remaining case was a stand-alone project that responded to a specific congressional mandate for information.

Psychotherapy

It is probably an understatement to note that the provision of psychotherapy is controversial. The hostile reception received by Freud when he first articulated theories of the unconscious has, despite the passage of almost a century and major differences in the nature of psychotherapy today, become a paradigm for reactions. In recent years, as pressures have intensified for governmental support of psychotherapy, controversy has raged. It is exacerbated, not only by the nature of psychotherapy, but by the multiple disciplines (primarily psychiatry, social work, and psychology) that lay claim to providing mental health services.

BACKGROUND

In 1979, the Senate Finance Committee held hearings and began a review of funding for mental health services. The Committee's interest was stimulated, in part, by the recently released report of the President's Commission on Mental Health (1978), which found numerous unserved groups and mental health problems unresolved due to lack of insurance coverage. Interest in mental health was also prompted by increasingly effective lobbying activities of mental health professionals. A related issue, in some ways the driving force behind the committee's actions, was recognition that the Medicare program (which provides health insurance for the elderly and disabled) was financially out of control and that restrictions on its benefits would be necessary.

OTA was already conducting a study at the request of the Senate Finance Committee on the use of cost-effectiveness/cost-benefit analyses (CEA/CBA) for health policy decision making. Under the umbrella of the CEA/CBA study, Senators Long and Talmadge asked OTA to conduct a study of the cost-effectiveness of psychotherapy. Their request letter stated that there were "over 130 psychotherapies" and that there was "an urgent need to determine which of those were effective, which were ineffective, and which were reasonable, given their costs and particular outcomes." Although the sentiment prompting the request was, as far as could be determined, a genuine interest in developing the best health policy, the request was regarded as "silly" by many involved in mental health services and research. For such experts, it was self-evident that no single entity could be called psychotherapy, nor could one identify 130 specific varieties. Some experts were also perturbed at characterizing psychotherapy as a technology, akin to computers and even medical procedures; and others were dismayed at the thought of psychotherapy procedures being evaluated at all.

Given the disjuncture between how legislators described the problem and how psychotherapy was seen by some mental health professionals, it was clear that a major focus of the report had to be an elucidation of the nature of psychotherapy and the ways in which different types of research information might be used to evaluate its effects. One advantage for the project director (senior author of this chapter) was that he was a social psychologist, rather than a clinician. Due to his background, he shared a common language with clinicians and clinical researchers (or, at least, understood their language), but his stake in the outcome was minimal and he had no theoretical or technical "ax to grind" (see also Banta & Saxe, 1983; Saxe, 1982).

OTA's function can be characterized as a "funnel" to provide scientific information to the Congress. Thus it was important for the research report to reflect broadly acceptable scientific understandings of the problem. Although scientific analysis is often contentious, as when one theoretical school "attacks" another, OTA's function is to stand above such internecine disputes and describe shared understandings. When that is not possible, then its responsibility is to identify where disagreement lies. In order to achieve neutrality in this project, it was important that the project director not reflect a particular bias. Also, outside contractors were employed to do initial project work, and the entire project was "kept honest" by a six-person advisory committee, which included psychologists, psychiatrists, an economist, and a citizen mental health activist.

FINDINGS

The report, in its final form, discussed four issues: (1) the definition and complexity of psychotherapeutic treatments, (2) the degree to which psychotherapy is amenable to scientific analysis, (3) the evidence of efficacy of psychotherapeutic treatments, and (4) the appropriateness and results of CEA/CBA studies of psychotherapy.

The essence of the report's conclusion was that psychotherapy is complex, yet evaluable by accepted scientific procedures. Its complexity was described in terms of the factors that determine its effectiveness. They included such elements as the theoretical orientation of the therapist, the nature of the problem, and the treatment setting. It was suggested that psychotherapy could not be described by simple labels. Nevertheless, various methods that have been used to evaluate the effectiveness of treatment (e.g., randomized designs) were described, and it was indicated how inferences could be developed across studies.

The report also attempted to summarize the substantive findings of psychotherapy outcome reasearch. This was perhaps the most difficult aspect of the study, in part because of the enormous number of studies that were potentially relevant. Thus, the review focused on a series of prominent reviews of the psychotherapy literature and commentary generated by these reviews. Surprisingly, at least to the study team, the conclusions of most reviews were found to be positive and there seemed to be a clear trend: The more recent the review, the more positive the finding. Although it is difficult to make global statements, the report suggested that available evidence seemed more supportive of psychotherapy than of alternative explanations and that treatment seemed demonstrably better than no treatment. It was not possible, however, to indicate under which conditions psychotherapy would be effective and which aspects of treatment were responsible for outcomes.

In essence, the assessment of psychotherapy involved explicating the nature of the interventions (i.e., technology) and marshalling evidence as to their effects. This effort differed from evaluations of psychotherapy typically conducted by mental health researchers in that it did not assume effectiveness and did not attempt to make the case for a particular treatment. As policy analysis, the technology assessment took a much broader focus than usual and attempted to be objective about the nature and outcomes of psychotherapeutic interventions. It also did not attempt to understand the process of therapy, but merely tried to develop a model that would explain its overall impact.

POLICY USE

The report was released in 1980 (OTA, 1980) and was completed in time to contribute to the evolving congressional debate about Medicare. The report was reviewed positively in the professional community, perhaps due to relief that a technology assessment could identify positive benefits. The report's conclusion, however, left Congress with a dilemma. Considerable scientific evidence was presented that psychotherapy is effective, at least compared with the alternative of not providing treatment. The report also indicated that the field of psychotherapy evaluation is relatively new and that only in recent years have substantial data accumulated. Because of the newness of rigorous evaluation efforts and changes in mental health treatments, many questions remained unanswered. Specifically, existing data did not indicate which type of psychotherapy in which setting would be optimal for which patient. From a policy perspective, such specific information is necessary.

Stimulated in part by the report and by discussions with OTA, Finance Committee staff working with their senators devised an ingenious approach to the problem. Coverage for psychotherapy would be expanded based on evidence of efficacy and safety. Because existing data were inadequate or not directly applicable, a special commission would be established to advise the government as to the conditions under which reimbursement should be provided. The commission would synthesize existing research data, consider them in light of clinical experience, and make specific Medicare coverage recommendations. Referred to as the "efficacy" amendment, this proposal was developed into a bill and introduced by Senator Matsunaga. It was an interesting solution because it satisfied many critics who thought psychotherapy would not meet the test of research scrutiny. Proponents were, of course, more sanguine that such positive evidence could be provided.

The efficacy amendment did not become law, however, in part because the elections of 1980 led to a change from Democratic to Republican control of the Senate and its committees. Since that time, the financial condition of the Medicare program has deteriorated and very few proposals for expanded coverage have been considered.

Alcoholism

OTA's alcoholism project was an outgrowth of the conditions that led to the demise of the efficacy amendment. By the time the 97th Congress organized in early 1981, it was clear that major changes would be made to Medicare. Costs of health care, and of the Medicare program in particular, were increasing faster than in any other sector of the economy; in addition, deliberate efforts were being made by the new administration to shift spending priorities. With control of the Senate shifting to the Republican party, there was the potential for far-reaching change.

BACKGROUND

Again, as with the psychotherapy project, the requesting committee for the alcoholism study was the Senate Finance Committee, this time chaired by Senator Dole. In the summer of 1982, as part of the budget process that required the Finance Committee to set spending targets, it was agreed to reduce the Medicare budget over a 5-year period by $13 billion. Such a reduction could not be achieved by administrative or even eligibility changes. In order to accomplish this reduction, it was necessary to review specific benefits.

Alcoholism treatment was, in the view of some, a likely target for cost-cutting. Treatment programs for alcoholics served a population believed to be responsible for their own problem. In addition, unlike some other patient groups, alcoholics were unlikely to have an organized lobby that could generate widespread public sympathy and support. Also, as a result of initial investigation by committee staff, several examples of fraud and abuse had been detected.

The most dramatic examples of alleged fraud concerned a proprietary hospital system, Raleigh Hills, located in a number of western states. Raleigh Hills had become well known because of its use of aversive conditioning techniques (e.g., pairing alcohol use with vomiting) as the centerpiece of its inpatient alcohol treatment program (Smith, 1982). Raleigh Hills had been highlighted by news reports in Los Angeles and Denver for alleged violations of Medicare rules, principally involving shifting patients from one facility to another to extend eligibility. Senate Finance Committee staff were convinced that the high cost of inpatient treatment provided by such facilities was not justified.

They were fairly open about seeking OTA's help in providing "scientific" documentation about the inefficacy of treatment for alcoholism.

STUDY

As with the psychotherapy project, this was a low-investment project and it was done as a "case study" within a larger study of the Medicare system. The charge was also similar to the psychotherapy project: the study focus was to synthesize scientific evidence on efficacy and to assess the cost-effectiveness of alcoholism treatment. Because of budget and time constraints, the study would be reviewed by the advisory panel of the larger study, along with a large group of ad hoc reviewers. The project team worked as outside consultants supervised by the staff of the Medicare project.

The report's organization paralleled the psychotherapy report. It began with an overview of the alcoholism problem and the multiple approaches to treatment. Even more explicitly than the mental health problems that are the focus of psychotherapy, alcoholism is dealt with by multiple disciplines, and much of the problem in understanding alcoholism stems from the question of to what extent it is a medical versus a social problem. The report attempted to sort out these issues and described the multiple etiological bases for alcoholism and how views of etiology affected treatment.

The report then reviewed both the range of research methods and findings about alcoholism. It suggested that because alcoholism had only recently been identified as a disease problem, research had been slow to catch up. The report found a substantial amount of evidence indicating that alcoholism can be treated. A major problem, however, is that we do not know which of the available treatment methods work with whom. The conclusion that an alcoholic is better off with treatment than without was sustained.

For policy purposes, probably the most important aspect of the report was its analysis of the costs of alcoholism and the effectiveness of treatments. Using data generated by economists, it estimated that alcoholism cost approximately $10,000 per alcoholic per year in 1980 dollars and, under such conditions, almost any investment in treatment was likely to be beneficial. Even those of us working on the report were surprised at the extent to which alcoholism had large and relatively easily measurable economic costs. Not only were data clear about the role of alcohol in traffic accidents and cirrhosis of the liver, but substantial evidence was available on the role of alcohol abuse in virtually every form of criminal and antisocial activity, as well as its pervasive impact on health care (costing up to 20 percent of our total health care expenditures).

As with the psychotherapy report, the conclusions of the alocholism case study were probably disappointing to requestors. They had sought ammunition to support funding cuts in alcohol treatment, and the evidence suggested otherwise. Perhaps the most important outcome of the report was that hearings were not scheduled before the Senate Finance Committee. The report suggested that the amount spent on alchoholism treatment was miniscule in relation to the cost of the problem, and it implied that increases in funding, rather than decreases, were required.

The alcoholism study, like the psychotherapy report, was a systems analysis and was influenced by a social psychological perspective. Alcohol was described as a multimodal problem requiring multiple treatments. An explicitly social psychological focus was not developed—no model of interpersonal processes was used. Nevertheless, the analysis implicitly assumed that alcoholism was a problem exacerbated by one's environment and amenable to treatment by taking the environment into account.

Polygraph Testing

A wholly different substantive problem was presented by the polygraph project. Its genesis was a change in polygraph regulations proposed by the Department of Defense (DoD) in 1982. The change would have resulted in the use of polygraphs for pre-employment and periodic security screening. This was followed by an even more far-reaching National Security Decision Directive issued by President Reagan in February, 1983, which instructed heads of agencies to develop policies to permit personnel with access to classified information to be subjected to polygraph testing in the event of information "leaks." The justification was the need to maintain secrecy of critical national security information.

The proposed DoD changes and the directive created an intense congressional reaction. Representative Jack Brooks, Chairman of the Government Operations Committee, was particularly concerned and asked both OTA and the General Accounting Office to study polygraph tests (see Brooks, in press). In his request to OTA, he specifically asked that the scientific validity of polygraph testing be investigated. Other representatives, including Patricia Schroeder, a member of the House Judiciary Committee, also called for investigations. In the Senate, the late Senator Jackson, ranking minority member of the Committee on Armed Services, was concerned and eventually engineered passage of an amendment to prevent the Defense Department from implementing expanded polygraph testing until Congress had reviewed the matter.

STUDY DESIGN

At OTA, although involvement in controversial issues was not new, the polygraph issue was novel. It was a relatively specific problem, but it was in an area that did not have a clear scientific disciplinary base and, to be sure, OTA had no prior experience with its assessment. Because of the emphasis of the request on the underlying scientific issues, which were assumed to be psychophysiological, the project was referred to the Health Program, and eventually the work was contracted out to the authors (OTA, 1983; Saxe et al., in press). We were selected because of our methodological expertise, our neutrality about the polygraph testing, and because of our "track record" with earlier OTA reports.

An important feature in this study was the use of an advisory panel. As with other OTA panels, its function was not to determine conclusions, but to provide nonbinding advice to OTA on the scientific issues. After a careful selection process, a panel composed of 12 individuals, most of whose members were scientists from psychology, medicine, and criminal justice, was formed. The panel included leading researchers on polygraph testing, as well as their critics, and several panel members had extensive experience as polygraph examiners. The number of proponents, opponents, and neutral scientists was carefully balanced.

STUDY RESULTS

The relatively specific focus of this study enabled us to deal with the complete population of relevant research. Using a number of bibliographic sources, we found that there were close to 4000 available references in the polygraph literature. It developed, however, that less than 10 percent of these sources were empirical investigations. Furthermore, of the 350 or so empirical studies, fewer than 40 were methodologically sound. Most empirical studies were case reports (e.g., from a police chief reporting on the number of examinations given by a particular department and their results). Despite the availability of a specific literature, however, in some respects the definitional problems and nature of the technology played an even more significant role in this study than in either the study of psychotherapy or alcoholism. As we immersed ourselves in literature about polygraph tests and held discussions with government and other experts, it became clear that little theory existed to explain polygraph test efficacy. Proponents and critics of testing often disagreed because they were referring to different aspects or uses of the technology.

As a result, much of our work consisted of trying to establish an understanding of how polygraph tests operated. On the surface, it appeared that there were various uses, which could be roughly classified as either screening (as in testing a large group of prospective employees for honesty) or specific incident testing (as in questioning a particular individual about a specific incident or crime). Although there are many nuances, it appears that screening uses very different techniques than specific incident testing. Screening tests use a version of what is called the Relevant/Irrelevant (R/I) test, in which physiological reactions to relevant questions are compared to reactions to irrelevant questions. A specific incident examination, in contrast, typically uses variations of the Control Question Test (CQT), in which reactions to questions that are supposed to be arousing for all subjects are compared to relevant questions about the specific incident being investigated.

An examination of the actual empirical data was revealing in a different way. First, despite extensive efforts, we were unable to find any evidence that directly investigated situations analogous to screening. Two studies came close, but there were enough differences to make them not generalizable. Almost all of the research evidence concerned the CQT, either from actual cases (field studies) or simulated situations (analogues). There were about 10 field studies of the use of the CQT and another two dozen analogue studies. Not only did the studies deal only with the CQT and specific incident situations, but they dealt mostly with criminal cases in which crime aganist persons was involved. With perhaps one exception, no studies investigated national security situations. This pattern suggested extreme restrictions to the generalizability of the available data.

Even more important, when we tried to develop an explanation for variability in accuracy rates across polygraph tests, it seemed clear that theory about testing was not well developed. Using social psychological data from the "bogus pipeline" studies, we developed our own tentative explanation. (The bogus pipeline is a procedure developed in the early 1970s to ascertain "true" attitudes by falsely convincing subjects in laboratory experiments that their verbal responses can be checked by a physiological "lie detector"; Jones & Sigall, 1971.) The findings with this technique suggest that the effects of a polygraph are due not to the test itself, but to the subject's perception of the test's efficacy. If a subject is convinced of the efficacy of the test, then it may be effective:

He or she will be afraid (aroused) when attempting to respond deceptively.

In addition to subjects' belief in the validity of the test, a number of other subject factors, either alone or in combination with belief, may affect outcomes. Thus, subjects' nervousness, sense of morality, intelligence, or psychopathy, as well as examiner training, may all affect test results. There may also be various ways for a subject to defeat the test. Perhaps the simplest countermeasure is to train individuals to believe that the polygraph can not detect them. Other means of defeating the test include physical movement in response to control questions, and the use of drugs to blunt responsiveness.

USE OF STUDY RESULTS

The political history of the polygraph study is not yet complete. Following release of OTA's report, findings were presented at hearings of the House Government Operations Committee. As a result, legislation was introduced that followed the line of argument of the report: namely, that there was no evidence for screening uses of the polygraph (see Brooks, in press). Parallel legislation was not introduced in the Senate although, as a result of the Jackson amendment, there was a need to hold hearings. The result of hearings held in the Senate and by the House Judiciary Committee—at both of which the OTA findings were presented—was that DoD did not go ahead with full implementation of polygraph screening.

The OTA study also generated other studies. The agency with the greatest stake in polygraph testing is the National Security Agency, a highly secretive component of DoD that conducts worldwide electronic surveillance (see Bamford, 1982). Under the auspices of the director of their polygraph program, Norman Ansley, a report (U.S. Department of Defense, 1984) was developed that purported to show the accuracy, but more important, the utility of testing. Early versions of the report reached very different conclusions from the OTA study, at one point claiming accuracy for polygraph testing of close to 100 percent (Ansley, 1983). Its final version, however, was much more circumspect and emphasized the so-called utility of polygraph tests.

It is not clear what will happen at this point. The government has begun a small-scale implementation. OTA staff and contractors continue to maintain contact with congressional staff involved in oversight of agencies that utilize polygraph tests. Interestingly, the use of the OTA report seems to have been very literal. From our perspective as authors, the most important conclusion had to do with the technique's lack of construct validity and the lack of research to validate most uses of testing. Yet, the common interpretation of the report was that there was limited validity for one type of use (specific incident testing) and no evidence for another (screening). In some respects, the important message about the lack of scientific theory underlying polygraph testing has been ignored. For proponents, it is an anathema and they cannot countenance the thought. Opponents of polygraph testing seem to regard concrete evidence (i.e., studies, however limited, or the lack of them) as the best offense. In the longer run, it is unclear what will be most important in influencing government policy. We would like to think that it will be the underlying ideas.

IMPLICATIONS

In the examples of social technology assessment described above, complex problems were attacked with a variety of problem-solving techniques. The analytic techniques were drawn in a loose way from social psychology. Although the problems addressed in these analyses were complicated ones, a number of implications of these assessments for applied social psychology and for the conduct of policy analysis can be suggested. The theme underlying our analysis is that the utilization of social science (and social psychology in particular) is greater than is usually acknowledged, but that utilization occurs in much more complex ways than are traditionally considered. Furthermore, we believe that social psychology provides a unique perspective for policy analysis. It facilitates explanation of complex phenomena from a frame of reference distinct from the problem, yet representative of societal concerns.

Traditions are changing, but for a long time social scientists have clung to the view that "if only" policymakers would better use our theories and data, the most deleterious social problems could be solved (see, for example, Lindbloom & Cohen, 1980; Weiss, 1977). To be sure, this optimism has not been unbounded. Many who have advocated the greater use of social science have called for major reforms in the way social scientists approach application (particularly, policy uses). Yet for some (e.g., Massad, Sales, & Acosta, 1983), improving the knowledge utilization process is mostly a function of getting more social science into the hands of policymakers. Massad et al. see this happening when social researchers develop a better understanding of the policy process. Such understanding is probably important, but it is insufficient. Successful use of psychological concepts and research by policymakers is dependent on a host of factors. These include how problems are defined, the credibility of researchers, the nature of the arguments developed by researchers, the quality and availability of the research evidence, the ability of analysts to communicate their ideas and research findings, and the timeliness of the policymakers' interest in the issue.

Although the policymakers affected by the projects described above are unique, as are the problems, an analysis of how they functioned suggests a view of the policy application process that has wide relevance to public policy. It is a view of problem-driven research that both adheres to standards of conceptual rigor and is sensitive to how psychological theory and data are used by policymakers. As will be described below, our analysis suggests a number of altenative ways of viewing social psychology's contribution and function in policy analysis.

The Assessment Process

The starting point for a policy analysis conducted by an organization such as OTA is a specific problem. Rarely is this problem clearly social psychological, as no technology (i.e., set of interventions) is uniquely associated with social psychology. Although social psychologists have made important contributions to intergroup problems such as racism and prejudice, as well as to understanding of mental health problems, education, and other fields, each area has its own substantive experts. Thus it should not be surprising that each of the technology assessment studies described above was not originally planned to be analyzed by social psychologists.

In some respects, this position of social psychology within policy analysis is no different than that of other fields. Health problems, for example, are often expressed by policymakers as economic ones, much to the chagrin of medical practitioners. And problems of school integration are often addressed as social justice problems rather than educational ones. It seems clear that, for policy purposes, the content of the problem may be different than the context within which it occurs. In many situations, a problem becomes a public policy issue because of the failure of substantive experts to solve it within their own domain. Each of the cases described above reflects such a failure.

Another feature of the way in which policymakers present questions is that they describe them in global terms: Is psychotherapy cost-effective? Is treatment for alcoholism effective? Does a polygraph test have validity? Such questions cannot be answered by single research studies. Although policymakers thrive on dramatic illustrations of problems (they make better media "news"), there is implicit recognition of the need to "weigh" the body of evidence. In the alcoholism project, for example, although charges of fraud and abuse were highlighted as part of Senate hearings, there was recognition that policy could not be altered without considering systematic evidence of effectiveness.

It is also true that policy problems can be reframed for particular groups to answer. Particularly in the case of OTA, requesting committees need to shape their questions in a way that is amenable to syntheses of scientific findings. This requires that questions be stated neutrally and with an emphasis on objective analysis. It is one of the side-benefits of OTA's bipartisan structure that congressional staff are guided to frame questions scientifically. Congressman Brooks, for example, had strong beliefs about polygraph testing before asking OTA to conduct its study, yet his study request was made in a neutral way and certainly did not necessitate a particular answer.

CREDIBILITY

Given that there are very few universally accepted principles in social science, how does one gain credibility for a particular position on a technology assessment issue? In OTA's case, there are several important mechanisms: the organization's structure, its reputation, and the use of advisory panels. Each of these played an important role in determining the influence generated by the assessments described above.

In contrast to research done by individual investigators, OTA reports are the result of a team effort. OTA is organized much like a university, with programs (departments) and divisions (colleges), yet a strong collaborative norm exists. Individuals work on multiple projects and there is extensive formal and informal review of projects (see Wood, 1982). This process operates both internally and externally and, for the most part, the feedback process is collegial. Although intense disagreements sometimes arise about project conclusions, the process is designed to resolve these conflicts and produce a product that has broad acceptability.

The use of advisory panels is also crucial to OTA's credibility. As described above, advisory panels, particularly on a project level, are important in the conduct of assessments. They do not, like panels established by the National Academy of Sciences, determine project conclusions, but they do provide critical input about the focus of the project and serve as quality-control reviewers of content, Anaysts attempt to incorporate the information provided by advisors and reviewers in the final product. Although this is not always possible because reviewers' information may be contradictory, irrelevant, or incorrect, reviewers' comments usually have a major impact on project reports.

The effect of the team nature of projects and the use of advisory panels is that OTA reports have a credibility that would not be possible in other situations. Reports are not merely the opinions of their authors, but have the imprimatur of the U.S. Congress. Even when reports are not reviewed by OTA's Board (as with each of the projects described above), most congressional staff have respect for the organization and seem to give OTA's views much weight. In part, the weight may be exaggerated, for there is an assumption that science has objective answers (hence the nonpartisan structure of OTA), and when opinions are delivered by OTA they are regarded as the "best" of current knowledge.

NEUTRALITY

OTA has been criticized (e.g., Dreyfus, 1977) for not having "the time, or perhaps temerity, to offer policy judgements on politically charged issue[s]" (p. 105). This is intentional, as noted earlier. Analysts are expected to take a neutral stance and OTA reports never include recommendations, per se. Dreyfus suggests that OTA's early work was characterized by presentations of undigested facts. Although the OTA goal of an "evenhanded" presentation might suggest dull and perhaps unhelpful analyses, in our view that was not a problem in the work we have conducted. The way in which one chooses to organize a problem, from its definition to the nature of evidence used to assess it, inherently involves an active and critical processing of information.

A key way in which evenhandedness is operationalized is in the choice of staff. Often project staff are chosen for their expertise in a particular problem area, but more often they are chosen because of generic methodological or policy analysis skills. In our case, we were not initially expert in any of the three project areas, yet we feel that this initial lack of substantive expertise worked to our advantage. Not having a wealth of information already schematized and a particular theoretical view of the problem allowed us to be more objective about analyzing data. In the psychotherapy study, it made it possible to conceptualize mental health treatments as an entity and not emphasize either behavioral, humanistic, or dynamic approaches. In the alcoholism project, it made it possible to examine the overall societal impact of alcoholism and not get entangled, as was the literature at that time, in disputes about such matters as controlled drinking and aversive conditioning. In the polygraph study, if we had been initial advocates of a particular position, it might not have been possible even to gather a group of advisory panel members to talk about the problem.

This is not to say that we were totally neutral. In fact, our perspective as social psychologists (see Saxe, 1983) played an important role in how our analyses were conducted. No doubt we were influenced by this perspective (both its substantive and methodological elements) to see problems as ones of interaction. In addition, we looked for data that had high internal validity according to the criteria of Cook and Campbell (1979). If we had had no perspective at all, we would have been incapable of conducting the studies.

In the psychotherapy project, the principal conclusion was that efficacy must be viewed as the product of interaction among a variety of factors: the treatment, setting, nature of the patient's problem, and characteristics of the therapist. Our solution to the policy dilemma was to propose establishment of a commission that could fund research and translate its results into reimbursement policy. In the alcoholism report, the conclusion was similar: that the problem was multiply caused and that any treatment system needed to reflect the various factors. In an even clearer way, the polygraph study employed a social psychological model. The report suggested that polygraph effects are due to what social psychologists have called the "bogus pipeline"—convincing subjects that they can be detected.

It has long been recognized (e.g., Berg, 1975) that the technology assessment process is not value-free or nonpolitical. What we are suggesting is that our analyses, although evenhanded, have been guided by a set of values and, to some extent, a conceptual framework. In our case, the values concerned improving social conditions, and the framework was social psychology. There is an important distinction between such a framework and the usual way in which problems are examined. To some extent, the work of OTA is to monitor and control the application of science. What is needed is a framework that allows (relatively) objective assessment of the implications of a technology from a perspective external to the technology.

Thus, mental health technologies need to be evaluated by criteria other than those used by mental health professionals, and the polygraph should be assessed by nonpolygraphers. This approach is, in a sense, the operational definition of taking a societal policy perspective on a problem. In this approach, social psychology is an important conceptual framework—one that is neutral precisely because there is no technology directly associated with it. It does have implicit assumptions, such as its focus on individual-organism interactions and its use of rational analysis, but these are consistent with the assessment needs that our society expresses.

Evaluation of Social Psychological Input

It is important to examine critically what we have accomplished as social psychologists and the degree to which social psychology has influenced our assessments. As noted above, no technology is uniquely social psychological and this has both positive and negative effects on utilization of our disciplinary perspective. Below, several ways of viewing social psychology's usefulness are described.

LIMITED ROLE

The tone of this chapter has been very positive with respect to the contributions that social psychology can make to national public policy. A caveat needs to be offered, however, before the theme of positive contribution is developed further. The caveat has to do with the peripheral role that social psychology has played at OTA. Despite its influence in the projects we have conducted, its role in other projects has not been widespread. Early in this chapter we noted that the projects described here were not full technology assessments, and that they were mostly done by personnel working outside of OTA (as consultants/contractors). To date, there has not been a large-scale technology assessment that was primarily social psychological, such as a study of leadership (e.g., in government agencies) or prejudice (e.g., in school busing). A number of current projects do come closer to requiring inputs from social psychology, such as studies of AIDS (the government's response) and of the Indian Health Services, but these are atypical. Probably, the most important areas in which social psychology could be used are in assessments of problems such as energy conservation and the impact of office technology, but to date contributions by psychologists to these problems at OTA have been minimal.

The reason for this lack of social psychological involvement has to do as much with how social psychologists view their work as with policymakers' views of who can contribute. We psychologists are often socialized to be defensive about our disciplinary identification and to carve out a unique position for our work. Thus, for example, research that does not derive from a social psychological theory may not be considered social psychological. We have not yet developed an appreciation of how a general orientation to problems yields useful understandings.

As social psychologists, we are also frequently sensitive about the limits of our abilities to understand particular problems. Again, without existing theory that bears on a problem, many researchers are unwilling to study the problem. Clearly, theory is important, but policy problems should be regarded as challenges to develop theory, rather than dead-ends because no theoretical explanation is readily available. Until social psychologists become more secure about their potential contributions, it may be difficult for their ideas to be respected. In addition, there will be reluctance on the part of policymakers to use our information unless we have credibility, and developing credibility is a long-term process.

We view this anomalous role of social psychology somewhat ambivalently. On the one hand, following Mayo and LaFrance (1981), we see strength in the marginal role played by social psychology. It is our marginality that allows us to view problems from a different angle and develop analyses that are both objective and useful in providing new information. It is, in a sense, social psychology's lack of a physical technology of its own that permits us to see problems in a unique way.

It should be clear that we advocate greater use of social psychology, and we hope this chapter has provided encouragement for greater use by giving concrete examples of the social psychological point of view and how it has functioned. We should not, however, be deluded into believing that our perspective can resolve every problem or even be a major influence. Social psychology is a point of view that needs to be heard, but as one of a number of perspectives.

DEALING WITH COMPLEXITY

To return to specifics of our studies, what have we accomplished? It seems clear that our work for OTA has not changed particular national policy decisions—at least we have no direct evidence of such impact. What we believe has happened, however, as a result of our efforts is that the debate about the issues we assessed is more informed. We have provided frameworks to understand complex problems, and our work has served an educative function. The level of debate in Congress has been affected, and we have provided policymakers with previously unavailable tools to understand important problems.

In some discussions, public policy is presented as a simple decision-making process, in which a series of yes/no decisions is made about very specific problems. Our experience in the policy world suggests a contrary view. First, decisions are inordinately complex, and the number of factors that have to be considered in any one decision is staggering. Even those who are cynical about the role of partisan politics need to acknowledge that partisan concerns (e.g., how will particular constituents react to my decision?) are very complex. Consequently, policymakers need to include a large number of factors in their decisions over and above the strength of evidence about a particular problem.

In the case of psychotherapy, although the initial question seemed simple (is psychotherapy effective or not?), even the policymakers did not expect that it could be answered in a simple fashion. More important, the associated political issues were not simple. As was indicated at one point in personal discussions, the congressional staff opposed to increasing reimbursement for psychotherapy did not consider themselves "Neanderthals" and were interested in the welfare of the greatest number of people. Their concerns about psychotherapy were that it was a potentially uncontrollable technology (because demand for services is dependent on the client and practitioner) and that its value was dubious. Cost-benefit analysis attracted them because it suggested a formal way of making sense of a difficult set of trade-offs.

The issues were similar in the alcoholism study: in particular, there was skepticism about the worth of treatment for alcoholism. Here the complexity of the treatment system (its medical, psychological, and social welfare bases) is apt to mislead policymakers as to the nature of the problem, and multifaceted treatment is confused with malfocused understanding of the problem. Debate within the mental health community about the best ways to deal with the problem naturally provides additional confusion. Our task was to develop a model of the problem, supported by data, that could explain this complexity and suggest how responsible social policy might be formulated.

We feel that conceptualization of such problems is critical. From our point of view, a principal benefit of the polygraph study was its conceptualization of the technology as more than a "gadget." Individuals have, perhaps, too much faith in physical technologies, and a central theme of the report was that it was subjective aspects, such as the way in which questions were structured and how examiners related to subjects, that determined the effectiveness of tests. Although we indicated earlier that policymakers did not utilize the conceptual information as much as we would have liked, nevertheless our analysis changed the context of the discussion. Partly as a result of our efforts, the discussion moved from an emphasis on values about privacy and civil liberties, to a focus on the nature of the technology and its function.

Our analysis partially contradicts Bickman's (1981) discussion of differences between basic and applied research, particularly in the purpose of research and the methods used. According to Bickman, basic research is characterized by a knowledge-driven search for relationships and causes, whereas applied research is focused on problem solving and prediction. Our contention is that applied research, in order to solve policy problems, must be driven by a conceptual search for relationships and causes. Thus, the distinction between basic and applied research may be overstated. Applied research can and should be conceptual.

This view is consistent with empirical data collected by Weiss and Bucuvalas (1977). In a survey of federal, state, and local mental health policymakers, their perceptions of the usefulness of various research studies were examined. The results of the survey suggest that research is useful both when it helps to solve specific problems and when it questions perspectives and definitions of a problem. Thus, research is useful when it challenges the conceptual status quo.

The Future

It should be clear that our work on national policy issues for OTA is only one of several options for social psychology. Social psychology needs to proceed on a number of tracks: theory development (traditional, basic research), applied problems (investigator- as well as policymaker-initiated research), and also policy analysis. A critical question is whether social psychologists engaged in this myriad of activities, ranging from basic research to policy analysis, and cutting across a variety of substantive problems, can continue to talk with one another and to cross-fertilize one another's efforts. The answer is important, not only to the health of our discipline, but also to our ability to solve social problems. Social psychology is a voice that needs to be heard. We need to maintain our disciplinary identity, while simultaneously learning how to use our analytic skills to study and help resolve various social issues. This is a challenge, we believe, that the whole discipline needs to accept.

The view presented here is that social psychological analysis can serve an educative function and offer policymakers useful understandings of their policy dilemmas. The above examples of our work for OTA indicate that such analysis is possible and that it can influence how national policy is formulated. We did not necessarily change policy, but we influenced policy by making complexity understandable. In a pluralistic society committed to democratic ideals, that is perhaps all one should expect. As suggested by Brickman et al.'s (1982) analysis of responsibility for social problems, identifying the cause of a problem and developing its solution may be quite different enterprises. As psychological researchers we are seekers of knowledge, and if we can fulfill that role and also facilitate the solution of social problems, we will have more than met our responsibilities.

REFERENCES

Ansley, N. (1983). *A review of the scientific literature on the validity, reliability, and utility of polygraph techniques.* Fort Meade, MD: National Security Agency.

Arnstein, S. R. (1977). Technology assessment: Opportunities and obstacles. *IEEE Transactions on Systems, Man, and Cybernetics, 7,* 571-582.

Bamford, J. (1982). *The puzzle palace.* New York: Houghton Mifflin.

Banta, H. D., & Behney, C. J. (1981). Policy formulation and technology assessment. *Milbank Memorial Fund Quarterly, 51,* 445-479.

Banta, H.D., & Saxe, L. (1983). Reimbursement for psychotherapy: Linking efficacy research and public policymaking. *American Psychologist, 38,* 918-923.

Baram, M. S. (1973). Technology assessment and social control. *Science, 180,* 465-472.

Berg, M. R. (1975). The politics of technology assessment. *Journal of the International Society for Technology Assessment, 1,* 21-32.

Bickman, L. (1981). Some distinctions between basic and applied approaches. In L. Bickman (Ed.), *Applied social psychology annual* (Vol. 2, pp. 23-44). Beverly Hills, CA: Sage.

Brickman, P., Rabinowitz, V. C., Karuza, J., Jr., Coates, D., Cohen, E., & Kidder, L. H. (1982). Models of helping and coping. *American Psychologist, 37,* 368-384.

Brooks, J. (in press). Polygraph testing: Thoughts of a skeptical legislator. *American Psychologist, 40.*

Cook, T. D., & Campbell, D. T. (1979). *Quasi-experimentation: Design and analysis issues for field settings.* Chicago: Rand McNally.

Dreyfus, D. A. (1977). The limitations of policy research in congressional decision making. In C. H. Weiss (Ed.), *Using social research in public policy making.* Lexington, MA: D. C. Heath.

Frank, J. D. (1966). Galloping technology: A new social disease. *Journal of Social Issues, 22*(4), 1-14.

Gibbons, J. (1984). Technology assessment for the Congress. *The Bridge,* 2-8.

Glass, G. V, McGaw, B., & Smith, M. L. (1981). *Meta-analysis of social research.* Beverly Hills, CA: Sage.

Hahn, W. A. (August, 1977). *Technology assessment: Some alternative perceptions and its implementation outside the United States.* Testimony before the Subcommittee on Science, Research & Technology of the House Committee on Science and Technology.

Jones, E. E., & Sigall, H. (1971). The bogus pipeline: A new paradigm for measuring affect and attitude. *Psychological Bulletin, 76,* 349-364.

Koppel, B. (1979). Evaluating assessment: A comment and a perspective. *Technological Forecasting and Social Change, 14,* 147-152.

Lindblom, D. E., & Cohen, D. K. (1979). *Usable knowledge: Social science and social problem solving.* New Haven, CT: Yale University Press.

Massad, P. M., Sales, B. D., & Acosta, E. (1983). Utilizing social science information in the policy process: Can psychologists help? In R. F. Kidd & M. J. Saks (Eds.), *Advances in applied social psychology* (Vol. 2, pp. 213-229). Hillsdale, NJ: Lawrence Erlbaum.

Masters, J. C. (1984). Psychology, research, and social policy. *American Psychologist, 39,* 851-862.

Mayo, C., & LaFrance, M. (1980). Applicable social psychology. In R. F. Kidd & M. Saks (Eds.), *Advances in applied social psychology* (Vol. 1, pp. 90-107). Hillsdale, NJ: Lawrence Erlbaum.

Office of Technology Assessment, U.S. Congress. (1980). *The efficacy and cost-effectiveness of psychotherapy.* Washington, DC: Government Printing Office.

Office of Technology Assessment, U.S. Congress. (1983). *Scientific validity of polygraph testing* (OTA-TM-H-15). Washington, DC: Government Printing Office.

President's Commission on Mental Health. (1978). *Report to the President* (Vol. 1, GPO Stock No. 040-000-00390-8). Washington, DC: Government Printing Office.

Rosenthal, R. (1978). Combining results of independent studies. *Psychological Bulletin, 85*, 185-193.

Riecken, H. W., & Boruch, R. F. (Eds.). (1974). *Social experimentation: A method for planning and evaluating social intervention.* New York: Academic Press.

Saxe, L. (1982). Public policy and psychotherapy: Can evaluative research play a role? *New directions for program evaluation: Making evaluation useful to Congress* (No. 14). San Francisco: Jossey-Bass.

Saxe, L. (1983). The perspective of social psychology: Toward a viable model for application. In R. F. Kidd & M. J. Saks (Eds.), *Advances in applied social psychology* (Vol. 2, pp. 231-255). Hillsdale, NJ: Lawrence Erlbaum.

Saxe, L., & Fine, M. (1981). *Social experiments: Methods for design and evaluation.* Beverly Hills, CA: Sage.

Saxe, L., Dougherty, D., & Esty, K. (in press). Alcoholism: A public policy perspective. In J. Mendelson & N. Mello (Eds.), *The diagnosis and treatment of alcoholism.* New York: John Wiley.

Saxe, L., Dougherty, D., & Cross, T. (in press). The validity of polygraph testing: Scientific analysis and public policy. *American Psychologist, 40.*

Smith, J. W. (1982). Treatment of alcoholism in aversion conditioning hospitals. In E. M. Pattison & E. Kaufman (Eds.), *Encyclopedic handbook of alcoholism.* New York: Gardner Press.

U.S. Department of Defense. (1984). *The accuracy and utility of polygraph testing.* Washington, DC: Dutton.

Varela, J. (1975). Can social psychology be applied? In M. Deutsch & H. Hornstein (Eds.), *Applying social psychology: Implications for research, practice, and training* (pp. 157-173). Hillsdale, NJ: Lawrence Erlbaum.

Weiss, C. H. (1977). Introduction. In C. H. Weiss (Ed.), *Using social research in public policy making* (pp. 1-22). Lexington, MA: D.C. Heath.

Weiss, C. H., & Bucuvalas, M. J. (1977). The challenge of social research to decision making. In C. H. Weiss (Ed.), *Using social research in public policy making* (pp. 213-230). Lexington, MA: D.C. Heath.

Wood, F. B. (1982). The status of technology assessment: A view from the Congressional Office of Technology Assessment. *Technological Forecasting and Social Change, 22*, 211-222.

PAUL R. KIMMEL

14

INFLUENCING SOCIAL POLICY
IN THE PUBLIC INTEREST

An increasing number of psychologists are becoming knowledgeable about public policy activities (Pion & Lipsey, 1984). There are several factors that explain the growing appeal of public policy, including the development of applied research (Weiss, 1977), a reduction in the number of more traditional academic and professional job opportunities (Stapp & Fulcher, 1982), and an interest in protecting established programs and funding in psychology at both the state and federal levels (Pallak, 1982). Another factor, more difficult to measure but of special interest here, is a growing concern among psychologists with the public interest—a concern that comes from a sense of social responsibility and perhaps also from what Bevan (1982) refers to as "professional patriotism." In this chapter, this motivation will be illustrated through case studies of four psychologists involved in public interest science.

Perl, Primack, and von Hipple (1974) coined the term "public interest science" to refer to the activities of physical scientists who brought technological information to the general public when they thought it necessary to have issues discussed outside industrial and government channels. A few social scientists have similarly called attention to industrial or governmental programs that they believed were not in the public interest, but others have been reluctant to do so because their data are not as "concrete" as those of the physical scientists. Thus, the public interest activities of most social scientists have been undertaken as private citizens and are not seen by them as being scientific or professional.

Rather than discuss the impracticality of separating private from professional activities (Bevan, 1970; Gouldner, 1970) or the role of values in most social science (Gouldner, 1969; Myrdal, 1972; Shadish, 1984), I will use the phrase "public interest science" as it pertains to the social sciences in a different sense than it has been used by the physical scientists. I will follow Sjoberg's definition of a social science "predicated upon respect for human dignity" that is "especially enhanced when humans are free to participate in the construction of structurally meaningful choices" (Sjoberg, 1975, pp. 43-44). Social scientists who become involved in public policy to enhance human dignity in this way are, by this definition, doing public interest science. This definition surely encompasses the activities of many psychologists.

To help clarify public policy issues and encourage the involvement of psychologists in public interest activities, the Board of Social and Ethical Responsibility in Psychology (BSERP) of the American Psychological Association (APA) established a Task Force on Psychology and Public Policy in 1980. As a member of that task force, I interviewed six psychologists recommended to me as having been involved in public interest science and influential in social policy issues. A condensation of several of those interviews was used in the task force's final report (Task Force on Psychology and Public Policy, 1984) to illustrate the variety of ways in which psychologists can influence the public policy process, and the complexity of that process. Case studies of the activities of four of these psychologists are presented here.[1]

METHOD

Three of these interviews were conducted by telephone and three were done in person, with five of the six conversations being recorded. I asked each respondent to tell me about an incident in their career in which they believed they had had an impact on public policy. All of them were able to identify such an incident except Dr. Gardner, who felt that it would be more useful to give a general overview of the role his psychological training played in his career. The interview method was a variation of the oral history approach, with the majority of my questions being requests for clarification or elaboration (McPherson & Popplestone, 1967). Three of the respondents gave me bibliographic references about the incidents they were discussing.

I wrote a draft of each interview from my notes and the available recordings and references. They were written in the third person with active verbs, and condensed and reorganized to provide chronological and topical coherence for the reader. Although this editing made the case studies more readable, it may in some instances have oversimplified and overdramatized the role of that individual in the complex and collaborative policy processes. To ensure that I had not distorted the facts as they were seen by the respondents, I sent the drafts to them within two weeks of the interview. All of their suggested revisions were incorporated in the BSERP Task Force's Final Report. I checked again with each of the six psychologists more than a year later in light of review comments on this chapter. Their reactions and suggestions were all used in writing the case studies that appear below.

Readers should keep in mind that differences of opinion and value are inherent in policy activities (Bauer, 1966). One person's fact is another's opinion; one person's idea of truth may not be the same as another's. These case studies describe the essential aspects of key incidents as seen by the respondents. Their interpretations would probably not always agree with those of other actors in these incidents but, to paraphrase Thomases' theorem, they are true for them and thus real in their consequences (Thomas & Thomas, 1928). All of the events described actually took place, and I have no reason to doubt the honesty and integrity of the respondents' reports.

The emphasis in all of these case studies is on social policy processes—from the identification and definition of the problem, through policy formation, adoption, and implementation, to the assessment of policy impact (Task Force on Psychology and Public Policy, 1984). As a result, there is a minimum amount of information provided about the substantive issues involved. Readers who want more detail on the legal, administrative, or research issues alluded to in these studies should consult the references and other public records.

In 1974, Primack and von Hipple reported, "Currently it takes an unusually adventurous and astute individual to be an effective public interest scientist" (p. 286). This is still true today and perhaps more so for social than for physical scientists (as most policymakers feel they already "know" about human behavior). These case studies are presented to provide stimulation and guidance to other social scientists who would like to develop or expand their work in public policy to promote the public interest.

DR. JOHN GARDNER—PUBLIC SERVANT

Former Secretary of Health, Education and Welfare (HEW)
Founder of Common Cause

Ph.D., Berkeley, 1938
General Psychology

Most people are not aware that John Gardner trained and worked as a psychologist. He taught at three universities, and worked for the Federal Communications Commission and the Office of Strategic Services from 1938 through 1945. After World War II, while he was with the Carnegie Corporation (where he served as President from 1955 to 1965), Dr. Gardner did 19 years of consulting with government agencies such as the National Aeronautics and Space Administration (NASA), HEW, the Air Force, and the State Department. From 1955 to 1960, he served on several boards and committees of the APA. Gradually, he moved away from psychology and into government service. Today, he would "never think" of holding himself out as a psychologist because he has not kept abreast of the field. However, he often dips back into the field and believes that his training has been quite useful in his career as a public servant. He still thinks "statistically" and often comes back to a preoccupation with motivation and personal development in his writing (Gardner, 1973).

Gardner stresses the need for developing citizen concern and support when "fighting battles" on social issues in the public arena, as he did at Common Cause. He became interested in forming this "Citizens' Lobby" when he headed the Urban Coalition at the time of turmoil in the cities in the late 1960s. He saw a need for a citizens' group to hold all levels of government accountable. His experience in opinion polling gave him a sense that there was a constituency for an organization like Common Cause, but even he was surprised to recruit 100,000 members in 23 weeks (membership is now around 250,000). In polling these members—a practice that continues within Common Cause— Gardner and his colleagues found more interest in Vietnam than in urban problems. Following where member interest led, Common Cause played a key role in getting congressional action to end United States involvement in Indochina.

In selecting later Common Cause issues, such as combating secrecy in government or corruption in campaign financing, Gardner looked at opinion surveys to find the points on which public education was needed. His background in survey research assisted him in assessing the reliability of various polls and in following public reactions over time. He feels that being in touch with public opinion was helpful in assessing the amount and type of public education required to generate the citizen support necessary to produce reforms.

When Gardner was working in the area of civil rights, he found his background in psychology very helpful for understanding the studies and reports done by social scientists like Coleman, Jencks, and Mosteller. The available data enabled him to become more knowledgeable about most aspects of the civil rights situation and to check out allegations as to what that situation was. His subsequent actions were taken in the light of available information and his best intuitions. Gardner has a preference for quantitative studies done by researchers who look at both the facts they like and the facts they don't like. He "feels at home" with quantitative research reports that illuminate various aspects of complex policy issues, but believes that research on social issues cannot provide "answers" to political questions and that the data will always be incomplete.

Another area in which Gardner finds his quantitative training helpful is in evaluation. As Secretary of HEW, he set up the Office of Planning and Evaluation in response to Bureau of the Budget requests for evaluations of programs. He hired highly trained social scientists such as William Gorham and Alice Rivlin, but he was always aware that some HEW programs would be extremely difficult to assess. For example, in the health field it was relatively easy to measure mortality, morbidity, and hospital visits. From these and other measures, the Office of Planning and Evaluation could do cost-effectiveness studies of different types of care. It proved much more difficult, however, to measure the outcomes of education and welfare programs. Gardner's background enabled him to help his staff plan and interpret HEW's evaluation efforts in a discriminating way.

Dr. Gardner considers psychology to be one of the great liberal arts subjects—a generalist subject. He says it has helped him to be sensitive to issues and opinions that are outside the fashionable categories created by the media and the government, and assisted him to be more precise in his thinking about complex policy options and program evaluations.

Common Cause does not employ psychologists. Their "research group" is primarily responsible for drafting brief policy memoranda that distill a great deal of material into policy alternatives for the Board of Directors. Like many policy groups, these researchers do not have time to do the kinds of primary research that psychologists do, but rely on the findings of other social scientists in developing policy alternatives.

John Gardner's and Common Cause's contributions to the public interest illustrate the value of having individuals with psychological training become public officials, and the importance of applied research on policy issues to such officials and their organizations.

DR. NATHAN S. CAPLAN—APPLIED RESEARCHER

Professor, University of Michigan   Ph.D., Case Western, 1961
Staff, Center for Research on the Utilization   Educational Psychology
  of Scientific Knowledge

Dr. Nathan Caplan has long been interested in the use of social science knowledge in national policy decisions, a subject on which he did a well-known and influential survey (Caplan, Morrison, & Stambaugh, 1975). His conceptualization of the policy process and the way in which problem identification and definition influence both research and policy are invaluable, though sometimes overlooked by other researchers (Caplan & Nelson, 1973; Nelson & Caplan, 1983). His work with the Commission on Civil Disorders (the Kerner Commission) in 1968 will be discussed here as a vivid illustration of his point that "how you go into research determines how you come out."

As a result of visiting the Detroit riot area in the summer of 1967, Dr. Caplan had strong feelings about what the Detroit *Free Press* characterized as a "police riot." He gladly accepted an Institute for Social Research (ISR) assignment to do a quick survey in Detroit's black community, in spite of the concerns of some colleagues who believed the results would be used to inflame the controversy, as the police were building a case for outside provocateurs. Caplan, however, believed that it was important to get all sides of the picture and that the public was not being fully informed. He carried out the study with the strong support of the Detroit paper that sponsored the survey and a great deal of volunteer professional time. He was gratified when the fears of some of his colleagues proved groundless and the survey data showed that the rioters were not outside provocateurs financed by the Soviet Union. The results of this survey became an important part of the *Free Press's* Pulitzer Prize winning series on the riots.

Dr. Caplan's work in Detroit was brought to the attention of the Commission on Civil Disorders by Dr. Robert Shellow, who was on loan from NIMH as a research director for the Commission. Caplan, believing it important to expand the survey, had written NIMH about his work and committed ISR funds to extend the enumeration which would serve as the basis for sample selection. Caplan was hired as a consultant to the Commission with the task of extending his Detroit research and developing similar surveys in Newark and possibly Milwaukee. Again he was cautioned by fellow researchers not to get involved with such a "hot potato" where political considerations might overrule empiricism. Some of their concern came from the dismissal of several social scientists, including Shellow, from the staff of the Commission in a controversy over an interim report. Caplan, however, found this report—which emphasized clinical and psychoanalytic theories about child-rearing by single parents—tangential to the concerns of the Commission and set out to gather more pertinent information.

It was important to Dr. Caplan that the work he was doing was sponsored by the Commission that he wanted to influence. He was given responsibility for all the survey research done by the Commission and assurances that the commissioners would listen to his findings. The cooperation and support of the Commission's chief-of-staff, David Ginsburg, and his assistant, Victor Palmieri, were instrumental in realizing these assurances. To ensure that the findings would be relevant,

Caplan listened to the commissioners' theories about the motivation of the rioters and structured the surveys to test their suppositions. He learned that the most popular theory was what he called the "riff-raff hypothesis": that the rioters were the dregs of society—poor, criminal, transient, undereducated, and emotionally disturbed.

In comparing the rioters with nonrioters in the Detroit and Newark surveys, Caplan found that there were few significant differences in income, education, employment, or emotional stability between the two groups and those differences favored the rioters (e.g., the rioters had higher GPAs in high school than the nonrioters). He reported these findings at a Commission meeting, and as he expected, several of the commissioners were startled. But rather than ignoring these results, as some critics predicted, these commissioners responded to the failure of the riff-raff theory by becoming more willing to listen to other explanations of the rioters' behavior. The hypothesis best supported by the data was that of closed opportunity. Those blacks who rioted had more pride in themselves and their race (high personal efficacy) than the nonrioters and, as a result, were more frustrated by discrimination (low political efficacy). These findings supported Deputy Commissioner John Lindzey's theory of social injustices (due to racism) that needed correction. Caplan's results aided Lindzey, who had a gift for charismatic writing, in creating the eloquent and influential introduction and conclusion of the final report.

Caplan and his associate, Jeffrey Paige, were given responsibility for the final editing of much of the Commission's report, some of which was premised on the findings of their surveys. Once again, to the amazement of many social scientists including Caplan himself, there was little rewriting of their work, with most of the edited copy going directly from them to the printer. The rumored censorship never took place, again thanks to the support of Ginsburg and Palmieri.

Dr. Caplan believes that the reason they had the trust of the Commission and its staff was their demonstrated competence and their responsiveness to the Commission's concerns. They had been observers of one of the riots and had contacted some of the participants. They had taken account of the Commissioners' preconceptions about the rioters and had dealt with them in a convincing empirical manner. And they had presented and validated a plausible interpretation of the rioters' motivation that was in concert with the ideas of one of the most influential members of the Commission. Dr. Caplan is convinced that he would not have taken this applied research approach if he had been working on a grant. The only academic payoff from his work with the Commission was an article in the *Scientific American* (Caplan, 1968).

But by not taking a more "academically interesting" approach to the riots, Caplan found a way to be heard and to influence the decisions of policymakers. The report of the Kerner Commission was instrumental in opening doors for more blacks to move into higher level positions in business, government, and academe.

DR. NANCY FELIPE RUSSO—ADVOCATE

Administrative Officer, Women's Programs,   Ph.D., Cornell, 1970
American Psychological Association   Social Psychology

As President of the Federation of Organizations for Professional Women (FOPW), head of its Task Force on the Equal Rights Amendment, and program officer for the Women's Program Office at APA, Dr. Nancy Felipe Russo has been involved in many public policymaking efforts, including passage of the women in science federal legislation in 1980. Although this legislation was officially introduced by Senator Edward Kennedy on March 7, 1979, a great deal of earlier work had been done by Dr. Russo and other women scientists in establishing networks and coalitions and gathering the data necessary for a successful legislative campaign.

Between 1975 and 1979, several conferences were held that were important sources of information and legitimization for the development of the women in science legislation. Two of the most important were held in February and March, 1978. The first, funded by the National Science Foundation (NSF), was designed to review the data gathered by Dr. Janet Brown of the American Association for the Advancement of Science (AAAS) on the participation of women in scientific research. The scientists at this meeting drafted policy recommendations to assist NSF in increasing the flow of women into science. At the end of the conference, the participants attended Senator Kennedy's press briefing on the Women in Science and Technology Equal Opportunity Act (later to become the National Science Foundation and Women in Science Authorization Act).

The second conference was sponsored by the Association for Women in Science's Educational Foundation and the New York Academy of Sciences. The powerful and prestigious participants there (such as Rosalyn Yalow, Estelle Ramey, and Charlotte Friend) demonstrated the support of government, academe, and industry for expanding the role of women in the sciences and provided comprehensive documentation on the issue, which became the basis for later legislative testimony. Dr. Russo stressed the importance of having such "clout" and "a network of powerful individuals to wield that clout" over the tortuous course of any legislative campaign.

In spite of their extensive preparation, the women working on the women in science bill had much to learn about the legislative process. They were assisted immeasurably in their efforts by legislative assistants, science fellows, and interns on Capitol Hill who worked with the legislators and committees considering the bill. On August 1, 1979, the Senate Subcommittee on Health and Scientific Research (which had held the only hearings on Kennedy's first bill in April, 1978) discussed the issue of equal opportunity for women in science in hearings on the health and needs of U.S. women. Women such as Dr. Russo, who represented multiple constituencies, worked diligently at mobilizing support for the Kennedy bill on the Hill and among scientific and educational groups. Seven months later the subcommittee held another day of hearings at which testimony was provided by well-known women scientists and officials at NSF.

In April, 1980, the subcommittee unanimously voted to send the Kennedy bill to the full Senate Committee on Labor and Human Resources that Kennedy chaired. Senator Hatch proposed a substitute bill that would have diffused the intent of the women in science legislation. The women's networks, working through Kris Iversen, Senator Hatch's legislative assistant on the bill, and Bob Knouss from Senator Kennedy's staff, persuaded Senator Hatch to modify his proposal so that the bipartisan compromise so necessary to the passage of any legislation could be developed. The information provided by the women's networks convinced the senator that parts of the original proposal would better meet his goals than would his own legislation.

The NSF and Women in Science Authorization Act passed the Senate on June 23, 1980. The women scientists had gained a victory, but now had to influence the House of Representatives and the House-Senate conference committee. In spite of their best efforts, they did not have the resources to keep up a sustained campaign in both houses simultaneously. However, their increasing political sophistication allowed them to support a strategy that would bypass the lengthy committee process in the House. They waited while the House passed the authorization legislation for NSF on September 4, 1980, including authorization levels stated as proportions of whatever amounts were appropriated (thus circumventing the normal appropriations committee procedures—a potential setback for the women in science funding).

With little time left in the 96th Congress (because any bill not passed and signed before a Congress adjourns must begin anew in the next

Congress), Dr. Russo and the other women scientists supporting the bill lobbied the House-Senate conference committee. Individual scientists were contacted to write committee members from their districts; scientific organizations such as the American Chemical Society and the American Physical Society were encouraged to support the bill; phone calls, letters, and follow-up visits were made to conference committee members; and President Carter was persuaded to make a personal commitment to the passage and implementation of the legislation by means of a telegram to Senator Kennedy signed by 44 women's groups urging him to ask the President "to clarify and emphasize the Administration's strong support for the bill."

During those last months of 1980, the women scientists learned about "horsetrading" on the Hill as they saw members of Congress trading votes on the women in science bill for votes on other issues. A move to include minority concerns in the legislation was mediated in a meeting with Representative George Brown of California, in which a minority woman scientist, Shirley Malcolm, pointed out the need for separate attention to minority and women's interests. A compromise reflecting the concerns of both minorities and women in science was developed. The women did some "horsetrading" themselves when they threatened to boycott a White House reception to celebrate the signing of the women in science bill unless they received a public commitment from NSF and the President's Office of Science and Technological Policy to implement the legislation. They got this commitment.

The conference report was agreed to by the Senate on November 21, 1980, and by the House on December 2, 1980. A somewhat ambivalent President Carter signed it into law on December 12, 1980. Because of his reservations and the change in the political climate after the 1980 elections, the support publicly promised by NSF for the women in science program was crucial. The change of administration meant that money for the program was not available in 1981, due to new Office of Management and Budget (OMB) regulations against starting new federal programs. However, even without the funding, the passage of the legislation caused many changes at NSF, such as the establishment of a Committee on Equal Opportunity in Science and Technology that provides ongoing surveillance of NSF's activities regarding women and minorities, and a program of visiting professorships for women in science and engineering.

In a chapter documenting the increased participation of women in organizing for equality in science and technology, Dr. Russo points out that the women in science bill was one of several results of women activists' growing realization that they have to work "together to document [their] needs, develop effective political strategies, and . . . articulate feasible solutions to [their] problems" (Russo & Cassidy, 1983, p. 250).

Dr. Russo looks back on the women in science bill as an educational process, extending the policymaking knowledge of those involved. They learned to know each other and gained the political skills necessary to attain their objective. They learned about raising money and organizing conferences to provide the documentation vital in Congressional testimony. They learned how to identify and influence people who could help them on Capitol Hill. And they learned what can happen to well-intended legislation when left to the vageries of the administrative bureaucracy. This knowledge will stand them in good stead in future campaigns in which, to quote Dr. Russo, "With a sustained and dedicated effort, an intelligent, prepared, and vigilant citizenry can influence policy directions."

DR. BRUCE SALES—LAWMAKER

Professor, University of Arizona   Ph.D., University of Rochester, 1971
Director, Law/Psychology Program, Psycholinguistics
University of Arizona   J.D., Northwestern, 1973

While developing the first fully integrated J.D./Ph.D. program (under an NIMH grant), Dr. Bruce Sales decided that it was important to show the students in this program that it was possible to influence public policy. He chose a topical, psychological issue and by "doing his homework" helped to rewrite the involuntary civil commitment procedures for the state of Nebraska, where he lived at that time. He found this exercise very influential in involving some of his students in other policy work.

In considering civil commitment procedures in Nebraska in 1974, Dr. Sales concentrated on *two legal* questions: (1) Was the current Nebraska law constitutional, and (2) Were patients' rights being protected; and *one scientific* question: Were committed citizens receiving the best and most appropriate treatment? Although there had been no legal rulings in Nebraska or its Federal District Court on the current law, several other federal court cases suggested that the Nebraska law probably was unconstitutional. Dr. Sales reviewed these cases and showed their relevance to the constitutionality of the Nebraska law. In a later suit brought by a member of a local legal aide society, the district court ruled the Nebraska law to be unconstitutional. This suit contributed to the adoption of Dr. Sales's bill.

On the scientific side, Sales was interested in the impact of different types of placements on rehabilitation. He studied the literature on psychiatric treatment and patient outcomes to construct a professionally respectable position for the treatment/placement sections of the proposed legislation. His background in psychology and the literature review he did were very useful when explaining the bill to the legislators and the State Medical Society.

After Dr. Sales had assured himself that the current legislation was unconstitutional and not in the best interests of the patients, he participated in organizing a committee to help draft new legislation. In an effort to be comprehensive, the committee included professionals who represented all of the important positions on the issue: a public defender, a prosecutor, a law professor, and a mental health administrator from the State Department of Public Health. They met for two hours every other week for three months and went through the legislation issue by issue. They looked at bills from other states and prior proposals in Nebraska. Sales used his knowledge of group dynamics to facilitate their work. Each section of their new draft was voted on, with a majority required for inclusion. The final vote on the entire bill had to be unanimous before the committee members' names would be used on the draft. By stressing the necessity for compromise to develop this important bill, and ensuring enough socializing, Sales got all of the members to endorse the final draft with enthusiasm.

Before the bill was introduced into the legislature, Dr. Sales decided to seek the endorsement of the Nebraska Bar Association. While researching state political and legislative processes, he had learned that the opinions of the State Bar and the State Medical Society would be important factors in the politicians' considerations of a new bill. He chose to approach the Bar Association because he believed they would be more sympathetic to his committee and its work and more influential with the legislators. He persuaded the Bar Association to form a committee on mental health (of which he was made chairman) to consider the new legislation and got the support of an ex-president of the association who had enough clout to help get the bill through the Bar Association's review process. As this was a legal review, Sales found it to be a good "rehearsal" for his later efforts with the state legislature. After two months of deliberation, the Bar Association agreed to endorse and introduce the bill to the legislature with Sales as their expert witness.

By the time Dr. Sales testified before the Nebraska State Legislature he had a thorough understanding of the legal and scientific issues involved in the bill and a good knowledge of the history of legislation on involuntary commitment in Nebraska. He told the legislators that the current law was very likely to violate the rights of defendants to due process and to be less than adequate in promoting their rehabilitation if they were committed. He also argued that the proposed bill would overcome the shortcomings of the current legislation and was a *new* and promising approach to the legal and scientific problems. He knew that Nebraska law had swung back and forth on civil commitment over the years and that legislators familiar with this history would want to be sure that any change in legislation would not be a "reinvention of the wheel."

The new bill that he testified for effectively related the general issues of civil commitment to "nuts and bolts" specifics of interest to a legislator. The work that had been done with the first committee and the Bar Association enabled Sales to present a clear synopsis of the key provisions of the bill and how it differed from the existing law in terms geared to the legislators (*not* to lawyers or scientists). As anticipated, the endorsement of the Nebraska Bar Asociation was very important. Other expert witnesses who testified against the bill with no organizational or constituent support did not have as much impact upon the legislators.

Although well-prepared for most of the questions raised by legislators about the bill and its impact on other laws affecting the mentally ill, Dr. Sales was not prepared when the legislators asked why the State Medical Society did not endorse the bill. He knew that the Society would be influential with the legislature, but he had hoped that the support of the Bar Association and the well-drafted bill he was presenting would overcome any reservations. However, the legislators had gotten some negative comments about the bill from the Medical Society and were insistent that Dr. Sales win its approval.

Rather than dealing directly with the Medical Society's objections before the legislators, Dr. Sales followed the committee chairman's suggestion to meet with representatives of the Society. He and the prosecutor from the earlier committee met with a group of psychiatrists from the Medical Society to go over their differences. They first agreed to put aside guild interests and try to work out a reasonable law in the best interests of the mentally ill. The psychiatrists were impressed with the interest of the Bar Association and the legislature in the new bill—a staff assistant had been assigned by the legislature to sit in on their meetings and help them draft a compromise—and by the commitment of the prosecutor, whom they trusted. When the psychiatrists listed their objections to the bill, Sales found that the majority were based on misunderstandings or were so minor that they could be easily remedied. Compromises were reached on a few main provisions, such as the patient's right to refuse treatment, and after three meetings the State Medical Society (and the State Psychological Association) endorsed the bill. Shortly afterwards, the Nebraska legislature adopted the new bill on involuntary civil commitment.

As a result of his experience, Dr. Sales encourages other psychologists to choose a topical project to work on, in which they can advocate the appropriate use of scientific information in public policymaking. He stresses the necessity for becoming an expert on both the issues and facts in your area of interest and the public policy process you want to influence. Unless the project is already a top priority of public officials, they will be too busy to do any work on it. The professional must do the homework and generate the support for his or her project. He or she would be wise to get as much help as possible from other professionals and organizations with a stake in the policy, and student involvement in such projects can also add markedly to their scope and influence.

CONCLUSIONS

In planning this project, I tried to find psychologists who represented certain roles mentioned in the literature on psychologists and public policy—roles such as activist/collaborator, translator, researcher, administrator, evaluator, and expert witness (Segall, 1976; Kiesler, 1983). In conducting these interviews, I learned that any one role did not fully capture the work of the respondents. For example, the role of expert witness is usually limited to government or legal testimony, but all of the respondents became experts in their areas and were effective translators of their ideas and of the supporting data, in both speaking and writing. The ability to communicate in a persuasive manner is vital in influencing public policy. Second, all of the respondents conducted research or made use of research findings. In some cases this research was not typical of the laboratory or field studies usually done in psychology, but the data the respondents presented were meaningful to the people they were trying to influence. Information must be seen as relevant and accurate to be influential in policy work. Third, although only one of the respondents had the job title of administrator, all had managerial responsibilities that were critical to their success. Policy work is usually a collaborative effort requiring good interpersonal relations. Finally, all of the respondents were critical evaluators of the institutions, programs, and people that they worked with. They did not completely accept or reject the status quo, but worked within the limits of the situation whenever possible. Effective public policy work cannot outrun the comprehension of policymakers or the acceptance of the public.

It is clear that all of the respondents possess broader skills and interests than those described by a single role definition or job description. In considering the motivation for their policy activities, I found a common characteristic to be their commitment to human dignity as Sjoberg (1975) defines it. Gardner's interest in accountable and responsible government, Caplan's interest in understanding the reasons for the urban riots, Russo's interest in equality for women in science, Sales's interest in civil commitment procedures that protect patients' rights and promote good treatment—all suggest an underlying commitment to enhancing the ability of individuals to control their own destinies. This commitment led them to find or create opportunities to utilize their skills, perspectives, and information as social scientists to change or initiate policies and programs that would help individuals help themselves.

It has been suggested that some of the case studies include activities that do not require training in psychology, whereas others suggest a need for more training than most psychologists have. Hopefully, the case studies have dispelled the myth that to be effective in policy work psychologists must be value-free and impartial social scientists, who influence policymakers through the scholarly presentation of empirical facts. But what about the "normal science" model (Kuhn, 1970) of the psychologist who uses the current concepts and techniques of the discipline to produce verifiable knowledge about the phenomena being studied—the psychologist who reviews the literature, constructs theories and derives hypotheses, develops and implements sophisticated research designs, and publishes only in professional journals? I suspect that this is the model that Dr. Gardner had in mind when he said that he would "never think of holding himself out as a psychologist," and the kind of approach that Dr. Caplan referred to as "academically interesting," but more applicable to grant research. Although all of the respondents were trained in this model and used aspects of it to gather the information that they needed, they also followed other models that require other skills of the psychologist. The role description that I find most applicable is that of the psychologist as an educator—bringing new concepts to policymakers and communicating them in a way that they can understand and accept. This approach has been called the "enlightenment model" (Janowitz, 1966).

Although the tactics the respondents used varied with the issues and the organizations involved, their general strategies were similar in most cases: Assess the current situation as defined by all the relevant parties, and then influence those responsible for the programs or policies to take more account of the definitions and needs of people they were serving. Some of this assessment was empirical; some was based on reviews of the literature. When the respondents needed information that they did not have, they learned what they needed to know to understand and influence the situation, often going outside of their discipline. Some of their influence came from their research and testimony, and some came from coalitions of professionals that they helped to mobilize. Whenever possible, the respondents worked to negotiate policies that would promote the vital objectives of all the parties involved. Their work illustrates Jackson's concept of the activist/collaborator who influences policies affecting human welfare through active, interactive involvement in the political process (Jackson, 1980).

It is important to note the difference between this approach to public policy and the more traditional approaches of working within the categories and norms of the established systems (e.g., consulting), or opposing those categories and norms (e.g., demonstrations). These more familiar approaches are less often instrumental in initiating new programs or changing established policies to the satisfaction of all parties concerned. The enlightenment strategy is more apt to mediate constructive changes. It produces social and organizational change by reshaping the definition of the problems and their solutions, thereby influencing the attitudes and behaviors of all concerned. This is best accomplished by working as an involved participant rather than as a disinterested observer or expert.

Although the four psychologists described above did not often develop theory, test hypotheses, or contribute directly to the professional literature in their activities, I believe that their approach to the analysis and change of human behavior in natural settings illustrates a type of applied psychology that meets the highest professional standards and ethical principles. As professionals they demonstrated a commitment to the well-being of individuals. They knew the importance of other individuals' definitions of situations and accepted the workings of social relativism. They understood the social nature of knowledge and of the policy process and realized that the provision of information in a scholarly manner would probably not influence the policies that they cared about. Instead, they collaborated with all the interested parties to create policies that they believed would enhance human dignity. They were willing to make the necessary value judgments and to take responsibility for their decisions. In short, they practiced public interest science.

Given the lack of professional rewards for this kind of activity (Tangri & Strasburg, 1979), it requires a commitment to particular issues and to the public welfare to become involved in the frustrating world of public policy. Certainly the dedication, creativity, and frustration tolerance of these psychologists were as important as their research and conceptual skills in enabling them to influence social policies. Undoubtedly other professionals also have this kind of commitment, but I think these case studies illustrate that psychologists can contribute a unique combination of skills and interests to this work. Their perspectives on human behavior, visions of what is possible in social organizations, techniques for analyzing social problems, and methods for mediating policy conflicts are all invaluable in public interest science.

In 1969, Wilbert McKeachie considered the question "What can psychologists contribute to public policy?" He answered, "When we [psychologists] withdraw from public affairs, the citizenry is left at the mercy of pseudo-scientists, less humble about their facts and less fearful of fighting for their values" (McKeachie, 1969, p. 595). Hopefully, the opportunities for new roles in the training and professional activities of psychologists that are illustrated in these case studies will encourage and enable more of us to become involved in public interest science.

NOTE

1. Interested readers can obtain the text of three additional case studies by writing the author. These cases describe the work of (1) Dr. Carolyn R. Payton, Dean of Counseling and Career Development at Howard University, and former Director of the U.S. Peace Corps; (2) Dr. Paul R. Kimmel, who served as program evaluator for the Agency for International Development (AID) to assess their International Training Program; and (3) Dr. Stephen J. Morse, a professor at the University of Southern California Law Center, who has helped to draft California and federal laws in the areas of diminished capacity, insanity defenses, and preventive detention, and often serves as an expert witness on those topics.

REFERENCES

Bauer, R. (1966). Social psychology and the study of policy formation. *American Psychologist, 21*, 933-942.

Bevan, W. (1970). Psychology, the university, and the real world around us. *American Psychologist, 25*, 442-449.

Bevan, W. (1982). A sermon of sorts in three plus parts. *American Psychologist, 37,* 1303-1322.

Caplan, N. (1968). A study of ghetto rioters. *Scientific American, 219*(2), 3-9.

Caplan, N., Morrison, A., & Stambaugh, R. (1975). *The use of social science knowledge in policy decisions at the national level.* Ann Arbor, MI: Institute for Social Research.

Caplan, N., & Nelson, S. (1973). On being useful: The nature and consequences of psychological research on social problems. *American Psychologist, 28,* 199-211.

Gardner, J. (1973). *In common cause.* (rev. ed.). New York: Norton.

Gouldner, A. W. (1969). Anti-minotaur: The myth of a value-free sociology. *Social Problems, 9,* 199-213.

Gouldner, A. W. (1970, May-June). Toward the radical reconstruction of sociology. *Social Policy,* 18-25.

Jackson, J. (1980). Promoting human welfare through legislative advocacy: A proper role for the science of psychology. In R. Kasschau & F. Kessel (Eds.), *Psychology and society: In search of symbiosis.* New York: Holt, Rinehart & Winston.

Janowitz, M. (1966). Foreward. In D. Street, R. D. Vinter, & C. Perrow, *Organization for treatment.* New York: Free Press.

Kiesler, C. A. (1983). Psychology and public policy. In E. M. Altmarer & M. E. Meyer (Eds.), *Applied specialities in psychology.* Reading, MA: Addison-Wesley.

Kuhn, T. (1970). *Structure of scientific revolutions.* Chicago: University of Chicago Press.

McKeachie, W. J. (1969). A public policy conference for psychologists. *American Psychologist, 24,* 593-596.

McPherson, M. W., & Popplestone, J. A. (1967). *Problems and procedures in oral histories.* Unpublished manuscript, University of Akron, Archives of the History of American Psychology.

Myrdal, G. (1972). How scientific are the social sciences? *Journal of Social Issues, 28*(4), 151-169.

Nelson, S., & Caplan, N. (1983). Social problem solving and social change. In D. Perlman & P. Cozby (Eds.), *Social psychology.* New York: Holt, Rinehart & Winston.

Pallak, M. (1982). Report of the executive officer: 1981. *American Psychologist, 37,* 621-624.

Perl, M., Primack, J., & von Hipple, F. (1974, June). Public-interest science—an overview. *Physics Today,* 23-31.

Pion, G. M., & Lipsey, M. W. (1984). Psychology and society: The challenge of change. *American Psychologist, 39,* 739-754.

Primack, J., & von Hipple, F. (1974). *Advice and dissent: Scientists in the political arena.* New York: Basic Books.

Russo, N. F., & Cassidy, M. M. (1983). Women in science and technology: Organizing for equality. In I. Tinker (Ed.), *Women in Washington: Advocates for public policy.* Beverly Hills, CA: Sage.

Segall, M. (1976). *Human behavior and public policy: A political psychology.* New York: Pergamon.

Shadish, W. R. (1984). Policy research: Lessons from the implementation of deinstitutionalization. *American Psychologist, 39,* 725-738.

Sjoberg, G. (1975). Politics, ethics and evaluation research. In E. L. Struening & M. Guttentag (Eds.), *Handbook of evaluation research* (Vol. 2). Beverly Hills, CA: Sage.

Stapp, J., & Fulcher, R. (1982). The employment of 1979 and 1980 doctorate recipients in psychology. *American Psychologist, 37,* 1159-1185.

Tangri, S., & Strasburg, G. L. (1979). Can research on women be more effective in shaping policy? *Psychology of Women Quarterly, 3,* 321-343.

Task Force on Psychology and Public Policy. (1984). *Psychology and public policy.* Washington, DC: American Psychological Association, Board of Social and Ethical Responsibility in Psychology.

Thomas, W. I., & Thomas, D. S. (1928). *The child in America.* New York: Knopf.

Weiss, C. H. (1975). Evaluation research in the political context. In E. L. Struening & M. Guttentag (Eds.), *Handbook of evaluation research* (Vol. 1). Beverly Hills, CA: Sage.

Weiss, C. H. (Ed.). (1977). *Using social research in public policy making.* Lexington, MA: D. C. Heath.

Author Index

ABC, 128-130
Ackerman, T. P., 9, 65
Acosta, E., 270
Adams, S., 78
Adams, W. C., 130-132, 153, 155
Adelman, L., 246, 248-249
Adler, A., 223
Alexander, Y., 200
Allison, G. T., 57
Allport, G., 21
Almqvist, K., 242
Alon, H., 197
Altman, L. K., 242
American Psychiatric Association, 207
American Psychological Association, 108
Anderson, B. F., 251
Anisman, H. L., 221
Ansley, N., 269
Argyris, C., 80
Armor, D. J., 107
Arnstein, S. R., 255
Atak, J. R., 42
Axelrod, R., 14, 50

Bachman, J., 11
Bachman, L., 220
Baer, D., 39
Bailey, T. A., 171
Balke, W. M., 243
Bamford, J., 269
Banta, H. D., 261
Barber, J. D., 161, 165, 170, 176
Bartlett, G. S., 113
Bartunek, J., 92, 100, 103
Bauer, R., 283
Baum, A., 13, 15, 159, 207, 223-225
Beardslee, W. R., 12, 113
Bennet, G., 223
Bennett, P. G., 113

Benton, A., 92
Berg, M. R., 274
Berman, L., 177
Berman, M., 88-89
Bethe, H., 64
Bevan, W., 281
Bickman, L., 277
Birch, H. G., 57
Blanchard, E. B., 219
Bonner, R., 212
Bordieri, J. E., 217
Boruch, R. F., 257
Borus, J. F., 211, 214
Boulanger, G., 218, 221
Bourne, P. G., 213
Boyd, H., 221
Bratton, D. L., 167
Brehm, J. W., 192
Brehmer, B., 235, 239-242
Brickman, P., 278
Brock, S., 199
Brock, T. C., 199
Bromet, E., 224
Bronfenbrenner, U., 8, 12, 49, 113, 121
Brookmire, D., 93
Brooks, J., 266, 269
Brown, C., 248-249
Brown, J. M., 155
Bruner, J. S., 58
Brunswik, E., 235
Brzezinski, Z., 82, 162
Bucuvalas, M. J., 278
Bundy, M. G., 63
Burn, S. M., 127
Burnstein, E., 123
Burris, B. C., 219
Byrnes, L., 113

Cacioppo, J. T., 11, 142, 199

299

Subject Index

Activism, 19, 34-36, 38-40
  activist psychologists, 283-294
  activist roles, 294-295
  commitment to human dignity, 295-296
  ethical issues, 40-41
  obstacles to, 36-38
  small wins, 37-38
  tactics, 296
  training for, 295
Advocacy, 9, 15, 20, 107-112
  groups, 9, 40
  nuclear disarmament, 117
  research in behalf of, 112-123, 124-125
Alcoholism treatment, 264-266
American Psychological Association, 108,
  110-112, 124, 282, 284, 288
  advocacy by, 108, 110-112
Arms control. See Disarmament
Arms races, 27-34, 43, 51, 53-54, 63
  reversal of, 53-54, 64-65
Attitude change research, 11
Attitude toward
  nuclear armaments, 107-125, 130-131,
    134-137, 151
  terrorism, 191-192, 197-198
  value of children, 118-123
Availability, cognitive, 51, 137

Bargaining. See Negotiation
Behavior analysis, 27-28, 38-40, 42
  behavior momentum, 43

Children's fears, 11-12
Civil commitment, 291-294
Civil Disorders, Commission on, 286-288
Common cause, 284-285
Commons, tragedy of, 14, 31-34

Conflict resolution, 233-252
  in policy disputes, 243-252
    government decentralization, 247-
     250
    implications, 252
    open space planning, 244-245
    police bullets, 245-248
    prediction of cancer risk, 250-251
  laboratory theory, 239-243
Contingency theory, 169-170

The Day After, 38, 47, 127-156
  detailed research findings, 132-153
    behavioral changes, 149-150
    changes in attitudes, 137-141
    persistence of changes, 144-149
  instant-analysis research, 128-131
  more comprehensive studies, 131-134,
    153-156
Decision making, 75-76
  criteria of decision procedure quality,
    66-68, 84
  defective patterns, 73-76, 85
  in crises, 57-58, 66-85, 181
  research assistance in policy disputes,
    243-252
  unsqueaky wheel trap, 81-85
Deterrence, 29-30, 49-50, 60, 64
Disarmament, 31-34
  American readiness for, 47-48
  attitudes toward, 112-123, 130-131, 136,
    151
  knowledge about, 118-123
  McCloy-Zorin Principles, 33

Fear arousal, 41-42, 46
  in terrorism, 190, 192-194

About the Authors

ANDREW BAUM is Associate Professor of Medical Psychology at the Uniformed Services University of the Health Sciences in Bethesda, Maryland. He has co-authored three textbooks (*Introduction to Health Psychology* with Robert J. Gatchel; *Environmental Psychology* with Jeffrey D. Fisher and Paul A. Bell; and *Social Psychology* with Jerome E. Singer and Jeffrey D. Fisher) and is co-editor (with Jerome E. Singer) of *Advances in Environmental Psychology* and the *Handbook of Psychology and Health*. He is currently editor of the *Journal of Applied Social Psychology* and associate editor of *Basic and Applied Social Psychology*. His research interests include stress, control, helplessness, and architecture.

SHAWN M. BURN received her M.A. in social psychology in 1984 from Claremont Graduate School. Her areas of interest include research on recycling of waste, political participation, and program evaluation.

PETER J. CARNEVALE is Assistant Professor in the Department of Management Sciences at the University of Iowa. He received his Ph.D. in social psychology from the State University of New York at Buffalo. His current research includes psychological approaches to the study of negotiation and mediation; in addition, he serves as a practicing mediator in labor-management disputes.

LAURA M. DAVIDSON is currently a doctoral candidate in medical psychology at the Uniformed Services University of the Health Sciences. She has recently co-authored several papers on the effects of perceived control on stress responses, as well as papers on the psychological consequences of exposure to disasters. Her interests include sympathetic nervous system reactivity, perceived control, and the relationship between psychological and physiological factors in stress responses.

DENISE DOUGHERTY is an analyst in the Health Program at the Congressional Office of Technology Assessment, and is currently completing her Ph.D. in social psychology at Boston University. Her research interests include the effects of political participation and the conduct of policy analysis. She has co-authored a number of chapters and monographs on the effectiveness of treatment for alcoholism and the scientific validity of polygraph testing.

SEYMOUR FESHBACH is Professor of Psychology and has served as department chair at UCLA. He has a long-standing theoretical and research interest in problems of human aggression, and an equally long-standing concern with the role and responsibilities of psychologists in regard to social issues, which stems from his association as a graduate student with the Yale Attitude Change Project.

NEHEMIA FRIEDLAND received his Ph.D. in social psychology at the University of North Carolina, Chapel Hill. Since 1974 he has taught at the Department of Psychology, Tel Aviv University. In the years 1975-1982 he served as senior research advisor to the psychology branch of the Israel Navy.

JANET GRASSIA received a master's degree in business administration from the University of Colorado. She has been a research assistant at the university's Center for Research on Judgment and Policy since 1980, and has co-authored several articles on judgment and decision making.

FRANK HAIST graduated from the University of California at Los Angeles and is planning to pursue graduate study in psychology.

KENNETH R. HAMMOND is Professor of Psychology at the University of Colorado and Director of the Center for Research on Judgment and Policy, a part of the Institute of Cognitive Science at the University of Colorado. His field of interest is judgment and decision making, particularly conflict resolution in public policymaking. He has done basic and applied research in these fields and has consulted for federal, state, and local governments and for multinational corporations. In 1982 he was awarded an honorary degree by the University of Uppsala.

IRVING L. JANIS, Professor of Psychology at Yale University, has long been a contributor to research on psychological stress and attitude change. More recently he has investigated the area of decision making through social-psychological studies of foreign policy decisions and fiascoes (reported in his book *Groupthink*) as well as through studies of personal decisions (reported in *Decision Making*, co-authored with Leon Mann). He received the AAAS Socio-Psychological Prize in 1967, APA's Distinguished Scientific Contribution Award in 1981, and SPSSI's Kurt Lewin Award in 1985.

ELIZABETH KANDEL finished her undergraduate work at the University of California, Berkeley, and is looking forward to graduate study in psychology.

PAUL R. KIMMEL is currently the first Public Policy Fellow at the American Psychological Association and the Association for the Advancement of Psychology in Washington, DC, where he represents the Society for the Psychological Study of Social Issues and promotes the involvement of psychologists in public interest science. In previous years he has served as a staff officer on a National Academy of Sciences' project evaluating the VA health-care system, done research at the U.S. Department of Labor, and been on the Iowa State University faculty.

JEANNE C. KING is working toward a Ph.D. in social/organizational psychology at Claremont Graduate School. She received an M.A. from California State University, Fullerton, and is a Lecturer in Psychology there. She has done research on the labor market impact of undocumented workers in Los Angeles and the social and physical environment of neonatal intensive care units. Her present interest is the application of ecological psychology to organizations, specifically in a study of the lifecycles of small retail/service businesses.

ALISON M. KONRAD received her M.A. in social psychology from Claremont Graduate School in 1984. Her research interests include organizational behavior, especially the work behavior of women and men.

ARIEL MERARI holds B.A. degrees in psychology and economics from the Hebrew University in Jerusalem and a Ph.D. in psychology from the University of California, Berkeley. In 1969 he was a Population Council Fellow at Stanford University, and since then he has taught at the Department of Psychology, Tel Aviv University, which he currently chairs. Since 1978 he has been a Senior Fellow and Head of the Project on Terrorism at the Jaffee Center for Strategic Studies, Tel Aviv University. For several years he has been a consultant on terrorism to the Office of the Prime Minister of Israel.

JOHN A. NEVIN received his Ph.D. in experimental psychology from Columbia University in 1963. He has taught at Swarthmore College, been Chair of the Psychology Department at Columbia, and finally moved to the University of New Hampshire in 1972. His research interests include reinforcement schedules, stimulus control, and signal detection, and he has served as editor of the *Journal of The Experimental Analysis of Behavior*. In addition to teaching and research in psychology, he coordinates an interdisciplinary course on nuclear war, and works with local groups on educational, political, and protest activities related to the nuclear arms race.

STUART OSKAMP is Professor of Psychology at Claremont Graduate School in California. He received his Ph.D. from Stanford University and has had visiting appointments at the University of Michigan, University of Bristol, and the London School of Economics and Political Science. His main research interests are in the areas of attitudes and attitude change, behavioral aspects of energy and resource conservation, and social issues and public policy. His books include *Attitudes and Opinions* and *Applied Social Psychology*. He is a past President of the APA Division of Population and Environmental Psychology and the current editor of the *Applied Social Psychology Annual* series.

JOHN A. POLLARD is a graduate student in the Psychology Department at the Claremont Graduate School. His areas of interest include program evaluation methodology and design, causal modeling, and concern for how social psychological knowledge can be used to prevent nuclear war.

LEONARD SAXE is Associate Professor of Psychology at Boston University and Associate Director of the university's Center for Applied Social Science. He received his Ph.D. in social psychology from the University of Pittsburgh, and in 1979 he held a Congressional Science Fellowship and was a staff member at the Office of Technology Assessment. In 1981, he was a Fulbright Lecturer in Psychology at the University of Haifa, Israel. His research concerns the evaluation of social interventions and public policy analysis. He is the co-author (with M. Fine) of *Social Experiments: Methods for Design and Evaluation*.

B. F. SKINNER is Professor Emeritus at Harvard University, where he taught from 1948 to 1974. He earned his Ph.D. at Harvard in 1931 and later taught at the University of Minnesota and served as department chair at Indiana University. Known as a pioneer of operant conditioning, the experimental analysis of behavior, and teaching machines, he received the APA Award for Distinguished Scientific Contributions in 1958. In addition to his many research publications, he has popularized scientific principles in his books *Walden Two* and *Beyond Freedom and Dignity*.

MICHAEL A. WHITE is a graduate student in the Psychology Department at the Claremont Graduate School, where he is working toward his Ph.D. in social/environmental psychology. He is employed as a research psychologist at the Navy Personnel Research and Development Center in San Diego. His research interests include organizational change, survey methodology, attitude assessment, and applications of attribution theory to organizations.

RALPH K. WHITE, long a student of Soviet behavior, is Professor Emeritus at George Washington University. Among psychologists he is perhaps best known as "the White of Lewin, Lippitt, and White" (autocratic and democratic atmospheres in children's groups), and for his book *Nobody Wanted War: Misperception in Vietnam and Other Wars*. Since retiring, he has written *Fearful Warriors: A Psychological Profile of U.S.-Soviet Relations* and edited a book of readings, *Psychology and the Prevention of War* (in press).

LAWRENCE S. WRIGHTSMAN is Professor of Psychology and former chair of the Department of Psychology at the University of Kansas, Lawrence. He is the author or editor of several books, including *Social Psychology in the Eighties* (4th Edition), with Kay Deaux; *The Psychology of Evidence and Trial Procedure*, with Saul M. Kassin; *Research Methods in Social Relations* (3rd Edition), with Claire Selltiz and Stuart W. Cook; and *Contemporary Issues in Social Psychology* (4th Edition), with John Brigham. He is a former president of the Society for the Psychological Study of Social Issues (SPSSI) and of the Society of Personality and Social Psychology (Division 8 of the American Psychological Association).